# JOSEPH E. BROWN
AND THE CONFEDERACY

# JOSEPH E. BROWN AND THE CONFEDERACY

By

LOUISE BILES HILL, Ph.D.

GREENWOOD PRESS, PUBLISHERS
WESTPORT, CONNECTICUT

*The Library of Congress has catalogued this publication as follows:*

Library of Congress Cataloging in Publication Data

Hill, Louise Biles, 1891-
    Joseph E. Brown and the Confederacy.

    Reprint of the 1939 ed.
    Bibliography: p.
    1. Brown, Joseph Emerson, 1821-1894. 2. Confederate States of America--History. 3. Georgia--History--Civil War. I. Title.
[E559.B876 1972]    973.7'13'0924  [B]    70-138612
ISBN 0-8371-5722-6

Originally published in 1939
by The University of North Carolina Press,
Chapel Hill

First Greenwood Reprinting 1972

Library of Congress Catalogue Card Number 70-138612

ISBN 0-8371-5722-6

Printed in the United States of America

# PREFACE

THE ULTIMATE success of the Confederacy depended in no small measure upon the extent of the support accorded to it by the individual Southern states. Because Georgia was a pivotal state, geographically, politically, and economically, the policies and activities of Joseph E. Brown, who served as governor throughout the War for Southern Independence, were of outstanding importance in the struggle. This study represents an attempt to examine his career and to indicate its effect upon the Confederacy as a whole. The examination of his course during the fifteen years following the war throws additional light on his character and conduct in the war period and justifies the inclusion of Chapters XI and XII.

For an appreciation of the dignities and duties of scholarship the author is indebted to the several teachers with whom it has been her privilege to study—Henry Johnson, Charles A. Beard, James T. Shotwell, William E. Dodd, David Seville Muzzey, Frederick A. Ogg, Edward M. Sait, Frank Lawrence Owsley, Curtis H. Walker; also the late William Archibald Dunning, James Harvey Robinson, John Spencer Bassett, and Carl S. Driver.

To Dr. Frank Lawrence Owsley the author is especially indebted for suggesting and directing this study and for his stern discipline in research and interpretation as for his inspiration and encouragement leading to its completion. To other members of the Department of History in Vanderbilt University appreciation is due for criticism in form and organization.

The author wishes to express her gratitude also to Dr. E. Merton Coulter for reading the manuscript; to Professor Ollinger Crenshaw of Washington and Lee University, Mr. Wirt Armistead Cate of Nashville, Mr. Thomas Robson Hay of New York, and Mr. James Houston Johnston of Atlanta

## PREFACE

for helpful suggestions in locating material; and to several citizens of Georgia, who prefer to remain anonymous, for special information.

Acknowledgment is gratefully made of assistance rendered by Mrs. James E. Hays, State Historian and Director, Georgia Department of Archives and History, her predecessor in office, Miss Ruth Blair, and their assistants, Miss Ruth Givens and Miss Murdoch Walker; by Miss Ella May Thornton, State Librarian, Georgia State Library; by Miss Jessie Hopkins, Librarian, Carnegie Library of Atlanta; by Mrs. Marie Bankhead Owen, Director, Department of Archives and History, State of Alabama; by Mrs. John Trotwood Moore, Librarian and Archivist, Division of Library and Archives, State of Tennessee; by Miss Isabel Howell, Reference Librarian, Vanderbilt University; by the secretaries of the Georgia Historical Society, the Tennessee Historical Society, the North Carolina Historical Commission, and the Historical Society of Pennsylvania; by the staffs of the Carnegie Library of Nashville, the Library of Congress, the New York Public Library, and the Library of Columbia University; and by those in charge of the Confederate Archives in the United States War Department.

To the United Daughters of the Confederacy appreciation is due for the honor the manuscript received in the award of the Mrs. Simon Baruch University Prize of one thousand dollars.

LOUISE BILES HILL

Nashville, Tennessee
March, 1939

# FOREWORD

WHO HAS NOT, at one time or another, believed that hidden away in an attic in an old trunk or darkly reposing in the secret archives of government is an all-encompassing document, which, could it be possessed by the curious one, would explain the baffling conduct of some individual or some government.

However, those who have sought the all-encompassing document have often been disappointed because the motivation of human action is complex and the records of this motivation are indirect, fragmentary, obscure, and inconsistent. It is, indeed, most unlikely that an individual or the representatives of a government, were they completely forthright, could completely explain the cause of their conduct at certain times. Causation in history is discovered by the synthesis of many fragments; by the rejection of many more that seem irrelevant. The resultant structure of cause thus assembled from chaos may be correct, it may be largely correct, or it may, by the process of rejection, be almost irrelevant and practically incorrect. Its soundness or unsoundness will probably depend upon the investigator's unbiased and careful appraisal of all available data and most particularly upon his ability to see the relationship between what may seem on the face of things to be unrelated.

Dr. Louise Biles Hill in her earnest and patient search for an understanding of the enigmatic character of Governor Joseph E. Brown of Georgia made no single discovery, as far as I know, that was spectacular or all-explaining. Indeed, she was greatly impeded in her study of Brown by a lack of documentary material of a private and personal nature. If such documents exist, the descendants of the remarkable Joseph E. Brown have not considered that the time was at hand to make this material accessible to Dr. Hill or to anyone else. However, Brown was a tireless speechmaker and letter writer; and if one possesses the patience the letters that Brown wrote his friends and his enemies (both very numerous) may be retrieved. This is what Dr. Hill has done to a remarkable degree. The letters, diaries, and speeches of other men with whom Brown associated and corresponded have been searched with satisfactory results. State and Confederate records have been levied upon for Brown's writings, and there is little doubt that the doughty governor of Georgia occupies more space in these records than even the militant Governor Vance of North Carolina who next to Brown caused more uproar in the Confederacy than all the other political leaders of the opposition. Newspapers, legislative journals, the Official Records of the Army and the Navy of the Confederacy have all yielded their fruit, and Dr. Hill has been able, despite the lack of a collected body of private and personal papers, to piece together with comprehension, craftsmanship, and objectivity a most satisfactory history and explanation of Joseph E. Brown as he traveled the political dial from doctrinaire state rights Democrat and secessionist to Radical Republican scalawag and finally to Bourbon Democrat without more than the temporary loss of face or fortune or his essential popularity in Georgia.

FRANK L. OWSLEY

Vanderbilt University
Nashville, Tennessee

# CONTENTS

| Chapter | | Page |
|---|---|---|
| | Preface | v |
| | Foreword | vii |
| I. | The Gubernatorial Campaign of 1857 | 1 |
| II. | The Secession of Georgia | 20 |
| III. | "Coming Events Cast Their Shadows Before Them" | 48 |
| IV. | Conscription: First Major Assault on the Richmond Government | 79 |
| V. | Factors in the Gubernatorial Election of 1863 | 107 |
| VI. | Opposition to Confederate Financial Measures | 138 |
| VII. | Local Defense | 162 |
| VIII. | Habeas Corpus: Second Major Assault on the Richmond Government | 194 |
| IX. | Peace Propaganda | 222 |
| X. | The Fall of the Confederacy | 243 |
| XI. | Reconstruction | 266 |
| XII. | Rehabilitation | 291 |
| | Bibliography | 329 |
| | Index | 347 |

# JOSEPH E. BROWN
# AND THE CONFEDERACY

## CHAPTER I

## THE GUBERNATORIAL CAMPAIGN OF 1857

EXCEPT for an unusually large number of able candidates for governor, the Democratic state convention which met at Milledgeville, Georgia's capital, on June 24, 1857, was in no wise different from those of previous years or those which were to follow. When, however, it had completed its work it had given to the party a candidate who was not only to succeed at the polls in the coming election, but who was to break all Georgia precedent by serving four consecutive terms, thereby affecting for weal or woe not only the fortunes of Georgia but those of the entire South and even of the United States.

Unconscious of the influence their work was destined to have on American history, delegates from one hundred and seven counties adopted rules and made nominations in the time-honored manner. Each county having two representatives in the legislature was entitled to five votes, and those with one representative, to three, making a total of three hundred and ninety-nine votes. A two-thirds majority was necessary for a nomination. As a platform a single resolution was adopted which condemned Robert J. Walker's inaugural address as governor of Kansas and endorsed President Buchanan's administration.[1]

In Georgia, as elsewhere before the War for Southern Independence, the office of governor was one of dignity and

---

[1] I. W. Avery, *The History of the State of Georgia from 1850 to 1881*, pp. 33-38, henceforth cited as Avery; *Augusta Constitutionalist*, June 26, 1857. Walker favored popular sovereignty.

honor and was sought only by those who had already established their reputations in public service. There were five such candidates before the convention at this time and in addition "any number of outstanding men ready to accept candidacy." [2] James Gardner, editor of the *Augusta Constitutionalist*,[3] desired the honor of "retiring under the *eclat* of a nomination by his party." Another candidate was H. G. Lamar, member of an influential family, who had served as judge of the superior court and member of Congress. No governor had ever been selected from North Georgia, the stronghold of the party, and the section now demanded the nomination of John H. Lumpkin, ex-judge of the superior court. Lumpkin was the son of a Baptist minister, a member of a powerful political family, and had represented his district several terms in Congress. Hiram Warner, a native of New England, was also in the race. He had lived long in the state and had served three terms as judge of the superior court, one term as judge of the state supreme court, and one term as a member of Congress. The fifth candidate was the "silver-tongued orator," W. H. Stiles, former member of Congress and minister to Austria in the Polk administration, who was the favorite of the Savannah aristocracy.[4]

In addition to the embarrassment to the party of so many able candidates, there was a complication of factions which went back almost a decade. In the trouble over the territorial adjustments following the Mexican War, Georgia and other Southern states had at first declared they would never accept the Wilmot Proviso or Clay's compromise measures. Resolutions advocating resistance to the point of secession and authorizing the calling of a state convention "to consider

---

[2] Herbert Fielder, *A Sketch of the Life and Times and Speeches of Joseph E. Brown*, p. 86, henceforth cited as Fielder.

[3] Avery, p. 610. Avery was editor of the *Atlanta Constitution* from 1869 to 1874 and was afterwards connected with the *Atlanta Herald*.

[4] For a description of the candidates, cf. William J. Northen (ed.), *Men of Mark in Georgia*, III, 76 *et seq.*, henceforth cited as Northen; Fielder, pp. 86-88, 487; Avery, pp. 30-32, 78, 825.

## THE CAMPAIGN OF 1857

the mode and measure of redress"[5] had been adopted in the 1849-50 session of the Georgia legislature by a vote of thirty-five to three in the senate, and ninety-two to twenty-eight in the lower house.[6]

Alarmed by the disunionist sentiment in the South, Robert Toombs, Alexander Stephens, and Howell Cobb, who had accepted the Compromise of 1850, hurried back from Washington to take part in the Georgia convention and endeavor to carry it for the Compromise and the Union. So successful were their efforts that a Unionist convention was elected which rode rough-shod over the Southern Rights group[7] and adopted a set of resolutions endorsing the Compromise as a final settlement of the sectional question. The Georgia platform,[8] as the resolutions came to be called, was the work of a coalition composed of a majority of Whigs and a minority of Democrats.[9]

As a means of combating secession sentiment throughout Georgia[10] and other Southern states, the coalition was transformed into the Constitutional Union party with the Georgia platform as its basis and organizations were perfected throughout the South.[11] Toombs and Stephens (Whigs)

---

[5] Herman V. Ames, *American Documents on Federal Relations*, pp. 259-61, henceforth cited as Ames.

[6] Avery, p. 20.

[7] Richard H. Shryock, *Georgia and the Union in 1850*, pp. 322-23, henceforth cited as Shryock.

[8] The platform may be found in the *Journal of the State Convention . . . 1850;* Ames, pp. 271-72; Henry Cleveland, *Alexander H. Stephens . . .* , pp. 75-77, henceforth cited as Cleveland; Alexander H. Stephens, *A Constitutional View of the Late War between the States,* Vol. II, Appendix B., henceforth cited as Stephens, *War between the States.*

[9] Fielder, p. 71; Ulrich B. Phillips, *Life of Robert Toombs,* p. 99, henceforth cited as Phillips, *Toombs.* The Democrats of Union sentiment were more particularly those of North Georgia—the "white belt."

[10] The popular vote for delegates to the convention was about 46,000 for the Union party, 24,000 for Southern Rights, which was quite a reversal of sentiment from the previous year.—*Chronicle,* Nov. 24, 1850; *Georgian,* Nov. 29, 1850; *Republican,* Dec. 15, 1850, cited by Shryock, p. 319.

[11] Cf. Lewy Dorman, *Party Politics in Alabama from 1850 through 1860,* pp. 48-50, henceforth cited as Dorman; Laura A. White, *Robert Barnwell Rhett: Father of Secession,* pp. 108-10, henceforth cited as White, *Rhett.*

and Cobb (a Democrat) were the leading spirits, the latter being the real organizer of the movement.[12] Cobb was nominated for governor and Toombs for the United States Senate.[13] The Southern Rights party—also a coalition, but with the proportion of Whigs and Democrats reversed—was defeated[14] all along the line and the secession movement was definitely halted throughout the South.[15]

The success of the party did not convince the Southern Rights group of the wisdom of the Unionist movement.[16] They felt that, aside from the unfairness to their section of the Compromise of 1850, the North would not accept the Compromise as a finality and that when the sectional question next arose—as it did arise ten years later—the North would be better prepared. Their bitterness toward the leaders of the Unionist movement was extreme[17] and when, after the breach in the Democratic party was supposed to be healed, Cobb was a candidate for the United States Senate, he re-

---

[12] Stephens, *War between the States*, II, 176, 332; Phillips, *Toombs*, p. 100.

[13] John M. Berrien, whose term was expiring, did not approve of the Georgia platform.—Ulrich B. Phillips, *Georgia and State Rights*, p. 165, henceforth cited as Phillips, *Georgia;* Shryock, p. 358.

[14] Fielder, p. 72.

[15] Georgia's location between South Carolina on the one hand and Alabama and Mississippi on the other was advantageous to the Union cause. Georgia was proclaimed throughout the North as the saviour of the Union.—Northern press cited by Shryock, pp. 337-41; White, *Rhett*, pp. 111 *et seq.;* Joseph Hodgson, *The Cradle of the Confederacy*, pp. 270-71, henceforth cited as Hodgson; William Garrott Brown, *The Lower South in American History*, pp. 133 *et seq.*, henceforth cited as Brown, *Lower South;* William E. Dodd, *Life of Jefferson Davis*, pp. 126-29, henceforth cited as Dodd, *Davis;* Dorman, pp. 60, 170.

[16] "If the great sectional conflict was indeed irrepressible . . . wisdom required that the South should hasten the issue."—Phillips, *Toombs*, p. 102.

[17] W. H. Hull wrote Cobb in 1853 that the hatred of the "fire-eaters" for him would end only with life: "I do believe that many of them will secretly drop Johnson [Democratic nominee for governor] only because he is understood to be your friend."—Ulrich B. Phillips (ed.), *The Correspondence of Robert Toombs, Alexander H. Stephens, and Howell Cobb*, p. 335, henceforth cited as Phillips, *Correspondence*. Cf. Dorman, p. 56.

## THE CAMPAIGN OF 1857

ceived but thirty-four votes in the legislature.[18]

Toombs and Stephens attempted to perpetuate and nationalize the Constitutional Union party to take the place of what had come to be considered an abolitionized Whig party, but their efforts were unsuccessful and as the presidential election of 1852 loomed on the horizon they returned to the Whigs for the time being.

Georgia politics was chaotic throughout the decade.[19] Each party had its scars and resentments from the conflict of 1850-51, but the condition of affairs in the two national parties on the sectional question was such as to strengthen the Democrats while it demoralized the Whigs. For the gubernatorial election of 1853 Toombs and Stephens revived the Constitutional Union party and, with the aid of Union Democrats who had refused to return to the fold, nominated for governor Charles J. Jenkins, Whig Unionist, and author of the Georgia platform.[20] So completely had conditions reversed themselves that Herschel V. Johnson, one of the Southern Rights leaders, was the Democratic candidate and had the support of Cobb, the erstwhile leader of the Constitutional Union party. Johnson was elected by a majority of five hundred and ten votes.[21]

It was the last effort of the coalition. Before the next gubernatorial election the national Whig party had wrecked itself on the question of the Compromise of 1850 as a "finality," and on the Kansas-Nebraska Act. Abolitionist

---

[18] Fielder, p. 79; Robert P. Brooks, "Howell Cobb and the Crisis of 1850," University of Georgia *Bulletin*, Vol. XVIII, Ser. 285 (Jan., 1918), pp. 279-98.

[19] For difficulties with reference to the presidential election of 1852, cf. *ibid.*; Phillips, *Georgia*, p. 168; Fielder, p. 75; Shryock, p. 361; Arthur C. Cole, *The Whig Party in the South*, pp. 265 *et seq.*, henceforth cited as Cole.

[20] Cole, p. 278.

[21] Fielder, p. 78; *Memoirs of Judge Richard Clark*, edited by L. B. Wylie, p. 286, henceforth cited as Clark, *Memoirs;* Percy Scott Flippin, *Herschel V. Johnson of Georgia*, p. 56, henceforth cited as Flippin; Shryock, p. 336, n. 1.

Whigs went into the newly created Republican party. Others united with the Democrats, joined the American party, or, as Stephens said of himself in his campaign for Congress in 1855, "toted their own skillets" and made no party affiliation. In Georgia the wreck was complete.[22] Toombs and some other leading Whigs went over to the Democrats, and Stephens soon joined them. Frances S. Bartow, Benjamin Hill, John M. Berrien, and Eugenius A. Nisbet went into the American party.[23] Johnson's reëlection as governor in 1855 was, therefore, a foregone conclusion.[24] The next year the nomination for president of a Democrat who was a "Northern man with Southern principles" led many Georgians, who had hitherto held back, into the Democratic party. Nationally the party was thought to be safe on the sectional question, locally it was a refuge for the "Anti-Know-Nothings."[25] Buchanan carried the state by a majority of fourteen thousand.[26]

The certainty of success for the Democratic party in the state elections in 1857, therefore, doubtless strengthened the determination of each group in the convention that its man should be the gubernatorial candidate, and made a deadlock inevitable. Six ballots were taken on the first day, with the votes rather evenly distributed among the favorites,[27] and for three days the situation continued without a nomination. There were appeals, trades, filibusters, the injection of other names, and unsuccessful attempts to abandon the two-thirds rule. The convention seemed permanently deadlocked.

Such a contingency had been foreseen by an astute young

---

[22] The situation in Alabama was similar.—Dorman, p. 170.
[23] Fielder, p. 79.
[24] Flippin, p. 69, n. 4; *Tribune Almanac for 1856*, p. 45.
[25] Fielder, p. 79.
[26] Edward Stanwood, *History of the Presidency, 1788 to 1897*, p. 276, henceforth cited as Stanwood.
[27] *Constitutionalist*, June 26, 1857.

politician, L. N. Trammell,[28] and as he drove to Milledgeville in a buggy with a sympathetic neighbor he unfolded his plans to make a fellow North Georgian the "dark horse" of the convention.[29] On the nineteenth ballot he made his first move, and three votes appeared for Joseph E. Brown, as again in the twentieth. There was no favorable reaction, but at any rate the name had been put before the convention. It was the entering wedge. The twentieth ballot revealed the hopelessness of a decision. Three strong candidates had been practically eliminated, but Lumpkin and Lamar continued in the field with 179 and 175 votes respectively, each having retained his strength since the fourteenth ballot. Neither side gave any evidence of yielding. North Georgia was particularly tenacious, but its candidate, Lumpkin, had been a Unionist in the crisis of 1850-51 and, in addition, he was thought to have had something to do with Buchanan's policy in sending Walker to Kansas to secure its admission as a free state.[30] The Southern Rights element would not accept him.

A compromise was the only way out of the impasse and a motion to put the matter into the hands of a committee was quickly carried. The committee consisted of twenty-four, three from each of the eight congressional districts, each district selecting its own representatives. Trammell of the sixth promptly secured the election of three men favorable to Brown.[31] The objections which the Southern Rights men

---

[28] Trammell later became a member of the lower house of the general assembly, president of its senate for two terms, member of the reconstruction convention of 1868, Tilden elector in 1876, and railroad commissioner in the eighties. He was Brown's candidate for Congress in 1874 in the "bloody seventh," whom Dr. Felton, the "fighting parson," forced to withdraw.—*Infra*, p. 306. Trammell was president of the Democratic state convention in 1880 which so bitterly fought the renomination of Governor Colquitt on the issue of his having appointed Brown to the United States Senate.—*Ibid.*
[29] Avery, p. 32.   [30] Clark, *Memoirs*, p. 327.
[31] Avery (p. 32) is mistaken in saying Brown's name had not been mentioned even in his own section except among a few friends. The *Constitutionalist* on

had to Lumpkin could not be raised against Brown. He had been the leader of the Southern Rights Democrats in the state senate in 1849-50 and had urged resistance and the calling of a state convention.[32] He had acquiesced in the Compromise of 1850 but he was not convinced of its finality.[33]

Judge Richard Clark related in his *Memoirs* that he was a member of the committee of twenty-four and in favor of Brown's nomination. On the way to the meeting he spoke to Linton Stephens of the availability of Brown and though Stephens replied that he had "no accurate idea of the style of man Joe Brown is," in the committee Stephens proposed his name and Clark seconded it.[34] The committee voted by ballot on various nominees, but before the ballots were counted Stephens succeeded by a viva voce vote in nominating Brown. As a matter of curiosity the ballots were afterwards counted and it was found that Alfred H. Colquitt had been nominated by a majority of one.[35] Brown's name was recommended to the convention and was quickly ratified.[36] Thus by a "scratch nomination," as Avery calls it,[37] Joseph E.

---

February 12, 1857, published his name in a list of possible candidates. No other mention seems to have been made of his availability.

[32] One of his speeches as given in the *Federal Union* of Feb. 5, 1850, may be found in Phillips, *Toombs,* p. 92. In the state convention of 1849, however, he had opposed approving Calhoun's *Address.*—Lumpkin to Cobb, June 6, 1849, Phillips, *Correspondence,* p. 161.

[33] Phillips, *Georgia,* p. 208.

[34] Pp. 325-30. Clark's version seems at variance with Linton Stephens' letter to his brother a few days after the convention adjourned in which he described Brown, whom he had known in the general assembly in 1849-50, as a man of decided ability and superior as a debater to any of the candidates before the convention. "He is quick, clear-headed, and a close reasoner, with considerable turn for sharp, witty remark. He was a firm Southern-rights man, and one of the most prudent among them. . . . He stands high in the up-country and deserves it."—James D. Waddell (ed.), *Biographical Sketch of Linton Stephens,* pp. 127-28, henceforth cited as Waddell.

[35] Northen, III, 70; Avery, p. 36.

[36] Fielder, p. 88; *Federal Union,* June 30, 1857; *Constitutionalist,* June 30, 1857.

[37] The whole story of the convention may be found in Avery, Chap. V.

## THE CAMPAIGN OF 1857

Brown was launched on his remarkable career.[38]

Toombs, candidate for reëlection to the United States Senate[39] and accordingly doubly anxious for the success of the party, was in Texas when he heard of the nomination. "Who the devil is Joe Brown?" he asked.[40] The opposition press echoed the question and Democrats throughout the state made inquiry of each other. The party press was kept busy with explanations.

The *Atlanta Intelligencer*, the *Columbus Sun*, and the *Atlanta Examiner* on June 29 published sketches of the nominee's life and descriptions of his personal appearance. Eight days later the *Examiner*, stung by "Know-Nothing" editorials, gave an account of his ancestry which was copied by the party papers. On June 30, the *Savannah Morning News* published a long letter signed "A Neighbor" giving a very full account of Brown's life which the *Constitutionalist*—that Democratic bulwark whose editor had been defeated in the convention—copied and used as the basis of an editorial. "Nature has endowed him with solid sense, and a sound, discriminating judgment," said the *Constitutionalist*, "and severe, continued and untiring personal application and laborious research have made him a most profound and able man." In the turbulent times of 1850 Brown was a Southern Rights Democrat, "believing the Federal Government to be the creature of the State Governments. . . . He loves the Union for the sake of the States, not the States for the sake of the Union." On the question of Temperance,[41] the

---

[38] The Cherokee country of North Georgia in which Brown lived acquiesced in his nomination with reluctance.—Clark, *Memoirs*, p. 329.

[39] Toombs to William M. Burwell, July 11, 1857, William M. Burwell Papers, henceforth cited as Burwell Papers.

[40] Avery, p. 39; Pleasant A. Stovall, *Robert Toombs; Statesman, Speaker, Soldier, Sage*, p. 154, henceforth cited as Stovall; Phillips, *Toombs*, p. 171. Toombs was worried—it would take a strong man to beat Ben Hill.—Stovall, p. 154.

[41] Brown was a member of the Sons of Temperance. The movement in Georgia, particularly strong among the Baptists, had been active since 1839.

*Constitutionalist* continued, "he is opposed to legislation and believes in moral suasion."[42]

Brown was probably the "best selection that could have been made to correct the abuses practiced on the State Road,"[43] thought the *Newnan Blade*, which predicted that he would make a good governor despite the uneasiness of the American party who had "never heard of him before." It hailed the nomination as a new era in which "a man of the people can obtain preferment over the heads of politicians, and without family influence and political wire-working."[44] The *Macon Telegraph* was of like mind. No intelligent man had been surprised at the result of the convention, it thought, hinting at the wrangling that had gone on, but it was pleased with a candidate who was "a self-made man—springing from the masses of the people—without family influence, wealth or potential friends to back him."[45] The *Southern Recorder* was restrained in its comment: "We cannot say that he has done anything very notable, or that he is a man of extraordinary ability . . . but he is a very worthy, honorable, intelligent gentleman, who is well known in his section of the State. . . ." The Union Democrats accepted Brown's candidacy, the *Rome Southerner* warned, only on condition that he would not side with the Southern Rights wing of the party. It took advantage of the occasion to deplore the practice of selecting an outsider, as in the case of Polk, Pierce, and Brown, whose virtues had not been canvassed and whose names were not before the convention.[46] The *Constitutional-*

---

—A. H. Stephens to Prof. Wm. Rutherford, Jr., March 17, 1857, Cleveland, p. 608. Cf. *Athens Southern Banner,* Aug. 16, 1839, cited by Phillips, *Georgia,* p. 139. Under the inspiration of the Maine Law the movement had advanced in 1855 to the point of putting into the field a candidate for governor.—Flippin, p. 69, n. 4; S. F. Miller, *The Bench and Bar of Georgia: Memoirs and Sketches,* I, 440-41, henceforth cited as Miller, *Bench and Bar.*

[42] July 2, 1857.

[43] The Western & Atlantic Railroad, built, owned and operated by the state.

[44] Quoted by the *Constitutionalist,* July 2, 1857.

[45] June 30, 1857.  [46] July 2, 1857.

## THE CAMPAIGN OF 1857

*ist* sought to reassure the Union Democrats, saying that while Brown had been a Southern Rights man in 1850, he had been chairman of a committee in the following year which had urged reunion of the two wings of the party. It also replied to objections that had been made to the inexperience of the nominee, to his not having been born in Georgia, and to his being comparatively unknown.[47]

Contemporaries agree upon the facts of Brown's life. His ancestors were Scotch-Irish and came to Virginia in the middle of the eighteenth century. His grandfather fought in the battle of King's Mountain, his father in the battle of New Orleans. Brown was the oldest of eleven children and was born in South Carolina in 1821, just previous to the family's removal to a farm in Union County, North Georgia. At nineteen he entered Calhoun Academy in South Carolina which he attended for about three years, paying his expenses with a yoke of oxen his father had given him and by teaching school. Afterwards he taught school for one year and at the same time studied law in Canton, Georgia. The following year he lived in the home of Dr. John W. Lewis, tutored the Lewis children, continued the study of law, and at the end of twelve months was admitted to the bar by public examination. With funds borrowed from Dr. Lewis he next attended Yale Law School for one year, graduated in 1846, and established himself in Canton. In the following year he married Elizabeth Grisham, daughter of a Baptist minister of South Carolina, and at the time he was nominated for governor he was the father of five children.

His political life began with his election in 1849 to the state senate[48] where he served one term and became the leader

---

[47] July 10, 1857.
[48] There were 47 senatorial districts, 46 of which were composed of two counties each. Brown represented the 41st, comprising Cobb and Cherokee counties.—Avery, pp. 16, 50. Cf. Stovall, p. 156; Fielder, p. 106. He was not a candidate in 1851, probably because the Constitutional Union party was

of the Southern Rights Democrats in that body. In the presidential campaign three years later he was an elector on the Pierce ticket, and in 1855 he was elected judge of the superior court of Blue Ridge circuit in which capacity he was serving at the time of his nomination for governor.[49] Three of Brown's most pronounced characteristics were in evidence by 1857: he was a vote-getter,[50] he was an able executive, and he was a money-maker.

His success as a candidate began with his first appearance in political life. In the campaign for the senate he defied the time-honored custom of treating with whiskey, causing gray heads to wag and predict his defeat. As candidate for presidential elector for his congressional district, he had the distinction of being the youngest man on the ticket and of receiving the largest number of votes. In the campaign of 1855 he carried eight out of the eleven counties in the circuit. He had, however, the advantage of an overwhelming Democratic electorate, and, in the campaign in 1855, some advantage in having been active in the senate in the formation of a new county, that of Pickens, which in gratitude endorsed him in its convention and voted for him at the polls. It is reasonable to suppose also that his affiliation with the Baptist denomination, particularly strong in North Georgia, was of value.[51]

---

dominant and there was little chance for a Southern Rights candidate in North Georgia. Cf. Brown to Governor Towns, Oct. 18, 1850, Joseph E. Brown Correspondence, Georgia Dept. of Archives and History, Atlanta.

[49] There were 16 superior courts in the state with a judge for each, elected by the people of the circuit for a period of four years. The court had exclusive jurisdiction over criminal and land cases, and concurrent jurisdiction in all other civil cases. The salary was $1,800 a year.—*American Almanac for 1858,* pp. 292-94.

[50] He was never defeated at the polls but was defeated by the legislature in 1868 for the U. S. Senate.

[51] Fielder (pp. 93-94) expresses the opinion that religion and politics did not mix in Georgia: "The politicians . . . are not over-zealous in religion; and the men of the church in turn forget or disregard its fellowship when they come to vote in party elections." Nevertheless when Brown became gov-

## THE CAMPAIGN OF 1857

As judge he kept perfect order, compelled jurors and counsel to be on hand promptly, cleared the dockets,[52] made up his mind with decisiveness, and in general corrected the easygoing practices that had previously obtained in the circuit.[53] Although lawyers' fees were small at the time, Brown made $1,200 in his first year's practice.[54] He invested $450 in a piece of land on which he developed a copper mine, a one-half interest in which he sold for $25,000. This in turn he invested in farms, "the basis of his afterwards immense fortune."[55]

In personal appearance Brown was tall and thin, with a large head and a large, determined mouth. His face was placid, "in marked contrast with his iron will and combative disposition." His manner was awkward but self-assured. His voice was nasal, his accent provincial,[56] and his clothes were lacking in fit and style. He did not drink or use tobacco or indulge in profanity, and he never "loitered or dissipated time or associated with the idle and vicious." When notified of his nomination for governor he was working in the harvest field.

---

ernor he was accused of employing only members of his own denomination on the state railroad.—Avery, p. 81.

[52] One of the objections to the reëlection of his opponent had been that he had allowed the docket to get behind.—Avery, p. 27.

[53] Avery (pp. 28-29) tells a number of anecdotes illustrative of Brown's firmness in keeping order in his turbulent mountain courts.

[54] A code by which lawyers regulated their charges before the war was known as the Augusta Fee Bill and may be found in Garnett Andrews, *Reminiscences of an Old Georgia Lawyer,* Chap. VIII. Brown's success during his first year of practice seems extraordinary.

[55] Avery, p. 14. Avery does not say at what time the copper mine was developed. No writer of the time has suggested it, but the advice and example of Dr. John W. Lewis, Brown's friend and patron, must have been of great value in maturing his judgment in investments. Cf. "Biographical Compendium," *History of the Baptist Denomination in Georgia,* pp. 332-33.

[56] He invariably pronounced "judgment" with the accent on the second syllable. His admirers were wont to speak of him affectionately as "Old JudgMENT." The author was told by L. A. Rosafy, chief clerk, Old Records Division, Adjutant General's Office, War Department, Washington, who was

## 14   JOSEPH E. BROWN

Such was the man who at the age of thirty-six had by chance[57] been nominated as the standard-bearer of the dominant party in the state.[58]

The American party was confident of success. Its nominee, young Benjamin H. Hill, was already recognized as a brilliant lawyer and had won a substantial political success in 1855 when, as a candidate for Congress in a Democratic stronghold, he had come within two dozen votes of wresting the prize from a seasoned campaigner.[59] But it was in the following year that Hill had established his reputation. As presidential elector for Fillmore he had toured the state and spoken at mass meetings where ten to twelve thousand were often in attendance.[60] The crowning success was the fact that he had successfully met in debate Toombs and Stephens, the oracles and political lords of the state.[61] A series of joint debates had been arranged between the thirty-three-year-old Hill and Alexander Stephens, the first of which was held at Lexington. In the words of a recent writer,

---

a page in the United States Senate when Brown was a member of that body, that he always addressed the presiding officer as M i s t e r  P r e s i D E N T.

[57] The accidents of Brown's nomination, it will be remembered, were: a deadlocked convention, the failure of the nominating committee to count the ballots, his having been a Southern Rights Democrat in the crisis of 1850, and his residence in North Georgia.

[58] Details of Brown's life may be found in the newspapers above quoted, and in Avery, Chaps. II and III, and pp. 48-49; Fielder, pp. 69-70, 88-90 and Chap. II; Northen, III, 76-79; Stovall, pp. 156-57; *Appleton's Cyclopedia of American Biography; National Cyclopedia of American Biography;* "Biographical Compendium and Portrait Gallery," *History of the Baptist Denomination in Georgia,* pp. 65-68; *Encyclopedia Americana; Dictionary of American Biography; Biographical Directory of the American Congress, 1774-1927.*

[59] The Democrats were accused of winning the election by bringing miners across the Alabama line to vote.—Benjamin H. Hill, Jr. (comp.), *Senator Benjamin H. Hill, His Life, Speeches, and Writings,* p. 18, henceforth cited as Benjamin H. Hill, Jr.

[60] Avery, p. 43.

[61] Haywood J. Pearce, *Benjamin H. Hill, Secession and Reconstruction,* p. 20, henceforth cited as Pearce; Stovall, pp. 145-50; Benjamin H. Hill, Jr., p. 19.

"Stephens lost his temper and the debate." [62] The joint debates ended then and there, and Stephens challenged Hill to a duel, which the younger man refused.[63] The admiration of the American party for its champion "arose almost to idolatry," [64] and his nomination for governor the next year was a matter of course.[65]

A contemporary describes the man who was soon to meet Joseph E. Brown in joint debate as "tall and of commanding presence, with a marvelously mobile face," who "never had a superior in oratory or pure mental power in the commonwealth." [66] The paths of the two candidates were destined to cross many times in the ensuing years.

Not only was a governor to be elected in 1857, but also members of Congress, a general assembly, and, by the latter, a United States senator. The issues were largely national. The Democrats condemned Walker's course in Kansas,[67] upheld Buchanan's administration, and advocated the retention of the State Road.[68] The Americans condemned Walker but held Buchanan responsible, and favored selling the State Road which they claimed had been used for party plunder. They endorsed the Georgia platform and the Dred Scott de-

---

[62] Pearce, p. 16.
[63] Correspondence regarding the duel may be found in Benjamin H. Hill, Jr., pp. 20-30. Stephens' version is in letters to his second, Thomas W. Thomas, in Phillips, *Correspondence*, pp. 384, 386, 389. Cf. Mrs. William H. Felton, *My Memoirs of Georgia Politics*, p. 30, henceforth cited as Felton.
[64] Fielder, p. 81.
[65] Cf. Fielder, pp. 69, 85; Phillips, *Toombs*, p. 171; *Avery*, pp. 40-41; Pearce, pp. 20-22; Benjamin H. Hill, Jr., p. 31; Phillips, *Correspondence*, p. 391.
[66] Avery, p. 41.
[67] According to George Fort Milton, *The Eve of Conflict—Stephen A. Douglas and the Needless War*, pp. 263-64, Walker's inaugural address, favorable to the principle of popular sovereignty, received the sanction of President Buchanan.
[68] Avery, p. 41; Brown's letter of acceptance, *Constitutionalist*, July 15, 1857; Brown's speech at ratification meeting, *ibid.*, July 18, 1857; Brown's speech at Rome, *ibid.*, Sept. 20, 1857; Brown's letter to W. H. Burton, *Intelligencer*, Sept. 17, 1857.

cision and condemned further agitation of the slavery question.[69] Committees of the two parties arranged a joint canvass between the gubernatorial candidates, beginning at Newnan in western Georgia on July 28. The terms of the agreement for the first meeting are interesting as showing the seriousness with which Georgians of that day took their politics and the importance, therefore, of able debate. Brown was to open in a one-hour speech, Hill to follow with one and one-half hours, after which Brown was to have a half-hour reply. Tidwell and Gartrell—American and Democratic candidates for Congress—were each to have one hour.[70]

The Democratic *Intelligencer* reported the debate and expressed surprise that the "man-eater Hill" did not swallow Brown "bodaceously," since Hill, the *Intelligencer* said, was reported to have made his meals in one day the previous year on Stephens, Toombs, and Gartrell of the Democratic party. Brown successfully "showed up" the Know-Nothings, it said, especially on the Kansas question and the inconsistency of their present platform with past professions. He indulged in no "flowery oratory," but in "plain, honest, unanswerable argument," and "the honest, straightforward look of his manly countenance charmed everybody." His opponent showed "vast ability in the management of a hopelessly bad cause" and indulged "in dexterous sophistry to deceive the people."[71] The *Intelligencer* neglected to say that Hill had shown the inconsistency of condemning Walker and at the same time upholding the president whose agent he was, and that Hill had dealt telling blows on Democratic management of the State Road.

The joint debates continued for a few days, the *Constitutionalist* reporting the Democratic nominee as bearing himself "gallantly,"[72] but the party press was not enthusiastic,

---

[69] Avery, p. 41; Fielder, pp. 87-88; *Federal Union*, July 14, 1857; *Columbus Sun*, July 11, 1857, *Savannah Morning News*, July 10, 1857, cited by Pearce, p. 23.
[70] *Intelligencer*, July 30, 1857. [71] *Ibid.* [72] July 31, 1857.

## THE CAMPAIGN OF 1857

and Toombs predicted that in a month the Democrats would be "fighting to carry the state." [73] Before the campaign began, Cobb in doubtful mood had written to Stephens: ". . . I know Judge Brown very well and he will conform to the judgment of his friends, but if left to his own may blunder. This canvass is deep water and it requires prudence . . . to conduct successfully." [74] Cobb's fears were soon realized. At Athens the Democratic nominee was so obviously unequal to meeting his opponent's argument and oratory that the joint debates were hastily called off and Cobb implored Toombs to take Brown in charge.[75]

Toombs and Brown went to southern Georgia where the people were likely to be less critical. And so it proved. After two or three speeches Toombs felt that Brown could take care of himself.[76] Now that he was no longer overshadowed by Hill, Brown's speeches were better received. As told years afterwards by a correspondent in the *Atlanta Constitution*, Brown "talked in a simple style, using the homeliest phrases. . . . There was a sympathy between the speaker and the people that not even the eloquence of Toombs could emphasize, or the matchless skill of Mr. Hill disturb. In Brown the people saw one of themselves. . . . Toombs left him . . . impressed with the fact . . . that a new leader had arisen." [77]

As the campaign progressed, Brown's ability in debate

---

[73] Toombs to Stephens, Aug. 4, 1857, Phillips, *Correspondence*, p. 409.
[74] July 23, 1857, in *ibid.*, p. 408.
[75] Avery, p. 45; Benjamin H. Hill, Jr., p. 36; Stovall, p. 155. Avery states that the meeting took place in Columbus, "a very fastidious place, used to city manners and college graces," which preferred Hill. The description might as easily fit Athens where the state university was located. Avery is evidently in error. Cf. correspondent in the *Atlanta Constitution*, no date given, quoted by Avery (pp. 39-40), stating that the meeting was in Athens. Pearce (p. 26) makes a similar statement. Brown was scheduled to speak in Columbus on Sept. 2 (*Constitutionalist*, Aug. 30, 1857), and it is not likely that he spoke in that city twice.
[76] Stovall, pp. 157-58.
[77] "H.W.G.," date not given, quoted by Avery, pp. 39-40.

improved. He developed a style which was "cool, adroit, conversational," [78] dealing always in facts. At a later time it was said of him, " . . . though his tone was nasal, his pronunciation provincial, and his manner on the stump awkward, yet with audiences justly appreciating Toombs, Stephens, Ben Hill, H. V. Johnson, and the two Cobbs, he was one of the most effective speakers of his day." [79] Along with a style in speaking Brown developed to an uncanny degree the ability to sense the popular mind, probe its depths, and with the precision of the chemist to gauge its reactions. Practically all writers agree with Avery that Brown "knew every popular influence and had the keenest powers of reaching the masses" of any public man the state has ever produced.[80]

In the presidential campaign of 1844 the Whigs by repetition of the query, "Who is James K. Polk?" succeeded in establishing the popular impression of Polk as an unknown and obscure person, an impression of which "even historians have not always succeeded in divesting themselves." [81] In like manner, Brown, in the campaign of 1857, by reiteration and the psychology created by his peculiar pronunciation of "judgment," [82] planted in the minds of his audiences the conviction that Hill was lacking in that quality. If his opponent was lacking in "judgment," "prudence," and "sagacity," and Brown called attention to the fact, it necessarily followed that he himself possessed these qualities, else how could he discern their absence in another? No quarter was given by either side, and the political antagonisms, which began between the two men at this time and

---

[78] Avery, p. 41.
[79] John C. Reed, "Joseph E. Brown," *The South in the Building of the Nation*, XI, 129.
[80] P. 48.
[81] E. I. McCormac, *James K. Polk: A Political Biography*, p. 722. Pearce (p. 309, n. 2) mentions Brown's characterization of Hill as lacking in judgment. An effective answer to the charge is given by Benjamin H. Hill, Jr., pp. 33-36.
[82] *Supra*, Chap. I, n. 56.

## THE CAMPAIGN OF 1857

which were intensified during the war and reconstruction, lasted until they met in the United States Senate two years before Hill's death.[83]

The election was held on October 5 and resulted in a Democratic victory. Only two of the American party's candidates were elected to Congress and a very small number to the general assembly. Brown's majority was more than ten thousand.[84]

---

[83] Pearce, p. 22; Benjamin H. Hill, Jr., p. 33.

[84] Avery, p. 46; Benjamin H. Hill, Jr., p. 36; *Constitutionalist*, Nov. 8, 1857; *Federal Union*, Oct. 20, 1857. Election returns by counties for governor and congressmen are given in the *Tribune Almanac for 1858*, p. 56. Brown received 57,631 votes, Hill 46,889.—*Ibid*. The Democratic majority was somewhat smaller than it had been two years before, which is surprising in view of the fact that the American party was disintegrating throughout the nation. Soon after the election it disappeared altogether in Georgia. Toombs was easily reëlected by the legislature.—Toombs to Wm. M. Burwell, Nov. 20, 1857, Burwell Papers.

Replying to a letter of congratulation Brown wrote: "It is true I have been very fortunate. I am in my 37th year. I was laboring on a farm and had scarcely any education at 20. I have been very attentive to business. Whatever I have undertaken I have never failed in any important enterprise. . . ."—To an unknown correspondent, Jan. 18, 1858, Library of the Historical Society of Pennsylvania, Philadelphia.

## CHAPTER II

## THE SECESSION OF GEORGIA

BROWN's election was a shock to the aristocratic element of the state for he had neither the social prestige nor the experience in public affairs usually associated with the office of governor.[1] The legislature, on the other hand, was able and experienced and many of the members felt themselves superior to Brown in ability,[2] a feeling, however, in which the Governor did not share. The situation was ideal for Brown if, as his friend Avery said, he had "a natural relish for a set-to with other folks." [3]

Brown's inaugural address foreshadowed what proved to be the important issue of his first term.[4] It was a "bombshell . . . that occasioned one of the . . . most dramatic public battles of his career, and that gave a startled State a pretty fair example of the extraordinary mettle of this untried and youthful country Governor." [5] In the general financial panic which had swept the country in 1857 banks had either suspended specie payment or closed their doors. Although Georgia law provided that any bank suspending specie payment should forfeit its charter, a number of banks had taken the step, and a committee of business men appealed to Governor Johnson to withhold action until the legislature

---

[1] Fielder, p. 110; Avery, pp. 47-48.
[2] Fielder, p. 111; Avery, pp. 50-52.
[3] P. 133.
[4] *House Journal, 1857*, pp. 33 et seq., henceforth cited as *H. J.* The address was published in the *Federal Union*, extra edition, Nov. 6, 1857, and the *Constitutionalist*, Nov. 8, 1857.
[5] Avery, p. 49.

should meet and legalize their course. The promise was given[6] and in his message of November 5 Governor Johnson recommended that the suspension be legalized and a day fixed for resumption.[7]

The new governor, whose attitude toward banks was similar to that of Andrew Jackson,[8] was of a different mind and in his inaugural address the following day he announced his intention to enforce the law.[9] Financial circles were thrown into a panic and hurriedly sent representatives to the capitol to appeal to the legislature. That body promptly prepared a bill suspending forfeiture proceedings for the period of one year, which passed by more than a two-thirds majority. In view of the size of the vote and the pressure brought to bear by the banks, it was not thought the Governor would dare to veto the measure. But whatever Brown's shortcomings, lack of courage was not one of them. With great care he prepared his message and "like a clap of thunder it burst upon the legislature." [10]

In the clear, vigorous style which characterized all his state papers Brown reviewed the history of the state's banking legislation and previous suspensions. Taking the position that the existing laws made bankers a favored class which was "contrary to the genius and spirit of our government," that there was no necessity for suspension, that the bankers had violated their contract with the people in refusing to meet "their solemn promises," and that they had openly defied a statute of the state for their own selfish purposes, he concluded that the banks had been guilty of "a high, commercial, moral, and legal crime," and had endeavored to "dictate the terms of their own pardon." He announced his

---

[6] Governor Johnson's letter, Oct. 15, 1857, Flippin, pp. 69-70.
[7] *H. J., 1857*, p. 12.
[8] E. Merton Coulter, *A Short History of Georgia*, p. 293, henceforth cited as Coulter, *Georgia*.
[9] *Minutes of the Executive Dept., 1855-59*, p. 221.
[10] *Atlanta Intelligencer*, Dec. 30, 1857.

intention to do his duty in executing the law to forfeit the charters of the offending banks and to pay the assets to their creditors. The bill designed to give them relief he considered unconstitutional.[11] The message was received by the legislature on December 22, and after a spirited debate, in which the president of the senate[12] took the floor in opposition to the veto, the bill was passed on the same day by a vote increased by five over the original passage.[13]

The reaction of the press to the Governor's veto was prompt. The *Augusta Chronicle* thought the question of the campaign, "Who is Brown?" could be answered with the reply that he is "a d—d fool!"[14] The *Savannah Republican* protested against poisoning the minds of the laboring class against the banks.[15] A correspondent to the *Constitutionalist* signing himself "Richmond" felt very bitter towards the Governor, but "Justice" replied sustaining the Governor's arguments that the bill was unconstitutional.[16] The *Albany Patriot* thought the Governor desired "to promote the best interests of the state," but that "any measures which would cripple or destroy the banks would react with destructive effect upon the interests of the people."[17] Although the *Columbus Times and Sentinel* was "not prepared to say that the veto was a wise and judicious act," it had no criticism to make of the Governor, "entertaining as he did contrary views . . . with regard to the bill's unconstitutionality."[18]

Several newspapers favored the veto but disagreed with

---

[11] *Senate Journal, 1857*, p. 558, henceforth cited as *S. J.* Extracts from the message and accounts of public reaction may be found in Fielder, pp. 121-23, and Avery, pp. 49-50, and Chap. VIII.

[12] John E. Ward, who the previous year had been president of the Democratic National Convention and was soon to be appointed minister to China. —Avery, pp. 50-52.

[13] *S. J., 1857*, pp. 577-78; *H. J., 1857*, pp. 449-50.

[14] Avery, p. 66.

[15] Dec. 25, 1857.

[16] Dec. 31, 1857; Jan. 3, 1858.

[17] Jan. 7, 1858.

[18] Jan. 5, 1858.

the reasons given,[19] while others thought that there were good arguments on each side of the question.[20] The *Savannah Georgian* had "abiding faith" in the Governor,[21] the *Clarksville Georgian* and the *Newnan Banner and Sentinel* believed the people would sustain him,[22] and the *Atlanta Intelligencer* pointed out that it "required *nerve* to thus stand by the people." [23]

Brown was confident that the people would sustain him[24] and he was not mistaken. Public meetings were held, praising the "Jacksonian firmness" of the Governor, who was "under all circumstances the friend of the people when their rights were threatened," and condemning as "hireling bank organs" the newspapers that opposed him.[25] On June 1 Brown issued a proclamation requiring banks to make their semi-annual returns in the manner prescribed by law, which provided that affidavits should accompany reports stating that the provisions of the act had not been violated.[26] When certain banks failed to comply, he issued a second proclamation listing those banks and forbidding the receipt of their bills at the treasury in payment of any debts due to the state.[27] This was the signal for another outburst of newspaper controversy.[28]

---

[19] *Macon Telegraph,* Dec. 20, 1857; *Constitutionalist,* Dec. 27, 1857.

[20] *Southern Recorder,* Dec. 29, 1857.

[21] Dec. 31, 1857.

[22] Quoted by the *Constitutionalist,* Jan. 10, 1858.

[23] Dec. 30, 1857. Avery (pp. 65-66) states that only the *Federal Union* stood by Brown at first, but as shown above, this was a mistake. A majority of the Savannah and Augusta papers naturally supported the banks.

[24] Brown to Stephens, Feb. 9, 1858, Phillips, *Correspondence,* p. 431. Stephens approved the veto.

[25] Avery, pp. 66-67. The banks resumed specie payment in the following May, although the law granted immunity until Nov., 1858.—Fielder, p. 123.

[26] *Minutes of the Executive Dept., 1855-59,* p. 414.

[27] *Ibid.,* p. 424; *Constitutionalist,* July 29, 1858.

[28] Editorial, *Constitutionalist,* July 27, 1858; letters from "Thankful" and "Fiat Justicia," *ibid.,* Aug. 1, 31, 1858. Cf. the Governor's recommendations to the legislature in the following November.—*H. J., 1858,* p. 6; *Constitutionalist,* Nov. 5, 1858. The legislature did not act on the recommendations.

When secession drew near and banks North and South began to suspend specie payment, Brown again vetoed a bill granting relief, using much the same arguments as in 1857, and severely castigated lobbyists.[29] The urgency for retaining specie in the South in the event of secession was a telling argument, however, and the legislature passed the bill over the Governor's veto.[30]

In his veto message the Governor intimated that the legislature had been bribed. The senate took offense and passed a resolution asking for information of any member who had taken money or any bank that had offered it. The Governor replied that he saw nothing in his message that he "desired to retract or modify," and his further remarks seemed to reflect upon the lower house. That body immediately passed resolutions to the effect that the Governor had evaded answering a charge that he could not sustain and ". . . his Excellency . . . has not only abused the privilege of this House but has failed to maintain in his official intercourse with this body, that dignity of deportment, which becomes the Chief Magistrate of Georgia." The Governor "who never declined a combat" [31] characterized the resolutions as "conceived in passion, prompted by a spirit of personal revenge, . . . undignified in their bearing, untrue in their statements, and unjust in the assault . . . upon a coördinate branch of the government." The legislature having adjourned, he ordered his message entered upon the minutes of the Executive Department.[32]

Brown used the veto power more freely than any executive in the state's history and it naturally created antagonisms

---

[29] *S. J., 1860*, pp. 161, 185.
[30] *Acts of the General Assembly, 1860*, p. 22. The law was extended from time to time during the war.—*Ibid., 1861*, pp. 18-19, 25-27; *ibid., 1862*, pp. 19-21.
[31] Avery, p. 131.
[32] *S. J. 1860*, pp. 185 *et seq.* Cf. Avery, pp. 131-34.

within and without the legislature.³³ In his message at the end of his first term he defended himself, saying that if a governor out of respect to the wishes of the two houses signed a bill of which his judgment did not approve, he deprived the people of that executive revision which they had a right to demand as a protection against hasty and unwise legislation.³⁴

Governor Johnson had urged upon the legislature the cause of public education, the promotion of railroads, and the employing of a state geologist and agricultural chemist with a view to the further development of the state's material resources.³⁵ Governor Brown made similar recommendations, but opposed the policy by which the state had promoted two railroads³⁶ through the purchase of stock. He recommended instead a general law under which the state should lend its credit by endorsing the bonds of railroad companies, secured by a mortgage upon the road and its appurtenances, with each stockholder made liable to the extent of his investment.³⁷ In the matter of public education, in which Governor Brown always took the keenest interest, he proposed a plan by which the public school fund might be increased and made permanent. The plan included a system of free scholarships to the state university for the education

---

³³ Avery, p. 101. He vetoed a joint resolution to pardon two women convicts (*S. J., 1857*, p. 205; *H. J., 1857*, p. 191; *Constitutionalist*, Dec. 15, 1857), a bill to commute the death sentence of John Black (*S. J., 1857*, pp. 372-74; *H. J., 1857*, pp. 457, 466), the Choice pardon (*H. J., 1859*, p. 220; *ibid., 1860*, pp. 215, 322; *S. J., 1859*, p. 264; *ibid., 1860*, pp. 281, 335). The Choice pardon case is discussed by Fielder, pp. 116-19; Avery, pp. 141-42; Benjamin H. Hill, Jr., pp. 36-37; Pearce, p. 34 *et seq.* Other vetoes included a bill granting a divorce, a bill to relieve a surety on a criminal bond, a bill to allow married women to conduct a business.—Avery, p. 21.

³⁴ Fielder, pp. 112-13.

³⁵ *H. J., 1857*, p. 10. Cf. Flippin, pp. 56-57.

³⁶ The Atlantic & Gulf and the Georgia railroads.

³⁷ *H. J., 1858*, p. 6. In 1868 the reconstruction legislature adopted this plan and Governor Bullock endorsed bonds with serious consequences to the state. See *infra,* Chap. XI, n. 105; Chap. XII, n. 58.

of teachers,[38] somewhat similar to that adopted twenty years later by the Peabody Education Fund. He pointed out that in this way the state could supply itself with teachers "raised in her midst and devoted to her interests and institutions— Southern men, with Southern hearts and Southern sentiments." [39]

The Western & Atlantic Railroad, popularly known as the "State Road," upon which was built much of Brown's reputation, played such an important part in his life as to make necessary a history of the road's origin. It was built entirely by the state, having been authorized by the legislature on December 21, 1838, and extended from Atlanta to Chattanooga. It was designed as a trunk line to connect with other Georgia railroads, to form a link of a general system within the state, and through its connections at its northern terminus to tap the great Northwest.[40] Early in May, 1851, the first train ran from the embryo city of Atlanta to Chattanooga, a distance of 137 miles.[41]

The road's location and connection were such as to make

---

[38] The South had difficulty in securing and retaining satisfactory teachers. Its own men went into other professions, into cotton raising, or politics, and its women did not seek to be self-supporting. Many of its teachers came from the North and oftentimes were abolitionists, while the women teachers usually married in a short time. Thus the "teacher turn-over" was heavy.

[39] *H. J., 1858*, pp. 6 *et seq*. The legislature did not adopt the recommendations but it did increase the annual appropriation for public schools, to be taken from the net earnings of the State Road.—*Acts of the General Assembly, 1858*, p. 59. The Governor subsequently recommended the establishment of a free industrial and normal school for girls whose parents were unable to educate them and generous appropriations to the state university.—*H. J., 1860*, p. 14.

[40] Ulrich B. Phillips, "Transportation in the Ante-Bellum South," *Quarterly Journal of Economics*, XIX (May, 1905), 449; *idem, Georgia*, p. 142; *idem*, "An American State-Owned Railroad," *Yale Review*, XV (Nov., 1906), 263-64; Cleveland, p. 612.

[41] James Houston Johnston (comp.), *The Western and Atlantic Railroad of the State of Georgia*, p. 21, henceforth cited as Johnston, *W. & A. R. R.*; Cleveland, p. 611; Phillips, "An American State-Owned Railroad," *loc. cit.*, p. 270.

it an invaluable asset to the state, not only in developing North Georgia, but in eventually bringing rich returns to the treasury.[42] But in the discouraging years of construction, which included the panic of 1837-39, this was evident only to the farsighted, and the people in general became weary of the continued drain upon the treasury with no immediate returns. The building of the road through the mountains at a time when the science of railroad construction was in its infancy had proved difficult, and the cost had exceeded expectations. Politicians seized upon the discontent as an issue, as politicians are wont to do, and made the State Road a football in gubernatorial campaigns. The Whigs in large part bore the onus of its building, the Democrats that of its operation. The "ins" favored the state's retaining the road, the "outs" advocated its sale or lease.[43]

By the end of 1857 the value of the road was apparent. Reviewing its operation over the period of his two terms, Governor Johnson in his retiring message showed in the period of four years gross earnings of $3,052,269.82, operating expenses of $1,329,411.51, and net earnings of $1,722,-849.31. After deducting expenditures for repairs, exten-

---

[42] The road is still owned by the state. It is operated by the N. C. & St. L. R. R. on lease at a monthly rental of $45,000 and a guarantee to add improvements to the amount of $5,000 per month.—Information given to the writer in 1934 by Mr. E. J. Little, chief clerk to the president of the N. C. & St. L. R. R.

[43] Exceptions were Governors Cobb and Johnson.—*H. J., 1853-54*, p. 19; *H. J., 1855-56*, p. 15. In the legislative session of 1853-54, a bill was introduced to lease the road.—*H. J., 1853-54*, p. 104; *S. J., 1853-54*, p. 195. The absence of graft in the building and operation of the road previous to the war was in striking contrast to its management in the period of reconstruction. Charges to the contrary in the ante-bellum period seem to have been merely for political effect, since none of the investigating committees unearthed anything more serious than a shortage of $53,000 due to fraud and collusion between the local agent and certain citizens of Chattanooga, and between the agent and a contractor who had built a woodshed at one of the stations. Cf. Phillips, "An American State-Owned Railroad," *loc. cit.*, pp. 273-74; Johnston, *The W. & A. R. R.*, pp. 49-50.

sions, rolling stock, and depots, he said that the state treasury had received:

| | | | |
|---|---|---|---|
| 1854 | $ 50,000 | 1856 | $ 43,000 |
| 1855 | 100,000 | 1857 | 100,000[44] |

The Governor pointed out that heavy expenditures would no longer be required and that the time had come for the patience of the friends of the road to have its reward. He expected the state treasury to receive in the future at least $390,000 annually. In comparison with other railroads in the matter of operation and maintenance he showed the Georgia Railroad as spending 45 per cent of its gross earnings, the Macon & Western 50½ per cent, the Central of Georgia 47¼ per cent, while the State Road had spent only 43½ per cent. He thought the "senseless clamor" against the management of the road, "for mere decency's sake, ought to cease."[45]

Early in January following his inauguration Governor Brown appointed as superintendent Dr. John W. Lewis,[46] giving him a written order to cut expenses, keep the road in repair, dismiss all "supernumeraries," reduce unreasonably high salaries, require obedience, dismiss all who were addicted to drink and gambling, and require conductors and agents to make reports promptly.[47] The new superintendent made sweeping changes in personnel and train schedules, which were attacked and defended in the press.[48] The wholesale removal of employees brought bitter condemnation, and Brown and Lewis were accused of filling the places with Baptists. A published official report of the religious affilia-

---

[44] *H. J., 1857*, p. 10 *et seq*. These figures agree with the financial summary in Johnston, *The W. & A. R. R.*, pp. 106-7.
[45] *H. J., 1857*, p. 10.
[46] *Supra*, Chap. I, n. 55.  [47] *Intelligencer*, Jan. 21, 1858.
[48] Cf. "Rip Van Winkle" in *Constitutionalist*, June 24, 1858, and reply of *Federal Union* quoted by Fielder, p. 133; official statement in defense of the policy of the superintendent, *Constitutionalist*, June 17, 1858; critical editorial, *ibid.*, Nov. 24, 1858.

tions of the employees showed 77 Baptists among 195 employees,[49] which was probably not an undue proportion from that denomination in view of its large membership in the state.

Among the spectacular economies effected by the Governor was that of gathering up the scrap iron along the road and selling it for $20,000.[50] It was heralded far and near and, whether so intended or not, served to focus attention upon the fact that the road was being conducted with the most rigid economy and efficiency, as indeed it probably was. There is no way of knowing whether the economies instituted by Brown—for the purpose of making a favorable showing in the state treasury, it was charged—seriously curtailed the services of the road. The "favorable showing" was not in evidence at the end of the road's fiscal year, September 30, 1858, in so far as the state treasury was concerned, since the state received only $175,000. This was an increase of $75,000 over the previous year, it is true, and a larger amount of bonds had been paid off, but in the last year of Johnson's administration there was almost twice as much expended for construction and the revenue from operations was more than $100,000 greater.[51]

In the remaining years of Brown's administrations the state received:

| | | | |
|---|---|---|---|
| 1859 | $402,000 | 1862 | 440,000 |
| 1860 | 450,000 | 1863 | 1,650,000 |
| 1861 | 438,000 | 1864 | 278,000[52] |

---

[49] For list, see Avery, p. 81.

[50] Brown to Stephens, May 7, 1858, Phillips, *Correspondence*, p. 434; Avery, p. 72.

[51] See Johnston, *The W. & A. R. R.*, pp. 106-7. The falling off of revenue is not easily explained. Not until 1862, when the demands of war and the inflation of the currency operated to increase them, did the revenues rise as high as in 1856-57. The panic of 1857 and its aftermath may have been responsible.

[52] *Ibid.* The small amount received in 1864 was due to the fact that after July 22 of that year until Sept. 25, 1865, the road was in the hands of the U. S. government.

Was Brown's management of the road extraordinary, as claimed? There is no doubt that the public thought so, but there were contributing factors in the successful showing which must not be overlooked. The cost of construction, equipment, and depots was a heavy drain upon the road's earnings in the earlier years, and connecting lines with consequent increase in traffic were not completed until near the outbreak of the war. When Brown became governor the road had just reached a point where the state could realize upon its investment—where, as Governor Johnson had said, the patience of the friends of the road could receive its reward.[53]

Brown based his claim to renomination in 1859 upon his successful operation of the State Road. There seems to have been no real opposition to him, despite his difficulties with the banks and with the legislature. He had without doubt shown himself to be an able executive and the masses supported him wholeheartedly, recognizing in him one of their own number and a champion of their interests.[54] It was also customary for a governor to serve two terms. A further reason undoubtedly was the threatening aspect of the sectional question. If there should be trouble between the two sections, Georgia wanted an executive of no uncertain temper on the subject.

The size of the vote Brown received in the election—the largest of any of his campaigns—was not wholly a tribute to him, but was in part due to political conditions outside of Georgia as well as within. The decline of the American party after its defeat in 1856, together with the break between Buchanan and Douglas in the Democratic party and the panic of 1857, for which as the party in power the Demo-

---

[53] Cf. opinion of *Federal Union,* cited by Phillips, "An American State-Owned Railroad," *loc. cit.,* pp. 273-74.

[54] His moral habits were no doubt pleasing to the stricter religious denominations. No drinks were served and no smoking allowed at the executive mansion. He had election day changed from Monday to Wednesday to obviate the necessity for Sunday preparations and recommended that no trains be permitted to run on Sunday.—Fielder, pp. 134, 161.

crats were held responsible, seemed to assure success to a conservative party which could draw support from both Democrats and Republicans. Whig-Americans, calling themselves the "Opposition," accordingly met in Washington in December, 1858, and perfected plans and an organization for the 1860 campaign. Southern conservatives—Whigs, Americans, and dissatisfied Democrats—claiming that the slavery question was settled and that the Democrats and Republicans used it merely as a political issue, went into the Opposition camp.[55]

In this state of affairs the executive committee of the American party in Georgia met and after much wrangling dissolved the party in that state and invited all opposed to the "maladministration" of the Democratic party in state and nation to meet in an Opposition convention to nominate candidates for state officers and for Congress. There were differences of opinion as to when and where the convention should be held, with the result that a second convention was necessary to get the delegates together. Hill was the leader of the movement and the object was to lay the foundation of a Constitutional Union party for 1860, in line with the Opposition throughout the nation. The convention endorsed the Federal Constitution and the Dred Scott decision, denounced squatter sovereignty, condemned agitation of the slavery question, and censured the "extravagant and corrupt democracy."

Opinion was divided on whether to nominate a candidate for governor, but it was finally decided to do so. Warren Akin, a Methodist minister and lawyer of North Georgia with only a local reputation, was chosen.[56] Brown made no

---
[55] Cole, pp. 333-36.
[56] Hill and other better known men than Akin did not wish to undertake a losing campaign, Brown's reëlection being conceded. For the Opposition convention in Georgia, cf. Fielder, p. 108; Avery, pp. 93-96; Northen, III, 76-79; Phillips, *Toombs,* pp. 175-76; *Southern Recorder,* July 26, Aug. 16, 1859, cited by Pearce, p. 34.

canvass, explaining that his health and official duties would not permit, and that $35,000 to $40,000 a month poured into the treasury from the State Road was an argument more potent than stump speeches.[57] He gave what was perhaps the true reason in a letter to Stephens: ". . . there are so many collateral issues that might be sprung in the canvas [sic] . . . upon which the public mind is divided, that I doubt whether any gains could be expected by the party from such a course." [58] Both the "woolhats" and the aristocrats supported the Democratic party,[59] and the Opposition elected only two members of Congress. Brown's majority was more than twenty-one thousand.[60]

Foreseeing the coming sectional conflict, Brown directed much effort from the time of his first inauguration to rehabilitating the militia, organizing volunteer companies, and strengthening the Georgia Military Institute.[61] On the subject of preparedness he said in his annual message of 1859: "We know not how soon we may be brought to the practical test of defending ourselves against the assault of foreign ambition, or the more unnatural attacks of those who ought to be our brethren, but whose fanaticism is promoting them to a course which is daily weakening the ties that bind us together as one people. The father of his country admonished us to prepare for war in time of peace." [62] The legislature followed his recommendation and appropriated $75,000 for military uses. Fielder states that the Governor ". . . exercised a vast and rapid influence in preparing the public mind for, and raising the public temper to the point of resistance and organized preparations for the public safety." [63]

---

[57] Speech before the Democratic state convention, Avery, p. 92. The *Republican* thought the speech was "puerile" and that "an ass could rule the people of Georgia as well as Brown was doing." It referred to him as "that inflated little demagogue Joe Brown."—*Ibid.*, p. 94.
[58] Phillips, *Correspondence*, p. 448.   [59] Avery, p. 99.
[60] *Tribune Almanac for 1860,* pp. 52-53.   [61] *Federal Union,* Nov. 9, 1858.
[62] *Ibid.*, Nov. 8, 1859; Fielder, pp. 164 *et seq.;* Avery, p. 129.
[63] P. 168.

## SECESSION OF GEORGIA

Brown had never been convinced of the finality of the Compromise of 1850 as a settlement of the sectional question,[64] and in his first inaugural he declared that Georgia would not remain in the Union unless accorded her full constitutional rights.[65] Shortly afterwards he expressed to Stephens the opinion that if the admission of Kansas were rejected "one of the contingencies of the Georgia platform will have happened," in which event he felt it would be his duty to call a convention to "determine the status of Georgia with reference to the Union." Nor was there any doubt in his mind as to the course the convention should pursue. "When the Union ceases to protect our equal rights, it ceases to have any charm for me," he said.[66]

In his second inaugural he expressed similar views: "Our fathers consented to enter the Confederacy of those States only upon terms of perfect equality; and we, as their sons, would be unworthy of our sires, if we consented to remain in the confederacy a day longer than this principle of equality is recognized." [67] Under the influence of their belligerent governor the legislature adopted a resolution on the John Brown raid which ended with the ominous declaration: "The State of Georgia holds herself ready to enter into any concert of action with the sister Southern States, which will secure their common rights under the Constitution in the

---

[64] See Phillips, *Georgia*, p. 182.

[65] *Ibid.* The South naturally stressed the importance of a strict adherence to the Constitution, believing with Calhoun that the purpose of a constitution is to protect the minority.

[66] Letter dated Feb. 9, 1858, Phillips, *Correspondence*, p. 431. Cf. *ibid.*, pp. 433, 434.

[67] Avery, p. 99; *Federal Union,* Nov. 8, 1859. In 1860 he wrote to two Savannah men whose newly invented rifle he had tested with a view to its manufacture by the state: "The legislature which places your 'Georgia Rifle' ... in the hands of every person in the State, qualified to do military duty, will have done more to protect the South against aggression than has been done by all the resolutions of its predecessors. ... Let us have no more compromises, and if the full measure of our rights is denied in future, let us stand by our arms."—Quoted by Avery, p. 125.

Union, or *if that be no longer possible, their independence and security out of it.*" [68]

It is interesting to note that with all his expressed determination to maintain the rights of Georgia and of the South, Brown did not favor the territorial plank which the Southern wing of the party insisted upon putting into the Democratic platform in 1860. After the Charleston convention had split he advised that the party adopt the Cincinnati platform with only an additional resolution such as the Northern wing would accept, merely recognizing the force of the Dred Scott decision.[69] When each wing of the party put up a candidate, the election of Lincoln became inevitable, though Georgians felt that somehow this would not happen.[70] Ben Hill, supporting the Constitutional Union party, made efforts for a fusion of the Bell-Douglas-Breckinridge forces in Georgia, but was opposed by Breckinridge supporters.[71] Brown favored Breckinridge and opposed fusion, doubtless thinking that Hill's judgMENT was again at fault.[72]

Although men like Rhett in South Carolina and Yancey in Alabama had long urged the futility of compromise and the necessity for prompt action by a united South,[73] leaders in Georgia up to the presidential election had not for the most part been so outspoken,[74] despite the continued excite-

---

[68] *Ibid.,* pp. 106-7.

[69] *Ibid.,* p. 118. The Cincinnati platform of 1856 represented Douglas' position on popular sovereignty, but in the meantime the Dred Scott decision had been rendered, which, in Southern opinion, changed the situation.

[70] *Ibid.,* p. 129.

[71] *Ibid.,* p. 128.

[72] In a few states fusion was accomplished. Under its terms the electoral vote was to go to the candidate receiving the largest number of popular votes.—Stanwood, p. 296.

[73] Yancey had long since proposed committees of safety.—John W. DuBose, *The Life and Times of William Lowndes Yancey,* pp. 361-64, henceforth cited as DuBose.

[74] Molyneux, British consul at Savannah, wrote to his home office in Dec., 1860, that if the state laws nullifying the fugitive slave act had been repealed and compensation guaranteed to owners of slaves unlawfully detained, a rupture of the Union might have been avoided.—Laura A. White, "The

## SECESSION OF GEORGIA 35

ment over the Kansas question, the returning of fugitive slaves, the refusal of the Republican party to accept the Supreme Court decision on slavery in the territories, and the John Brown raid.[75] Senator Iverson in 1859 declared the Northern Democracy paralyzed and powerless to aid the South and favored secession in the event of the election of a free-soil president in 1860. His opinion of the seriousness of the political situation was denied by Alexander Stephens,[76] and Iverson was not reëlected.[77]

Toombs had given warning in his "door-sill" speech[78] in the United States Senate in January, 1860, of the effect upon the South of the election of a party hostile to that section's interests, but after the election he had advised delay "to test Republican willingness to do the South justice."[79] T. R. R. Cobb and Toombs did not make their pleas to the Georgia legislature until November 12 and 13, and the address, "To Our Constituents," by a committee of Southern senators and representatives in the United States Congress, declaring that "the argument is exhausted," was not issued until December 13.[80] Not until December 24, after the Crittenden compromise had failed to win Republican support and the Georgia legislature had called a state convention, did Toombs send his well-known telegram from

---

South in the 1850's as Seen by British Consuls," *Journal of Southern History*, I (Feb., 1935), 46.

[75] Robert Bunch, British consul at Charleston, described to his government the feeling of terror which the John Brown raid inspired in the South.—*Ibid.*, p. 44.

[76] That Stephens deliberately misrepresented the situation is shown in a letter to a friend in 1860, in which he admitted retiring from Congress in 1859 because he "saw the shadows approaching and felt helpless to avert them."—Cleveland, p. 669.

[77] Avery, pp. 105-6. In 1862 Iverson declined appointment to the Confederate Senate for which he had been a candidate against Toombs and in a published letter reminded the electorate of his predictions in 1859.—*Ibid.*, p. 243.

[78] *Cong. Globe*, 36th Cong., 1st sess., Appendix, pp. 88-93.

[79] Phillips, *Toombs*, pp. 209-10.

[80] *Ibid.*, p. 206.

Washington saying that secession by the fourth of March ought to be thundered from the ballot box by the unanimous vote of Georgia.[81]

It was Joseph E. Brown, therefore, who, in his special message to the legislature on November 7, 1860, and in his subsequent pronouncements, crystallized sentiment and laid the foundation for the secession of the state.[82] The occasion of Brown's message was to lay before the legislature the invitation of South Carolina to a convention of Southern states "to concert measures for united action." The result of the presidential election, held the previous day, was as yet unknown, but the election of Lincoln was expected. Governor Brown opposed South Carolina's proposal, but in doing so he did "not wish to be understood as expressing a willingness to acquiesce in the repeated aggressions of the non-slaveholding States." [83]

He reviewed the history of slavery in the United States— the legal and illegal importation of slaves by Northern people, the abolition crusade with its doctrine of Negro equality and amalgamation and its incitement to servile insurrection, the denial by abolitionists to slaveowners of their right to carry their property into the territories—and characterized as nullification of the Constitution the so-called personal liberty laws of the Northern states. As remedies for the violation of the fugitive slave law he recommended reprisals by

---

[81] *Ibid.*, pp. 209-10.

[82] Coulter (*Georgia*, p. 296) says that Brown would have liked Georgia rather than South Carolina to lead in secession. Rhett's biographer states that Brown's speech caused the committee of the South Carolina legislature to bring in a bill calling for the election of delegates on Dec. 6 to a convention to meet Dec. 17.—White, *Rhett,* pp. 180-81. Governor Vance stated that Georgia more than any other state except Virginia influenced North Carolina in secession.—*Confederate Records of Georgia*, III, 702-4, henceforth cited as *C. R.*

[83] Those who opposed immediate secession and hoped for a compromise within the Union advocated a convention of all the Southern states and were known as coöperationists. See White, *Rhett,* pp. 98-99, 176, n. 41. Unionists, unable to stem the tide of secession and hoping that in a general convention secession might fall, also became coöperationists.

seizing, wherever found, the property of such states and of their citizens, and trade discriminations against their manufactured goods.[84] Should these measures prove ineffective, he suggested a repeal of that part of the penal code and other laws which protected the lives, liberties, and property of citizens of the states in question residing or traveling in Georgia. He thought the time had come for "bold, decided action." He was no disunionist per se, but the Union could not endure unless each section would accord to every other section "the full measure of its constitutional rights."

Justifying secession upon the concept of the Union as a business partnership, he said that whether the will of the people of the Southern states should be ascertained by a general convention of all the states, or whether each state should decide for herself, was a question upon which a diversity of opinion might exist. For himself, he had "no doubt of the right of each State to decide and act for herself." In agreement with the theme developed by Webster in his Capon Springs address, Brown said: "It is an essential part of the law of contracts, that both parties are bound or neither is bound."

He denied that secession was revolution or that there was any analogy between the separation of the colonies from Great Britain and that of a state's withdrawal from the Federal Union. States of the Union were "not the subjects of the Federal Government, were not created by it, and do not belong to it," but the States created that government, "from them it derives its powers, to them it is responsible." If, therefore, Georgia should secede and any other govern-

---

[84] For similar reasons the Democratic convention in Georgia in 1855 adopted a resolution asking the legislature to pass retaliatory measures. The legislature took no action, but a voluntary boycott resulted and purchases of commodities in the North and subscriptions to Northern newspapers fell off to such an extent as materially to add to the business depression in New England in 1858.—Editorial in *Boston Herald*, cited by Phillips, *Georgia*, p. 183.

ment should interfere and take the lives of any of her citizens upon a charge of treason, he would retaliate promptly "by seizing and hanging upon the nearest tree, two of the subjects of such Government for each citizen of Georgia. . . ."

The "King Cotton" theory he developed in the well-known argument that should the Southern states secede there would be no war, since the people of the North, dependent upon the South for cotton and the trade and employment connected with it, could not afford to fight. He insisted that the mutual and reciprocal relations existing between the South and Great Britain, which also was dependent upon Southern cotton, together with the rivalry in manufacture and trade between that country and the North, would act as a further deterrent of war. "An invasion of our soil," he said, "would shake the pillars of the English throne, and the cry of 'bread or blood' would . . . control the action of the Government, the Army, and the Navy . . . in our favor." He recommended in the event of the election of the Republicans that a state convention be summoned. For the purpose of defense and to prepare for an emergency, "which must be met sooner or later," he asked for an appropriation of a million dollars as a military fund. His message ended with the challenge: "To every demand for further concessions, or compromise of our rights, we should reply, 'The argument is exhausted,' and we now 'stand by our guns'." [85]

The effect of the Governor's message,[86] reaching the public as it did with the news of Lincoln's election, was electri-

---

[85] *C. R.*, I, 19-57; *Federal Union,* Nov. 13, 1860.

[86] Brown also addressed a military convention of volunteer companies in Milledgeville about the same time and repeated his threat to hang two Federal soldiers for every Georgian who should be executed for treason in the event of secession. He urged that it was the duty of every other Southern state to sustain South Carolina.—Horace Greeley, *The American Conflict* . . . I, 337, henceforth cited as Greeley; Joseph I. Derry, "Georgia in the Confederacy," *The South in the Building of the Nation,* II, 172, henceforth cited as Derry.

## SECESSION OF GEORGIA

cal. Public meetings were held throughout the state and resolutions poured in upon the legislature.[87] On November 12, 13, 14, 15, in response to invitation, T. R. R. Cobb, Toombs, Stephens, Hill, and others addressed the legislature.[88] On the sixteenth the million-dollar appropriation bill was signed,[89] and on the seventeenth the legislature issued a call for a constituent convention.[90] On December 7 the Governor in an open letter advocated immediate secession, whereupon the legislature, in response to his earlier recommendations, created the office of adjutant and inspector general, incorporated volunteer companies, and authorized the Governor to accept ten thousand troops. It also authorized the incorporation of, and state aid to, a shipping company to ply between Georgia ports and Europe and requested the Governor to appoint a commissioner to negotiate arrangements.[91]

While excitement was at its height in the campaign for the election of delegates to the state convention, Brown pub-

---

[87] These resolutions may be found in *C. R.*, I, 58-156. Letters poured in also from manufacturers in the North, imploring the legislature not to carry out the Governor's recommendations.—Avery, p. 130.

[88] Cobb and Toombs favored immediate secession. Stephens and Hill, while conceding the right of secession and admitting that sufficient cause existed, thought secession inexpedient. Stephens' speech led to some correspondence with Lincoln in the following month. Cf. Cleveland, pp. 150-53; Stephens, *War between the States,* II, 265-67.

Cobb's address may be found in *C. R.*, II, 157-82. Stephens' address, *ibid.*, pp. 183-205; Richard M. Johnston and William H. Browne, *Life of Alexander H. Stephens,* Appendix B, henceforth cited as Johnston and Browne; extracts, Stephens, *War between the States,* II, 265 *et seq.* Hill's address, Benjamin H. Hill, Jr., pp. 265-70. A copy of Toombs' address is in the Library of Congress; extracts, Stephens, *War between the States,* II, 321 *et seq.* Cf. Phillips, *Toombs,* Chap. IX.

For attitude of various leaders in Georgia, see Dwight L. Dumond, *The Secession Movement 1860-61,* pp. 142-44, henceforth cited as Dumond.

[89] *C. R.*, I, 741-42.

[90] *Ibid,* pp. 206-8; *Minutes of the Executive Dept., 1860-66,* p. 126. Horace Greeley thought the Governor's "impassioned message" was responsible for the unanimous vote in the legislature.—Greeley, I, 347.

[91] *C. R.*, I, 740-47; *ibid.*, II, 3-5, 6-8.

lished the above mentioned letter, written in response to the request of the state's presidential electors[92] for an expression of his views. He said that the election of Lincoln merely as a successful candidate would not justify secession, but as a tool in the hands of a fanatical abolitionist party it was ample justification. Submission to his inauguration would make future resistance futile, and would result in the abolition of slavery and the ruin of the South in twenty-five years. If abolition should be accomplished by the government's purchase of the four and one-half million slaves, two and one-fourth billion dollars would be required, enormously increasing taxes. Discussing the question of what would be done with the Negro after abolition, he pointed out the cost of colonization and the still more undesirable alternative of his remaining in the South. In the latter event his competition in the labor market with the poor white man, whom he would underbid, would lower the white man's standard of living and force him into tenantry or reduce him to a day laborer. Legal, economic, and social equality of the races would result, and crime would increase with probably one fourth of the Negro population kept constantly in jails.

The South could not live in peace with the North without new constitutional guarantees, he continued, and these he felt the North would never grant so long as the South remained in the Union. Secession before Lincoln's inauguration, on the other hand, might lead the North to make concessions and permit of reunion. Secession would not lead to war, he felt confident, referring to Buchanan's recent statement that the Federal government had no right to coerce a state, while submission at this time might lead to war in the

---

[92] The vote in Georgia was such that no party received a majority of the whole and the selection of presidential electors devolved upon the legislature, although it was recognized that the vote of the state could not affect the result. Brown was so indignant over Lincoln's election he advised the legislature not to choose electors.—Coulter, *Georgia*, p. 296. The vote in Georgia stood: Breckinridge 51,889, Bell 42,886, Douglas 11,590.—*Tribune Almanac for 1860,* p. 50; Stanwood, p. 297.

## SECESSION OF GEORGIA 41

future. Let wise men be sent to the convention, he urged, and let them act for the best to protect the rights and preserve the liberties of the people.[93]

To Governor Gist of South Carolina Brown sent a message to "put South Carolina out of the Union high and dry, as quick as possible." [94] Writing to the commissioner to Georgia from the state of Alabama Brown said: ". . . The Federal Government denies the right of a sovereign state to secede from the Union, while it refuses to make any concession or to give any guaranties which will secure our rights in the future. If we yield this right we become the subjects and the pro-slavery States the provinces of a great centralized empire. . . ." [95] He urged that each state secede promptly and unite on a common platform to form a more perfect union.[96]

Brown's every utterance had been in favor of immediate secession, and his official position and immense popularity with the masses combined to give weight and influence to his opinions. But his seizure of Fort Pulaski—Federal property—before the state had seceded must have had still greater influence, particularly upon the members of the state convention. From the standpoint of the Federal government, it was an act of treason for which the Governor might be arraigned. The fort was situated at the mouth of the Savannah River, commanded the approach to the city of Savannah, and was the chief fortification on the Georgia coast. Its pos-

---

[93] Avery, p. 134; *Federal Union,* Dec. 11, 1860, cited by Phillips, *Georgia,* p. 194. The letter was extensively published throughout the South, and exercised a powerful influence on the people of the slaveholding states.— Fielder, p. 262. The *Chronicle and Sentinel* said that South Carolina had "created a collision" with the Federal authorities "for the purpose of arousing the South from her slumbers."—Quoted by Greeley, I, 347.

[94] The message was given to the commissioner from Alabama who was on his way to South Carolina and had stopped in Milledgeville to ascertain Georgia's attitude toward secession.—Commissioner J. W. Garrott to Governor Moore, Dec. 7, 1860, Miscellaneous Papers of Governor A. B. Moore.

[95] Letter to the Hon. John Gill Shorter, Jan. 5, 1861, *C. R.,* III, 13-17. The letter was written six days before Alabama seceded.

[96] *Ibid.*

session by the state in the event of war was a military necessity.

In violation of the understanding with the South Carolina commissioners, the Federal government had moved its garrison from Fort Moultrie to the stronger position of Fort Sumter in Charleston harbor, causing great uneasiness in the South. When news came from Washington that Southern members of the cabinet were being replaced by coercionists, the occupation of other Southern forts with increased Federal forces was thought to be imminent.[97] Governor Brown accordingly gave an order on January 2, 1861, the day of the election of delegates to the state convention, to seize Fort Pulaski and on the following day one of the volunteer companies took possession without resistance.[98] The Governor's prompt action was applauded and his return to the capital was celebrated with music and a torchlight parade.[99] On the day on which he gave the order Governor Brown telegraphed to the governors of Mississippi, Alabama, and Florida, states in which conventions had been called, telling them of his action and urging them to take possession of Federal forts in their respective states. Florida, having only a few troops, asked assistance of Alabama in taking Pensacola. Brown in great anxiety telegraphed Governor A. B. Moore of Alabama: "Have you ordered troops to Pensacola to aid in taking forts? Answer quick." [100]

---

[97] See Toombs' telegram to the *Augusta True Democrat*, Jan. 1, 1861, quoted by Phillips, *Toombs*, pp. 215-16, stating the facts and calling attention to the danger to Fort Pulaski. According to Phillips, a project was on foot among citizens of Savannah to seize Pulaski, and Brown's action was due to these facts.

[98] *C. R.*, II, 7; *Savannah Morning News*, Jan. 3, 1861; Avery, pp. 145-46; Derry, p. 173. Brown's statement is given in the Executive Minutes, published in *C. R.*, II, 9-16. A description of the fort may be found in Fielder, pp. 178-79. The fort was occupied at the time by an ordnance sergeant and his assistants.

[99] Avery, p. 147; *Constitutionalist*, Jan. 16, 1861.

[100] Telegram to Governor Moore in Samuel W. Crawford Papers, 1860-1873; Governor Moore's message to the legislature, Jan. 14, 1861, *Official Records of the Union and Confederate Armies*, Ser. IV, Vol. I, p. 48, hence-

## SECESSION OF GEORGIA

The seizure of Fort Pulaski was no doubt a wise precaution, but the act was, to say the least, "unconstitutional," and the fact is interesting to remember in connection with the Governor's numerous controversies with the Confederacy over alleged violations of the Confederate constitution.

Public approval was also with the Governor in his controversy with the state of New York in which he seized vessels belonging to citizens of that commonwealth. Individuals and newspapers in the South had long advocated reprisals against Northern states for the illegal detention of slaves, but the policy had never been widely adopted and never in so dramatic a form as that employed by Governor Brown in the winter and spring of 1861. A shipment of guns, purchased by a Georgia firm and by the state of Georgia, was seized by the New York police on board the "Monticello" in New York harbor and placed in a state arsenal. When Governor Morgan refused to release the arms, Governor Brown ordered all vessels in Savannah harbor belonging to New York citizens to be seized and sold and the proceeds used to indemnify the owners of the arms. A few days before the date advertised for the sale the arms were released and Governor Brown rescinded his order.[101]

---

forth cited as *O. R.;* Dumond, p. 179. On Jan. 18 Governor Brown transmitted to the assembled state convention a copy of a resolution passed by the New York legislature tendering aid to the president of the United States in putting down the "insurgent State of South Carolina" and other states where Federal property had been seized, Georgia among the number. Toombs promptly offered a resolution in the convention thanking the Governor for taking Fort Pulaski and instructing him to hold it "until the relations of Georgia to the Federal government be determined by this Convention," and ordered a copy sent to the governor of New York.—*C. R.*, I, 241-44. The fort was held until March 20, when by ordinance of the convention it was transferred with other former Federal property to the Confederate States of America.—*Ibid.*, pp. 501-2. Brown also seized the United States arsenal at Augusta, but this was not done until Jan. 24—after the state had seceded.— Avery, pp. 161-63; Derry, pp. 175-76; Fielder, p. 182.

[101] *C. R.*, II, 24-31; *Cong. Record*, 47th Cong., sp. sess., pp. 106 *et seq.;* *Constitutionalist,* Feb. 16, 1861; Avery, pp. 171-79; Fielder, pp. 182-83, 631-32; editorial in *Savannah Republican* quoted by New York *Evening Post,* Feb. 15, 1861; *Governor's Letter Book, 1861-65,* eleven entries during Feb.,

The story of Georgia's secession has often been told and need not be repeated in detail. Practically every prominent man in the state was a member of the convention except Governor Brown, Howell Cobb, and Charles J. Jenkins, and they were invited on the floor. Four states had already seceded[102] but as in 1850-51,[103] Georgia held the key to the situation.[104] If she refused to secede, the movement would collapse. The deliberations of the Georgia convention were, therefore, watched with anxiety, North and South. On the question of the right of secession, the convention was practically unanimous, but there was a large minority of "coöperationists" who favored delaying action until measures could be agreed upon in a Southern convention, which meant another attempt at compromise.[105] Contrary to the general impression, Herschel V. Johnson and not Alexander Stephens led the fight against immediate secession.[106] He was aided by Benjamin H. Hill. Johnson's motion for a convention of all the Southern states, which was lost on the first test by a vote of 166 to 130, was offered again the next day by Hill as a substitute for the ordinance of secession, and the vote stood 133 to 164 against it. Seeing the futility of further op-

---

1861; *Minutes of the Executive Dept., 1860-66,* pp. 198-210. The mayor of New York wrote an apology to Toombs which was published in the New York *Herald,* Jan. 8, 1861. Authority over the police was at that time held by the state of New York.

[102] South Carolina, Mississippi, Alabama, and Florida.

[103] Dorman (pp. 63-64) claims that Alabama was not in favor of secession in 1850-51, believing in it as an abstract principle rather than as a policy to be put into practice at that time.

[104] *Cf.* Felton, pp. 26-27; Milton, *The Eve of Conflict,* p. 516.

[105] Among the coöperationists were Hershel V. Johnson, Benjamin H. Hill, Alexander and Linton Stephens, Hiram Warner, A. H. Kenan, and Dr. Alexander Means of the Atlanta Medical College. Leading the immediate secessionists were Toombs, T. R. R. Cobb, E. A. Nisbet, Francis S. Bartow. Johnson, Toombs, Cobb, and Nisbet had reversed their positions since the crisis a decade earlier.

[106] Johnson's *Autobiography,* cited by Flippin, pp. 177-79. Stephens spoke in favor of Johnson's resolution, *War between the States,* II, 305 *et seq.*

## SECESSION OF GEORGIA

position, Hill and forty-three others[107] patriotically joined the majority in adopting the ordinance, which was carried on January 19 by a vote of 208 to 89.[108]

Georgia had seceded. A Southern Confederacy was assured. The news "stirred the state to delirium," and ratification meetings were held everywhere, with guns firing and cannon roaring.[109] Ben Hill, who believed in the right of secession but thought it inexpedient at this time, could see no cause for rejoicing and was hung in effigy by jubilant throngs. To represent the state in the Provisional Congress at Montgomery the convention elected a delegate from each of the eight congressional districts, with two—Toombs and Howell Cobb—from the state-at-large. Among the number were Hill, A. H. Kenan, and Alexander Stephens, who had opposed immediate secession, and who were chosen "to give an air of moderation and responsibility," a recent writer thinks.[110] No doubt the object was to unify the sentiment of the state.

Well might the seceded states breathe a sigh of relief when the action of the Georgia convention was known. The state's four divisions produced almost everything to make it self-sufficing—North Georgia with its corn, wheat, stock, provisions of all kinds; the cotton belt with its cotton, grains, and sugar; the pine barrens, producing lumber, grains, livestock, cotton, rice, and sugar; and the coast lands with their rice and incomparable sea-island cotton.[111] Georgia's aggregate wealth in 1860 was more than $672,000,000. Her

---

[107] Dr. Alexander Means also joined the majority, but Johnson, the Stephens brothers, and Hiram Warner continued to vote with the minority.
[108] The election of delegates and the proceedings of the convention may be found in *C. R.,* I, 213 *et seq.;* Fielder, pp. 174 *et seq.;* Avery, pp. 149 *et seq.*
[109] Avery, p. 157.
[110] Phillips, *Georgia,* p. 222; *C. R.,* I, 294-95.
[111] See map in Phillips, *Georgia,* p. 140.

447,000 slaves represented a value considerably greater than her more than 33,000,000 acres of taxable land and city property. Her bonds were quoted at a higher premium than those of any other state in the cotton belt, she led also in the manufacture of textiles, and her comparatively small public debt was being rapidly liquidated by her Midas—the State Road. Her voting population of 97,000 in 1857 had increased to 110,000 and her property values accordingly. Her twenty-five banks represented a capitalization of $17,000,000.[112]

From 1817, when the first steamer to cross the Atlantic, the property of Savannah citizens, had left from the port of Savannah, the state's shipping had grown to enormous proportions. By 1843 she possessed a greater railroad mileage than any other state in the Union,[113] and by 1860 she had the distinction of being the only state that owned and operated a railroad. In public men of national repute, she was the peer, if not the superior, of any state in the Union. The state's influence upon the secession movement was accordingly very important. In the words of a contemporary: "The decisive act of Georgia settled the revolution. Whatever doubts had existed as to the policy or purpose of the South were dissipated. . . . In the sister states of the South the effect was electrical . . . and the secession crusade became irresistible." [114]

The influence of the state's chief executive was necessarily

---

[112] *American Almanac*, 1857, 1858, 1859, 1860; Report of State Comptroller, 1859, 1860; United States Census 1860; Tax Returns, *Federal Union*, Feb. 17, 1857. Price of slaves, *ibid.*, June 12, 1860. Cf. George White, *Statistics of Georgia, 1849*, p. 58.

[113] *Niles Register*, LXV, 272, cited by Phillips, *Georgia*, p. 142, n. a. The state did not long retain her pre-eminence in the matter of railroads.

[114] Avery, pp. 136-37. The terms "secession" and "revolution" were often used synonymously, there being in Southern minds no incompatibility between the two. Secession was a civil right, based upon the Constitution; revolution was a natural right, recognized in the Declaration of Independence and resting upon the law of God. Cf. Jesse Thomas Carpenter, *The South as a Conscious Minority 1789-1861*, p. 196, henceforth cited as Carpenter.

## SECESSION OF GEORGIA

far-reaching. Fielder states that the Governor's communications, in connection with those of Georgia's leading statesmen holding office in Washington, were read and accepted in every part of the South.[115] Of Brown's influence upon the masses within the state, particularly in the "white belt," in comparison with Hill's, a well-known author says: "Benjamin H. Hill emerged as a new leader in 1857, denying the expediency of secession, but he was more than offset by Joseph E. Brown, . . . sprung from yeoman stock and swaying thousands of mountaineers and other non-slaveholders. . . . As Governor, Brown did much to hasten secession." [116] Louisiana and Texas were the next states to fall in line and on February 4 the Provisional Congress met at Montgomery to inaugurate the Southern Confederacy of which Troup, Quitman, Yancy, and Rhett had so long dreamed.

Having failed in three lines of policy developed for her protection as a minority[117] since the United States was established, the South was now to try a fourth, that of independence. These policies had, however, left their imprint so deep upon the collective mind that from being a defense, they were to become, under the new policy of independence, like the fabled Ouroboros, a means of self-destruction. Perhaps upon the mind of no one person had this imprint been so deep as upon that of the governor of Georgia—and Georgia was the "Empire State of the South," whose geographic position and economic security gave her a leadership not equaled perhaps even by that of Virginia. It was a fateful combination.

---

[115] Pp. 168, 262.

[116] Ulrich B. Phillips, "Georgia in the Federal Union 1776-1861," *The South in the Building of the Nation*, II, 169-70. The difference between the attitude of the two men toward secession, according to Benjamin H. Hill, Jr., (p. 34) was that Brown advocated it as a constitutional right and a perfect remedy, while Hill recognized the constitutional right but believed it was not a practical remedy.

[117] See Carpenter, p. 5. The three lines of policy were local self-government until the Missouri Compromise, the principle of te concurrent voice until the end of the Mexican War, constitutional guarantees from 1850 to 1860.

## CHAPTER III

## "COMING EVENTS CAST THEIR SHADOWS BEFORE THEM"

IMMEDIATELY upon the state's secession Governor Brown set to work with energy to prepare for any contingency. Indeed, he had not waited for secession. In November he had written the secretary of war for samples of various military equipment with a view to having them manufactured by the state,[1] and before the end of 1860 he had placed orders in the North and in Europe for military supplies which more than exhausted the $75,000 appropriated by a previous legislature.

He appointed a commander for the state forces, a commodore lately resigned from the United States Navy to command the vessels which the convention authorized for coast defense, and a commissioner to Europe. The duties of the latter were to make arrangements for a line of steamers to Georgia ports, purchase supplies, and set before the nations the true cause of Georgia's secession.[2] After Lincoln's policy of coercion became evident, Brown redoubled his efforts to secure arms. Through proclamations offering two dollars each for old guns that might be repaired and by appeals to citizens to lend their private firearms for the term of the war, he secured practically every gun within the limits of the state.[3]

---

[1] It developed that he had already exhausted the state's quota for 1861 and the samples had to be purchased.—*C. R.*, III, 3-6.

[2] Georgia was a *de facto* independent republic from Jan. 19, 1861, until the Confederacy was organized.

[3] *C. R.*, II, 3-5, 6-8, 19-24, 45-46, 48-49, 116, 137-38; *ibid.*, I, 735; Avery, pp. 129, 189-90; Fielder, p. 184. For the commissioner's activities in Europe, see *C. R.*, II, 324-28.

Toombs declared that Brown had "more guns than the whole Confederacy." [4]

Indeed this may well have been true. The South as a whole was totally unprepared for war and the Confederacy was so short of guns that until shipments from Europe arrived in December, 1861, it was compelled to turn away thousands of eager volunteers.[5] President Davis said there were only 15,000 rifles and 120,000 muskets within the limits of the Confederacy when the war began, and that these had been taken in large part from United States arsenals and were old models and out of repair.[6] The people of the South had for the most part expected secession to be peaceful.[7] Many people of the North took the same view, among them being the powerful New York *Tribune* which favored "letting the erring sisters depart in peace," and hoped "never to live in a republic, whereof one section is pinned to the residue by bayonets." [8] Under the circumstances the Confederate Congress was slow to adopt measures of defense that might create antagonism and as a result the military measures of the first year were hastily improvised and often in conflict.

---

[4] Stovall, p. 284; *C. R.*, III, 106.

[5] Out of a population of 8,000,000 white people, 600,000 offered their services in the first year of the war.—Frank L. Owsley, "Defeatism in the Confederacy," *North Carolina Historical Review*, III (July, 1926), 446.

[6] Jefferson Davis, *The Rise and Fall of the Confederate Government*, I, 471, henceforth cited as Davis, *Rise and Fall*. A newspaper reporter traveling from Washington to Montgomery in the early days of March, 1861, was struck with the lack of preparation everywhere apparent.—Thomas C. DeLeon, *Four Years in Rebel Capitals*, p. 23, henceforth cited as DeLeon. Volunteers in training, unable to procure guns, used "Joe Brown's pikes"—a rude sort of bayonet or steel lance fastened to a handle—which the Governor had manufactured in large quantities in 1861. See John B. Gordon, *Reminiscences of the Civil War*, pp. 5-6, henceforth cited as Gordon.

[7] White, *Rhett*, p. 205. Davis did not share this view.—*Rise and Fall*, I, 230; DeLeon, p. 175.

[8] Nov. 10, 1860; Laura A. White, "Charles Sumner and the Crisis of 1860-61," *Essays in Honor of William E. Dodd*, Chap. VII. An English correspondent found the North very much in favor of peace, with Confederate commissioners in Washington in high favor in fashionable society.—W. H. Russell, *My Diary North and South*, I, 92-96, henceforth cited as Russell, *My Diary*.

On February 28 the President of the Confederacy was authorized to assume control of all questions of peace and war for the new government, to receive from the several states the arms and munitions in forts and arsenals seized from the United States, and to form a provisional army. The army was to be composed of such forces as might be tendered by the states for a period of twelve months and were to be received, with their officers, by companies, battalions, or regiments, the President with the advice and consent of the Provisional Congress appointing the general officers.[9] Georgia's contribution to the peacetime army was two regiments which the convention authorized in January.[10] After President Lincoln's policy of coercion was announced it became necessary to put the Confederate army on a war basis, and by May 4 Brown had organized six regiments and two battalions.[11] By the end of the year he had furnished fifty regiments.[12]

Brown's understanding of the psychology of the mountain people and his tact in dealing with them at this time was of great value to the state. Jasper County raised the United States flag, causing enraged Confederates to demand that troops be sent to tear it down. "By no means," the Governor replied. "It floated over our fathers, and we all love the flag now. We have only been compelled to lay it aside by the injustice that has been practiced under its folds." In a short time the flag was quietly removed by the people themselves.[13] By such methods, and by giving preference in place, arms, and equipment to companies from mountain counties, the Governor soon had the situation in hand and Union sentiment disappeared.[14]

---

[9] Act of Feb. 28, 1861, *O. R.*, Ser. IV, Vol. I, p. 117; *C. R.*, III, 18-19.
[10] *Ibid.*, p. 68; *ibid.*, I, 710-11.  [11] *Ibid.*, III, 68.
[12] *Ibid.*, II, 140. There was great enthusiasm in volunteering, particularly among the wealthy. See Avery, pp. 191-97.
[13] Avery, p. 188. Cf. *ibid.*, pp. 186-87.
[14] Disloyalty in the mountain section reappeared later, however, and continued in an aggravated form until the end of the war.—Georgia L. Tatum,

Although there was no difficulty in getting men to fill the President's requisitions, a small cloud appeared on the horizon in filling the very first call. The Governor had not been able to work harmoniously with the legislatures of his administrations, perhaps for the reason, as Avery says, that nature had put into him "an over rather than an under stock of combativeness." [15] In the storm and stress of war his inclination to dominate was naturally accentuated despite his avowed zeal for the cause. On March 9, following Lincoln's inaugural address foreshadowing his course toward secession, the Confederate Secretary of War under the act of February 28 sent requisitions to five states for troops for immediate service at points on their coasts. Georgia was requested to send one thousand men to Fort Pulaski and an equal number to Pensacola, "the troops to be sent forward . . . with as little delay as possible, and on their arrival . . . to be mustered into service of the Confederate States." [16] Out of this call grew the "skeleton regiment" dispute between the Governor and the Confederacy, which had to do with the appointment of officers—a subject upon which Brown warred with the administration from this time until the surrender of the Confederate armies.

Although the Secretary of War urged haste, Brown did not send the men forward. Instead, he entered into correspondence with the Secretary, proposing that the Confederacy accept, not companies as they arrived, but incomplete, or "skeleton," regiments along with their full quota of officers, leaving in the state those officers not necessary to the command to continue the enlistment of the remainder. "If the Confederacy will accept them in this manner," he wrote, "they are now at your service and subject to your order." [17]

---

*Disloyalty in the Confederacy*, p. 76, henceforth cited as Tatum. Not all mountain people shared the Union sentiment by any means. Cf. Gordon's amusing experience with the "Raccoon Roughs," *Reminiscences*, p. 9.

[15] P. 133.
[16] *C. R.*, III, 20.   [17] *Ibid.*, p. 24.

The point was of course that if the men went as companies the President would organize them into regiments and appoint the regimental officers; if as fully organized regiments, the Governor would commission the officers.

The Secretary replied that "to receive officers without men would not be . . . within the scope of the law," but the Governor made it clear that he would not send the men forward by companies. "If you should think proper to receive the regiments [in the manner proposed] you would have no further embarrassment about troops from this State," he added as an inducement. The Secretary explained that "to receive either a company, a battalion, or a regiment not organized and in existence would do such violence . . . both to the letter and spirit of the law as to put it altogether out of the question." [18]

The Governor next endeavored to have the troops mustered into service at Macon, Georgia, instead of Pensacola to which point the Confederacy was paying transportation. The Secretary said that no other governor had objected to the arrangement, and he did not feel that he could make an exception in favor of Georgia troops. "I desire to know without delay whether the arrangements will suffice," the harassed Secretary telegraphed. The need was so obviously urgent that the Governor finally gave in, a month after the requisition had been made, and the troops were mustered at Pensacola.[19] But the question was by no means settled. The Confederacy was to learn in the four years of its life that no question with Governor Brown was ever settled until it was settled in his way. On April 11 Brown wrote the Secretary of War that he could not recognize as a precedent the instance of the regiment lately sent "under peculiar circumstances," and added: "I think it best to notify you of my conclusion in advance . . . so that you may designate the officer

---

[18] *Ibid.*, pp. 24-25, 27, 30, 31-32, 34.
[19] *Ibid.*, pp. 37-38; Avery, pp. 194-95.

## "COMING EVENTS" 53

who will perform the service [of mustering the men into the Confederate army] in advance of a call by me for the rendezvous of troops." He said that he wished to be obliging, and that Georgia would at all times be ready to do her part, "but she will insist on having her rights and wishes respected when she is claiming the recognition of a principle of justice to her troops, as well as of obvious propriety." [20]

For the same reason the troops for Fort Pulaski were delayed. The Lincoln government was endeavoring to reinforce Fort Sumter when on April 13 the Secretary of War telegraphed Brown, "I must beg of you at once without more delay to furnish my requisition for troops of March 9. If you still refuse to transfer the enlisted men except upon the terms heretofore suggested by you, I must earnestly insist that you issue a call for 1,000 volunteers for the defense of Fort Pulaski. I trust you will concur with me in the opinion that the emergency of the case demands instant action." [21] The troops were sent, but on the Governor's terms. The Secretary of War acquiesced "for the sake of harmony" and because he thought "technicalities must not stand in the way of preparation." [22]

To impress upon the Secretary that he intended this method of mustering Georgia troops into Confederate service to apply to all future requisitions, Brown replied to the Secretary's call of April 22 for two regiments for Virginia by stipulating that each company should be mustered in upon its arrival at Augusta, Georgia, and when all the companies reached Richmond they should form a regiment and

---

[20] *C. R.*, III, 46-47.

[21] *Ibid.*, p. 48.

[22] *Ibid.*, p. 55. The arrangement had been made possible by the intervention of the Georgia convention—still in session—which requested the President to receive fragments of regiments with the necessary number of officers to command them, allowing them later to be assembled under officers appointed by the state.—*O. R.*, Ser. IV, Vol. I, p. 185. This was not quite the arrangement Brown had demanded, in that the full quota of officers was not at once to be accepted.

elect field officers. The Secretary telegraphed in reply: "They will be mustered into service at such places as you may designate." [23] The Governor had won his first round with the Confederacy.

The controversy with reference to the appointment of officers took on a more serious aspect a short time afterwards. Lincoln's call for three-year volunteers made it necessary that the Confederacy increase its armies more rapidly than the acts of February 28 and March 6 permitted,[24] and on May 8 a law was passed authorizing the President to accept, for the term of the war, volunteers in companies, without regard to the place of their enlistment, to organize them into larger units, and to appoint the field and staff officers and commission the elected company officers.[25] Three days later Congress authorized the President to accept companies, battalions, and regiments directly, "without the formality and delay of a call upon the States." [26]

The military laws of the Confederacy up to this time provided that when regiments were tendered already organized, the men should elect their field officers (colonel, lieutenant colonel, major). When companies were tendered, the President organized them into regiments and appointed all officers except company officers (captain, first and second lieutenants), who were elected by the men and commissioned by the President. At all times the President appointed the general officers (lieutenant general, major general, brigadier general) and staff officers of regiments (assistant quartermaster, commissary, surgeon, assistant surgeon). Officers of militia were appointed or elected, according to the laws of the various states, and commissioned by the governors. In Georgia the law provided for election. When called into service of the Confederacy the officers were in no way af-

---

[23] *C. R.*, III, 57.
[24] *O. R.*, Ser. IV, Vol. I, pp. 117, 126-27.
[25] *Ibid.*, p. 302.
[26] *Ibid.*, p. 310.

fected, since the constitution reserved to the states the appointment of militia officers.

Brown took the position that the Confederacy could raise troops in only two ways—through individual enlistment in the regular army and through requisitions upon the governors of states. He contended that volunteers who joined the provisional army through requisition were militia and the officers, therefore, subject to state appointment.[27] The crux of the question lay in the definition of militia. If, as Brown contended, militia meant "all the arms-bearing population of a state," [28] whether or not the population was organized, then the Confederacy, when it called out the militia, could appoint none of the officers. Brown admitted that in practice the United States government had always appointed the general officers, but this, he said, was not originally intended.[29] He stated to the legislature that the May laws were plainly unconstitutional and if allowed to stand would enable the President to control "the whole military force of the Confederacy," and with the central government thus in possession of both the "sword and the purse," he feared it might

---

[27] C. R., II, 85. The election of officers by the men and the appointment by the governors of those of regimental rank in the North (Cf. Fred A. Shannon, *The Organization and Administration of the Union Army, 1861-1865*, I, 158 et seq.; ibid., II, 162 et seq., henceforth cited as Shannon; James G. Randall, *Constitutional Problems under Lincoln*, p. 418, n. 20, henceforth cited as Randall), as in the South, gave rise to laxity of discipline, straggling, the shirking of duty, and favoritism. See Dodd, *Davis*, p. 293. The Confederate Secretary of War found that election made for popularity seeking and electioneering which were not conducive to discipline.—*O. R.*, Ser. IV, Vol. II, p. 1001. General Taylor said "the vicious system . . . struck at the very root of the stern discipline without which raw men cannot be converted into soldiers."—Richard Taylor, *Destruction and Reconstruction*, p. 15. For Mark Twain's amusing colloquy between a private and an elected officer, see "The Private History of a Campaign that Failed," cited by Shannon, I, 223. Senator Ben Hill stated that the military laws of May, 1861, were made necessary by complaints that the governors were using their power of appointment under the former acts to put forward their friends and promote their own political fortunes.—Benjamin H. Hill, Jr., pp. 251 et seq.

[28] C. R., III, 360 et seq.

[29] Ibid., II, 294.

become "the uncontrollable master instead of the useful servant of the States."[30]

Brown wrote the Secretary of War that he regarded the policy of authorizing the President to accept troops independent of state authority "as a very dangerous infringement of State rights."[31] When in June a requisition was made under these acts he protested so strongly against the right of the President to appoint field and staff officers[32] that the Secretary hastened to write a conciliatory letter. It was not intended to oppose the policy of the state in the matter of appointing the officers, he said, but merely to get companies quickly into camps of instruction. "The appointing power," he told the Governor, "is one the exercise of which is far from desirable with the President. . . ." If, however, the Governor preferred to tender regiments under the earlier acts of Congress, he could do so, but he hoped there would be no delay or loss of efficiency by the substitution. As a further concession, the Secretary asked Brown to suggest persons suitable for quartermasters and commissaries for instruction camps.[33] Brown had won again.

A recent historian states that Brown "began his refractory course in June, 1861,"[34] but a month earlier Howell Cobb had written to his wife: "I can say to you rather confidentially that there is a fair prospect of a quarrel between President Davis and our *worthy* Joe Brown. The latter is trying to ride the high horse about certain acts of Congress which take out of his hands all control of the Georgia troops. I shall sustain Davis and our Congress, and if they show the right spirit we will thoroughly put down the miserable demagogue who now disgraces the executive chair of Georgia."[35]

The conciliatory method of the Secretary of War did

---

[30] *Ibid.*, pp. 83-88.
[31] *O. R.*, Ser. IV, Vol. I, p. 332.
[32] *C. R.*, III, 108-10.
[33] *Ibid.*, pp. 112-13, 124-25.    [34] Dodd, *Davis*, p. 300.
[35] May 18, 1861, Phillips, *Correspondence*, p. 568.

"COMING EVENTS" 57

not appease the Governor or abate his determination to circumvent the statutes in question. If a "sovereign state" could not control the troops furnished to the Confederacy it could at least see that those who volunteered directly took with them no arms belonging either to the state or to themselves individually, and he issued a proclamation to that effect.[36] Brown had supplemented his own supply of arms[37] by taking some from the Augusta arsenal before turning it over to the Confederacy,[38] while the Confederacy's supply, never anything but small, had been exhausted in arming troops already in the field.[39] The *Republican,* indignant over the Governor's order, said: "From the beginning a misunderstanding seems to have existed between him and the Confederate authorities, to be found with no other State, and it is high time it were brought to a close." [40]

Northern troops were massing on the border for the first drive on Richmond. The Secretary of War, aware of the danger, wrote to Brown explaining at length the neces-

---

[36] *O. R.,* Ser. I, Vol. LII, Pt. II, p. 97.

[37] The Georgia convention authorized the Governor to transfer to the Confederacy all arms in the forts and arsenals taken from the U. S. government, but left it to the Governor's discretion whether state arms should also be transferred. He did not think best to transfer them, he said in his message to the senate on Nov. 19, 1861.—*C. R.,* II, 141.

[38] See Brown's proclamation of July 26, 1861 in *ibid.,* pp. 48-49. Brown had been extremely slow in turning over to the Confederacy the arms, munitions, and other ordnance which the arsenal contained.—See Walker's letters to Brown, Mar. 1, Apr. 10, Apr. 17, *ibid.,* III, 17-18, 44-45, 51-52. The transfer was not made until May 1.—*Ibid.,* II, 140. T. R. R. Cobb wrote to his wife that Brown took all the best arms from the arsenal at Augusta and shipped them secretly to Savannah.—"Correspondence," *Publications of the Southern History Association,* XI, 318.

[39] Toombs asked Stephens, who was at this time in Georgia, to see whether there were among the citizens any private arms to be had, saying that the situation was very serious and that "arms is the cry everywhere."—June 8, 1861, Phillips, *Correspondence,* pp. 569-70. DeLeon (p. 127) states that the 6,000 stands of arms captured at First Manassas in July, 1861, enabled the Confederacy to put a dozen new regiments on an effective war footing.

[40] Quoted by Frank Moore, *The Rebellion Record,* Vol. I, Pt. I, p. 72. T. R. R. Cobb wrote to his wife, "Governor Brown is interfering again."—"Correspondence," *Southern Historical Society Papers,* XXVIII, 288.

sities which had led Congress to adopt the laws to which the Governor objected and begged him to withdraw the order.[41] But Brown was obdurate and on May 25 the baffled Secretary gave in and permitted Brown to furnish troops under the earlier acts of Congress with state-appointed officers. He telegraphed the Governor that ". . . all the regiments . . . armed and equipped will be received into the Confederate service for twelve months, although it is highly desirable they should be enrolled for the war." [42] General Lee added his plea to that of the Secretary, begging for the good of the "common cause" that Brown allow Georgia troops to bring their guns and equipment.[43] President Davis also telegraphed, urging that troops be sent forward with all possible haste. Lee's and Davis' pleas were unnecessary, however, for after the Secretary of War had consented to his terms Brown furnished the troops promptly, well armed and equipped.[44]

But "requisitioned" troops was one thing, and "direct

---

[41] *C. R.*, III, 87-88.      [42] *Ibid.*, pp. 88-89.

[43] Brown through his aide-de-camp informed Lee that he had sent into service every regiment for which he had received requisition, that every one had been armed and equipped, and that he would continue to fill requisitions in this manner as long as his arms held out. But "any volunteers from Georgia now in Virginia without arms have not been sent under the requisitions upon this department, and have to look for their supply to the Confederate States."—*O. R.*, Ser. IV, Vol. I, pp. 366-67. Cf. Douglas S. Freeman, *R. E. Lee*, II, 30.

[44] *C. R.*, III, 89, 90. The last requisition made upon Brown for troops for general service, with the exception of that of Aug., 1864, which Brown refused to honor, was that of Feb. 2, 1862, for twelve regiments (*O. R.*, Ser. IV, Vol. I, pp. 902-3) under the act of Jan. 23 of that year, which authorized the President to call upon the several states for troops to serve three years and permitted the election of officers (*ibid.*, p. 869). This being a "requisition" and not a "direct tender," the Governor threw all his energy into raising the troops, and tendered to the Confederacy 18 instead of 12 regiments.—Brown's proclamation, *C. R.*, II, 187-95; *Federal Union*, extra ed., Feb. 12, 1862; *Republican*, Feb. 14, 1862. Senator Hill on Dec. 11, in his address to the legislature defending the conscription acts, called attention to the expedients to which the Governor had been compelled to resort in order to raise the troops: illegal draft, compelling the Secretary of War to stop the raising of independent regiments by officers commissioned for that purpose, threat to seize the men and deprive them of their suffrage.— Benjamin H. Hill, Jr., pp. 261-62.

tender" troops quite another, and on June 1 Brown sent a dispatch direct to the President requesting him to see that arms in the possession of companies received under "direct tender" be left in the state, otherwise he would arrest the officers. "I deprecate anything like conflict between State and Confederate authority," he said, "and I feel sure you will not encourage any company to disobey my orders. . . ." [45] In June the Floyd Sharpshooters eluded the Governor's watchful eye by shipping their sixty guns to Virginia and themselves going out of Georgia unarmed. Brown immediately demanded that the President return the guns by express.[46] A volunteer company of Newton County was not so successful. A rumor reached the Governor of its intention and he promptly made demand upon the officers for the return of the eighty muskets which they had received from the state arsenal.[47]

One of the bitterest controversies over the question is described by Avery, who was himself a participant.[48] When the law permitting direct enlistments was passed, Captain Francis S. Bartow, of the Oglethorpe Light Infantry in which Avery was a private, telegraphed the news from Richmond to his company, which wanted to be the first to offer its services for the term of the war. The men were escorted to the station by "soldiery and citizens," with flags flying and banners waving—the men carrying arms belonging to the state.[49] An acrimonious correspondence between Brown and Bartow followed, in which Bartow wrote to the Governor: "God forbid that I should ever fall so low as to think it necessary to obtain *your* consent to enter the service of my country." [50]

---

[45] *C. R.*, III, 92-93. Cf. *ibid.*, pp. 94-95.  [46] *Ibid.*, pp. 98-99.
[47] *Ibid.*, II, 43-44.  [48] Pp. 198-99.
[49] *Governor's Letter Book,* May 29, 1861, pp. 47-49; *Intelligencer,* May 31, 1861; *Southern Recorder,* June 4, 11, 1861; *Republican,* July 30, 1861.
[50] Coulter, *Georgia,* p. 309; Derry, p. 180. Cf. Walker's letter to Brown, *O. R.*, Ser. IV, Vol. I, pp. 473-74, and John Beauchamp Jones, *A Rebel War*

Secretary Walker had pointed out to Brown the inefficiency and expense of short-term troops and the administration's embarrassment in the matter of equipment,[51] but probably even he did not suspect the lengths to which the Governor would go in the matter of retaining the state arms. Walker's successor in office, Secretary Randolph, was the recipient of a startling request from Governor Brown in April, 1862, to the effect that as the terms of the twelve-months men expired they should return to Georgia and bring their arms. He was unwilling, he said, that the arms should be thrown into Confederate arsenals and distributed to troops from other states while inferior arms were placed in the hands of new levies of troops from Georgia. "If I have not mistaken your character," the Governor continued, "you belong to the class of statesmen known as States rights men. I cannot, therefore, doubt what will be your decision of this question." [52]

The Governor must have received a shock from Secretary Randolph's reply. He reciprocated most cordially Brown's wishes for harmonious action between state and Confederate governments; he felt that mutual patience and forbearance were necessary to insure good understanding; but he thought the conscription bill in the act of passage would render a redistribution of arms unnecessary. The exigencies of war require many things otherwise unjustifiable, he explained, and the Provisional Congress had, therefore, passed an act[53] in January requiring that arms of volunteers should be kept within the control of the President. "Nothing but the extreme peril to be apprehended from the dispersion of the arms in the hands of the troops, and the belief that the states would acquiesce in a measure absolutely essential to their safety,

---

*Clerk's Diary at the Confederate States' Capital*, I, 57, henceforth cited as Jones, *Diary*.
[51] *C. R.*, III, 112-13.
[52] *Ibid.*, pp 178-79.
[53] *Statutes at Large of the Provisional Government, C. S. A.*, p. 282.

"COMING EVENTS" 61

would induce the Government to adopt a measure at first sight arbitrary . . . ," he wrote.[54] On the day the conscription act passed, Brown turned over the state troops to General Lawton, Confederate officer at Savannah, but stipulated that their arms should not be taken out of the state.[55] It must be said in fairness to Brown that some of the other governors insisted upon keeping a good part of their arms. One historian has pointed out the disastrous result of this policy[56] when, because of the Confederacy's inability to arm its volunteers, Albert Sydney Johnston had to retreat from Bowling Green for lack of troops.[57]

The months of June and July of the Confederacy's first year of existence were filled with correspondence in which Brown endeavored to have the government accept a brigade as such, along with its state-commissioned field, staff, and general officers, which Confederate law did not permit. The Georgia legislature in December, 1860, had authorized the Governor to raise a force of ten thousand troops,[58] but after the organization of the Confederacy the Georgia convention felt that the state should not keep troops and turned over to the central government the two regiments which it had itself authorized. Brown did not share the views of the convention with reference to a state army, and he set to work early in the spring of 1861 to raise the troops which the legislature had authorized.[59] Under this doubtful authority[60]

[54] *C. R.*, III, 184.   [55] *Ibid.*, p. 188.
[56] Frank L. Owsley, *State Rights in the Confederacy,* pp. 7-8, 23.
[57] Brown and the Confederacy had some further difficulties in regard to arms when the latter on more than one occasion inadvertently obtained shipments which he had ordered from Europe.—*C. R.,* III, 171-74, 176-78, 180, 192-96, 211, 225-26, 233; *ibid.,* II, 253-54. In each instance the Confederacy hastened to make amends. It could not afford to offend the powerful state of Georgia and its irascible governor.
[58] *Ibid.,* I, 744-47.
[59] The law under which these troops were authorized (*ibid.*) provided that each company should elect its commissioned and non-commissioned officers, that the commissioned officers should elect the field officers, and that general officers should be appointed by the governor and confirmed by a two-thirds vote of the senate.   [60] Avery, p. 239.

a brigade was ordered into a camp of instruction where it remained from June 11 until August 2, despite all the efforts of the hard-pressed Confederacy to secure these armed and well trained troops.[61] The Confederacy could not accept an organization larger than a regiment, and the Governor claimed that state law forbade his breaking up the brigade.

Finally, twenty days before the battle of First Manassas, the Secretary of War made requisition for two regiments of infantry, armed and equipped, to be sent to the field as quickly as possible. Brown replied with what he called a "frank proposition": "If you will receive the brigade as it is, armed and equipped, with General Phillips in command, or if there is any question about your right to receive a brigade, then receive the regiments and battalions and appoint him to the command, I will consent that you appoint all his staff officers except one confidential aide, and I will, at any cost of labor or expense to myself or the State, within ten days from the date of your acceptance of this proposition, furnish you in addition to the brigade two other regiments, as fully armed and equipped for the field as have been former regiments furnished by me." [62] "Though [Brown] felt unauthorized to violate Georgia law, he . . . suggested how Walker might evade the Confederate law. . . ." [63]

On July 13 the Secretary again appealed to Brown to send the two regiments forward: "The crisis of our fate may depend upon your action. . . . For the sake of our cause and the country I beseech you to send them, without standing upon the point of the brigade organization. The President has no power to accept a brigade. If you refuse you will regret it." [64] But the appeal did not move the Governor and he took offense at what he termed the Secretary's attempt to

---

[61] *C. R.*, III, 96-97, 101-2, 107-8, 109-10.   [62] *Ibid.*, p. 111.

[63] Owsley, *State Rights*, p. 93. Brown sought the influence of the Vice President to whom he made the same suggestion.—Phillips, *Correspondence*, p. 572.

[64] *C. R.*, III, 114.

"COMING EVENTS" 63

intimidate him. He had not intended to convey a threat, Walker hastened to assure the Governor, but "to make an appeal to your well-known patriotism, based upon facts known to the Department but which it would be highly impolitic to make public." [65] Four days later the battle of First Manassas was fought, as the Secretary had foreseen, and Brown's brigade was still in Georgia. The *Republican* savagely attacked the Governor for withholding the troops.[66] Doubtless public criticism had its effect for on August 1 the Governor yielded, telegraphing to the President that he did so "in view of the emergency," [67] although the emergency for the time being had passed. "For the sake of controlling the appointment of a brigadier-general and his aide," this well-equipped brigade had remained idle "when it might have changed the history of the Confederacy." [68]

The question of the appointment of officers arose again under the law of December 11, 1861,[69] which provided for the reënlistment and reorganization of the twelve months troops which had originally been organized and officered under state authority. Governor Brown demanded to know who should commission the company and field officers and what construction should be placed upon the phrase in the Confederate constitution, "reserving to the States respectively the appointment of officers." He said that he wished to avoid all conflict between state and Confederate governments, since there was no hope "for the future permanence of our institutions unless each confines itself within the sphere assigned to it by the Constitution." [70] Secretary of War

---

[65] *Ibid.,* pp. 116-17, 118.
[66] July 31, 1861. Criticism of Brown for the "Camp McDonald experiment," as the brigade controversy was called, continued for months. Cf. *Southern Confederacy,* Sept. 28, Oct. 1, 1861.
[67] *C. R.,* III, 119-20.
[68] Owsley, *State Rights,* pp. 93-94. Brown's report to the legislature, *C. R.,* II, 91-98. On another occasion Brown sought to have even a division accepted, with its state-appointed officers.—*Ibid.,* III, 146-47.
[69] *O. R.,* Ser. IV, Vol. I, pp. 825-26.  [70] *C. R.,* III, 149-50.

Benjamin replied that the officers were to be commissioned by the President and that the constitutional phrase applied to militia and not to forces raised by virtue of an act of Congress.[71]

In the meantime another difficulty[72] had arisen between

---

[71] *Ibid.,* p. 162. In the spring and summer of 1863 Governor Brown carried on a heated correspondence with Secretary of War Seddon regarding the alleged right of the Fifty-first Georgia Regiment to fill by election the vacancy caused by the death of Col. Slaughter.—*Ibid.,* pp. 359-60, 360-68, 377-82, 394-99. Cf. Avery, pp. 264-65. The vacancy had been filled by the Confederate government through promotion, which Brown said was "in palpable violation of the plain constitutional rights of the regiment."—*C. R.,* III, 360. The troops were militia, he said, and "it doesn't matter what Congress calls them."—*Ibid.,* pp. 394-99. The regiment had been raised under the law of Jan. 23, 1862, which authorized the President to call upon the states for volunteers to serve 3 years.—*O. R.,* Ser. IV, Vol. I, p. 869. Toombs was impatient with Brown's contentions and expressed himself forcibly on the subject: "What the devil has Joe Brown to do with it? I cannot imagine. After the troops go into Con[federate] ser[vice] the governor's power over them is at an end."—Phillips, *Correspondence,* p. 592. The confusion arising out of the somewhat conflicting military laws and practices previous to conscription was in part responsible for Brown's position in the matter. See Benjamin's postscript to Brown and Seddon's interpretation.—*C. R.,* III, 162, 377-82.

[72] Trouble between Brown and the Secretary of War over the State Road was averted by a narrow margin in the fall of 1861. The Secretary was not aware that the Western & Atlantic Railroad belonged to the state of Georgia and ordered its rolling stock impressed, if the road should refuse to sell, for the use of the Virginia & East Tennessee Railroad in transporting troops and supplies. Upon discovering his mistake, the Secretary revoked the order, but in the meantime Confederate officers had made requisition upon the road. Brown telegraphed the administration that he would "resist the impressment by military force if necessary."—*C. R.,* III, 132, 133-34. Throughout the war there was more or less friction between Brown and the Confederacy over the road, which Brown never permitted the government to take over as a part of a unified transportation system. In 1863 there was trouble when Bragg was at Tullahoma and unable to get supplies from Atlanta (Dunbar Rowland [ed.], *Jefferson Davis, Constitutionalist: His Letters, Papers and Speeches,* VI, 149-50, henceforth cited as Rowland), and two months later when Bragg threatened to use force. On the latter occasion Brown indignantly telegraphed the President: "The road is as absolutely the property of the State as is the State House. If he may seize the one, he may the other." At this time Brown pointedly stated that all operations on the road would cease until Bragg's orders were revoked.—*C. R.,* III, 329-31; Davis' conciliatory reply, Rowland, V, 449-50, 453, 490. There was further friction in 1864, when, after the loss of Chattanooga, Johnston had some difficulty in getting supplies.—*C. R.,* III, 450-51, 453-58, 463-66; *Weekly Chronicle and*

"COMING EVENTS" 65

Governor Brown and Confederate authorities. The state of Georgia had some powder stored in the Confederate arsenal at Augusta, which the military storekeeper thought belonged to the Confederacy and refused to release.[73] On June 5, 1861, Brown took the matter up with the Secretary of War, demanding the powder—39,000 pounds. The military storekeeper, to whom Brown's complaint was referred, took inventory and concluded that about 29,400 pounds really did belong to Georgia.[74] Before his report could go through the proper channels, an ordnance officer at Savannah telegraphed his chief that Governor Brown had ordered the state arsenal in that city not to issue anything to Confederate officers, which, he stated, "ties up half a million caps and stops cartridge-making." [75] Meanwhile the chief of ordnance had received the report on the powder at Augusta and passed it on to the Secretary of War who at once ordered it released. Upon receiving word of Brown's action at Savannah the Secretary telegraphed Brown to know why he had closed the Savannah arsenal to Confederate authorities, to which Brown replied by inquiring why the state's powder was withheld at the Augusta arsenal.[76]

The year 1861, the last of Brown's second term in office, was as we have seen one of ceaseless activity. Fielder, who at the time was a clerk in the state executive department, says the Governor was active "day and night, barely taking time for refreshment and sleep." [77] The million-dollar appropriation of the previous year, supplemented by $842,500 borrowed from the banks,[78] he spent for coast defense and other war purposes. He purchased boring and rifle machines and turning lathes, converted a part of the machine shops of the State Road to the purpose of forging gun barrels, established

---

*Sentinel*, Feb. 3, 1864; Rowland, VI, 178-81; Phillips, *Correspondence*, p. 632.
[73] *C. R.*, III, 93-94.
[74] *Ibid.*, pp. 100-1.
[75] *Ibid.*, p. 98.
[76] *Ibid.*, p. 107.
[77] P. 266.
[78] Avery, p. 214; *C. R.*, II, 98-99.

factories for making clothes, shoes, and blankets, and, in an effort to conserve the supply and keep down prices, impressed salt and tin.[79] By the end of October the state had furnished to the Confederacy forty regiments and three battalions of which the latter and twenty-one regiments had been armed, accoutered, and equipped by the state. The battalions and thirty-three regiments had gone into service under requisition; the remaining ten regiments had been raised independent of state authority.[80]

Throughout the year the Governor was in constant communication with the Secretary of War, demanding men, arms, cannon, and even the return of Georgia troops from Virginia for the defense of the Georgia coast.[81] After his state troops—the brigade—had been absorbed by the Confederacy, he set to work to organize another state army which when called out in the autumn consisted of seven regiments and three battalions.[82] Whether the policy of the Governor in calling into existence a state army was legal, wise, or expedient when the Confederate government was itself defending the coast, was hotly debated in the press and in the legislature when it met in November. But the gubernatorial campaign was on and no doubt much pressure was brought to bear upon the Governor, making the strengthening of the coast defense a political if not a military necessity.[83]

The Governor's assistance to the Confederacy had without doubt been considerable. On the other hand he had had

---

[79] *Governor's Letter Book, 1861-65,* pp. 135, 140-41; Fielder, p. 266; Avery, pp. 213 *et seq.*

[80] Message to legislature Nov. 6, 1861, *C. R.,* II, 87; *Federal Union,* Nov. 8, 1861; Benjamin's report to president of the Provisional Congress, Dec. 14, 1861, *O. R.,* Ser. IV, Vol. I, pp. 788-90.

[81] *Infra,* p. 163.

[82] *C. R.,* II, 87.

[83] Owsley is of the opinion that the Governor himself was responsible for much of the hysteria.—*State Rights,* p. 19. Cf. "Justice," in *Federal Union,* Nov. 7, 1861; editorial, *ibid.,* Nov. 8, 1861.

"COMING EVENTS" 67

numerous conflicts with the administration and had criticized its policies freely. It was feared that his course might seriously affect the conduct of the war and jeopardize the success of Southern independence.[84] As the end of Brown's term drew near there was much speculation regarding a successor.[85] No governor of Georgia had within fifty years been elected for a third term,[86] and it was felt that a candidate must be selected, regardless of party considerations, who could unify the people and coöperate wholeheartedly with the Confederacy.[87]

Brown seems to have determined quite early to become a candidate to succeed himself, and he was never at any time, previous to the election of 1863, more astute in political management than in his campaign of 1861. He knew that his controversies with the Confederate administration—"certain policies had awakened opposition," as a friendly biographer puts it[88]—together with the long-established custom with respect to a third term would arouse determined opposition, and he was well aware that he could not be nominated in a convention. He accordingly arranged with a group of political friends[89] to oppose a convention as "distracting" in the midst of war. The important part of the strategy was to

---

[84] Avery (p. 201) thinks it was natural that a man "so fearless in assuming responsibility, and so constitutionally combative" should "get into more or less turmoil. . . ."

[85] See Underwood to Cobb, in Phillips, *Correspondence*, p. 560.

[86] *C. R.*, II, 126; *Southern Confederacy*, July 16, Aug. 22, 1861.

[87] *Southern Recorder*, Apr. 9, 23, July 2, 9, 16, 23, Aug. 25, 28, Sept. 14, 18, 1861; *Chronicle and Sentinel*, July 30, 1861. Several newspapers opposing Brown also opposed a convention, including the *Southern Recorder* (Apr. 23, July 2, 9, 16, 23, 1861), *Columbus Enquirer, Chronicle and Sentinel,* and *Southern Confederacy* (Aug. 13, 25, 28, Sept. 14, 1861). They advocated a free-for-all with the General Assembly choosing the governor from the two highest candidates. They claimed this plan would avoid party strife but it may have seemed a surer method to defeat Governor Brown.

[88] Northen, III, 76-99.

[89] A delegation from only three counties, the *Macon Telegraph* and the *Savannah Republican* declared, Sept. 28, 1861.

emphasize the Governor's support of and perfect accord with the Confederate administration,[90] together with the value of his knowledge of the organization of troops and of war finance and the danger in making a change at a time so critical to Southern independence.[91]

In pursuance of this plan Jared Whitaker, owner of the *Intelligencer*, wrote to Brown inquiring (1) whether under the existing circumstances it was wise to hold a state convention, and (2) whether, if it should be the wish of the masses, he would in the present critical period consent to serve for a third term.[92]

Brown replied from Camp McDonald on August 13. He thought that party differences had passed away in the mighty conflict in which the people were engaged, involving not only their lives, liberty, and property, but the destiny of their posterity. A convention would destroy that unity by renewing party divisions and strife.

In reply to the second question Brown wrote that he had been solicited repeatedly by persons in both political parties to offer himself for a third term, but that neither his personal interest nor his inclination prompted him to consent. However, he felt there was precedent in Georgia history for a third term and in Tennessee the people had elected a governor for a third term "being unwilling to put in a new man" at a time so critical. He said that his friends had urged his familiarity with the duties of his office, with taxation, and with the management of the State Road "whose earnings of $400,000 a year would have to be raised by taxation if the

---

[90] Brown's letter to the people of Georgia asking for clothing and blankets for soldiers and praising President Davis was perfect. The letter was published by the *Republican,* Sept. 4, 1861, and by the *Southern Confederacy,* Sept. 24, 1861.

[91] Mrs. Felton (pp. 24-25) says that her husband supported Brown in his four gubernatorial campaigns, at first because he liked his policies, and later because he feared to "swap horses in the middle of the stream."

[92] Whitaker was appointed commissary general of Georgia shortly afterwards and the editor of the *Intelligencer* was made surveyor general.— *Republican,* Nov. 7, 1861.

road were not satisfactorily operated." They had shown the risk of putting in a new man wholly unacquainted with the conditions of the military and financial affairs of the state when the Confederacy was fighting for its existence. His services in withdrawing Georgia from the wicked and oppressive abolition government of the United States had been given by his friends as another reason why he "should remain at the helm and endure, without complaint, all the responsibilities, toils, and hardships, to carry the old ship of state triumphantly through the storm." Furthermore, these friends believed that his name would tend to harmonize conflicting claims and prevent divisions when unity and harmony were of vital importance. Feeling that there might be some force in the arguments the Governor consented.[93]

Brown's published letter was followed by editorials in the *Intelligencer* and *Federal Union*, the only newspapers of any importance that supported him in the campaign.[94] They praised the Governor's management of the state government under difficult war conditions and urged his reëlection. The *Republican* replied that "beyond two newspapers in the bounty of the present administration, we have seen no indication of a popular desire for the reëlection of the present Executive."[95] The *LaGrange Reporter* declared it would "support the man whose chances seem best against the present incumbent," and the *Republican* and *Cassville Standard* started a campaign for E. A. Nisbet. They asserted that of all the governors of the Confederate States Governor Brown alone had been unable to act in perfect accord with President Davis.[96]

The *Macon Telegraph* accused the Governor of "shouting his own praises" and the *Columbus Enquirer* observed that

---

[93] *Southern Confederacy*, Aug. 15, 1861. Cf. Brown to Stephens, Aug. 22, Phillips, *Correspondence*, p. 574.
[94] Avery, p. 209.
[95] July 18, 1861.
[96] *Republican*, Aug. 5, Sept. 23, 1861.

the desire to serve beyond the customary two terms "argues an inordinate estimation of his own abilities by any governor." The editor of the *Southern Recorder* quoted a prominent citizen as suggesting Charles J. Jenkins for governor since he wanted "once more to see an elevated, high toned, true, virtuous, talented, and patriotic man in the executive chair of Georgia." The press in general refuted the Governor's claim for Georgia precedent for a third term and endeavored to show that the Union party in Tennessee, which did not exist in Georgia, was responsible for Governor Harris' third term in that state.[97]

Regardless of the recommendations of the Governor and his political friends, plans were made for a state convention.[98] It met on September 11 with delegates from 58 of the 132 counties, and promptly nominated Eugenius A. Nisbet, author of Georgia's ordinance of secession, member of the Provisional Congress, and ardent supporter of the Confederate administration.[99] Practically the entire press of the state announced its enthusiastic support of the candidate.

Brown's refusal to abide by the action of the convention led to much bitter comment. As in 1859, the Governor made no canvass, but in a published address he defended his action on the ground that he had announced his candidacy before the convention was called and that to retire would embarrass his friends; that not all of the counties were represented in the convention and therefore its action was not binding; and that the delegates had not condemned his administration. He charged that the whole movement was merely an effort of politicians to rekindle the fires of party strife when the people should be a unit "for the protection of life, liberty,

---

[97] *Republican,* Aug. 16, Sept. 24, 1861; *Southern Recorder,* July 23, 30, 1861; *Southern Confederacy,* Aug. 22, 27, Sept. 8, 18, 19, 22, 1861.

[98] *Republican,* Aug. 19, 1861.

[99] Avery, p. 208; Northen, III, 89. Nisbet's letter of acceptance, *Macon Telegraph,* quoted by the *Republican,* Sept. 18, 1861; *Southern Confederacy,* Sept. 18, 1861.

"COMING EVENTS" 71

property, and all that is dear." With reference to the two-term custom, he said that it was also not the custom to have war and for Georgia to have thirty thousand men in the field, "called out by her executive whose duty it is to know when and with what preparation each company went to the field, what had been supplied to them and what they lack, and to know the conditions of the finances of the State, and her present means of affording the most speedy assistance to her suffering troops . . ." which it would be difficult for a new man to know.[100]

The attacks of the press were savage. It charged that Brown had failed to support the administration, that he had quarreled with all his legislatures, that he was ambitious, unconstitutional, self-opinionated, greedy of power, inflated, and vain. The arms controversy was aired as was that relating to the brigade.[101] The Governor was accused of trying to perpetuate himself in power[102] and of speculating in munitions.[103] In August the Governor wrote Stephens that while the "press and the politicians" were against him he was confident that the people would sustain him,[104] but in September he regretted having entered the race. "Had I known the opposition . . . would have been so bitter," he wrote, ". . . I

---

[100] "To the People of Georgia," Sept. 19, *Southern Confederacy,* Sept. 24, 1861.

[101] *Republican,* Sept. 18, 20, 23, 24, 25, 27, 28, 1861; *Constitutionalist,* Sept. 30, 1861; *Columbus Times,* Sept. 30, 1861.

[102] There was a great deal of opposition to a third term. Cf. *Republican,* July 8, Aug. 20, 1861; *Southern Recorder,* July 16, 1861; *Southern Confederacy,* Aug. 13, 22, Sept. 20, 22, 29, Oct. 1, 1861; *Gazette* and *Dalton Times,* cited by *Republican,* Sept. 23, 1861.

[103] The last charge probably had reference to the fact that Brown had purchased for the state and resold to the Confederacy a quantity of saltpeter and sulphur, making a profit of $22,132.70.—*C. R.,* II, 73-74, 110-11. The *Intelligencer* was quite proud of the Governor's bargaining power and boasted of the 50 per cent profit which had accrued to the state. The *Republican* hoped the legislature would refund the money, and the *Macon Telegraph* regretted to know that such a thing could happen.—Sept. 2, 3, 1861. The *Federal Union* thought the Governor had been very liberal with the Confederate government.—Nov. 8, 1861.

[104] Phillips, *Correspondence,* p. 574.

should not have consented to the use of my name. . . ."[105]

The Governor need not have had any disquieting moments, if indeed he did have, for the masses voted for him on this occasion as they had done previously and would do again, while the press and most of the leading men opposed him. The election took place on the first Wednesday in October,[106] giving Brown 46,493 votes and Nisbet 32,802.[107]

A month after his reëlection Brown delivered his annual message to the legislature reviewing the events of the year.[108] He defended himself with reference to the brigade and arms controversies, criticized the Confederate government for not more adequately defending the Georgia coast, and justified himself in calling out the state troops. The message began with a dissertation on State Rights—of the particular brand which Brown professed—which defined his attitude toward the central government and gave warning of the bitter conflicts which were to follow. He characterized the military acts of May 8 and 11 as unconstitutional, inconvenient, and dangerous.[109]

---

[105] *Ibid.*, p. 577.

[106] *C. R.*, I, 730-31; *ibid.*, II, 125.

[107] *Federal Union*, Nov. 10, 1861; *Republican*, Nov. 11, 1861; Avery, p. 211. Several factors seem to have been responsible for Brown's reëlection: (1) the danger of putting in a new man at a time so critical to Southern independence, (2) the fact that no clear-cut issue could be made between the two candidates, each professing to support the administration and ardently to favor independence, (3) the splendid record to which Brown could point in filling the President's requisitions, (4) the consummate skill with which Brown and his supporters planned and carried on the campaign, (5) the calling out of the state troops just before the election, indicating the Governor's determination to give the state all the protection possible, and (6) the unwavering support which the masses always gave to Brown whatever the issue.

Brown's attitude toward the Confederate administration was already being commented upon in the North. The *Tribune Almanac for 1862* (p. 59) said with reference to the election: "Governor Brown having shown a little restiveness under the despotism of the Rebel National Government, the leaders of the conspiracy held a convention and nominated Nisbet, but Brown . . . was triumphantly elected."

[108] Nov. 6, 1861, *C. R.*, II, 78-125.

[109] *Ibid.*, p. 83.

Conceding to the President the right to appoint all officers of the regular army,[110] he quoted the clause of the constitution reserving to the states the right to appoint officers of the militia, which, he argued, the acts in question violated. He defined militia as "volunteers and other military forces not embraced in the regular army." [111] The acts were dangerous, he said, in that they gave to the President "an imperial power, which in the hands of an able, fearless and popular leader, if backed by a subservient Congress in the exercise of its taxing power, would enable him to trample under foot all restraints and make his will the supreme law of the land." [112] He disclaimed any fear that President Davis would abuse the power, but "some future Napoleon" might "assume the imperial robes and seat himself upon a throne." To guard against usurpation and "prevent the consolidation of the power and sovereignty of the States in the hands of the few," he besought the people to "watch, with jealous eye, every act of their representatives" and to "condemn . . . every encroachment made by the general government upon either the rights or the sovereignty of the States." [113]

Just how the Confederacy was to create an effective army without the powers to which he objected and how it could achieve independence without other centralizing measures, the Governor did not then, or ever, explain. That he was ardently patriotic and determined upon independence at this time there can be no doubt. In the same message in which his criticisms of the Confederacy planted doubt and suspicion in the minds of the people toward their newly established government he said: "If the people of the South are true to their own interests, they will never in the future have any political connection with the people of the North, nor permit

---

[110] That is, an army made up of enlisted men. The Confederacy provided for a regular army, but it was never organized.—*O. R.*, Ser. IV, Vol. I, pp. 127-31.
[111] *C. R.*, II, 85.   [112] *Ibid.*, p. 88.
[113] *Ibid.*, p. 89; *Federal Union*, Nov. 7, 8, 1861.

their commercial relations to be controlled by Northern legislation or Northern capital. . . ." [114]

After discussing the value of the institution of slavery to the Southern white laborer and to republican government and picturing the results to each should the South be conquered, he ended with the words: "Sooner than submit to this I would cheerfully expend in the cause the last dollar I could raise and would fervently pray, like Sampson of old, that God would give me strength to lay hold upon the pillars of the edifice and enable me, while bending with its weight, to die a glorious death beneath the crumbling ruins of the temple of Southern freedom. . . ." [115] In his message at his inaugural two days later,[116] at which he appeared in a full suit of homemade cloth with Georgia-made hat and boots to show the independence of the South from the manufacturing East,[117] he made an eloquent plea for coöperation in winning the war: "Let us lay aside all past differences upon minor questions—as brethren confer freely together, and as a band of patriots, bury in one common grave every personal aspiration and every feeling of ambition, pride or jealousy which may tend to hinder united and harmonious action, for the defense of our beloved old State, the triumph of our glorious arms, and the independence of that grand constellation of Southern Confederate States, in which Georgia shines as one of the most brilliant stars." [118]

It is just such inconsistencies—his intense desire for political and economic freedom for the South, and his unrelenting hostility to the means necessary to achieve that freedom—that puzzle historians.

Friction between Governor Brown and the Confederacy during the year 1861 had created difficulties for the new

---

[114] *C. R.*, II, 118.
[115] *Ibid.*, p. 125.
[116] *Ibid.*, pp. 125-30; *Federal Union,* Nov. 9, 1861; *Republican,* Nov. 11, 1861.
[117] *Federal Union,* Nov. 10, 1861; Avery, p. 214.
[118] *C. R.*, II, 129.

"COMING EVENTS" 75

government at a time when the utmost harmony should have prevailed. As the war progressed and military necessity forced upon the administration the adoption of the usual war measures, difficulties with the Governor multiplied. Unfortunately for the new nation he received encouragement from men from whom the Confederacy had every right to expect unselfish interest and loyal support. The effect of these dissensions, though it cannot accurately be measured, may yet be conjectured.

The opposition of this powerful group to Richmond policy was perhaps not unnatural, for the organization of the Confederate States of America had unavoidably left the wreck of many ambitions. Indeed, the circumstances under which it was established and the unusual number of able men, who, because of their ability and their contributions to the cause of Southern independence, might each look forward with good reason to filling the highest office, hampered the government from its beginning and in the end contributed no little to its downfall. Yancey and Rhett,[119] who had earliest believed in the necessity for Southern independence and had suffered at the hands of the people of their respective states who had not their ability to foresee the trend of events, might well expect to lead when at last their policy was vindicated and their predictions fulfilled.

In Georgia three leading statesmen held similar ambitions,[120] and to Georgia as the pivotal state the presidency was at first conceded. Robert Toombs and Howell Cobb had come late to Rhett's and Yancey's way of thinking, but their influence in the end helped to make possible the secession of Georgia and with it a Southern Confederacy. Alexander Stephens had opposed secession but unable to stem the tide had seemingly entered wholeheartedly into the new order of things. Each of the three men was considered for the

---

[119] Cf. White, *Rhett*, pp. 13-42, 106, n. 9, 77, n. 32, 105, 136, 139, 146; DuBose, *passim*.

[120] Milton, *The Eve of Conflict*, p. 518.

presidency, along with others outside the state, but the prize went to a Mississippian who did not want it.[121]

Jefferson Davis' election by the Provisional Congress was unanimous and gave general satisfaction. According to Fielder's description of the new president, he "united in himself in the opinion of his people in a rare degree the qualities of unsullied honor, devotion to the South, moral and physical courage, ability as a statesman and no ordinary military talents, with a firmness and integrity of purpose and strength of will seldom to be found, as well as energy and perseverance equal to the crisis." [122] On the surface the utmost harmony prevailed and possibly no one of the defeated candidates ever consciously realized how much of his subsequent opposition to Davis was due to the disappointment of that February day.[123]

Governor Brown in congratulating Stephens upon his election to the vice presidency said of Davis: "I have not the pleasure of a personal acquaintance with the President, but regard the selection as a good one, as his wisdom and states-

---

[121] Davis, *Rise and Fall*, I, 230. Davis' preference for a military position and the facts of his election as president may be found in Stephens, *War between the States*, II, 329 *et seq.*; Johnston and Browne, pp. 389-91; Fielder, pp. 187-89; Avery, p. 181; Howell Cobb to his wife, in Phillips, *Correspondence*, p. 537; T. R. R. Cobb to his wife, in *Publications of the Southern History Association*, XI, 163-72; Varina Davis, *Jefferson Davis ... A Memoir by His Wife*, II, 18, henceforth cited as Davis, *A Memoir*; Stovall, p. 218; DuBose, p. 586; Dodd, *Davis*, pp. 220-22; Flippin, pp. 208 *et seq.*; Phillips, *Toombs*, pp. 223 *et seq.*; John C. Reed, *The Brothers' War*, pp. 283 *et seq.*

[122] P. 188. After describing Davis' popularity in 1861, DeLeon (p. 103) says: "Cavil, jealousy and partisan intrigue, in which he and the cause finally went down together, had not yet done their work." Lee, when asked after the war who could have done better than Davis, answered: "I know of no one."—Quoted by Gen. Morris Schaff, in an address before the Massachusetts Historical Society, Feb., 1924, Dunbar Rowland (ed.), *Reviews of Jefferson Davis, Constitutionalist*, pp. 39-41.

[123] "While there was general acquiescence in the election of Jefferson Davis it was not unnatural to expect that some of the many conspicuous and ambitious men of the South would not be willing to heartily co-operate with the Confederacy under his leadership."—Flippin, p. 209. Cf. Henry W. Cleveland to Jefferson Davis in Rowland, IX, 603-5; X, 32. For Toombs' disappointment, cf. Phillips, *Toombs*, pp. 226-27; Owsley, *State Rights*, p. 233.

"COMING EVENTS" 77

manship are known to all to be of the most profound and highest order."[124]

The closest intimacy existed between Toombs and the Stephens brothers and between the Stephens brothers and Governor Brown. Toombs and Alexander Stephens—friends since 1834—were the "Castor and Pollux of Georgia,"[125] and usually agreed on every public question. Linton Stephens had begun the practice of law in Toombs' office and was his political follower. The tie between Alexander Stephens and his half-brother was unusually close. They corresponded regularly, thought alike, and never accepted cases where they would be opposing counsel.[126] Brown owed his first nomination for governor in large part to Linton Stephens[127] and the two were warm friends. From the beginning of his first term Brown had assiduously cultivated the friendship of Alexander Stephens, frequently asking his advice on matters of state policy and delicately showing his high appreciation of Stephens' judgment.[128] If this powerful combination should wholeheartedly coöperate with the Confederate administration the effect would be great.

In making up his cabinet it was natural that President Davis should offer first place to Toombs, although Toombs was far better fitted for secretary of the Treasury[129] and would probably have been happier in that position. In a short time Toombs disagreed with the foreign and financial policies of the administration,[130] left the cabinet, and in July entered the army. His military career was not satisfying and

---

[124] Phillips, *Correspondence*, p. 543.
[125] Cleveland, p. 56.
[126] Waddell, p. 309.
[127] *Supra*, p. 8.
[128] An examination of Phillips, *Correspondence*, shows that Brown wrote Stephens fourteen letters between 1858 and 1861, two in 1862, eight in 1863, fifteen in 1864, two in 1865, and one in 1866. The more confidential letters were without doubt destroyed.
[129] Phillips, *Toombs*, p. 227.
[130] See James F. Rhodes, *History of the United States from the Compromise of 1850*, V, 376, henceforth cited as Rhodes.

he resigned, later serving with the Georgia state troops.[131]

That Stephens fully realized the importance of harmony and coöperation in the new government is evidenced on numerous occasions before and during 1861.[132] In his speech on the evening of his serenade after his election to the vice presidency he said, ". . . all republics, to be permanent and prosperous, must be supported by the virtue, intelligence, integrity, and patriotism of the people. . . . Resting ours upon these, we need fear nothing from without or within." [133] In his "Corner Stone" speech a short time later he said the success of the new-born Confederacy depended upon the people themselves, "but if unwise counsels prevail—if we become divided—if schisms arise—if dissensions spring up—if factions are engendered—if Party spirit, nourished by unholy personal ambition, shall rear its hideous form, I have no good prophesy [sic] for you." [134] Before many months had passed, Stephens, like Toombs, was in opposition to the policies of the Confederacy.[135] By the end of the year he was "an unsympathetic critic of the administration," [136] and was himself being criticized.[137]

---

[131] Cf. Phillips, *Toombs*, pp. 237-51; Stovall, pp. 235 *et seq.; infra*, Chap. V, n. 72.

[132] Writing a secessionist friend in New York on Nov. 25, 1860, Stephens said: ". . . whatever fate befalls us, I earnestly hope that we shall be saved from the worst of all calamities—internal divisions, contentions, and strifes." —Quoted by Cleveland, pp. 162-63.

[133] *Ibid.*, p. 158.

[134] *War between the States*, II, 522; Cleveland, pp. 721 *et seq.;* Avery, p. 196.

[135] Cleveland, pp. 169-77; Rhodes, V, 381; Henry D. Capers, *The Life and Times of C. G. Memminger,* p. 349, henceforth cited as Capers.

[136] Rhodes, V, 376.   [137] *Federal Union,* Nov. 7, 1861.

## CHAPTER IV

## CONSCRIPTION: FIRST MAJOR ASSAULT ON THE RICHMOND GOVERNMENT

BROWN's controversies with the Confederacy had heretofore been mere skirmishes. With the passage of the first conscription act on April 16, 1862,[1] he began a pitched battle which continued throughout the next three years. He opposed conscription as unconstitutional and unnecessary, claimed that it was a scheme of the President to secure to himself the command of the state troops and the appointment of officers in order to establish a military despotism, and threw every obstacle in the way of its enforcement.[2] Brown's position was stated to the legislature on November 6, 1862, and to this position he adhered throughout the period of the war: "We entered into the revolution in defense of the rights and sovereignty of the States, and sundered our connection with the old government, because State Rights were invaded

---

[1] *Public and Private Laws of the C.S.A., 1862-64*, pp. 29-32; *O. R.*, Ser. IV, Vol. I, pp. 1095-97. Cf. *Republican*, Apr. 19, 1862. For a discussion of conscription in the U. S. government, see Randall, Chap. XI.

[2] The administration made every effort to placate Brown. In the fall of 1862 the President sent circular letters to all the governors asking their coöperation in filling the depleted ranks of the army, and Col. Wm. M. Browne was selected to see Governor Brown in person and explain to him the critical military situation.—*O. R.*, Ser. IV, Vol. II, pp. 141, 211, 216; Rowland, V, 379. Cf. *C. R.*, III, 306-8. On another occasion Col. A. H. Kenan, Georgia representative in the Confederate Congress, was sent by the President to secure Brown's coöperation. Avery (pp. 233-34) states that in this interview "it was intimated to Governor Brown that a place in the cabinet would be at his command if all went harmoniously," but that the discussion was "very animated, and at times stormy."

and State sovereignty denied. The conscription Act, at one fell swoop, strikes down the sovereignty of the States, tramples upon the constitutional rights and personal liberty of the citizens, and arms the President with imperial power." [3]

Although Governor Brown had resorted to a draft without legal authority and continued to use the threat throughout the war,[4] he began at once a correspondence on conscription with President Davis which extended from April through July.[5] There was no necessity for the law, Brown wrote, at least so far as Georgia was concerned, since the state had at all times furnished her quota. The act put into the hands of the President "the power . . . to disorganize Georgia's troops[6] . . . and . . . to destroy her State Government, . . ." he said. He called attention to the constitutional provision which reserved to the states the training of militia and the appointment of officers, which he claimed conscription violated. He would "throw no obstructions" in the way of enrollment but he declined to permit the militia officers to aid "in the execution of a law which virtually strips the State of her constitutional military powers, and, if fully executed, destroys the legislative department of her Government. . . ." [7]

---

[3] *C. R.*, II, 301. Reasons for conscription: Albert Burton Moore, *Conscription and Conflict in the Confederacy*, pp. 1 *et seq.*, henceforth cited as Moore; President Davis' message, Mar. 28, 1862 in James D. Richardson (comp.), *A Compilation of the Messages and Papers of the Confederacy*, I, 205-6, 449-50, henceforth cited as *Messages and Papers;* Frank L. Owsley, *King Cotton Diplomacy*, Chap. XIX *et passim*. The Federal government had not yet resorted to conscription, but it had a larger population from which to draw its armies which were also increased by the importation of foreigners. Cf. Senator Wilson's speech, *Cong. Globe,* 38th Cong., 2nd sess., p. 607; *O. R.,* Ser. III, Vol. IV, pp. 455-58; Shannon, II, 78, n. 809, 140-41; Owsley, *King Cotton Diplomacy*, p. 517. The North was also able to pay enormous bounties. Cf. *O. R.*, Ser. III, Vol. I, p. 153; Shannon, II, 55 *et seq.*, 80; Rhodes, V, 430, n. 5, 431 *et seq.*

[4] Cf. *C. R.*, II, 464-68; *ibid.*, III, 374-75; letter to Benjamin, *ibid.*, p. 154; *Republican* Mar. 18, 1862; *supra*, Chap. III, n. 44; *infra*, pp. 168, 170-71.

[5] The correspondence may be found in *C. R.*, III, 192-98, 200-1, 212-21, 233-46, 251-82, 284-86, 286-91.

[6] The state army, *supra*, p. 61; *infra*, pp. 183, 189.     [7] *C. R.*, III, 192-98.

## CONSCRIPTION

Although the President sent a copy of the exemption law[8] and explained that the constitutionality of the conscript act was not derived from the power of Congress to call out the militia,[9] Brown argued that the power of Congress to raise armies meant merely "regular armies" of enlisted men and not "armies composed of the whole militia of the States." He repeated that he would have nothing to do with enrollment and would not permit civil or military officers of the state to be conscripted. If, however, the President should make requisition for troops, "to be organized and officered as the Constitution directs," he promised hearty coöperation. The people of Georgia will "watch with jealous eye, even in the midst of revolution, every attempt to undermine their constitutional rights," he warned.[10] Brown's argument thus hinged upon his definition of militia as the whole arms-bearing population of a state.[11]

President Davis submitted Brown's letter to the cabinet, required a written opinion from the attorney general which he sent to Brown, and in his reply made a lengthy and carefully prepared constitutional argument. The President intended his letter as a reply not only to Brown, but to "other eminent citizens" who entertained similar views.[12] He showed that the power of the Confederacy to raise armies was unqualified; that Congress is the judge of whether a law is necessary; that the term militia is applied to "a body of soldiers in a State enrolled for discipline" and not to separate

---

[8] The exemption law may be found in *O. R.*, Ser. IV, Vol. I, p. 1081. Cf. *Republican*, Apr. 26, 1862; Moore, p. 52; Brooks, "Conscription in the C.S.A.," University of Georgia *Bulletin*, XVII, No. 4 (1917), 421 *et seq.*

[9] *C. R.*, III, 200-1.

[10] *Ibid.*, pp. 212-21.

[11] This was also the view of the Stephens brothers. Linton Stephens said that militia meant the arms-bearing people of the states and not a mere organization. He objected to conscription because it "robbed the soldiers of their right to elect officers and robbed the States of their appointment of officers," the effect being to "decitizenize the whole army."—Waddell, p. 246.

[12] *C. R.*, III, 234.

individuals; that the right of the states to officer the militia had not been interfered with and would not be under conscription; and, finally, that the right to raise an army and call out the militia were separate and distinct powers. In conclusion the President conceded that the conscription law was not necessary as far as Georgia was concerned, expressed his appreciation for the manner in which the state had responded to his several calls for troops, and acknowledged his indebtedness to the Governor personally for "prompt, cordial, and effective coöperation." [13]

In the long and tedious letters which Brown subsequently wrote with the assistance of Alexander Stephens,[14] he developed no new arguments. He merely went into detail, repeating now in this form, now in that, the points which he had previously made. He published the correspondence in the newspapers and in pamphlet form.[15]

In his letter of June 21 Brown accused the President of making Congress the sole judge of the constitutionality of the law, a proposition which he said had never been more broadly stated "by Webster, Story or any other statesman or jurist of the Federal school." [16] The President denied that he had made such a statement. "Neither in my letter to you," he said "nor in any sentiment ever expressed by me, can there be found just cause to impute to me the belief that Congress is the final judge of the constitutionality of a contested power. . . . I never asserted, nor intended to assert, that after the passage of such a law it might not be declared

---

[13] *Ibid.*, pp. 233-46; Rowland, V, 254-62; *Republican*, June 21, 23, 1862.

[14] See Brown's letters to Stephens, in Phillips, *Correspondence*, pp. 598, 611.

[15] The 52-page pamphlet, *Correspondence between Governor Brown and President Davis on the Constitutionality of the Conscription Act*, was printed by the *Atlanta Intelligencer* in 1862. A copy may be found in the Jefferson Davis Papers. It was this pamphlet which Pollard says Brown "hawked about the streets of every city in the South."—Edward A. Pollard, *Life of Jefferson Davis, with a Secret History of the Southern Confederacy*, p. 211, henceforth cited as Pollard, *Davis.*

[16] *C. R.*, III, 262.

unconstitutional by the courts, on complaint made by an individual. . . ."[17]

Brown instructed militia officers to call out military forces to protect themselves from enrolling officers,[18] and the Secretary of War was compelled to exempt militia officers,[19] the ruling of necessity applying to all states.[20] Brown gave to the press the telegrams on the subject which had passed between himself and the Secretary of War, whereupon a correspondent of the *Republican* said that the Secretary had yielded to the Governor "just as you or I . . . would have yielded to a madman who stood over a barrel of powder with a lighted match." Brown, the correspondent charged, had threatened "to light the fires of civil war in Georgia."[21] The *Macon Telegraph* likened the Governor to a man who, when aroused by a fire bell at night and found his neighbors fighting the flames, stopped them and demanded documentary evidence that they were acting under regular orders from the fire department.[22] Those not in sympathy with the Governor referred to the exempted officers as "Joe Brown's Pets," and facetiously inquired what force the Governor would use in protecting his officers since, if the militia were called out, there would be only officers to report.[23] Yancey, though a state rights advocate, sarcastically referred to Brown's doctrine as a "new phase of State Rights."[24]

In Georgia, Brown, Toombs, and the Stephens brothers

---

[17] *Ibid.*, p. 285. The correspondence led to much discussion not only in Georgia but throughout the South. Cf. A. H. Kenan's letter to the *Federal Union*, quoted by the *Republican*, May 15, 1862; letter from Simpson Fouche to H. A. Gartrell, published in the *Rome Southerner* and quoted in the *Republican*, May 18, 1862; letter from "Family Friend," *Republican*, May 26, 1862.

[18] *C. R.*, II, 224; *ibid.*, III, 229-30, 248, 249.

[19] *Ibid.*, pp. 249, 250, 283.

[20] *O. R.*, Ser. IV, Vol. I, pp. 1105, 1120, 1123, 1154, 1155, 1169.

[21] "Middle Georgia," *Republican*, June 28, 1862.

[22] Cited by Moore, p. 261, n. 17.

[23] Cf. letter from "Confederacy" in the *Republican*, June 10, 1862; Owsley, *State Rights*, p. 206; Moore, p. 71.

[24] DuBose, pp. 671 *et seq.*

were a unit in opposing conscription and their influence was felt throughout the South.[25] It no doubt had much to do with the wrangling and delay in Congress over the act of September 27, 1862, by which conscription was extended to include all who were forty-five years of age, which President Davis had recommended two months earlier.[26] The Senate favored the President's recommendations, but the House, impressed with the opposition to conscription, wished to return to the former system of calling upon the states for troops.[27] The law was a compromise. It extended conscription to include those forty-five years of age, but authorized the President to suspend the operation of the two conscription acts in any locality where it was impractical to execute them and to receive troops under the acts passed prior to April 16.[28]

This provision of the law opened Pandora's box. Brown immediately seized upon the clause giving the President an option in the matter and urged him to obtain troops by requisition. He said that he had permitted conscription under the first act with the exception of militia and civil officers because of the "emergencies of the country," due to the "neglect of the Confederate authorities to call upon the States for . . . additional forces to supply the place of the twelve-months troops." [29] But he flatly refused to allow the second conscription act to be executed in Georgia until the legislature should meet and pass upon it. No act of a President of the United States, prior to the secession of Georgia, "struck a blow at constitutional liberty, so fell, as had been

---

[25] Phillips, *Toombs*, p. 248; *idem, Correspondence*, pp. 597-98; Waddell, p. 246; Cleveland, p. 765. For Stephens' idea of military duty as expressed by Gen. Richard Taylor, see Taylor, p. 29. Stephens states his position on conscription in *The War between the States*, II, 572-73.

[26] *Messages and Papers*, I, 234-35; *O. R.*, Ser. IV, Vol. II, p. 54.

[27] Moore, p. 139.

[28] *O. R.*, Ser. IV, Vol. II, p. 160.

[29] One of the chief reasons for the conscription law of April 16 was the necessity of retaining the twelve-months men at the time of McClellan's preparations for the peninsular campaign.

CONSCRIPTION    85

stricken by the conscription acts," he said. He warned that the people of Georgia, having entered into the revolution freemen, "intend to emerge from it freemen." [30] After writing his letter to the President, Brown notified enrolling officers that he would not permit men between the ages of thirty-five and forty-five to be enrolled in the state of Georgia.[31]

Brown's refusal to allow a Confederate law to be executed was serious. He took the step on his own initiative, he was not sustained by public opinion as subsequent events proved, and he made his declaration at a time when Lee, Bragg, and Van Dorn had failed in their objectives[32] and were in retreat. In view of his ardor for secession, his action in thus jeopardizing its success is, like so much else in Brown's life, inexplicable.

There was no Confederate supreme court to pass upon the question of the constitutionality of the law,[33] but Judge A. G. McGrath of the Confederate district court of South Carolina, as early as June, 1862, had declared the law constitutional,[34] as had some of the state supreme courts. Since Brown paid not the least heed to these decisions, President Davis suspended enrollment in Georgia and took steps to have the law tested in the courts of that state.[35]

In the meantime in a special message of twenty-five printed

[30] *C. R.*, III, 294-302; Fielder, pp. 292 *et seq.;* Pollard, *Davis,* p. 211.
[31] *O. R.*, Ser. IV, Vol. II, p. 170.
[32] See Nathaniel W. Stephenson, *The Day of the Confederacy,* p. 44, henceforth cited as Stephenson.
[33] For reasons for no Confederate supreme court, see symposium by contemporaries in *Publications of the Southern History Association,* IV, 81-101. The question is also discussed by Sidney D. Brummer, "The Judicial Interpretation of the Confederate Constitution," Chap. V in *Studies in Southern History and Politics Inscribed to William Archibald Dunning . . . by His Former Pupils, the Authors,* henceforth cited as Brummer; Moore, Chap. VIII; Benjamin H. Hill, Jr., p. 12; Pearce, pp. 79-82; J. C. Schwab, *The Confederate States of America, 1861-1865,* pp. 219-20, henceforth cited as Schwab; DuBose, pp. 689 *et seq.,* 700 *et seq.;* Flippin, pp. 248 *et seq.;* Carpenter, pp. 243 *et seq.*
[34] Schwab, pp. 195, 219.
[35] *O. R.*, Ser. IV, Vol. II, pp. 123-24, 130, 141. In a lower court in Georgia, Judge Harris, in the case of Asa C. Jeffers, conscript, against John Fair,

pages Brown described to the legislature the operation of the conscription laws. The persons of "freeborn citizens" had, he said, been claimed "as the vassals of the central power" and disposed of "like chattels." [36] The bad faith of the government in breaking its contract with the twelve-months men could not be justified, "no matter how great the emergency may have been," he declared. He repeated his interpretation of the constitution to the effect that Congress could raise armies only by enlistment or by calling out the militia. He defined militia as all the arms-bearing population of a state, and pointed to the possibility of the complete destruction of the states through conscription. Congress "might be influenced by ambition, interest or caprice," and conscript "every Executive in every State in the Confederacy, every member of the Legislature in every State, every militia officer and other State officers, to enter the armies in times of peace or war, as privates under officers appointed by the President. . . ."

Thus, "at one fell swoop," he said, conscription "strikes down the sovereignty of the States, tramples upon the Constitutional rights and personal liberties of the citizen, and arms the President with imperial powers." He called attention to his letter to the President refusing, until the legisla-

---

enrolling officer, sustained the constitutionality of the law, but in a similar case Judge Thomas W. Thomas, friend of Governor Brown and of the Stephens brothers, took an opposite view. The case of *Jeffers* v. *Fair* was appealed to the state supreme court where the decision of the lower court was unanimously upheld.—33 Ga. 347. The arguments of opposing counsel were practically those of the Brown-Davis correspondence. The opinion was applauded so vigorously that the chief justice threatened to clear the room.—Moore, p. 170. Cf. Avery, p. 249. "Such a rehash of old Federalist doctrine . . . I have not met with in many a day," Alexander Stephens wrote to his brother.—Johnston and Browne, pp. 229-30.

[36] A little earlier Brown had written to Governor Vance: "We are in the midst of perilous times, where I fear we have more to apprehend from the consolidation tendencies of the Government than from the common enemy. All look to you, with confidence, for the maintenance of the integrity of the Government and the sovereignty of the State over which you preside."—Joseph E. Brown Correspondence, Library of Congress.

ture should meet, to allow conscription to operate upon those between thirty-five and forty-five years of age, and demanded that the legislature sustain him. "Shall the pompous pretensions of imperial power . . . but acquiesced in, or shall the Government be compelled to return to the exercise of the powers delegated to it by the Constitution?" he demanded to know. "The solemn question now presented for your consideration is," he concluded, "shall we continue to have States, or shall we, in lieu thereof, have a consolidated military despotism?" [37] The Governor's recommendations produced a bitter struggle in the legislature.[38]

In the meantime the state supreme court had rendered its decision on conscription and Brown sent a message to the legislature[39] in which he charged that the decision had been "rendered under heavy outside pressure, and if not *ex parte* under most peculiar circumstances." [40] The insinuation created a furor and "in the stormy moments that followed, Linton Stephens soared to the plane of Seward's higher law doctrine," [41] by declaring the decision of the court not binding on the legislature as a coördinate branch of the state government.[42]

A joint committee of the legislature which reported on the recommendations of the Governor was almost evenly divided. The majority took the Brown-Stephens position that conscription was unconstitutional and that armies could be raised only through requisition. The minority declared conscription to be constitutional and recommended that the Confederate government countermand all orders suspending the execution of the conscription acts.[43] At this point friends of the administration invited Senator Benjamin

---

[37] Message of Nov. 6, 1862, *C. R.*, II, 283-308; *H. J., 1862,* pp. 33 *et seq.*
[38] Moore, p. 170, citing *Southern Confederacy,* Nov. 13, 16, 19, 25, 28, 1862.
[39] Nov. 13, 1862, *C. R.,* II, 317-21.
[40] *Ibid.,* p. 320.
[41] Moore, p. 170.
[42] Avery, p. 250. Cf. Waddell, pp. 245-48.
[43] Avery, p. 251; Coulter, *Georgia,* p. 310; Pearce, p. 67.

Hill, who had come to Georgia to counteract the disaffection which the Governor had aroused,[44] to speak before the legislature on the subject. Hill took up in turn each military law that had been passed prior to conscription, showing how it had operated to place a double burden upon the patriotic while shirkers escaped service. He proved to the satisfaction of the members that conscription was just, constitutional, and effective,[45] and, in the words of Avery, "handled Brown with gloves off." [46] The legislature adjourned without acting upon the committee's report and the Governor's recommendations.[47]

Both the legislature and the state supreme court having failed him, Brown permitted the conscription laws to be executed in Georgia but he exempted all state officers. Out of the wreck of his hopes he salvaged a miniature state army.[48]

Brown then demonstrated one of his strong points—his ingenuity in devising new methods of accomplishing a pur-

---

[44] *Ibid.*

[45] Benjamin H. Hill, Jr., pp. 251-72. Cf. *supra*, Chap. III, n. 44.

[46] P. 255. Brown's published letter in reply, DuBose, p. 672; Avery, p. 256.

[47] Pearce, p. 67, n. 45; Moore, pp. 258-59. The legislature passed a resolution against the principle of conscription "as a precedent for the future."—Avery, pp. 251, 255; Dodd, *Davis,* p. 300.

[48] On Dec. 13 the legislature authorized the Governor to organize two regiments of 1,800 to 2,000 men, to be raised from volunteers from any militia not in actual service in the Confederacy, the regiments to be used within the state.—*C. R.,* III, 319-20. This "state army" existed until the end of the war.—*Ibid.,* pp. 317-19; *ibid.,* II, 674, 824. Cf. state supreme court decisions, *ex-parte Bolling, in re Watts,* 39 Ala. 609; and *Simmons* v. *Miller,* 40 Miss. 19. Two attempts were made later to disband the regiments that the men might be conscripted or to transfer the regiments, as organized, to the Confederacy. In the spring of 1863 a bill to this effect passed two readings but was defeated on the third by a vote of 50 to 35. Figures were submitted to show that the expense of keeping the two regiments was $700,000 per regiment.—*Southern Recorder,* Apr. 21, 1863. In the stormy session one year later a similar resolution was introduced. It described the troops as "hale and vigorous young men, living at ease and in luxury, secure from the dangers of the battlefield." The bill failed of passage by a vote of 8 to 101.—*H. J., 1864,* pp. 62-90.

# CONSCRIPTION 89

pose in which he had been thwarted. He turned his attention to exemptions as a means of crippling conscription.[49] The exemption law of May 1, 1863, left to each legislature the question of deciding what civil officers were necessary to the proper administration of the state government, but, until the legislatures should meet, permitted governors to certify what officials were indispensable.[50]

Brown promptly certified that all civil and military officers were "indispensable,"[51] and on December 14, 1863, the new legislature, which was more in harmony with the Governor than its predecessors had been,[52] by joint resolution ratified the Governor's action.[53] Although all the governors exempted a larger number than was necessary,[54] Brown and Governor Vance of North Carolina were the chief offenders.[55]

The law of February 17, 1864, gave to the governors rather than the legislatures the right to determine what officers were essential to the operation of the state govern-

---

[49] Brooks, "Conscription in the C. S. A.," *loc. cit.,* p. 432.

[50] *O. R.,* Ser. IV, Vol. II, pp. 160-62.

[51] The Governor advanced this "admittedly broad claim in no spirit of opposition," but merely "as the best method of avoiding unnecessary discussions and of securing without acrimony the just rights of the State and of the Confederate Government," he said.—*Ibid.,* p. 569. The provision exempting ministers in charge of churches Brown interpreted to include ordained local ministers as well.—*C. R.,* II, 671-72. Attempts made in the North to exempt ministers did not succeed, although ministers could pay the $300 commutation and avoid service. Some of the members of the U. S. Congress, feeling that ministers had had no small part in bringing on the war, thought they should "fight, pay, or emigrate."—Shannon, II, 259.

[52] Brown had been elected governor for the fourth time.—*Infra,* Chap. V.

[53] *O. R.,* Ser. IV, Vol. III, p. 345.

[54] For the abuse of the courtesy, cf. Moore, pp. 265-67, 298, n. 5; Schwab, p. 198.

[55] Brown wrote to Vance that the joint resolution of the Georgia legislature requiring the governor to exempt all civil and military officers of the state left him no discretion, as he felt "bound to carry out the will of the legislature."—Mar. 23, 1864, Joseph E. Brown Correspondence, Library of Congress. Brown frequently recommended legislation and then posed as "bound by the law."

ments,[56] it being supposed, as Cobb later wrote to Brown,[57] that governors would patriotically exempt only those absolutely necessary. Brown's exemptions, as listed in his proclamation of April 9, 1864, included every civil and military officer of the state from the highest to the lowest. "If I have omitted any officer whom the law makes it my duty to protect," the proclamation continued, "the fact will be made public when the omission is discovered." [58] It was found that he had omitted the attorney general, the solicitors general, and the masters of chancery. They were added to the exempted list on April 20.[59]

Governor Brown's wrath may easily be imagined, when the law of February 17, 1864, lowered the conscription age limit to seventeen and raised it to fifty. Those between the ages of seventeen and eighteen and between forty-five and fifty were to be organized as reserves for their respective states and for detail duty, thereby releasing men between eighteen and forty-five for general service.[60] The reserves were not to be required to leave their states and were to be detailed to their vocations when no emergency existed.[61]

Aside from Brown's unyielding opposition to the policy of conscription, he objected to the law because it would disrupt his newly organized militia, which included all between sixteen and sixty years of age.[62] This fact had much to do with the call for the special session of the Georgia legisla-

---

[56] *O. R.*, Ser. IV, Vol. III, pp. 178-81.

[57] *C. R.*, III, 503 *et seq.*

[58] *Ibid.*, II, 683-87.

[59] *Ibid.*, p. 690. The Governor seemed suddenly to have found his administration in need of a large number of "state agents."—*Ibid.*, pp. 679-80, 682-83, 688, 697-98, 700, 701, 782, 788-89, 799. ". . . Brown exempted any man whom he wished to [exempt] by attaching him to some shadowy and elusive official position."—Owsley, *State Rights*, p. 206.

[60] *O. R.*, Ser. IV, Vol. III, pp. 178-81. President Davis' recommendations, *Messages and Papers*, I, 404.

[61] This was the type of organization Seddon had tried to secure the previous summer.—*Infra*, pp. 167 *et seq.*

[62] *Acts of the General Assembly, 1863-64*, pp. 51-58.

ture the following month,[63] in which Governor Brown and the Stephens brothers attempted to carry out a well matured program to cripple the Confederate administration.[64]

In his message of March 10 Brown told the legislature that the late act of Congress proposed to take from the state her entire military force, which he claimed was unconstitutional. He said that the state supreme court had ruled that Congress had the power to raise armies by conscription, not that it had the power to enroll the whole population of a state.[65] Arguing the military advantages of the South in comparison with the North, he said the ratio was four to one in favor of the South, and that the South could by properly husbanding its resources keep two hundred thousand men in the field for twenty years. If this were done, production kept up, and pitched battles avoided, an enemy even of a million would in the end be defeated or would "melt away." It was for the legislature to say whether the "necessities of the State, her sovereignty and dignity and justice to those who are affected by the Act," do not forbid that the militia organization be broken up.[66]

Since the legislature was about to adjourn on Saturday, March 19, without having taken action on any of Brown's major recommendations, he sent a message on that date convening the legislature in another extra session on the following Monday unless it should in the meantime pass upon the question of conscription and other matters for which it had been called.[67] In the question of whether the Confederacy should be allowed to break up the militia organization was involved "the sovereignty, and probably the existence, of the State," he said.[68] It is remarkable that in view of the pressure brought to bear upon the legislature

---

[63] *C. R.*, II, 675.  [64] *Infra*, p. 200.
[65] *C. R.*, II, 601-2.  [66] *Ibid.*, pp. 605-7.
[67] The other questions were the habeas corpus and peace.—*Infra*, p. 209.
[68] *C. R.*, II, 673-76.

in this March session it successfully resisted the Governor's recommendation and voted to turn the militia over to the Confederacy.[69]

Brown, however, continued his policy of obstruction, and General Howell Cobb was sent to the state to organize the reserves in the hope that his popularity might counteract the influence of the Governor. Sherman's invasion was imminent but Brown seemed willing to jeopardize the safety of the state for the sake of his own preconceived opinions. Cobb wrote to the adjutant general on April 23, 1864, that the number in the reserves was likely to fall below the estimate on account of the Governor's course.[70] And so it proved. The number was insufficient to guard the thirty thousand Federal prisoners in the state during Sherman's invasion and had to be supplemented by a battalion of Brown's numerous militia.[71]

The Cobb-Brown correspondence of April and May[72] gives an illuminating picture of Brown's methods in rendering conscription ineffective. On April 21 Cobb protested to Brown against his sweeping exemptions, which, he said, the law did not contemplate. There was no necessity, Cobb contended, for the large number of deputies exempted, in view of the fact that the business of the courts was almost suspended, nor for the retention of 2,000 justices of the peace, 1,000 constables, and 3,000 military officers. He asserted that there were districts where there had not been a justice of the peace for years but where men capable of military service were now shielding themselves from such duty, and that the retention of men for sinecure offices made it neces-

---

[69] *O. R.*, Ser. IV, Vol. III, p. 244.
[70] *C. R.*, III, 503.
[71] Brown to Seddon, in *ibid.*, p. 660.
[72] The correspondence may be found in *ibid.*, pp. 504-9, 515-27, 529-40, 541-58, 562-66, 568-73.

sary to call into the field farmers and mechanics who were needed in production.[73]

Cobb's letter offered opportunity to the Governor for the exercise of his talent for carrying on a controversial correspondence. He called Cobb's attention to the fact that the state legislatures, and not Congress, had jurisdiction over state officers and the exemption was not, therefore, claimed by the state under the act of Congress "nor accepted as a matter of grace or favor." [74] Anyway, there was nothing he could do about it, he said, the legislature having sole jurisdiction and his own duty being merely "to commission those who are legally elected. . . ."

In reply to Cobb's plea of the urgent need for men to meet the enemy pressing upon the state from the northwest and from the seacoast, Brown said that the arrangement for reserves to continue their pursuits when not actually in service was inadequate for the production of provisions. The detail system, he said, required so much of a farmer's time "in keeping his papers right" as to cripple the agricultural interests operating under the system of making bread "by permission of the Government." The Governor fired a parting shot by affirming that "the outcry against the State government and State officers comes up from the almost countless swarms of Confederate officers, agents, and detailed men,[75] who as the favorites of power, have obtained safe and

---

[73] *Ibid.*, pp. 504-9.   [74] *Ibid.*, pp. 515-19.

[75] These were favorite expressions of the Governor when referring to Confederate officers or agents connected in any way with conscription. In his message of Nov. 5, 1863, he referred to the "swarms of enrolling officers."—*C. R.*, II, 495. In that of Mar. 10, 1864, they were designated as "thousands of young officers in gold lace and brass buttons."—*Ibid.*, p. 607. In a letter to Seddon on Nov. 14, 1864, the Governor referred to them as a "corps of conscript officers."—*Ibid.*, III, 660. Rhodes (V, 441) quotes Brown as estimating the "able-bodied men . . . acting as clerks, etc." as forming 50 per cent of the army, and comments that Brown's statements must be taken with allowance.

comfortable positions in the rear, . . ." who were engaged in their own private business and in speculation, "or in earnest, industrious efforts to manage and control the policies of the State." [76]

Brown had sought to put upon the legislature the responsibility for withholding the officers, but Cobb thought the public would be curious to know why the Governor did not arrest the action of the legislature "by his favorite resort to the veto power," and suggested that in an extra session Brown's hands "might be untied." The act of Congress conformed strictly to the doctrine of the Georgia supreme court, Cobb said, but "neither Congress nor our Supreme Court, nor anybody else but your Excellency, ever conceived the idea that justices of the peace who never held a court, constables who never served a warrant, and militia officers who have no men to command, were necessary for the proper administration of the state government. . . ." [77] Referring to Brown's allusion to Confederate officers' taking part in politics, Cobb thought Brown would have viewed the matter in a different light "if they could have found in the Governor's course more to approve and less to condemn." [78] As the correspondence continued it grew more bitter and degenerated further into personalities.

Meantime the commandant of conscripts in Georgia, Colonel William M. Browne, in charge of enrolling for general service those between the ages of eighteen and forty-five, was having difficulties. On May 10 he made a plea to the Governor for coöperation in preventing enrolled men from accepting civil offices to which they had been elected subsequent to enrollment in Confederate service, "under the erroneous impression," the commandant tactfully said, "that you will protect them in their claims." [79] Brown took

---

[76] *C. R.*, III, 526. The reference was to Cobb and other administration supporters who prevented the consummation of the Brown-Stephens brothers' plans in the special session of the legislature. See *infra*, p. 210.

[77] *C. R.*, III, 534-35.   [78] *Ibid.*, p. 540.   [79] *Ibid.*, pp. 528-29.

CONSCRIPTION                                     95

the position that any citizen not in military service might accept any office to which he had been elected, and that he was not in service until actually enrolled and personally notified of his enrollment. He said that he would adhere to this rule until the courts should decide otherwise.[80]

As the difficulties with Brown increased during the crisis of Sherman's invasion, the Secretary of War became "weary of vain attempts to obtain his good will or assistance." He wrote the commandant that the "spirit and temper of the Governor, especially in the late correspondence with Cobb, precludes all hope of a change in policy, and renders further attempts at conciliation useless." He thought "a course of firmness and decided action" in dealing with Brown would be "wiser and more effective." [81]

After the fall of Atlanta, President Davis visited General Hood in Georgia "to try to fill up the depleted ranks of the army, to bring the absentees and deserters back to the ranks, and induce the Governor and State officials to coöperate . . . with the Confederate Government. . . ." [82] He estimated Brown's "inordinate exemption" as embracing 15,000 men between the ages of eighteen and forty-five.[83]

It is difficult to arrive at a satisfactory conclusion with reference to the number of exemptions in Georgia or in other states, for the reason that, for the most part, blanket exemptions were made by the governors. Only when a state exempt was caught in the toils of a Confederate enrolling officer was an individual certificate issued. The reports of the Bureau of Conscription were, therefore, at no time conclusive, but were, as the superintendent explained, "progressive." [84] On the basis of certificates issued under these circumstances,

---

[80] *Ibid.*, pp. 559-62.
[81] *O. R.*, Ser. IV, Vol. III, p. 530.
[82] *Infra*, p. 188.
[83] *Rise and Fall*, II, 565. Cf. Jones, *Diary*, II, 333. Owsley thinks Davis' estimate of 15,000 exemptions approximately correct.—*State Rights*, pp. 205-8.
[84] *O. R.*, Ser. IV, Vol. III, p. 867.

the commandant of conscripts in Georgia reported in November, 1864, 2,751 militia officers and 5,478 civil officers exempted. General Cobb, who enrolled the reserves, reported more than 6,000 militia and civil officers in addition to employees of state industries. The Bureau of Conscription reported 8,000 exempted up to November, 1864, and 8,229 up to February, 1865. The nearest figures from other states were 5,589 for North Carolina and 1,894 for Virginia.[85]

Brown stated to the legislature on February 15, 1865, that "the whole number of State officers in Georgia who have been held by me under the legislation of the State to be exempt from military service, was only 1,450, of whom a large proportion are over military age."[86] An examination of Brown's *Letter Book* shows that on December 9, 1864, there were 15,000 men exempted, all but 1,450 being in the militia.[87]

The opposition to conscription of Brown, Alexander Stephens,[88] and Toombs tended to place a stigma upon those who were drafted and no doubt accounts for the fact that from the first conscription act to February, 1865, Georgia furnished only 8,992 conscripts, while 26,400 within that time volunteered. In other states no such proportions are found.[89] The fact cannot be ignored, however, that the fear

---

[85] *Ibid.*, pp. 344-49, 869-70, 1102-10. Cf. *ibid.*, pp. 75, 871; Moore, pp. 81-113.

[86] *C. R.*, II, 822.

[87] P. 738.

[88] Stephens said the policy of conscription was dangerous and might be fatal, because it tended "to check the ardor of the people by appearing to slight their spontaneous patriotic service." He expressed his views to the Secretary of War, to members of Congress, to his friends in private letters, to the public through speeches and through the press, and schemed with his brother how best to put through the legislature resolutions condemning conscription.—Johnston and Browne, pp. 409, 415, 418, 434-35, 461, 462. Later Stephens was to be reminded of his support of Brown when doubtless he would have preferred that the matter be forgotten.—Cf. Brown's speech, De Gives' Opera House, Nov. 15, 1880, Fielder, pp. 540-41.

[89] Report of the superintendent of conscription, *O. R.*, Ser. IV, Vol. III, p. 1101. The report was not wholly reliable, as the superintendent himself said.

## CONSCRIPTION

of conscription had added materially to the volunteer spirit.[90]

Because of his policy of exemption, Governor Brown was without doubt an important factor in preventing favorable action on the President's recommendations for a stricter Confederate exemption law.

The law exempting entire classes worked badly and the President several times recommended its repeal and the enrollment of all within conscription ages, with military details for industrial and agricultural purposes.[91] His recommendations were only in part acted upon, although the law of February 17, 1864,[92] repealed all former exemptions, made a different classification, and authorized the President to make details in certain cases. When Congress met in November, 1864, the military situation was critical. Lee was being hard-pressed in the siege of Petersburg; Sherman was in possession of Atlanta; and Hood had started on his ill-fated Tennessee campaign. Knowing the desperate need for men the President returned to the subject of strengthening the conscription laws. He said that the exemption of entire classes afforded the temptation and the means of escaping service by fraudulent devices and was one of the principal obstructions to the efficient operation of the conscript laws. Pointing out that those exempted in the various occupations and in the "numerous other classes mentioned in the laws" could not be equally necessary in their several professions nor distributed throughout the country in such proportion that only the exact number required were to be found in each locality, he again recommended that the mat-

---

[90] See report of Nov. 26, 1863, in which the Secretary of War stated that conscription had brought into the army three volunteers for every conscript. —*Ibid.*, II, 995. In the North there was a similar attitude toward conscription. "A stigma was placed upon the person who was drafted though not at all upon the person who volunteered solely to escape draft or upon the mercenary recipient of enormous bounties or substitute fees."—Shannon, II, 57.

[91] *Messages and Papers,* I, 295, 371. Cf. Davis, *Rise and Fall,* I, 515.

[92] *O. R.,* Ser. IV, Vol. III, pp. 178-81.

ter be left to the military authorities of the Confederacy to distribute them by details.[93]

Brown seized upon the President's recommendation as a means of making a demagogic appeal to the masses. In a message devoted exclusively to the subject[94] he entered his "solemn protest" against the "monstrous proposition." [95] The effect of the policy would be to invest the President with such power that "no man could cultivate his fields . . . or run his factory . . . or work his blacksmith shop . . . or follow other industrial pursuits without . . . a *detail* from the President." [96] It would enable the President to determine how many members might attend the legislature, their ages and their political sentiments; how many judges each state might have, and what should be their ages.[97] Nor could a newspaper be published without the President's consent. It would make the editors the President's tools and prostrate at the President's feet the public press of the country—"the great bulwark of Constitutional Government and advocate of civil and religious liberty." [98]

Calling especial attention to the President's phrase, "numerous other classes mentioned in the laws," Brown inquired who were these classes "of whom the President seeks to get the absolute and unlimited control, without startling the country by the designation of them in this message." Brown found within them ministers of religion, whom he said the President would not exempt "*as a class*, but only such of them as he, in his 'discretion' may deem a sufficient number to be *detailed* to *continue* to *exercise* their *pursuits* or *profession* that only the *exact numbers* required may be found in each locality." This would, he asserted, give the President power "to determine not only how many may be

---

[93] *Messages and Papers*, I, 491.
[94] Nov. 17, 1864, *C. R.*, II, 792-98.
[95] *Ibid.*, p. 798.
[96] *Ibid.*, p. 794.
[97] *Ibid.*, pp. 795-96.   [98] *Ibid.*, pp. 794-95.

## CONSCRIPTION 99

necessary, but to select the localities . . . and to prescribe . . . the denominations . . ." and thus violate the constitutional provision guaranteeing freedom of religious worship. "Even the Lincoln government, despotic as it is, has not dared to attempt any such encroachments upon the liberties of the people of the United States," he declared. He recommended a joint resolution of the legislature instructing Georgia's representatives in the Confederate Congress to oppose the passage of such a law.[99]

Before the message could be delivered the approach of Sherman's army led to a hurried adjournment of the legislature. Later the Governor ordered the message printed and distributed, feeling that "the people and the presses of the country should speak out boldly" against the proposed law.[100] Editors were in the exempted class and those favorable to the Governor outdid themselves in praising his message and warning the people against allowing the destruction of the freedom of the press. The *Columbus Sun* thought the Governor's message ought to be read by every free man in the Confederate States,[101] and the *Montgomery Appeal* invited its readers to consider the thought of allowing some officer of the government to decide what divine should continue to serve his congregation, what physician should heal the sick, and who should till the earth.[102] The President's recommendations were not carried out.[103]

---

[99] *Ibid.*, pp. 797-99.
[100] *Ibid.*, p. 792.
[101] Copied by the *Weekly Chronicle and Sentinel*, Dec. 21, 1864.
[102] *Ibid. Cf.* Moore's discussion of the subject, pp. 105 *et seq.*
[103] Governor Brown objected also to the policy of substitution (*C. R.*, II, 433-37, 490-92), and so, it is interesting to note, was in agreement with President Davis (*Messages and Papers*, I, 370). The President's recommendations were carried out in the laws of Dec. 28, 1863; Jan. 5 and Feb. 17, 1864. —*O. R.*, Ser. IV, Vol. III, pp. 11, 12, 178-81. All principals were made subject to conscription except those who were exempted for religious reasons and had paid the commutation of $500.—*Ibid.*, II, 160-62. No other commutation was permitted in the Southern army, unless the "20-nigger" clause of the act of May 1, 1863, and the "15-nigger" clause of that of Feb. 17, 1864, may be so construed. These provisions were designed to secure adequate ag-

The last step in the policy of conscription was that of including the slaves. Brown opposed the measure as a matter of course.[104] As conditions in the Confederate States became more desperate, the use of slaves in the army became a burning question. General Lee voiced the growing sentiment when he said: "We must decide whether slavery shall be extinguished by our enemies and the slaves used against us, or use them ourselves at the risk of the effects which may be produced upon our social institutions." [105] President Davis, in his message of November 7, 1864, cautiously raised the question of their status should they be so used—whether they should be retained in servitude or be freed, whether freedom should be granted at once or at the end of their public service. He said nothing of using slaves other than as laborers, but he suggested that if the alternative were subjugation there would be no doubt of their use as soldiers.[106]

---

ricultural production and reasonable prices through "bonded exempts." The first mentioned law required the payment of $500 a year to the government, the second repealed the money payment because of the depreciation of the currency and stipulated a certain amount of produce which was to be delivered to the government at fixed prices.—*Ibid.,* pp. 553-54; *ibid.,* III, 175-81.

The evils of the policy of substitution never reached the proportions in the South that they attained in the North where excessive bounties and commutation aggravated the situation and where substitution was never abolished. —Cf. Shannon's chapter on "The Concession to the Bourgeoisie," II, 20, 24, 34-35, and 219-37; *ibid.,* I, 302-8; *O. R.,* Ser. III, Vol. II, p. 26; *ibid.,* IV, 631. For number of substitutes in the Northern army after 1862, see Shannon II, 179, n. 1024.

[104] Negroes had served as soldiers in the U. S. Army from the beginning of the war. After the Emancipation Proclamation and the enrollment act of Mar. 3, 1863, the recruiting of Negroes was regularly carried on. Of the 186,017 Negro soldiers, 104,387 were recruited from slaves in Confederate territory.—Shannon, II, 160. President Davis referred to this fact when he said that broad distinction existed between the use of slaves as soldiers in the defense of their homes and the incitement of them to insurrection against their masters. Such was the judgment of all writers on public law, he continued, as well as that expressed and insisted upon by the U. S. government in all previous wars. That government had denounced the practice in the Revolution and in the War of 1812, and one of the charges in the Declaration of Independence against George III was that he had "incited domestic insurrection among us."—*Messages and Papers,* I, 493-96.

[105] *O. R.,* Ser. IV, Vol. III, p. 1012.   [106] *Messages and Papers,* I, 493-96.

## CONSCRIPTION 101

Governor Brown replied to the President in his message of February 15, 1865: "The administration, by its unfortunate policy of having wasted our strength and reduced our armies, and being unable to get freedmen into the field as conscripts, and unwilling to accept them in organizations with officers of their own choice, will, it is believed, soon resort to the policy of filling them up with the conscription of slaves." [107] Brown opposed freeing the slaves as a reward for their fidelity to the Confederate cause, and thought independence was not worth while with "personal liberty," "state sovereignty," and slavery lost. He denied that the Confederate government could "either directly or indirectly" abolish slavery. Such a monstrous doctrine had not been advocated even in the old Congress by any of the more rational abolitionists, he declared.[108]

Before the adoption of conscription Brown's methods had often enabled him to circumvent the military laws and secure the privilege of appointing the officers.[109] The conscription laws, in order to settle the question of appointment and secure as commanders men of military training and experience, provided for the whole provisional army a regular method of appointment and promotion according to seniority.

This feature was evidently Brown's chief objection to conscription. One of the "palpable injustices" of which he complained in his special message of November 6, 1862, was that the laws deprived volunteers who had gone into the army through state requisition of the right to elect their officers and have them commissioned by their state authorities, established a system of promotion in violation of this right, and authorized the President to issue the commis-

---
[107] *C. R.*, II, 832.
[108] *Ibid.*, pp. 832-35. The act of Mar. 13, 1865 (*O. R.*, Ser. IV, Vol. III, p. 1161) was never executed.—Brooks, "Conscription in the C. S. A.," *loc. cit.*, p. 621; Dodd, *Davis*, p. 343.
[109] *Supra*, pp. 51, 53, 58, 61; *infra*, p. 172.

sions.[110] He demanded of the legislature on several occasions that it take action to "vindicate the dignity and sovereignty of the State."[111] Even as late as 1863 Brown attempted to secure for a Georgia regiment in Confederate service the right to fill a vacancy.[112] When in August, 1864, the President made requisition upon him for troops, Brown charged that the President's object was to place in power "his own partisans and favorites . . . in place of the distinguished officers who were appointed . . . in conformity to the constitution of the country and the laws of the State. . . ."[113]

In detailing, in his last message to the legislature, the sins of omission and commission of the Confederate government, Brown adverted to the appointment of officers. Contrasting the old and "constitutional" method of raising troops with that of conscription, he stated that the conscription policy was desired by the President for the sake of the patronage in the appointment of thirty thousand officers. "Thus, in violation of the Constitution," he concluded, "the President was substituted for the States, and like the King of England, made the foundation of all honor."[114]

When the Confederacy was nearing its end Brown devoted a large part of his message of February 15, 1865, to a scathing denunciation of the administration, taking up in turn each policy from the beginning of the war and showing to his own satisfaction its futility and imbecility.[115] He was by no means discouraged, however, and expressed an emphatic belief in the ultimate success of the Southern cause if his own recommendations would be but heeded. Heading the list of reforms was the repeal of conscription, the "return

---

[110] *C. R.*, II, 287.
[111] *Ibid.*, pp. 335-44.
[112] *Supra*, Chap. III, n. 71.
[113] *C. R.*, III, 618.
[114] *Ibid.*, II, 842-45. If the Governor were living today, it would be interesting to know his opinion of the National Guard Status Act of June 15, 1933, which, in amending the National Defense Act of 1916, makes the National Guard—embracing the ages of 18 to 64, enlisted for 3 years—a reserved component of the regular army of the United States.
[115] *C. R.*, II, 835-53.

# CONSCRIPTION 103

to the Constitutional mode of raising troops by the States," and the reorganization of the armies "under officers appointed by the respective States as the Constitution directs." [116] The legislature at last acted upon his recommendation and requested the Georgia delegation in Congress to work for the repeal of the conscription acts.[117]

Brown returned to the theme in his message just one month before Lee's surrender. "Let the Conscript Act be repealed, as you have wisely resolved that it should be," he said, "let us return to the principles upon which we entered the contest. . . ." [118] It was the Governor's swan song—his last message before the fall of the Southern Confederacy which he had himself hastened. His proclamation on May 3 convening the two houses in extra session[119] led to his arrest six days later by the United States authorities.[120]

The effect upon the army of the fight on conscription can only be conjectured. Pollard—editor of the anti-administration *Richmond Examiner* and certainly no friend to President Davis—says that conscription was seized upon as political capital "by men who had a much deeper design than that of contesting a particular measure." He calls Brown the "Prince of Southern demagogues," who under cover of excessive "Yankeephobia" and devotion to state rights, merely "raised a false clamor" and by "appealing to old political prejudices against a centralization of power" and "marshalling the old elements of the Union faction distributed through Georgia, Tennessee, and North Carolina," sought to weaken

---

[116] *Ibid.*, pp. 848-49. Brown reminded President Davis of the fact that when President Polk had tendered to the then Col. Davis the appointment of brigadier general for distinguished service in the Mexican War, the appointment had been refused on the ground that the President had not the right under the constitution to appoint a brigadier general to command state volunteers employed in the service of the United States.—*Ibid.*, III, 289-90. Cf. Davis, *A Memoir*, I, 360.
[117] *Acts of the General Assembly, 1865,* p. 89.
[118] *C. R.,* II, 869.
[119] *O. R.,* Ser. IV, Vol. III, pp. 1182-83.
[120] *Infra,* p. 247.

and betray the Confederacy.[121] Dodd says that by the end of 1862 Brown had brought the state of Georgia to a condition of mind akin to open revolt.[122] A recent writer in a study on disloyalty in the Confederacy says that Governor Brown "gave much comfort to conscript evaders and made desertion from the army seem less odious," and that his criticisms of the Confederacy "soon began to bear fruit," the disloyal determining to keep out of the army and many of the volunteers deciding to come home.[123] This opinion is borne out by the experience of the commandant of conscripts in Georgia who wrote to General Cobb: "The Executive . . . and his officials and partisans, aided by a few prominent and influential public men in the State, have persistently labored to oppose the execution of these laws and to create public opinion not only hostile to their execution, but commendatory of their evasion. . . . Instead of finding their security condemned as dishonorable, [those evading conscription] find it approved, if not connived at, by some whose positions ought to be a warrant of a different course of conduct." [124]

When Sherman invaded Georgia "the disloyal were greatly encouraged . . . because of the disaffection shown by Governor Brown and Vice President Stephens. . . . No man in the state openly showed more disaffection than the Governor." [125] A writer dealing with desertions in both the Northern and Southern armies shows 6,797 men and 79 officers as deserters in Georgia.[126]

From the beginning of the controversy over conscription

---

[121] *Davis*, pp. 211-12.
[122] *Davis*, p. 300.
[123] Tatum, p. 75.
[124] *O. R.*, Ser. IV, Vol. III, p. 1049.
[125] Tatum, p. 77.
[126] Ella Lonn, *Desertion During the Civil War*, Appendix, p. 231, henceforth cited as Lonn, *Desertion*. Longstreet felt that many of the desertions among Georgia troops were due to inducements offered them to join the local organizations.—*From Manassas to Appomattox*, p. 651, cited by Lonn, *Desertion*, p. 55.

## CONSCRIPTION

to the end of the war there was trouble in the mountain counties, which Governor Brown tried in vain to put down. He sent troops to that section in 1863 and again in September, 1864, and January, 1865, besides asking in various messages for additional legislation to enable him to deal with the problem—even to a law to confiscate the property of shirkers and deserters and to refuse aid to their families.[127] The opposition to conscription in the mountain section in February, 1863, came to open rebellion and was so serious, particularly in Brown's home county,[128] that General Lee had to be called to the state to aid in quelling it.[129] The Governor's attitude toward conscription was the cause of these conditions, said friends of the administration. Toombs, on the other hand, voicing the opinion of Stephens and Brown, said: "We never had a desertion until we had conscription, for the very good reason that there were thousands outside who wanted to take the places of those inside, and besides men who felt an interest in the cause stepped forward full of energy and enthusiasm. . . . Conscription and conscription alone destroyed all that feeling." [130]

There were of course various factors entering into the situation—the lukewarm or Union sentiment in the mountains which existed from the beginning, high prices, insecurity of families, invading armies, hardships of camp life, and toward the last, the waning fortunes of the Con-

---

[127] Brown's message of Nov. 6, 1862, *C. R.*, II, 257-58; his proclamation, Jan. 17, 1863, *ibid.*, pp. 359-60 and *O. R.*, Ser. IV, Vol. II, pp. 360-61; letter of Aug. 10, 1863, *ibid.*, p. 753; messages, one in Nov., 1863, two in Nov., 1864, one in Mar., 1865, *C. R.*, II, 493-94, 594-95, 772, 804, 868; his telegram to President Davis, *ibid.*, III, 704-5. In 1863 the legislature passed a law designed to check desertions.—*Acts of the General Assembly, 1863,* p. 61. Cf. *O. R.*, Ser. IV, Vol. II, p. 786; *ibid.*, III, 393 *et seq.;* Jones, *Diary,* II, 28, 34-35; Lonn, *Desertion,* pp. 109-10; Moore, p. 152; Tatum, pp. 75-76; *Chronicle and Sentinel,* Sept. 28, 1864; Rhodes, V, 442.

[128] *Infra,* p. 126.

[129] Cf. *O. R.*, Ser. I, Vol. XXIII, Pt. II, p. 632; *Republican,* Feb. 14, 1863; *Richmond Enquirer,* Feb. 12, 1863; Brown's message, *O. R.*, Ser. IV, Vol. II, pp. 360-61.

[130] Phillips, *Correspondence,* p. 629.

federacy. Fielder thinks the "alienation of the feelings of the people by the course of the Confederate Government and her authorities, civil and military," was an important factor.[131] No doubt Fielder is right, but a question arises as to who aroused their opposition to Confederate measures? Who sowed the seed of distrust against the administration? It is not reasonable to suppose that the Governor's influence and popularity functioned only at election time. Backed as he was by no less a personage than the Vice President of the Confederacy and by a leader so admired as was Toombs, the Governor's opinions carried weight. It would be strange indeed if his picture of President Davis as a "military despot," resorting to conscription without constitutional authority and gathering unto himself "imperial power," should not have been taken seriously by the unthinking masses.

It seems safe to conclude that Governor Brown was the most important single factor in crippling conscription and thereby weakening the Confederacy.

---

[131] P. 258.

## CHAPTER V

## FACTORS IN THE GUBERNATORIAL ELECTION OF 1863

Citizens of no state were more intensely patriotic toward the Southern cause than were those of Georgia, nor did any make more sacrifices in blood and treasure.[1] Why, then, did they continue to reëlect a governor who throughout the four years of war was out of harmony with the Confederate government and used every means at his command to thwart and discredit its two most essential measures for winning the war?[2]

A partial explanation undoubtedly is to be found in the fact that Brown administered the affairs of the state in a most efficient manner. His program of state relief showed vision in its conception and unusual energy and resourcefulness in its execution. Whether it was a matter of relieving the salt famine, supplying soldiers with clothing, giving aid to soldiers' families, or curbing the distillation of whiskey in the interest of food conservation, the Governor never relaxed his efforts. Those who were in close contact with him during the war testified to his industry.

From the early part of 1862 until the end of the war Brown was deeply concerned with the problem of preventing the distillation of grain. During the time, he closed distilleries by proclamation, made numerous recommendations to

---

[1] According to Avery (p. 183) Georgia furnished more men in proportion to her population than any other state in the Confederacy—120,000 soldiers out of a voting population of 100,000.

[2] Conscription and the suspension of the writ of habeas corpus.—*Infra*, Chap. VIII.

the legislature, issued and revoked licenses, prosecuted offenders, and through some of these policies came into conflict with the Confederate government. Kentucky and Tennessee, from whence Georgia and the Confederate government had been accustomed to obtain whiskey, had in large part fallen into the hands of the enemy, and the distillation of grain in Georgia thereafter assumed alarming proportions. In one county alone seventy distilleries were in operation. On February 29, 1862, the Governor took matters in hand—in a manner which in Toombs' estimation was as "unconstitutional and as foolish as anything that Davis or Lincoln [had] ever done." [3] By proclamation he closed all distilleries, under penalty of confiscation, until the next meeting of the legislature. He directed the superintendent of the State Road to refuse all shipments of liquor from other states and requested the presidents of other railroads to do likewise. Militia officers were instructed to confiscate and empty on the ground all intoxicating liquors brought near the soldiers under their commands.[4]

In response to the Governor's recommendation[5] a law was passed on November 22 which prohibited the distillation of grain except as authorized by license issued by the Governor and at prices designated in the statute. The Governor was authorized to determine the quantity of alcohol and whiskey necessary for medical, chemical, and mechanical purposes and no more than that amount was to be permitted for state use. The Governor was further authorized to issue licenses to Confederate contractors up to one million gallons, but the

---

[3] Phillips, *Correspondence,* p. 609.

[4] *C. R.,* II, 202-7; *Republican,* Mar. 4, June 5, 1862; *Southern Confederacy,* Nov. 5, 1862; Brown to Vance, Sept. 26, 1862, Joseph E. Brown Correspondence, Library of Congress. A militia officer, who evidently did not take the Governor's proclamation seriously and continued to operate his distillery, was court-martialed and fined $500.—*Republican,* June 5, 1862; Avery, p. 241. A citizen of Franklin County was sentenced in April, 1863, to pay a fine of $2,000 and costs and to serve twelve months in jail. He served the term, but as he was insolvent the Governor remitted the fine.—*C. R.,* I, 706-7.

[5] *Ibid,* pp. 259-61.

purchase of grain within twenty miles of a railroad or navigable stream was forbidden. To prevent speculation, distillers were required to deliver every gallon to the government.[6] Violators of the law were subject to a fine of not less than $2,000 nor more than $5,000 and to imprisonment for a term equal to each day the distillery ran, the informer getting half the fine.[7] When it was found that people were distilling other things than grain—sweet potatoes, pumpkins, molasses, peas, dried fruit[8]—the Governor secured at the spring session of 1863 a law to prohibit the distillation of all food stuffs.[9] In the following November and in March, 1864, he asked for more stringent regulations.[10]

A liberal supply of whiskey was essential to the Confederate army. It was not a regular ration, but it was issued under circumstances of great exposure and protracted fatigue,[11] the supply of coffee having been cut off by the blockade. Whiskey was even more essential in the hospitals. The Federal government had made medicines contraband and operations in Confederate hospitals had often to be performed without the use of ether, chloroform, or morphine.

The Georgia law interfered with the government's arrangements with contractors in that state, where, because of the abundance of grain, the government secured its supply. Seddon asked the Governor to except government contracts from the operation of the act, "if consistent with your sense of public duty."[12] The law was accordingly modified to permit the Confederacy to complete its contracts by purchasing small grains—rye, shorts, and ship stuff—within

---
[6] It had been customary for the government to make contracts by which it received four quarts to the bushel, the distiller retaining the remainder.
[7] *Ibid.*, pp. 356-58, 479; *Acts of the General Assembly, 1862*, p. 25.
[8] Whiskey at $30 to $40 a gallon in Confederate currency was a great temptation to evade the law.
[9] *C. R.*, II, 370-72.
[10] *Ibid.*, pp. 541, 591-92.
[11] Report of the commissary general of subsistence, *O. R.*, Ser. IV, Vol. II, p. 971.
[12] *C. R.*, III, 309.

twenty miles of a railroad or navigable stream.[13] The government furnished its own corn, quantities of which it had on hand from the tax-in-kind[14] and much of which had spoiled and was fit only for distillation. The government changed its contracts to meet Georgia law by requiring five quarts of whiskey per bushel of corn and purchasing the excess at commissioner's prices. The "slops" were fed to government hogs and cattle.[15]

During January and February, 1864, when Johnston's army was at Dalton, Georgia, and meat was difficult to obtain, the General, thinking it advisable to make a more generous allowance of whiskey to the troops, called upon Commissary of Subsistence Cummings for the necessary supply. Cummings wrote to Brown that he had arranged his contracts to comply with the state laws and asked whether any other steps were necessary to enable the contractors to carry out their agreements. He explained that he would use only corn of the tax-in-kind and wished to make whiskey near a railroad or navigable stream for the sake of easy transportation.[16]

Brown's reply figuratively lifted the Commissary off his feet. It was as much a violation of the criminal laws of the state for a Confederate officer to make whiskey without a license as for any other person to do so, he said. The law forbade the use of corn for the purpose of distillation, and it mattered not, said the irate Governor, whether the corn was tithe corn or not; for if the Confederate government might distill tithe corn, it might also impress the bread out of the mouths of wives and children of soldiers and distill that too. No such pretensions would be acquiesced in for a moment. There was not enough corn for both bread and whiskey, he said, and intimated that he intended to allow only enough

---

[13] *Ibid.*, II, 552-54.
[14] *Infra*, p. 146.
[15] *C. R.*, III, 468, 471, 478-79.
[16] *Ibid.*, pp. 467-70, 472, 473.

## THE ELECTION OF 1863

to be distilled for hospital purposes and that only under license and from grain grown at least twenty miles from a railroad or navigable stream. The Governor next resorted to insinuations. He said that a bushel of corn would make not merely four or five quarts of whiskey, but ten quarts. "Thus you give the distiller, if no Government officer has any part of the profits, $75 a bushel[17] to distil the Government corn, and he can make one gallon for you and one and one-half gallons for himself. . . . The laws of Georgia and regulations of this department have wisely . . . provided against this kind of favoritism or fraud. . . . Why should a Confederate officer object to having the distiller put upon these terms, and prefer to give him a bushel of corn for a gallon of whiskey?" Whoever engages in or encourages such unreasonable speculation, "if not peculation," in defiance of the penal laws must expect to suffer the penalties, he warned.[18]

Since the officer had not expected to make whiskey without a license and had corrected all contracts requiring only four quarts of whiskey to a bushel of corn, Brown was knocking down a straw man. Cummings had the desire to reply "in the same tone and spirit," but a "sense of duty" prevented, he reported to his superior officer.[19] Instead he wrote a dignified reply to Brown, being convinced, he said, that the Governor had misconstrued both his motives and his action. He had written the original letter "couched in respectful and courteous language." His contracts were in strict accord with the law and would not consume three thousand bushels of corn per month, a large portion of which was totally unfit for bread or for stock to eat. The insinuations of fraud and corruption were false and slanderous, and he demanded the names of the parties who made them.[20] For once the Governor did not have the last word.

---
[17] Whiskey was by that time selling at $50 a gallon.
[18] *C. R.*, III, 474-77; *O. R.*, Ser. IV, Vol. III, p. 119.
[19] *C. R.*, III, 469.     [20] *Ibid.*, pp. 478-79.

Cummings wrote to Northrop, commissary general of subsistence, on February 13, 1864: "In common with other departments I have experienced unlooked-for opposition from the State authorities. They seem bent on subordinating the best interests and success of the Confederacy to their self-conceived notions of justice and patriotism, and an insane desire to preserve the material interests and welfare of all citizens." [21]

Although Brown intimated, in asking the legislature for a more stringent law with respect to Confederate distillation, that the government had abused its privileges,[22] his attitude was no doubt inspired in large part by his religious and moral sentiments. In carrying out the terms of the law with respect to the state he ascertained from the various civil officers the least amount of alcohol and whiskey necessary for their respective counties and let the contracts to the lowest bidders, requiring them to give bonds. He did not expect any of them to make a profit, but to take the contracts at a little less than the actual expense. "Hundreds who are writing me for licenses," he said, "put their application upon the ground that they wish to distil for medical purposes, as a public benefit." He added with grim humor that he hoped "to see ample proof of their sincerity when they come to bid against each other for the privilege to confer this *public benefit*." [23]

The problem of obtaining a sufficient quantity of salt for soldiers and civilians was a serious one for both the Confederacy and the states. It was particularly difficult for the governors of Georgia and Mississippi because those

---

[21] *Ibid.*, p. 470. Meanwhile the Georgia delegation in Congress took the matter up with the Secretary of War. The endorsement on the letter by the commissary general called attention to Cummings' report, which indicated no shortage of corn as had been claimed, and the Secretary of War dismissed the matter with the statement, "Whiskey must be distilled somewhere, and nowhere can [corn] be found more abundantly."—*O. R.*, Ser. IV, Vol. III, pp. 105-7; Cummings' report, *C. R.*, III, 469-70.
[22] *Ibid.*, II, 235, 260.     [23] *Ibid.*, p. 357.

THE ELECTION OF 1863 113

states had no saline resources within their boundaries—other than the seacoast. An enormous amount of salt was required everywhere[24] because of the lack of refrigeration. Pork, beef, mutton, fish, and eggs were preserved by salting, packing in brine, or smoking.[25] Because of the low cost of imported salt,[26] the South had not, to any great extent, developed its own resources. With the breaking out of hostilities the blockade cut off the foreign supply and the domestic sources on the Great Kanawha in Virginia and those of Goose Creek in Kentucky were early in possession of the enemy. Only the great wells at Saltville in southwest Virginia remained.

When in the first year of the war the packing season approached, salt prices soared and profiteers swarmed. Whereas Liverpool salt had sold in New Orleans at fifty cents a sack, the staple was selling in Richmond in September, 1861 at $6.00 and in Raleigh at $8.00.[27] Governor Brown acted promptly and vigorously to check profiteering, hoarding, and the exportation of salt from the state for higher prices elsewhere. On November 20 he ordered the state commissary general to seize for the use of the state troops all salt in Atlanta, Macon, and Columbus offered for sale at more than $5.00 a sack, which amount the officer was instructed to pay to the owners as "just compensation." [28] He telegraphed the mayor of Augusta to seize a shipment of salt at the station and to take from dealers 2,000 sacks which he understood were to be shipped out of the state. Next he ordered the railroads to hold all shipments unless

---

[24] The subject has been exhaustively treated by Ella Lonn, *Salt as a Factor in the Confederacy,* henceforth cited as Lonn, *Salt.*
[25] *Ibid.,* p. 16.
[26] English vessels brought salt as ballast and took out cotton. Salt sold on board at about one fourth of a cent per pound.—*Ibid.*
[27] *Ibid.,* pp. 43-44.
[28] *C. R.,* II, 145; Brown to Vance, Sept. 26, 1862, Joseph E. Brown Correspondence, Library of Congress. Cf. *Republican,* Nov. 23, 30, 1861; *Macon Telegraph,* Nov. 30, 1861.

it should be shown by affidavit that the salt was for personal use.[29]

One of the companies from whom 1,000 sacks had been seized brought suit to recover them from one of the state military storekeepers. The storekeeper was arrested but Brown ordered the man's release, saying: "While I hold the military authority of this State subject to the civil, in times of peace . . . in times of war . . . I cannot permit the military operations of this State to be delayed or hindered by the arrest or detention of persons in military service by any civil officer . . . under civil process issuing from any Court of this State; nor can I permit the military stores of this State . . . to be seized or interfered with by any civil tribunal whatever." [30] When the legislature met in November, 1861, the Governor recommended a law authorizing him to seize and appropriate provisions or other supplies, the compensation to be determined by "competent valuing agents." He said that prices thus established by the state would soon become the general market price, and argued that such legislation would not violate the constitutional right of the speculator, since "just compensation" did not mean "unreasonable prices." [31] The legislature passed a law to aid in prosecuting extortioners and speculators, but, like the "Law of the Maximum" in the French Revolution, it was difficult to enforce.

The Governor's recommendation and his action in freeing the storekeeper are interesting in view of his later position toward Confederate impressment, price fixing, and the suspension of the writ of habeas corpus.

---

[29] For the difficulties arising out of this order, cf. *Republican,* Dec. 5, 1861, Apr. 4, 5, June 18, 1862; *Constitutionalist,* Dec. 30, 1861.

[30] *C. R.,* II, 182-84; Avery, pp. 241-42. Rumors having reached the Governor that the sheriff was about to disobey his order and imprison the storekeeper, Brown ordered the commanding officer of the First Brigade to ascertain the facts, and if necessary to use military force to break open the prison, free the storekeeper, and arrest the sheriff.—*C. R.,* II, 186.

[31] *Ibid.,* p. 106.

## THE ELECTION OF 1863

The legislature appropriated $50,000 to aid private concerns in establishing salt works. The Governor offered a $5,000 reward for the discovery of a salt well and urged citizens near the coast to make their own supply. After several discouraging failures to contract for large supplies, the Governor through his friend, Senator John W. Lewis, made arrangements at Saltville for the manufacture of salt on state account. As no appropriation had been made for the purpose, the Governor ordered the treasurer of the State Road to honor the drafts which were later repaid from a legislative appropriation of $500,000.[32]

The State Road and other Georgia railroads carried the salt free of charge. Brown drew up a plan of distribution by means of which one-half bushel was donated to widows of soldiers and to those who had lost a son in service, and each family of a soldier was allowed one-half bushels for $1.00. After these were supplied, heads of families could each purchase a bushel for $4.50.[33]

In the meantime a magnificent mine of rock salt was discovered at New Iberia, Louisiana,[34] and Brown contracted with a Georgia company to take all it could import from that point at $7.50 a bushel.[35] He also contracted with two Georgia companies at Saltville to furnish salt on state account.[36]

Owing to the difficulties of transportation at Saltville, shortage of labor, speculation, and the confusion that arose

---

[32] *Ibid.*, pp. 223-24, 231, 277; *Republican,* April 7, 1862; Lonn, *Salt,* p. 96; Coulter, *Georgia,* p. 314.

[33] *C. R.*, II, 223-24, 277-78, 281-82. There were at least three such distributions to soldiers' families—the first in the summer and fall of 1862, another one year later, and the third in September, 1864.—Directions to the commissary general, July 31, 1862, *C. R.*, II, 227-31; proclamation of the Governor and letter of commissary general to justices of the inferior courts, *Southern Confederacy,* Aug. 5, 1863; Governor's instructions to commissary general, Sept. 26, *Weekly Chronicle and Sentinel,* Oct. 12, 1864. Cf. *C. R.*, II, 229, 728-32.

[34] Lonn, *Salt,* pp. 30-33; *ibid.,* Chap. II, n. 43.

[35] *C. R.*, II, 280.     [36] *Ibid.,* p. 281.

at the wells among state and private companies, contractors and sub-contractors, there was never enough salt available to carry out the Governor's plans. This was especially true after the state of Virginia entered the field for the purpose of supplying her own needs and those of the Confederate army in her state.[37] The Governor recommended that a warehouse be built at Bristol in which to store the salt and trains or cars be impressed from railroads in Georgia to haul it from that point.[38] The legislature gave the desired authority but the threat of impressment alone was sufficient to obtain the necessary rolling stock. The State Road sent the locomotive "Texas" to operate on the branch line of the Virginia & Tennessee Railroad to haul supplies to, and salt from, the works.[39]

Throughout the entire period of the war the Governor gave especial attention to supplying salt to soldiers' families and to the poor and needy, including refugees, but despite his exertions there was never a sufficient amount for all citizens. A recent historian estimates from the incomplete data on the subject that the state supplied to the civilian population of Georgia annually about six pounds of salt per capita.[40]

As the blockade became more effective the problem of clothing also became acute, the factories of the state being unable to supply the demand, and the legislature appropriated $100,000 for a state factory to manufacture cotton cards to be used in the home production of cloth. The Governor established the factory in the state penitentiary, swept the state clean of sheep, goat, deer, and dog skins, and of wire and tacks, and sent an agent to Europe to pro-

---

[37] *Ibid.*, pp. 281-82, 420-27.
[38] *Ibid.*, pp. 413-16, 431-33, 444-45.
[39] *Ibid.*, pp. 477-78.
[40] Lonn, *Salt*, p. 214. In Richmond in the winter of 1862-63 the civilian population was allotted one pound per month per person.—Jones, *Diary*, I, 183-84. Records of Georgia's salt transactions fill four enormous volumes in the Georgia Dept. of Archives and History.

## THE ELECTION OF 1863

cure more of these raw materials to be used in the manufacture of the cards. By March, 1863, 1,777 pairs of cards had been turned out and one year later the factory had a capacity of 100 pairs per day.[41] The supply was, however, insufficient, and the Governor recommended an appropriation of $1,000,000 for the purchase of cotton for exportation, a part of the proceeds to be exchanged for cotton cards manufactured in Europe and for raw materials for the state factory.[42]

The supply of cards was not at any time adequate to meet the demand. As with salt, the Governor arranged that soldiers' families and the needy should be supplied first. Cards for the purpose were allocated to the different counties and paid for out of the relief fund.[43]

With husbands, sons, and fathers in the army, with few slaves to till the fields in the mountain counties, and with no adequate provision for caring for needy families such as the United States adopted in the World War, private contributions and individual charity were unable to cope with the problem of relief. The Governor recommended that the state take the matter in hand. Toombs, who was opposed to all paternalism, remarked sarcastically that Brown's hobby was soldiers' families.[44]

The Governor never failed to make recommendations to the legislature for caring for the poor, and as the need increased, his demands increased. On November 6, 1862, he recommended a bounty of $100 to the family of each soldier whose property was less than $1,000—the funds to be raised from the net proceeds of the State Road and from freight rates increased by 25 per cent, together with a tax

---

[41] *C. R.,* II, 395-98, 452-53, 666-67; Brown to Vance, Feb. 4, Mar. 14, 1863, Zebulon B. Vance Correspondence, II, 120-21, 176-77; Lucius L. Knight, *A Standard History of Georgia and Georgians,* II, 765, henceforth cited as Knight; Avery, p. 251.
[42] *C. R.,* II, 520-21, 666-67.
[43] *C. R.,* II, 360-64.
[44] Phillips, *Correspondence,* p. 600.

of 33⅓ per cent upon the net incomes of speculators.[45] The legislature responded with an appropriation of $2,500,000. Three months later the Governor reported more than $869,-000 expended among 84,000 persons.[46] An unfavorable season and the presence of contending armies for a part of the year of 1863 left portions of North Georgia desolate. The appropriation having been spent, the Governor used the contingent fund to purchase supplies and sent a train from the State Road to haul corn from southwest Georgia. From his own farm he gave to the poor of Cherokee County $4,000 worth of corn and fodder.[47] In November of that year he asked an appropriation of $5,000,000 and in 1864 and 1865 each, $6,000,000.[48]

The Governor was no less diligent in behalf of his troops. Because of his efforts and recommendations and generous appropriations by the legislature, no troops in Confederate service, except perhaps those of North Carolina,[49] were better clothed throughout the war than were those from Georgia.

Before the quartermaster department of the Confederate States was organized it was necessary for the states to clothe their own troops. The law of March 6, 1861, provided that volunteers furnish their own clothing and those in the cavalry their own horses, for which the government allowed additional compensation.[50] When later the Confederacy was ready to clothe its troops,[51] some of the states insisted upon

---

[45] Brown warred on speculators throughout the entire four years of war.

[46] *C. R.*, 263-65, 402-6; Avery, p. 251. Cf. *C. R.*, II, 450-51.

[47] *Ibid.*, pp. 372, 503-6; *Intelligencer*, Feb. 22, 1863; *Southern Confederacy*, Mar. 4, 1863; Avery, p. 253.

[48] *C. R.*, II, 503-4, 588-89, 765; Coulter, *Georgia*, p. 314. The legislature made the appropriations, added $800,000 especially for counties that had been overrun by the enemy, and in March, 1865, supplemented the fund with an additional $2,600,000.—*C. R.*, II, 862-67, 873, 874-77.

[49] See Owsley, *State Rights*, pp. 119-27.

[50] *O. R.*, Ser. IV, Vol. I, pp. 125-27.

[51] Commutation for clothing was discontinued by the act of Oct. 8, 1862.—*Ibid.*, II, 229.

## THE ELECTION OF 1863

continuing the custom, although the administration opposed the policy.[52]

With his usual thoroughness Governor Brown set about the task of supplying Georgia troops. He asked and received large appropriations from the legislature,[53] and in November, 1862, he was given authority to seize all factories and tanneries in the state and appropriate their products "till a good pair of shoes and a good suit of clothes are furnished every Georgia soldier in the service." [54] A month before the fall of the Confederacy the Governor recommended an appropriation of $3,000,000 for a clothing fund and for the transportation of corn to destitute sections.[55]

Early in the war he sent agents to Savannah, Vicksburg, and to Texas to secure leather, hides, and wool for the manufacture of shoes and clothing, and as late as February, 1865, agents were still purchasing these materials. State purchasing agents in Europe sent blankets, clothing, shoes, and other supplies for Georgia troops. Early in 1864, acting under authority of the legislature, Brown chartered a line of steamers to export cotton and import supplies.[56] Up to November 17, 1864, he had exported 1,614½ bales of cotton, of which only 58 were captured by the enemy. Brown had purchased the cotton with the rental received in three months from the rolling stock of the State Road not engaged in government transportation, the road itself being at this time in possession of the enemy. The state obtained for the cotton, less the freight, a credit in Europe of more than $5,000,000 in currency, and had on hand at Nassau on that date 30,000 soldiers' blankets among other things,

---

[52] *Ibid.*, III, 928-29, 948-53. Cf. Owsley, *State Rights*, pp. 110-49.
[53] *C. R.*, II, 94, 96, 142, 501, 502, 766. Cf. report of state quartermaster, *ibid.*, pp. 408-13.
[54] *Ibid.*, pp. 266, 354-55.
[55] *Ibid.*, p. 864.
[56] *Ibid.*, pp. 412, 581, 782; Brown to Vance, Mar. 23, 1864, Joseph E. Brown Correspondence, Library of Congress. Cf. *infra*, p. 157.

and was expecting on December 1 about 5,000 suits of soldiers' clothing, 18,000 yards of cloth, and 5,000 pairs of army shoes. The legislature appropriated $1,500,000 for the state's shipping business in 1865.[57]

The Federal government having agreed with the Confederacy to allow cotton to go through the blockade to New York to pay for relief to Southern soldiers in Northern prisons, the Governor on March 2, 1865, recommended an appropriation to purchase 1,000 bales for this purpose.[58]

Ever watchful of the comfort and well-being of the soldiers, Governor Brown recommended to the legislature that soldiers be relieved of the poll tax and that each be given $1,000 exemption on his property tax. He thought that it was just that the wealthy of the state and those who remained in the enjoyment of home comforts should bear the burden of taxation necessary to support the government and the families of those in the field.[59]

The Governor next directed his attention to securing increased pay for soldiers. Privates received only $11 a month,[60] which, however adequate at the beginning of the war, was no longer so by April, 1863, when he devoted an entire message to the subject. He pointed out that the majority of the soldiers were poor men and non-slaveholders upon whose labor their families depended for support. He thought that the operation of the conscript act as between the poor and the rich had been unfair and unjust. There were also rich speculators who remained at home "preying like vultures upon the vitals of society," and turning a "deaf ear to the cries of soldiers' families." He wanted the pockets of these men reached through the tax gatherer, and he recommended a joint resolution requesting the Georgia delegation

---
[57] *C. R.*, II, 756, 784-86, 799, 872, 874; Fielder, pp. 307-8.
[58] *C. R.*, II, 861-62; Rowland, VI, 525. Cf. *C. R.*, III, 710-12, 880-81.
[59] *Ibid.*, II, 265-66, 761.
[60] In the North, $13.

THE ELECTION OF 1863          121

to bring the matter before Congress.⁶¹ In the following November the Governor returned to the subject and flayed Confederate senators who had refused to sanction the bill.⁶²

In caring for the sick and wounded, as in the matter of clothing the troops, the states at first were compelled to look after their own soldiers. For this service patriotic associations were formed to collect funds and make the necessary arrangements, a custom which was in part continued throughout the war. Governor Brown gave much of his attention to this phase of relief work. In 1861 he contributed $5,000 from the military fund for this purpose, and in November and thereafter he recommended liberal appropriations by the legislature.⁶³

Well might Georgians at the front cheer for "Joe Brown." He could always be depended upon to look after their comfort and the protection of their families. In supplying salt and cotton cards he had seen that soldiers' families and poor widows should be first served. Relief was quickly given, whether in the form of food, clothing, or shelter—as in the case of citizens driven out of their homes in Atlanta when Sherman so ruthlessly and wantonly burned the city. As Cobb suggested,⁶⁴ all the credit should not be claimed for the Governor—the legislature and the taxpayers were generous and equally concerned. Upon the Governor, however, lay the responsibility of initiative and that of administering the funds, and he performed these duties with sympathy, understanding, and efficiency.

The policy of restricting the cultivation of cotton for the sake of compelling recognition of the independence of the

---

⁶¹ *C. R.*, II, 433-37. The resolution was passed and the matter was brought before Congress.—*O. R.*, Ser. IV, Vol. II, pp. 485-86, 1043; *C. R.*, II, 498; *ibid.*, III, 332-33; Fielder, pp. 278-80.

⁶² *C. R.*, II, 498-500. On June 9, 1864, the pay of privates was increased to $18; on June 30, 1864, in the Federal army, to $16.—Schwab, p. 182.

⁶³ *C. R.*, II, 108.

⁶⁴ *Ibid.*, III, 563-64.

Confederate States[65] ultimately gave place to restriction for the sake of increasing the production of food supplies. Governor Brown took up the matter in his message of November 6, 1862, and urged planters to cultivate only enough cotton for home consumption and to concentrate upon raising grain and other forms of provisions. With Confederate ports blockaded he thought that there would be no foreign market for the staple,[66] and that if it were raised and stored it would tempt the enemy, suffering a cotton famine, to penetrate to the interior to obtain it.[67] The legislature responded by prohibiting the cultivation of more than three acres per hand.[68] President Davis in a personal letter congratulated the Governor upon his part in securing the measure.[69]

In the following March, the enemy having overrun a large part of the productive lands of the Confederacy and the remaining portions having to support many refugees, the Governor felt the need of further restriction. Expressing the fear that the cultivation of so much cotton would result in "subjugation by hunger, and the utter ruin of the Confederacy," he recommended that the amount of land to be planted in cotton be reduced to one-fourth acre per hand.[70] He made similar recommendations in November of that year and again in March, 1864.[71]

It seems clear that such accomplishments in state administration were a strong inducement to citizens of the state to continue the energetic Governor in power, in spite of his opposition to measures of the Confederate administration.

[65] *Infra*, p. 152.
[66] Blockade-running had not at that time developed into the proportions it later assumed.—*Ibid.*
[67] *C. R.*, II, 268-69. Cf. Avery, p. 252.
[68] *Acts of the General Assembly, 1862*, pp. 5-6.
[69] *O. R.*, Ser. IV, Vol. II, p. 376.
[70] *C. R.*, II, 367-68, 505. Brown to Governor Gill Shorter of Alabama, Mar. 11, 1863, Miscellaneous Papers of Governors A. B. Moore and John Gill Shorter.
[71] *C. R.*, II, 504-7, 591.

# THE ELECTION OF 1863

Without such a record of achievement, he would doubtless have been retired in short order. Herschel V. Johnson could not be elected to the Confederate Senate in 1862 until he had assured the legislature of his wholehearted support of conscription, and the popular Toombs was three times denied the honor of election to the Confederate Senate, as well as the nomination for governor, because he was not in accord with administration measures.[72] Other factors in Brown's favor were, of course, his cleverness in political strategy; his popularity with the masses, in the mountain region in particular where more or less Union sentiment had persisted and where conscription was especially opposed; and the fact that he had the support of Toombs and the Vice President. In addition, Brown had the advantage of being already in office and the prestige which the power of appointment always

---

[72] For the failure of Toombs to secure the nomination for governor in 1863, cf. Avery, p. 260; Toomb's explanation to Wm. M. Burwell, Jan. 10, 1863, Burwell Papers. In Nov., 1861, the Georgia legislature, resenting Toombs' attitude toward the administration, chose Benjamin Hill for the full term in the Confederate Senate by a vote of 127 to 68.—*H. J., 1861*, pp. 118-20. After five ballots had been taken to fill the short term, with no one of the candidates receiving a majority, former U. S. Senator Alfred Iverson, Toombs' nearest competitor, withdrew his name and on the sixth ballot Toombs was elected. He was so humiliated by the evident reluctance of the legislature to elect him that he refused to serve, saying that he preferred to remain in the army. Governor Brown appointed Dr. John W. Lewis to the position.—Benjamin H. Hill, Jr., pp. 42-43; Federal Union, Nov. 20, 1861; Avery, p. 222; Phillips, *Toombs*, pp. 241-42.

For the vacancy created in 1862 by the resignation of Dr. Lewis, Toombs received only 24 votes on the first ballot and 14 on the second. He wrote Linton Stephens shortly afterwards that he felt "a deep resentment against the present legislature."—Phillips, *Correspondence*, p. 608; Avery, pp. 250-51. The friends of Herschel V. Johnson had expected to elect their candidate on the first ballot but not until Johnson promised to give his undivided support to the administration and its war measures would the legislature accept him. He was elected on the second ballot.—Avery, p. 250; Flippin, pp. 236-37; Rhodes, V, 448.

Toombs was a candidate for the Senate in 1863. On Nov. 13 he spoke before the legislature, denouncing Confederate war measures. He was defeated through the efforts of administration supporters led by Senator Hill who came from Richmond for the purpose. Herschel V. Johnson was elected at the same time for a full term.—Pearce, pp. 84-85; Phillips, *Toombs*, p. 250; Owsley, *State Rights*, pp. 235-36; Rhodes, V, 376.

bestows. Those officeholders, civilian and militia alike, who may have been averse to going into the army naturally supported the man who made it possible for them to retain their comfortable berths.

The odium which had rested upon Brown for the exemption of his "pets" (the militia officers) was in part removed in the latter part of the winter of 1863 when the Governor ordered them to aid General Beauregard in the defense of Savannah, with instruction to serve in any capacity—even as privates. If any refused to obey, their exemption from conscription was to be withdrawn. The Governor's order expressed the hope that their conduct would disprove the unjust charges that had been made against their valor. Avery states that a "grin" spread over the state.[73]

The gubernatorial campaign of 1863 may be said to have commenced, as far as Brown was concerned, almost nine months before the election. On January 30—when conscription had been less than a year in operation and when other measures of the Richmond government had also aroused his opposition—Brown wrote Stephens on the subject of the campaign. He said that he did not intend to be a candidate, but that he felt a deep interest in seeing someone elected "who, while he does his whole duty to the Confederacy, will contend for and sustain to the extent of his ability the rights and sovereignty of the State." He thought that a few "who are friends and agree upon the great issues which are likely to come before the country should confer in advance about the matter." He suggested Linton Stephens for the position. "The contest may be a hot one," he continued, "and it will be best to give the proper direction to the public mind through the proper channels at no very distant day." [74]

Evidently Stephens urged Brown to stand for reëlection,

---

[73] Pp. 256-57; Brown to the legislature, *C. R.*, II, 496; orders of adjutant and inspector general, *Southern Confederacy*, Mar. 4, 1863. Cf. *ibid.*, Mar. 11, 1863.

[74] Phillips, *Correspondence*, p. 610.

for on February 16 Brown wrote: "I have not said publicly that I will not under any circumstances be a candidate for another term ... but I do not think there is any state of facts likely to arise which can induce me to change my purpose." [75] In the event that Linton Stephens would not agree to be a candidate, he favored Toombs, in whose patriotism, ability, "and soundness on the vital question of state sovereignty" he had the highest confidence. He had heard the names of two men mentioned "by the advocates of arbitrary power," and he thought it "a matter of first importance that a friend to constitutional liberty be selected." [76]

A month later Brown was regretting that Linton Stephens had refused to make the race and fearing that Toombs' cotton crop of the previous year[77] had jeopardized his chances.[78] He reported A. H. Kenan as saying that should Toombs be a candidate, President Davis would come to Georgia and take the stump against him.[79]

Toombs had angrily resigned from the army, believing that the President, whom he now called a "false and hypocritical wretch," [80] had prevented his promotion.[81] He ex-

---
[75] *Ibid.*, p. 611.  [76] *Ibid.*
[77] When in 1862 the Southern states were seeking through voluntary agreement among planters to restrict the cultivation of cotton in favor of cereals, Toombs refused to coöperate and instructed his overseer to plant a full crop of cotton. To his brother he wrote: "As to what I shall choose to plant on my estates, I shall neither refer it to newspapers nor to public meetings, nor to legislatures." In reply to a protest from two committees of public safety he telegraphed from Richmond on June 11, 1862: "You may rob me in my absence but you cannot intimidate me."—Phillips, *Correspondence,* p. 595; *idem, Toombs,* p. 247; *Federal Union,* June 17, 1862; Stovall, p. 275; Mary Boykin Chesnut, *A Diary from Dixie,* p. 120, henceforth cited as Chesnut, *Diary.*
[78] Brown would not, of course, admit it, but it was Toombs' opposition to the administration rather than his cotton crop that was most likely to prevent, and did prevent, his nomination. See Avery, p. 260.
[79] Phillips, *Correspondence,* p. 614.
[80] *Ibid.,* p. 611.
[81] Davis had refused to make Toombs a major general, promotion depending upon the recommendation of the commanding general. For Toombs' difficulties in the army, cf. Stovall, pp. 235 *et seq.;* Phillips, *Toombs,* pp. 237 *et seq.*

pressed the conviction that the real control of affairs in the Confederacy was narrowing down into the hands of the President and the "old army," [82] and that when it should get there entirely the cause would collapse. He said that the only question in his mind for a patriot was whether resistance or acquiescence would do the most harm to the public cause. He thought the latter would do so, and would "act accordingly." [83] The attitude of Toombs toward the administration no doubt accounts in part for Brown's advocacy of him as a candidate for governor.

The majority of the press sought, as in 1861, to prevent Brown's nomination. In the winter of 1862-63 opposition to conscription in Brown's home county of Cherokee had come to open rebellion and the state authorities had much difficulty in restoring order. The *Republican*, commenting on the fact on February 14, disclaimed any intention of charging the Governor with "heading a rebellion," nevertheless it thought his course towards the Confederate administration, his denunciation of Congress and his proclamations on the recruiting acts of that body, his repeated attempts to poison the minds of the people toward their government by exhibiting it as their enemy, all "tended towards rebellion and towards nothing else." Whether so intended or not, the *Republican* continued, the Governor's course had "done more to breed disloyalty and desertion than all other causes combined."

It was rather generally believed that the Governor and the Vice President were preparing to head a party in opposition to the Confederate administration.[84] "P. W. A.," the army correspondent of the *Republican*, wrote to his paper on March 12, 1863, that every real friend of the cause of Southern independence would deplore such a move, without

---

[82] The "old army crowd" was Toombs' designation for West Pointers.
[83] Letter to Wm. M. Burwell, Aug. 29, 1863, Burwell Papers.
[84] Cf. Senator Johnson's letters to Stephens warning him against such a course.—*Infra*, pp. 201, 204 *et seq.*

## THE ELECTION OF 1863

reference to the merits or demerits of the administration. It would embarrass the army and give substantial aid to the enemy, he warned.

Soon afterwards an anonymous circular was sent out condemning conscription and giving notice that an opposition political organization was about to "spring into existence." The circular stated that the friends of the administration had tried in every way

to make the conscript act lie upon the stomachs of the people, but all in vain. They have explained it by all the laws of necessity and emergency, declared it constitutional and patriotic; but still it was a bitter pill to a free people and could not be swallowed. Nothing but the strong arm (the tyrant's arm) of military power could enforce it. . . .

What is a State government worth when the very power which sustains it is pulled from under it and held at the discretion of a foreign Executive? Are the Governors of these States and their cabinets mere puppets suspended upon the stage to amuse the women and children and the few noncombatant diseased old men left by the operation of the conscript act? . . . they have the name of Governor, but the President only can chuckle over the power. . . . It is idle to call a State sovereign and yet acknowledge the constitutional right of a foreign Executive to divest it at any moment of the power to execute its sovereignty. . . .

The old system of drafting [by the states] was not objectionable to the people and was amply sufficient to send out ablebodied men to the defense of the country and the Governor possessed ample authority to fill promptly every requisition of the President. . . .[85]

Through the winter and spring there was a careful "build up" of Brown for a fourth term by the newspapers that supported him. Brown's wise management of state finances and of the State Road, his care in looking after the comfort

---

[85] A copy of the circular came into the possession of Governor Milton who on Apr. 15, 1863, sent it to the President.—*O. R.*, Ser. IV, Vol. II, pp. 489-90.

of Georgia soldiers and their families, his ardor for Southern independence and his energy in raising troops were kept constantly before the people. The *Constitutionalist* emphasized the Governor's virtues as an administrator, pointed to the danger of making a change in a crisis, and asserted that he had "aided largely to bring the great struggle . . . to a successful and triumphant issue." [86]

The *Southern Confederacy*, which had supported Nisbet in 1861, felt confident on April 15 that the Governor would again be a candidate, but it thought his recent proclamation asking for greater coöperation with the Confederacy would not convince the people of his sincerity. Brown was not at all the financial genius and statesman that his friends proclaimed him to be, the editor said, and he saw no reason to give him a perpetual term of office. On May 5 the *Intelligencer* reported the people in general as favoring Brown for another term, to which the *Republican* retorted three days later that there was no end to the capacity of the people for being duped. The *Southern Recorder*, which was also opposed to the Governor, said that Brown's confidential organs had long been preparing the public mind for his fourth candidacy. The editor recalled that it was in reply to a letter from a man who controlled the *Intelligencer* in 1861 "and who is now State Commissary" that Brown had declared himself in that year for a third term.[87]

The political strategy of Brown in 1863 was a repetition of that of 1861: nomination by a few friends, early announcement of his candidacy, and emphasis upon his patriotism and warm support of the Confederate administration. On May 16 James Gardner, owner of the *Constitutionalist*, and three other citizens of Augusta,[88] addressed a letter to Brown asking him to serve for another term. They placed their plea solely upon the ground of patriotism, being ac-

---

[86] Avery, pp. 259 *et seq.;* Northen, III, 98-99.
[87] May 12, 1863.   [88] George Schley, B. H. Warren, and Robert H. May.

## THE ELECTION OF 1863

tuated, they said, only by consideration of the issue between the United States government and the Confederacy. They believed the Confederacy could best be served by retaining him in office and thereby preventing any controversies that might otherwise arise throughout the state through individual preferences or political prejudice. They had often differed with the Governor in the past, they admitted, but they appreciated his honesty of purpose and his care for and devotion to the interests and comfort of Georgia's brave sons now pouring out their life blood on the battlefields.[89]

On May 21 the Governor replied. He said that he had received similar letters from a number of people, many of whom had formerly opposed him. It had been his intention to retire, but he admitted the right of the people "to determine otherwise." He had desired the position of executive in peace time, and now that he was familiar with the financial and military affairs of the state, the necessities of her brave sons, and the management of the State Road, "which by the end of the year will have paid to the state treasury an average of more than $550,000 a year" during his administrations, he felt that it was his duty to contribute his knowledge and experience to the state in view of the gigantic war in which it was engaged.

"I have constant assurance," he continued, "that the people of Georgia do not wish a change of administration, a change of faithful and experienced officers in different departments of government, a change in the management of the State Road, a change in the financial management of the state government, or a change of the liberal policy of the state towards her glorious troops in the field or their families at home. . . ."

It had also been suggested, the Governor said, that his retirement would open the door for a number of new and

---

[89] *Southern Recorder,* June 2, 1863. The *Constitutionalist* had heretofore opposed Brown.

untried men, which would again divide the people into parties and factions "when unity and harmony among ourselves are of the utmost importance." Nothing in his judgment could be more unfortunate than for political aspirants at this time to harangue the people and distract their attention from the common defense.

Referring to rumors of the formation of a party in opposition to the Confederate government, he said that nothing could be more unwise. He did not approve of every act of the administration, "but it does not follow that we can make war on an administration because it may have committed some errors." Nevertheless, "having entered into this struggle in defense of the great doctrine of State Rights and State sovereignty, we would be untrue to ourselves and our posterity were we to permit these great fundamental principles to be disregarded...." While the Confederate government should be confined within the sphere which the constitution had assigned to it, "we should give it our last dollar and never consent to a reconciliation of the old Union upon any terms." He had differed with President Davis on conscription, he admitted, but his opposition had been "conscientious" and under "an honest difference of opinion." [90]

Writing to Alexander Stephens regarding his candidacy, Brown said: "Your message . . . had much to do with shaping my course." He had consented to make the race because his friends thought that "no other State Rights man who would consent to run could carry the State." He thought it "would never do for Georgia to back down from her position" and he was willing to "submit to any personal sacrifice"

---

[90] *Ibid.* Avery had from Col. P. Thweatt what he calls "inside information" regarding Brown's candidacy. He states (p. 260) that Brown called a group of his friends to the executive mansion and informed them of his desire for Toombs to make the race. A committee appointed to canvass Toombs' chances reported that Toombs' differences with the President made him unavailable. Brown still refused to run and a committee of his friends was named to determine upon a candidate. Col. Thweatt refused to serve on the committee, urged Brown to make the race, and the Governor finally consented.

## THE ELECTION OF 1863

rather than see her do it.[91] He thought there would be no difficulty in his reëlection, but believing that "the only certain rule is to work all the time," he begged Stephens to "write to friends in the army[92] and do all you can for me." He said that he had negatived the idea of an anti-administration party in his letter of announcement, which he thought would be "something in the way of the administration candidate who might expect success on that ground." [93]

Brown's letter is interesting in view of his assumption at all times that the state was behind him in his opposition to administration measures. He was in reality as opposed to the administration as was Toombs, but, unlike Toombs, he was too clever a politician to make it a political issue.

As in 1861, the announcement of Brown's candidacy brought a storm of opposition. The *Southern Recorder* declared that to vote for Brown was to endorse his opposition to conscription, his "foolhardy correspondence" with the President, his "slanderous message" to the legislature concerning the supreme court decision on conscription, and his "unjust protection of the militia officers." [94] Governor Brown "has warred against the Confederacy at home as fiercely as we have warred for it in the field," a soldier wrote to the *Republican*.[95] The *Southern Recorder* on June 23 and 30, 1863, published articles two columns each in length in which the writer reviewed Brown's conduct toward the Confederate administration and denounced his war on President Davis. He asserted that Brown had struck the administration "whenever he dared, caring only to see that the lick struck President Davis and did not rebound and strike himself." With reference to Brown's opposition to conscription he said

---
[91] Brown frequently and oftentimes mistakenly identified the state with himself.
[92] A law had been passed to permit Georgia soldiers to vote.—*Acts of the General Assembly, 1861*, p. 31.
[93] Phillips, *Correspondence*, pp. 617-18.
[94] Cited by Moore, p. 265.
[95] June 20, 1863.

that "but for the legislature, the Supreme Court, and the people, he would have had a little sectional war of his own ... which would have brought ruin upon the whole country."

Brown's early announcement of his candidacy had somewhat taken the opposition unawares. The absorption of the people in the war made a convention impracticable and no candidate had been agreed upon. Various names were now put forward in the press, but those who might successfully oppose Brown, as Senator Hill or General Cobb, could not be spared from their posts of duty.[96] Brown thought Hill would "hardly be willing to resign his seat in the Senate for the chance he would have to be elected Governor," and that if he made the race without resigning "he would not be a formidable candidate." [97]

In late August the *Atlanta Gazette* and the *Rome Southerner* announced the candidacy of Joshua Hill. Hill's name provoked a storm of opposition only a degree less violent than that of Brown. Hill had been a Whig Unionist in 1860-61 and had angered the people of Georgia by a speech in the United States Congress condemning Brown's seizure of Fort Pulaski. He had caused still further resentment by refusing on January 23, 1861, to withdraw from Congress with the Georgia delegation and by sending in his formal resignation to the Speaker, "thereby acknowledging the authority of the Federal government over a representative of Georgia in Congress." [98] Brown thought the movement to place such a man in the field was a "bold one." [99]

A private in the army, signing himself "Newton," enthusiastically supported Hill. He pointed out that Hill had opposed secession and had predicted that it would mean war and the abolition of slavery, while "no man contributed more to bring on secession than Governor Brown." The corres-

---
[96] Pearce, pp. 83-84; *Republican,* June 20, 1863.
[97] Phillips, *Correspondence,* p. 618.
[98] Fielder, p. 108. Cf. Avery, p. 180.
[99] Letter to Stephens, Aug. 22, 1863, Phillips, *Correspondence,* p. 628.

THE ELECTION OF 1863      133

pondent stated that although he intended to fight to the end of the war, he thought the election of Brown would be far worse for the state than the election of Hill and the possible reconstruction of the Union.[100] The *Southern Confederacy* was in a quandary. It had already expressed its opposition to Brown, and it could not, of course, support Hill. It, therefore, announced on August 26 that it would not for the present support either candidate and that all articles pertaining to them would be inserted as advertisements.

Hill's supporters hastened to publish a letter from him defining his position toward the administration and reconstruction,[101] and the *Republican* four days later announced its intention to support him. Hill's letter, the *Republican* said, was in striking contrast to the "frothy fulminations and demagogical appeals which we are so accustomed to receive from the public men of the present day." [102] Others, however, were not so enthusiastic. A. A. Adams probably expressed the opinion of one group when he announced that he would withdraw his support of Hill's candidacy because in his judgment Hill's letter pledged him (1) to oppose reconstruction of the Union upon one ground only—that of subjugation and the abolition of slavery as proposed by Lincoln; (2) his position regarding the prosecution of the war was not satisfactory; and (3) his statement was not sufficiently strong with respect to supporting the administration.[103] The *Republican* valiantly defended Hill on all these points,[104] but it is evident that the journal was supporting him merely as a choice of two evils. Others, however, felt that Hill would sincerely coöperate with the Confederate administration.

In the meantime the candidacy of Timothy M. Furlow had been announced, but for some reason the *Republican* could

---

[100] *Southern Confederacy*, Aug. 26, 1863.
[101] Letter dated Aug. 31, published in the *Republican*, Sept. 4, 1863.
[102] Sept. 4, 1863.
[103] *Republican*, Sept. 12, 1863.
[104] *Ibid.*

not support him. The journal extricated itself from a political situation it evidently did not relish by announcing on September 25 that it would take no further part in the contest. The explanation was that while its editor wished to support Hill, its proprietor was not satisfied with Hill's position on reconstruction and that "if [the proprietor] cannot support Hill, he cannot support Brown." The names of the three gubernatorial candidates—Hill, Furlow, Brown—were carried at the *Republican* masthead in the order shown. Although it took no position with reference to Hill and Furlow, the *Republican* continued its opposition to Brown.

Timothy M. Furlow's candidacy was promoted by the *Southern Recorder*.[105] He had had very little experience in public affairs and was not, therefore, a strong candidate. He was a wealthy planter and had been a state senator during the two preceding years. In 1850 he had been a Southern Rights man, and as a member of the state convention in 1861 had voted for secession. He was a strong supporter of the President and the policy of Congress and believed in prosecuting the war until the independence of the Confederate States should be fully established. "Before we yield to reconstruction," he said in his letter to the voters on September 8, "let every place in the Confederacy be a battlefield, and every warrior bite the dust." [106]

Supporters of Furlow could not hope to elect their candidate on a straight vote of the electorate, but as the state constitution provided that a gubernatorial candidate to be elected must receive a majority of all the votes cast, they hoped by the three-cornered contest to split Brown's vote and throw the election into the legislature, where Brown's defeat was assured.[107] Thus Hill represented the conservative

---

[105] Avery, p. 261.
[106] *Republican,* Sept. 16; letter to R. M. Orne & Son, Sept. 5, published in the *Republican,* Sept. 11, 1863. R. M. Orne & Son were proprietors of the *Southern Recorder.*
[107] Avery, p. 261; Fielder, pp. 109, 541.

## THE ELECTION OF 1863

or Union sentiment, Furlow the other extreme, and Brown somewhere between and presumably opposed to reconstruction. Brown had, however, agreed with Stephens that independence without constitutional liberty was not worth the sacrifices the people were making,[108] and he had several times stated that conscription had destroyed constitutional liberty.

There was no active campaigning on the part of any of the candidates, published letters and editorials for the most part being depended upon.[109] People were too much occupied with the war to take any active interest in politics, although on election day they seem to have voted rather generally.[110] During the summer Vicksburg had been surrendered and Lee's invasion of the North turned back. The battle of Chickamauga was fought only a few weeks before the election. The Baptist press seems to have been of some assistance to Brown,[111] but of much greater value perhaps was Toombs' speech in Sparta on June 17. Toombs took the same position as the Governor on conscription, martial law,[112] the tax-in-kind, the necessity for the Confederacy to pay market prices for provisions, and opposition to state endorsement of the Confederate debt.[113] In excusing Brown's conscription fight Toombs said that people were a unit as to independence but differed as to the means, and that conscription was unconstitutional because it did not permit the states

---

[108] Phillips, *Correspondence,* pp. 618-19.

[109] Brown appointed the editor of the *Morning News* aide-de-camp, thereby presumably securing the support of that journal.—*Republican,* Sept. 30, 1863.

[110] This was true of citizens at home, who cast 64,804 votes, but only 15,223 Georgians in the army cast their ballots. This was probably due to the difficulty of taking the soldier vote. The voting population of the state in 1860 numbered 100,000.

[111] See Brown's campaign letter to the Rev. A. E. Dickinson, which was forwarded by Dickinson to "Brother Boykin" and published in the *Christian Index* with the Rev. Dickinson's comment that Brown had made "a handsome pecuniary donation to army colportage" and his "noble sentiments deserve serious consideration of all who desire the permanent good of the land."—*Intelligencer,* June 19, 1863.

[112] *Infra,* p. 196.

[113] *Infra,* p. 142.

to officer the militia. He ended with the statement that the independence of the South was worthless without liberty.[114]

A letter from Senator Hill to J. A. Billups in opposition to the election of Brown was widely published. Hill charged that Brown bred constant confusion and quarrels, that his patriotism did not include the Confederacy as a whole, and that he should have retired and allowed someone to take the helm who could unit the people. Hill expressed no choice as between Furlow and Joshua Hill but thought if either were elected the army would be increased and the state united.[115]

There was no anti-administration campaigning whatever. The *Republican* ironically commented a month before the election that the champions of each candidate for Governor had vied with each other in putting their heroes in "as close coöperation and as cordial relations with the Confederate administration as possible." As for the organs supporting Brown, the editor said that every one had "paraded in every issue, and some of them many times in the same issue, evidence over the signature of President Davis to establish the most friendly relations and the most cordial and thorough understanding and coöperation between the Governor and the President." President Davis' certificate to Governor Brown's "faithful coöperation" had, the *Republican* continued, been "paraded in big type and little type. . . ." [116]

As was to have been expected, Brown carried the army vote by a large majority. The election returns showed: [117]

---

[114] Phillips, *Toombs*, p. 248. The publication of the correspondence between the Governor and Fullarton, British consul at Savannah, was doubtless of some value to Brown, since in it he so vigorously upheld the dignity of the state and of the Confederacy.—*C. R.*, II, 464-68; *ibid.*, III, 372-75, 383-89, 392, 403-9; Owsley, *King Cotton Diplomacy*, p. 503.

[115] *Republican*, Oct. 6, 1863.

[116] Oct. 5, 1863.

[117] Avery, p. 261; Northen, III, 98-99. The *Republican* gave somewhat different figures on Nov. 6—probably before all the returns were in. County

## THE ELECTION OF 1863

|        | County Vote | Army Vote<br>73 regiments |
|--------|-------------|---------------------------|
| Brown  | 36,558      | 10,012                    |
| Hill   | 18,222      | 3,324                     |
| Furlow | 10,024      | 1,887                     |

Brown's vote was, therefore, 6,556 more than the necessary majority.

---

vote for Brown, 21,984; Hill, 12,684; Furlow, 6,562. Army vote for Brown, 13,454; Hill, 4,664; Furlow, 2,797.

## CHAPTER VI

## OPPOSITION TO CONFEDERATE FINANCIAL MEASURES

ALTHOUGH Governor Brown criticized practically every method to which the Confederate government resorted to obtain funds and supplies to carry on the war, most of the financial sins of which the Governor complained he himself committed in state financing, at least in the first two years of the war. There was at Milledgeville as at Richmond the same hesitancy to tax, the resort to borrowing, the issuing of treasury certificates and notes, the establishment of maximum prices, and impressment.[1] Brown opposed state endorsement of the Confederate debt and criticized the government

---

[1] The million-dollar appropriation by the Georgia legislature on Nov. 16, 1860, was not raised by taxation but by the issue of 6 per cent bonds, which later had to be raised to 7 per cent.—*C. R.*, II, 96-99; *Republican*, Sept. 30, 1861. On Nov. 6, 1861, the Governor recommended an appropriation of $3,500,000 of which $2,500,000 should be raised by the issue of bonds.—*C. R.*, II, 94-95, 99-100. He recommended (*ibid.*, p. 114) that the Confederate war tax (*O. R.*, Ser. IV, Vol. I, pp. 567-94), of which Georgia's part was $2,494,-112.41, be paid through the issue of 8 per cent bonds.—*C. R.*, II, 245, 247-48; Schwab, pp. 285-89; Davis, *Rise and Fall*, I, 490 *et seq.*

During 1862 the Governor issued treasury notes to the amount of $2,320,000 and the State Road $80,000 in change bills, the latter of which the Governor asked on Nov. 6, 1862, to be increased to $300,000.—*C. R.*, II, 243, 254, 256. The state also issued change bills in denominations between five cents and four dollars.—*Ibid.*, pp. 243, 254, 256.

By the end of 1863 the Governor was alarmed at the amount of outstanding paper and recommended taxation for both state and Confederacy because the currency of both, as he said, was so much depreciated.—*Ibid.*, pp. 509-10, 541-46, 760-61. At the end of the war Georgia's debt was $18,035,775, of which $3,308,500 was in bonds and the remainder in treasury notes, treasury certificates, and change bills.—Schwab, pp. 150, 303, 307; Clara M. Thompson, *Reconstruction in Georgia, Economic, Social, Political, 1865-1872*, pp. 28-31, henceforth cited as C. M. Thompson.

## FINANCIAL MEASURES

for not resorting to heavy taxation, but he later condemned the Confederacy's most effective tax law as unconstitutional, and his opposition to the government's enlightened policy of controlling foreign trade was only a degree less than his opposition to conscription.

The Confederate fiscal system was in the beginning based upon the theory of peace, or at most upon a short war. Its success depended upon an uninterrupted foreign commerce. The $15,000,000 loan of February 28, 1861, provided for interest to be paid in coin to be obtained from an export duty on cotton.[2] The "produce loan" of May 16 was designed to secure coin and bills of foreign exchange. It provided also for a property tax of $10,000,000.[3] The two measures were at first thought to be adequate to meet the needs of the new government, but the necessities of war forced an increase in the property tax and the issue of treasury notes. To prevent depreciation of the currency the law provided that holders of the notes might at any time convert them into 8 per cent bonds,[4] the high interest rate being designed to encourage conversion. The success of the whole financial plan, therefore, depended upon the ability of the government to pay interest in coin,[5] which in turn depended upon the regular exchange of goods with foreign countries.

The Confederacy was, however, unable to keep the channels of foreign trade open, since the United States government had bluffed Great Britain and France out of building a Confederate navy,[6] and soon the Federal blockade had

---

[2] *O. R.*, Ser. IV, Vol. I, pp. 116-17.
[3] *Ibid.*, pp. 328-29. The provisional constitution did not require that a direct tax be apportioned.
[4] The "war tax" of Aug. 19, *ibid.*, pp. 567-74.
[5] Davis, *Rise and Fall*, I, 489 et seq.
[6] *Messages and Papers*, II, 34, 42; *Official Records of the Union and Confederate Navies*, Ser. II, Vol. III, pp. 393, 397, 481, 500-4, 574, henceforth cited as *O. R. N.*; *ibid.*, II, 431-38, 464, 590, 691; James D. Bulloch, *The Secret Service of the Confederate States in Europe*, I, 307 et seq., 386-460, henceforth cited as Bulloch; *ibid.*, II, 18-19, 23 et seq.; Virginia Mason, *The Public Life and Diplomatic Correspondence of James M. Mason*, pp. 479-82, 487,

demoralized commerce and put a premium upon specie.[7] The situation became serious. The scarcity of specie and the lack of credit in Europe slowed up the shipment of arms and munitions, while the inflated currency led to high prices and speculation at home. The Confederacy was faced with the choice of heavier taxation, the pooling of the resources of the country through state guarantee of the Confederate debt, or the issue of more treasury notes, the latter of which would increase the evils.

The levy of an adequate tax was difficult, since the permanent constitution required that direct taxes should be apportioned and war conditions made a census impracticable. No doubt the controversy over the constitutionality of conscription served to increase the timidity of Congress, with the result that no tax after 1861 was levied until April, 1863, and the Confederacy was in the meantime buried under an avalanche of treasury notes.[8] The states—Georgia among the number—had contributed no little to the dangerous situation by the method in which they had paid the "war tax," [9] and by resort to treasury notes and borrowing in general.[10]

---

489 *et seq.*, henceforth cited as Mason; John T. Scharf, *History of the Confederate States Navy*, p. 784, henceforth cited as Scharf; James M. Callahan, *The Diplomatic History of the Southern Confederacy*, pp. 101, 265, 216 *et seq.*, Chap. IX; John H. Latane, *A History of American Foreign Policy*, p. 373, henceforth cited as Latane; Owsley, *King Cotton Diplomacy*, Chap. XIII; Samuel B. Thompson, *Confederate Purchasing Operations Abroad*, p. 40, henceforth cited as S. B. Thompson; Ephraim D. Adams, *Great Britain and the American Civil War*, Vol. II, Chap. XIII, henceforth cited as Adams; Pierce Butler, *Judah P. Benjamin*, pp. 339, 356, henceforth cited as Butler.

[7] See Schwab, p. 43.

[8] Cf. Duncan Rose, "Why the Confederacy Failed," *Century*, LIII (Nov., 1896), 34-35; the reply in the *Century* for February, 1897; Capers, pp. 429 *et seq.*; Stephenson, p. 45.

[9] Only South Carolina, Mississippi, and Texas raised the funds by taxation. —*O. R.*, Ser. IV, Vol. II, p. 1036; Capers, p. 243.

[10] Schwab (p. 153) estimates that by 1863 probably more than $20,000,000 had been issued in paper by states, municipalities, banks, corporations, and individuals. This was probably unavoidable, since there was only about $27,000,000 in specie in the Confederacy when the war began (*ibid.*, p. 43), much of which had to be spent in Europe.

## FINANCIAL MEASURES 141

Since the states had credit in foreign countries which the Confederate government lacked, Virginia, Alabama, Florida, and South Carolina now proposed plans by which Confederate bonds should be guaranteed by all the states and thus find a market in Europe.[11] The Secretary of the Treasury embodied the suggestions in a report which he presented to Congress on January 10, 1863. The Secretary's plan was designed to enable the Confederacy to fund its debt, reduce the interest from 8 per cent to 6 per cent, call in its redundant treasury notes, and sustain the credit of its securities or purchase them. To accomplish this purpose a heavy war tax and a loan to be guaranteed by the states were proposed. The Secretary pointed out that if the states would extend the guarantee to cover $500,000,000 of the debt, a saving in interest charges of $10,000,000 annually would be available to apply to the reduction of the principal.[12]

On January 12 President Davis recommended the measure[13] and on March 23 Congress adopted it. The law authorized the Secretary to sell $200,000,000 worth of thirty-year, 6 per cent bonds, guaranteed by the states, for treasury notes which were not to be reissued.[14] It was intended to increase the amount to $500,000,000 at a later date.

Three days after the President's recommendation Alexander Stephens went into action against state endorsement.[15] There was considerable sentiment in the state favorable to the measure and as the special session of the legislature drew near Stephens was worried.[16]

---

[11] *O. R.*, Ser. IV, Vol. II, pp. 219, 237-38, 320.   [12] *Ibid.*, pp. 347-48, 376.
[13] *Ibid.*   [14] *Ibid.*, p. 452; Davis, *Rise and Fall*, I, 489.
[15] Stephens wrote to Linton that he had written Mr. Gardner, editor of the *Constitutionalist,* in opposition to the plan and that Gardner had begun a campaign against it, using Stephens' ideas and in many instances his very language.—Johnston and Browne, p. 430. A short time previously Stephens had said that Confederate finances were on the verge of collapse. A biographer intimates that Stephens was satisfied to let the Confederacy fall.—Louis B. Pendleton, *Alexander H. Stephens,* pp. 308-9, henceforth cited as Pendleton,
[16] Johnston and Browne, p. 441.

Just two days after Congress passed the law, state endorsement received its death blow. In his message to the legislature[17] Governor Brown took the same position that Stephens had taken. The measure was in his judgment unfortunate, unjust, and unwise, since it would array capital against the Confederacy and level the credit of all the states to an equality, injuring the credit of those states "who have managed their financial affairs better than others." Among these he placed Georgia and he thought that her people were "entitled to the benefits of her economy, her wise management and her far-seeing statesmanship." If Georgia should adopt state endorsement then the people of other states would "reap the benefits of her credit, to which the people of Georgia alone are entitled." [18]

One of the state rights arguments in favor of state endorsement was that since the states were morally bound for the payment of the Confederate debt and their people legally bound to submit to taxation, the states should make the endorsement and take upon themselves the legal obligation to pay. As an advocate at all times of the priority of the states over the central government Brown should have appreciated the argument,[19] but he replied that the constitution had imposed upon Congress the responsibility of devising the means of meeting its obligations. State endorsement in his opinion would strengthen the central government at the expense of the states and "power once usurped, with acquiescence, is

---

[17] *C. R.*, II, 381-94.
[18] *Ibid.*, pp. 382-83.
[19] Indeed, in his message of Nov. 6, 1861, he had expressed the hope that the Confederacy would apportion the taxes among the several states [as under the Articles of Confederation], allowing each to make its own collection. In the same message he recommended that the state "act upon a principle alike compatible with her dignity and sovereignty" by collecting the tax by its own authority and paying it to the government, thereby preventing "the Confederate tax-gatherers from making their appearance among us."—*C. R.*, II, 114. To obtain funds quickly for the infant treasury the states were allowed to anticipate the war tax within their borders and by paying it to the Confederate government before Apr. 1, 1862, receive a rebate of 10 per cent.

## FINANCIAL MEASURES 143

never relaxed but at the point of the bayonet. . . ." He asserted that the remedy for the financial troubles of the Confederacy was taxation by Congress, and recommended a joint resolution to this effect, in which he asked other states to join.[20]

On April 2 James P. Boyce addressed the Georgia legislature in the interest of the measure. His own state of South Carolina was one of the originators of the plan and he had been requested by the Secretary of the Treasury to visit the several states and explain its terms to the legislatures. Boyce said that it was to the interest of debtors, creditors, and consumers alike that the excess currency be reduced. He asserted that the proposed plan would accomplish this result by enabling the Confederate government to retire its treasury notes, now at a discount of four to one in gold, to a point where they would be on a par with specie. State endorsement would in his judgment insure for Confederate bonds a market in Europe and place sterling exchange to the amount of $250,000,000 at the command of the treasury.[21]

All eyes were turned to Georgia, where it was generally conceded the question of state endorsement would be decided. Several states had passed the necessary laws but they were all dependent upon the acceptance of the plan by all the states. A bill in the lower house to authorize the Governor to endorse Georgia's quota of $50,000,000 passed by a majority of six but the senate voted twenty-two to ten to refer the proposal to the people in the October election. The next day the matter was indefinitely postponed.[22]

The question was agitated during the summer, but on November 5, Governor Brown referred the legislature to his former message and added that the proposition of state endorsement was a virtual declaration that the Confederate

---

[20] *Ibid.*, pp. 389-91.
[21] *Southern Recorder*, Apr. 7, 1863.    [22] *Ibid.*, Apr. 14, 1863; Avery, p. 252.

government was either a failure, or its officers were incompetent to the task of establishing a wise financial system. Let the states and the Confederate government each move within the sphere assigned to it by the constitution, he said, since when either undertook to discharge the duties which properly pertain to the other it not only took responsibilities not its own but assumed the incompetency of the other.[23] Memminger, secretary of the Treasury, blamed Governor Brown for the failure of the plan and declared that state endorsement would have created a sure market in Europe for Confederate bonds.[24]

The Confederate government had attempted to avoid redundancy by offering inducements to voluntary funding, but its inability to pay interest in coin defeated its efforts and the funding act of March 23, 1863, because of this fact and because of the failure of state endorsement, came to nothing. By December of that year the circulating currency amounted to $600,000,000, which was three times more than was required for the business of the country,[25] with the usual results of a redundant currency—speculation and high prices. The President, therefore, recommended compulsory reduction of the currency, pledging no further increase,[26] and on February 17, 1864, the compulsory funding bill became a law.[27] Like that of the Continental Congress of March, 1780, the funding act was a virtual repudiation of a part of the Confederacy's obligations, but the drastic measure seemed to be a stern necessity and even anti-administration men and newspapers favored it.[28]

---

[23] *C. R.*, II, 512.

[24] See Ernest A. Smith, "History of the Confederate Treasury," *Publications of the Southern History Association*, V, No. 2, 110. Toombs issued a public letter on Aug. 12, 1863, advocating funding and adequate taxation.—Phillips, *Toombs*, p. 249. Cf. opinion of Herschel V. Johnson, in Flippin, pp. 181, 228-30.

[25] Davis, *Rise and Fall*, I, 490; Capers, p. 340.

[26] Davis, *Rise and Fall*, I, 495; Cf. O. R., Ser. IV, Vol. II, pp. 1008, 1010-11, 1017.

[27] *Ibid.*, III, 159-61.  [28] Schwab, p. 66; Cf. Davis, *Rise and Fall*, I, 489.

FINANCIAL MEASURES 145

To the special session of the legislature, on March 10, 1864, Governor Brown said that the measure had shaken the confidence of the people in the justice of Congress and its competency to manage financial affairs. He thought history furnished few more striking instances of "unsound policy combined with bad faith." The measure was the result of a secret session of Congress, he charged, which was resorted to in order that the representatives might not be annoyed by "the murmurs of public disapprobation." He asserted that "secret sessions" were becoming the blighting curse of the country and were being used as a convenient mode of covering up from the people such acts of their representatives as would "not bear investigation in the light of day." [29]

The *Marietta Rebel*, commenting upon the Governor's message, was impressed with its "want of candor and fairness." It charged that he had shown "a studied design to bring the Government into disrepute and destroy public faith in its issues"; every objectional feature of the funding act was harped upon "and every justification or excuse ignored"; the subject was treated "as though there were two distinct parties having no identity of interest with each other, the Government, incurring obligations which it failed to meet, and the people most grievously wronged." [30] No less critical of the Governor was the *Columbus Times* which accused him of having "a little and spiteful mind" and of attempting to "create a sensation and bring about the condition he complained of." [31]

Heavy taxation had been demanded by Brown, Toombs, and Stephens, but when, on April 24, 1863, Congress overcame its constitutional scruples and passed a drastic tax law,[32] each of the three objected to some phase of it. The law

---

[29] *C. R.*, II, 595-600. Brown returned to the subject just before the fall of the Confederacy.—*Ibid.*, pp. 839-40.
[30] Quoted by the *Macon Telegraph*, Mar. 21, 1864.   [31] Mar. 29, 1864.
[32] *O. R.*, Ser. IV, Vol. II, pp. 513-24. The constitutionality of the law was never passed upon by any state supreme court.—Brummer, p. 131, n. 2.

did not directly tax land and slaves—in which two thirds of the capital of the South was invested—but it levied a tax-in-kind on practically all farm products. By this method of obtaining supplies the government hoped to avoid the necessity for increasing the volume of treasury notes, keep down prices, and enable the farmer to pay most easily his share of taxation.[33] Toombs condemned the law as placing an undue burden upon farmers[34] and predicted it would be "the winding sheet of poor Hunter." [35] Stephens favored the tax-in-kind, or tithe, as it was usually called, but complained that it was not undertaken in time and was mismanaged.[36] Brown thought the tithing system was an "unfortunate error" and that it was wasteful, worked badly, led to general dissatisfaction, and placed a burden on one class alone.[37] He recommended to the legislature a joint resolution asking the repeal of the law and the substitution of taxes to be paid in currency, which he said would absorb any redundancy caused by the payment of just compensation for property purchased by the government.[38] Later he complained that Congress had levied direct taxes of an "enormous burden" without the census or enumeration "imperatively required by the Constitution." [39]

The Secretary of War reported at the end of the year that the tax-in-kind had been of great value, in part obviating the necessity for impressment, and recommended that it be increased.[40]

Inflation of the currency, inadequate transportation, and war conditions in general led to high prices, speculation, and

---

[33] Smith, "History of the Confederate Treasury," *loc. cit.,* pp. 204-5.

[34] Phillips, *Toombs,* pp. 246, 248.

[35] Letter to Wm. M. Burwell, June 10, 1863, Burwell Papers. Robert M. T. Hunter was senator from Virginia and had voted for the measure.

[36] *War between the States,* II, 569-70.

[37] As a matter of fact the law of which the tithe was a part taxed heavily every class and individual.

[38] *C. R.,* II, 541-46.

[39] *Ibid.,* p. 836.      [40] *O. R.,* Ser. IV, Vol. II, pp. 1011-12.

## FINANCIAL MEASURES

an illusive business prosperity. Owners of commodities necessary to the army preferred to hold them on a rising market and the Confederacy was faced with the necessity of compelling sales to the army at reasonable prices. At first the government acted under military authority in impressing supplies,[41] but complaints of alleged abuses[42]—which no doubt occurred in some instances despite strict instructions from the War Department[43]—led to the law of March 26, 1863, and the amendment of April 27, regulating the manner in which impressment should be made and appeals heard.[44] The President reported in the following December that the law had checked rising prices and caused products to come into the market for fear of impressment. He regretted the necessity of the policy, but pointed out the remedy, which was the restoration of the currency to such a basis as would enable the War Department to purchase in the open market.[45]

Although Governor Brown had himself resorted to impressment and continued to do so throughout the life of the Confederacy,[46] he waged unrelenting warfare against Confederate impressment from the beginning, oftentimes no

---

[41] *Messages and Papers,* I, 374 *et seq.;* Owsley, *State Rights,* p. 220; Schwab, p. 183; Rhodes, V, 373.

[42] *O. R.,* Ser. IV, Vol. I, pp. 646, 666; *ibid.,* II, 904; Jones, *Diary,* I, 194, 198.

[43] General Orders, Nos. 56 and 104 of 1862, No. 31 of 1863, *O. R.,* Ser. IV, Vol. II, pp. 39, 234-35, 441-42.

[44] *Ibid.,* pp. 469-71, 904; General Orders, Nos. 37 and 138, *ibid.,* pp. 471-72, 897-98. Cf. *ibid.,* p. 127. Report of board of appraisers, *ibid.,* pp. 616-17, 898-906. Schedule of prices established for South Carolina, *ibid.,* pp. 836-38.

[45] *Messages and Papers,* I, 374.

[46] In 1861 he seized salt; in 1862 block tin (*C. R.,* II, 202); in 1861 and 1862 he asked authority to seize tanneries, factories, and manufactured articles (*ibid.,* pp. 106, 332-35); in his "Letter to Planters," Nov. 1, 1862, he threatened impressment of slaves if they were not voluntarily supplied (*ibid.,* pp. 238-39; *Southern Confederacy,* Nov. 12, 1862); in 1863 he asked authority to impress slaves (Jones, *Diary,* I, 387); on Mar. 10, 1864, Feb. 15, and Mar. 3, 1865, he recommended laws to enable state officers to impress provisions for soldiers' families, refugees, and the destitute in general (*C. R.,* II, 593, 829-30, 862-64). On Nov. 3, 1864, and in the following February he recommended and finally secured a law to enable him to impress agricultural products from Confederate bonded exempts.

doubt with justice, at other times, it is suspected, merely as a part of his opposition to the administration.[47] Whether or not they were so intended, the Governor's pronouncements made impressment in Georgia increasingly difficult, and the Confederate government found it almost impossible to supply Bragg's army which was at the time besieging Rosecrans at Chattanooga. Seddon explained the emergency to Governor Brown on October 31, 1863, and begged for his help in "removing all impediments to the free action of Commissary officers." Seddon stated that people would not sell even at market prices, preferring to hold their produce for a still higher market, and that impressment was the only mode of getting supplies.[48] The Governor replied that he had no desire to interfere with legal impressment, but complained of impressment by unauthorized persons, for purposes of robbery, and of acts of "partiality, injustice, and oppression," by those who were properly authorized. He thought the government need not resort to impressment if it would pay market prices.[49]

President Davis himself replied to Governor Brown's numerous complaints, saying that if at any time subordinates acted rudely or illegally they should be reported to the local commanders, but that accusations against undescribed persons afforded no means of bringing them to justice. He thought that a general, in the face of the enemy, should be charitably judged if in providing for his troops he inadvertently exceeded his authority. He felt sure the people of Georgia would prove themselves, as on the field of battle, equal to these trying tests.[50]

[47] Cf. *ibid.*, p. 308; *ibid.*, III, 328; *ibid.*, II, 473-76; *Republican*, Sept. 25, 1863. War Department instructions as to Georgia, *O. R.*, Ser. IV, Vol. II, p. 912. Owsley thinks Governor Brown merely wished to bring the Confederacy into disrepute with the people, since he never gave to the authorities specific instances of unauthorized impressment but made only general charges of such.—*State Rights*, p. 252.
[48] *C. R.*, III, 426-27; *O. R.*, Ser. IV, Vol. II, p. 915.
[49] *C. R.*, III, 429-30; *O. R.*, Ser. IV, Vol. II, pp. 943-44.
[50] Rowland, VI, 260-61.

## FINANCIAL MEASURES 149

Governor Brown savagely denounced impressment in his message of November 5, 1863, claiming that agents were acting illegally or engaging in "moral robbery and plundering." He recommended a law making it a felony to be punished by ten years in the penitentiary for any one to impress property in violation of the provisions of the act of Congress, and the same punishment with thirty-nine lashes on the bare back for any one making impressment without proper authority.[51] Although the legislature did not comply with the Governor's request, it did pass a resolution asking that impressment officers subject to conscription be removed and that citizens of the various counties not subject to conscription be appointed.[52] In the meantime the Georgia supreme court had passed on the question of impressment and had declared that a scale of prices arbitrarily fixed was not a proper criterion of the value of articles seized subsequently by agents of the government;[53] which meant practically that the government must pay the market price. A collision between Confederate and state authorities in Georgia was probably averted by amendments to the impressment act in the following February.[54]

Brown's next objective was to prevent Confederate details from delivering their provisions to the government, for

---

[51] *C. R.*, II, 514-17.

[52] *Ibid.*, III, 438-39; Jones, *Diary*, II, 92, 99. The War Department replied that its policy had always been to use those not subject to service in the field and to give preference to citizens of the state in which they were to serve, but that the exigency of the support of the army precluded the department from revoking the appointments requested.—*C. R.*, III, 442-43.
Toombs spoke before the legislature on Nov. 13, 1863, saying that impressment violated the fundamental principles of the constitution in that it was not uniform, falling only upon agriculture, while "capitalists, merchants, manufacturers, speculators, and extortioners" who remained at home and made money escaped.—Owsley, *State Rights*, pp. 235-36; *Appleton's Annual Cyclopedia, 1863*, pp. 207-8, cited by Tatum, p. 19; Rhodes, V, 376.

[53] *Cox and Hill* v. *Cummings*, 33 Ga. 555; *Cunningham* v. *Campbell, et al.*, 33 Ga. 625.

[54] Schwab, p. 208; Jones, *Diary*, II, 111; act of Feb. 16, 1864, *O. R.*, Ser. IV, Vol. III, pp. 198-99. See also act of Feb. 17, 1864, *ibid.*, p. 249.

which purpose they had been exempted from military service and had given bond for the faithful performance of their duties.[55] He attacked the policy in his message of November 3, 1864, on the grounds that the schedule of prices which the bonds of these men required was below the market price,[56] and that provisions could not be purchased from them. "In this way," he said, "the Confederate Government prohibits citizens of Georgia from selling . . . to their own State, when the State needs these productions and is ready to pay just compensation for them." [57] He recommended a law authorizing the impressment of such supplies, saying: "A Confederate regulation cannot be defended upon any principle of reason or justice which drives a State out of her own markets for the purchase of her necessary supplies." [58] He returned to the subject three months later,[59] and this time the legislature complied with the Governor's wishes. When Toombs heard of the action of the legislature he remarked to Stephens: "I see Brown has got him an impressment law too. How catching is thieving!" [60]

The ability of the War Department to obtain provisions for the army was seriously impaired in Georgia by this law and elsewhere by the law of Congress limiting the power of impressment. President Davis pleaded one month before the fall of the Confederacy that restrictions be removed. He admitted that impressment was liable to abuse, but he thought that all objections should yield to stern necessity.[61] The plea was made in vain. Criticisms of the administration in regard

---

[55] *Supra,* Chap. IV, n. 103.

[56] This was true, but it was the commutation, so to speak, which they paid for the privilege of exemption.

[57] The fact that Sherman's army reveled in plenty while Lee's army was starving would seem to indicate that there was no lack of provisions in Georgia.—See Rhodes, V, 385.

[58] *C. R.,* II, 766-77.     [59] *Ibid.,* pp. 829-30.

[60] Phillips, *Correspondence,* p. 660.

[61] *Journal of the Congress of the Confederate States of America,* IV, 704, henceforth cited as *Journal of the C. S. A.*

# FINANCIAL MEASURES 151

to impressment, conscription, taxation, appointment of officers, and what not had done their deadly work. Intimidated or disaffected congressmen ignored the President's recommendation and passed a totally inadequate measure which defined "just compensation" as the market price and otherwise emasculated the impressment laws.[62] Brown and his allies had won their fight on impressment.

No doubt impressment oftentimes worked badly,[63] but as the administration claimed, it was an "inexorable necessity," and performed an invaluable service.[64] Without it the Confederate treasury would probably have broken down in 1863. In his report of November 26 of that year the Secretary of War admitted that impressment was "harsh, unequal, and odious," and that it was perhaps the sorest test of patriotism, which "no other people . . . would have endured . . . without undue manifestations of discontent and resistance," but that because of hoarding it had been the only method of obtaining supplies. Like the President, he thought the difficulty was due to the depreciation of the currency.[65]

The most important and successful financial measure of the Confederacy—government control of blockade-running—also failed to win Governor Brown's approval. Indeed, it was but another evidence to his mind that the central government intended to destroy the states.

---

[62] Act of Mar. 18, 1865, *O. R.*, Ser. IV, Vol. III, p. 1170.

[63] Cf. Herschel V. Johnson's letters to the secretaries of Treasury and War, *ibid.*, pp. 594, 662; Gen. Joseph E. Johnston's letter to Brown, *C. R.*, III, 575. Complaints from other states, *O. R.*, Ser. IV, Vol. II, pp. 863, 976, 1061-62, 1066; *ibid.*, III, 2-3, 43, 402-3, 407-8, 689, 932; *ibid.*, Vol. XXIV, Pt. II, pp. 865, 929, 975. Owsley, *State Rights*, pp. 226-27, gives a valuable discussion of the subject.

[64] Cf. statement of board of commissioners, Oct., 1863, *O. R.*, Ser. IV, Vol. II, p. 901; report of the Secretary of War, Nov. 26, 1863, *ibid.*, p. 1009; opinion of the Secretary of War, *ibid.*, Vol. III, pp. 3, 111, 337, 562, 689; Davis to Governor Vance, *ibid.*, p. 824; opinion of General Lee, *ibid.*, pp. 33, 114; Davis to Congress, *Messages and Papers*, I, 374.

[65] *O. R.*, Ser. IV, Vol. II, pp. 1007-11.

When the "King Cotton" policy, upon which the Confederacy had built its hopes during the first year of the war,[66] failed to bring recognition, an opposite policy was adopted. The government lifted the embargo[67] on cotton and during 1862-63 encouraged blockade-running. The object was twofold: to obtain funds for its purchasing agents in Europe and to demonstrate to the nations of the world that the blockade was ineffective.[68] A paper blockade being contrary to international law in general and to the Declaration of Paris, to which treaty the Confederacy had adhered,[69] it was supposed that foreign nations would intervene either in a peaceful mediation, in an armed intervention, or in an outright recognition of Southern independence.[70]

While the policy demonstrated the paper quality of the blockade,[71] it did not bring the hoped-for results in diplomacy.[72] It did, however, show surprisingly important results in the field of finance,[73] for by the end of 1862 the stock of

---

[66] Brown's message to the legislature, Nov. 7, 1860, *C. R.*, I, 19-57; Latane, pp. 361-62; Adams, II, Chap. X; message of President Davis, Dec. 7, 1863, *O. R.*, Ser. IV, Vol. II, pp. 1026-34. Owsley shows that the policy was sound but for certain conditions in the foreign market which could not be foreseen.—*King Cotton Diplomacy*, Chaps. I, II, V, XIX. For opposition of Toombs and Stephens to the policy, cf. Cleveland, pp. 756 *et seq.;* Stephens, *War between the States*, II, Appendix Q; Phillips, *Toombs*, p. 249. For Memminger's defense of the policy, cf. Capers, pp. 348-51, 356-57; Pollard, *Davis*, p. 308; Jones, *Diary*, I, 382; Rhodes, V, 381; Schwab, p. 234.

[67] No Confederate law had been necessary, public opinion for the most part setting up and maintaining the embargo. Cf. Owsley, *King Cotton Diplomacy*, p. 43. The *Charleston Mercury* launched the campaign (White, *Rhett*, pp. 211-14) and it was recommended by the Georgia legislature (*Acts of the General Assembly, 1861*, p. 137) and by other state legislatures.

[68] Cf. *O. R.*, Ser. IV, Vol. I, pp. 1007-8; *O. R. N.*, Ser. II, Vol. III, pp. 1077-79.

[69] With the exception regarding privateering.—Latane, p. 369 *et seq.*

[70] Owsley, *King Cotton Diplomacy*, pp. 1, 51.

[71] Mason, p. 291; Owsley, *King Cotton Diplomacy*, Chap. VIII; S. B. Thompson, pp. 24, 44; Scharf, pp. 477-79, 488; James Russell Soley, *The Blockade and the Cruisers*, p. 165, henceforth cited as Soley; Butler, p. 267.

[72] Cf. President Davis' remarks upon Great Britain's not standing by the Declaration of Paris, *O. R.*, Ser. IV, Vol. II, pp. 1026-34, and Owsley's explanation, *King Cotton Diplomacy*, Chap. XIII.

[73] Scharf, p. 476; *O. R.*, Ser. IV, Vol. II, pp. 99-105; *O. R. N.*, Ser. II, Vol. III, pp. 568-72, 590-97, 605.

## FINANCIAL MEASURES 153

cotton in Europe had been exhausted and the price had risen to 50 cents a pound; within another year it was 60 cents.[74] The enormous profits to be had by shipping cotton attracted a fleet of small vessels which ran the blockade to Nassau, Bermuda, Havana, and Matamoras, Mexico, from whence their cargoes were transhipped to Europe. Supplies were brought back in the same manner. The Confederacy's four small vessels went and came "with almost the regularity of packets."[75] The correspondent of the New York *Herald* wrote from Nassau on June 24, 1863: "Charleston and Savannah in their palmiest days were never so overrun with cotton as is the city of Nassau at the present time. . . . It is piled up six and eight bales deep on all the wharves, vacant lots, and even on some of the lawns. It is literally 'laying around loose'."[76]

By 1863 it had become evident that in encouraging blockade-running the Confederacy had created a Frankenstein. Large British companies had entered the business, their swift, low, greenish-gray vessels—built especially for the purpose[77]—replacing the nondescript fleet which had been hastily improvised in the beginning,[78] and shares in these corporations were being regularly quoted on the market. Actuated only by motives of gain, these companies found it to their interest to import luxuries rather than the bulkier war materials.[79] They crowded the government out of its own markets, drained the country of gold, and set a standard of display that was demoralizing. Indignant citizens demanded that the traffic be regulated or suppressed.[80]

---

[74] Owsley, *King Cotton Diplomacy*, p. 387; S. B. Thompson, p. 86.
[75] *O. R.*, Ser. IV, Vol. II, p. 1014.   [76] Scharf, pp. 478-79.
[77] *Ibid.*, p. 483; Callahan, p. 171. At the close of the war there were 35 British blockade-runners at Nassau valued at $15,000,000.—Scharf, pp. 487, 491.
[78] See Charles Cawley, *Leaves from a Lawyer's Life Afloat and Ashore*, pp. 112-13, cited by Scharf, p. 475, n. 1.
[79] Scharf, pp. 474, 483; Butler, p. 333. Cf. *Journal of the C. S. A.*, IV, 373-76; *ibid.*, VII, 368-71.
[80] *Ibid.* Cf. Scharf, p. 470.

Making bad matters worse, seaboard states had entered into the business and were competing with the Confederacy for shipping space. Freight rates ranged from $300 to $1,000 a ton.[81] The government attempted to remedy these conditions in the summer and fall of 1863 by requiring owners of vessels to carry one third to one half of their cargoes for government account, but it was compelled to pay the exorbitant freight rates.[82] Shipowners and seaboard states then combined to evade the ruling by arranging for states to purchase shares in vessels or to charter them[83] and continue to carry a large part of the cargoes for the private owners.[84]

Conditions in Europe were equally chaotic. There Confederate agents were compelled to compete in the markets with speculators and agents of railroads and seaboard states. The government was compelled to use its cotton in payment of cotton certificates and cotton bonds which stipulated a price in the Confederate States, usually 6 cents and 10 cents a pound,[85] while its competitors shipped cotton direct and received Liverpool prices. During the first nine months of 1863, 100,000 bales of cotton were shipped to England, bringing $200 a bale, or $20,000,000.[86] The *London Index*, commenting upon the fact, said: "Had the cotton been exported for its own account, instead of, for the most part, private speculators, the Confederate Government might have dispensed with foreign loans, might have bought its warlike stores at the lowest cash rates and supplied its citizens with

---

[81] *Ibid.*, pp. 473, 474, n. 1.
[82] *O. R.*, Ser. IV, Vol. III, pp. 28, 554; *ibid.*, II, 1013-14.
[83] Cf. President Davis' message, *Messages and Papers*, I, 466 *et seq.*; *O. R.*, Ser. IV, Vol. II, p. 60; *ibid.*, III, 77-78; Owsley, *State Rights*, pp. 127 *et seq.*; *idem, King Cotton Diplomacy*, pp. 411-12.
[84] Owsley, *State Rights*, p. 131.
[85] *O. R. N.*, Ser. II, Vol. III, pp. 529-32, 590-93, 675-77, 730-31. For Erlanger bonds, cf. Davis, *Rise and Fall*, I, 495-97; Owsley, *King Cotton Diplomacy*, pp. 394 *et seq.*; Schwab, pp. 30-43.
[86] S. B. Thompson, p. 75.

## FINANCIAL MEASURES 155

commodities of prime necessities at a moderate advance on cost."[87]

Under these circumstances there developed among Confederate agents in Europe and among citizens at home a public opinion favorable to government ownership of vessels and strict control of all exports and imports.[88] On February 6, 1864, Congress accordingly passed two laws, which, with the regulations shortly afterwards issued, revolutionized the shipping business. One of the laws prohibited the importation of luxuries, the other forbade the exportation of cotton, tobacco, military and naval supplies, sugar, molasses, and rice, except under regulations to be issued by the President. Section five of the latter law provided that nothing in the act should be construed to prohibit the Confederate States, or any one of them, from exporting any of the enumerated articles on their own account.[89]

The regulations—issued on March 5—were designed to remove the difficulties which the Confederacy had experienced in the two previous years. Vessels desirous of carrying out any of the enumerated articles were required to carry one half their tonnage on outbound and homeward voyages for the government at fixed rates and to bring back at least one half the proceeds of the owner's cargo in goods not prohibited by Confederate law. Vessels owned by states and employed for the exclusive use of states were not subject to the regulations, nor were states subject to the regulations in the event they chartered the other half of vessels privately owned.[90]

---

[87] Dec. 24, 1863, p. 552, quoted by Owsley, *King Cotton Diplomacy*, p. 416.
[88] Bulloch, I, 109-27; *ibid.*, II, 223-26, 236-37; *O. R.*, Ser. IV, Vol. II, pp. 982 *et seq.*; *O. R. N.*, Ser. II, Vol. II, pp. 568, 578, 594, 702; Scharf, p. 481; S. B. Thompson, p. 84. Cf. *Richmond Enquirer*, cited by Scharf, pp. 483-84; opinion of Governor Milton, *O. R.*, Ser. IV, Vol. II, pp. 487-89; letter of Vernon & Co. to the President, quoted by Scharf, p. 474.
[89] *O. R.*, Ser. IV, Vol. III, pp. 78-80, 80-82.
[90] *Messages and Papers*, I, 417-20.

According to a later interpretation chartered vessels were also subject to the rules. The laws were strictly enforced and vessels complied or they were refused clearance or forfeited bonds to the amount of more than double the value of the vessels.[91]

The government's new plan made a decided impression in Europe. Confederate credit rose, enabling its agents to purchase or contract for the construction of a fleet of fourteen blockade-runners,[92] six torpedo boats, and four specially designed steamers, the latter to be used to cover the approach of blockade-runners and to make attacks on the blockading squadron.[93] In addition, munitions, arms, medicines, and other supplies were shipped to the Confederate States.[94] Confederate bonds in Europe rose from 42 in the spring to 77 in midsummer.[95] European bankers proposed to establish a Franco-Confederate bank, with branches in the Confederacy, and to float a large loan to aid the government in prosecuting the war.[96] From March 1, 1864, to December 10 of that year the government shipped cotton to the net value of $5,296,006, the equivalent of $132,500,000 in Confederate currency, and this despite the fact that the system did not get well under way until August and only a part of the fleet of blockade-runners had arrived.[97]

This remarkable success had been made possible through (1) the elimination of competition in the purchase of cotton and the centralization of the function east of the Mississippi River under Colonel Thomas L. Bayne, with a corresponding centralization under P. W. Gray in the trans-Mississippi department;[98] (2) government control of freight rates and

---

[91] *Ibid.*
[92] Bulloch, I, 108; *ibid.*, II, 237-40; *O. R.*, Ser. IV, Vol. III, p. 525.
[93] Bulloch, II, 241-43; S. B. Thompson, pp. 93-94.
[94] *Ibid.*
[95] *Ibid.*, p. 95.
[96] *Ibid.*, pp. 99 *et seq.*
[97] Report of the Secretary of War, *O. R.*, Ser. IV, Vol. III, pp. 928-30; S. B. Thompson, p. 126.
[98] *Ibid.*, pp. 91-92, 117-18; Owsley, *King Cotton Diplomacy*, pp. 413-14.

FINANCIAL MEASURES 157

tonnage; (3) the receipt and sale of all cotton in Europe by one agent, General C. J. McRae;[99] (4) the purchase of war supplies on a cash or stable credit basis by Confederate agents directly responsible to McRae; and (5) the prohibition on the importation of luxuries.

But the old laissez-faire policy was not to be set aside without a struggle. Seaboard states and shipping companies again joined forces to compel a modification of the regulations. The latter threatened to transfer their vessels to the states, with which they expected to make better terms. They even went on strike for several weeks[100]—just when Grant's campaign against Lee and Sherman's against Johnston were beginning.

Governor Brown had previously purchased shares in shipping companies for the state of Georgia,[101] and on March 1, 1864, he chartered four vessels and prepared to engage in a more extensive shipping business.[102] It was not a mere coincidence, one suspects, that two days later Congressman Hartridge of Georgia introduced in the House of Representatives a resolution inquiring "whether ... the secretary of the treasury had the right to prevent the sailing of vessels owned or chartered by any of the states" in the event the vessels refused to obey Confederate regulations.[103] After the regulations were published Governor Brown had the "Little Ada" loaded with state cotton and telegraphed for clearance. As the vessel was not owned by the state and did not offer one half its tonnage to the Confederate government, his request was refused.[104] He immediately sent dispatches to

---
[99] *O. R.*, Ser. IV, Vol. II, pp. 824 *et seq.;* Bulloch, II, 222-23, 417; S. B. Thompson, p. 83.
[100] *O. R.*, Ser. IV, Vol. III, p. 554.
[101] *Ibid.*, p. 1060; *C. R.*, II, 752.
[102] *Ibid.*, pp. 581, 752-53.
[103] *Journal of the C. S. A.*, VII, 13.
[104] *C. R.*, II, 753; *O. R.*, Ser. IV, Vol. III, p. 416. One half the tonnage was of course controlled by the company to whom the vessel belonged.—*C. R.*, II, 754.

the governors of other states, saying that the Confederate government had "refused to permit the States to export their own products upon their own ships," unless they would allow the government half the space of each vessel—which was not quite accurate—and asking them to unite with him in a protest to Congress against the regulations. Governors Smith of Virginia and Milton of Florida refused, the latter writing:

... Most respectfully I decline. ... I am not sensible of the propriety of the Governor of a State, or the Governors of States, asking Congress to legislate upon that or any other subject. ...

I am not convinced of the necessity of any further legislation of Congress upon the subject. ...

Might not attempt on the part of the states, separately, to relieve the necessities of the armies and citizens by trade with citizens of foreign nations destroy the confidence and respect which those nations entertain for the ability of the Confederate States as belligerents under a government of their own choice; embarrass Congress. . . ; cause our armies and citizens to suffer; and endanger the stability of the Confederate Government, if not entirely destroy it, by a separation of the States?

The safety of the people ... demands the utmost confidence and generous support [by] the State governments to the maintenance of the Confederate Government in the execution of the sacred trusts which have been confided to it. It is best, therefore, where it can be honorably done, to avoid all conflicts and competition between the State and Confederate authorities for political power, or commercial privileges, at all events during the existing war. When the independence of the Confederate States shall have been achieved, ... the rights of the States and the constitutional powers of the Confederate Government will be adjusted by an intelligent, brave, and free people. ...[105]

Having secured the coöperation of the governors of Mississippi, North Carolina, and Alabama, and the protest hav-

---

[105] *C. R.*, III, 497-500.

## FINANCIAL MEASURES 159

ing been forwarded to Congress,[106] Brown made three more unsuccessful efforts to send the "Little Ada" to sea.[107] On May 21 he demanded "clearance as a right, not as a favor." [108]

The Hartridge resolution finally led to a bill to exempt from the regulations all vessels owned or chartered by states.[109] In his veto message of June 10 President Davis reviewed the conditions that had led to the restrictions and pointed out that the regulations placed the states on an equal footing with the Confederacy, except that while the government imposed a forced charter for one half the tonnage of privately owned vessels, "it had no authority to do more for the States than to leave the other half subject to their use by charter obtained by consent of the owners." To change the regulations in the manner proposed by Congress would permit the states to charter the entire tonnage of vessels and "thus deprive the Confederacy of a resource now at its disposal, and without which very serious embarrassment to the public service would ensue." States and Confederacy would thus again be brought into competition to the advantage of shipowners, with the risk of depriving the government of "an indispensable means of carrying on the war." [110]

The Governors' Conference, meeting in Augusta, Georgia, in October, of which Governor Brown was an influential member, adopted a resolution to the effect that states had the right to export and import supplies "upon any vessel owned or chartered by them," and requested Congress to remove all restrictions on the states.[111]

Brown reported to the Georgia legislature his difficulties

---
[106] *Ibid.*, p. 753; Avery, pp. 281-82.
[107] *O. R.*, Ser. IV, Vol. III, p. 416; *C. R.*, III, 527-28, 558-59, 562.
[108] *Ibid.*, pp. 558-59.
[109] *O. R.*, Ser. IV, Vol. III, p. 552; *Richmond Examiner*, June 3, 1864, cited by Schwab, p. 218.
[110] *Messages and Papers*, I, 470.
[111] *C. R.*, II, 780.

with the Confederate government in the matter of blockade-running. He declared that the President's regulations misinterpreted the law,[112] and that the state had been seriously embarrassed in its shipping operations by the "Lincoln blockade" and the "partial blockade of our own Executive." He said the "Little Ada" had been threatened "by Confederate guns in the harbor and by the Federal guns outside." To refuse clearance to vessels owned or chartered by states, except upon terms dictated by the Confederate executive, was to his mind "a palpable assumption of power, and an utter desregard of every principle of State Rights and State Sovereignty." He hoped that at its next session Congress would remove the obstacles "by enactments too plain and too stringent to be disregarded." [113]

The continued agitation of the subject led the two houses of Congress in the December session to inquire of the President regarding the restrictions placed upon the states and the possible modification of the regulations.[114] Fortified by reports from the secretaries of Treasury and War and their opinions of the value of the system,[115] the President made a strong argument for the retention of the laws and regulations. Repeating what he had said in his veto message of June, he pointed out that the Confederate government was charged with the duty of supplying the army with clothing, subsistence, and munitions. He thought one could well imagine the feelings of soldiers from interior states if the soldiers of seaboard states standing beside them should be well supplied while they were deprived of what they now receive. He saw no justice "in the demand that all the States should sacrifice a common right for the profit of a single State, nor in diminishing the necessary comforts of the

---

[112] There is no doubt that the President took all the latitude the law allowed in restricting the states. It was the only way to correct the evil of collusion between them and the shipowners.
[113] *C. R.*, II, 752-58.
[114] *O. R.*, Ser. IV, Vol. III, p. 897.     [115] *Ibid.*, pp. 928-30, 953-58.

## FINANCIAL MEASURES

soldiers for the benefit of those who remain at home." The shipping laws had enabled the government to secure supplies to a much greater extent than formerly, meet installments on its foreign loan, and put an end to a wasteful and ruinous contract system. "Instead of being compelled to give contractors a large profit on the cost of their supplies, and to make payment in cotton in our own ports at 6 pence per pound," he said, "we now purchase supplies abroad by our agents at cost in the foreign market, and pay there in cotton, which sells at a net price of 24 pence per pound." Allowing for the capture of 66 bales out of 600—the proportion shown in the treasurer's report—he showed that the remaining 534 bales would yield 21,360 pounds sterling while the same 600 bales delivered in payment at a home port would yield less than 6,000 pounds sterling. He was convinced that the effect of the legislation had been "salutary" and that any modification of the regulations would be "calamitous."[116]

The movement for repeal was halted for the moment, but the agitation of Brown and his supporters was effective in the end. On March 4 and 8, 1865, Congress passed a bill removing all restrictions, which "left the Confederacy stripped of all its means of exportation and importation." [117]

---

[116] *Messages and Papers,* I, 505-13; *Journal of the C. S. A.,* IV, 373-76; *ibid.,* VII, 368-71. With further reference to the success of the government's shipping operations, cf. S. B. Thompson, pp. 98-99; Scharf, pp. 488-89, 490.

[117] Owsley, *State Rights,* p. 149. *Journal of the C. S. A.,* VII, 694, 720. Cf. Louise Biles Hill, *State Socialism in the Confederate States of America, passim.*

## CHAPTER VII

## LOCAL DEFENSE

THE DIFFICULTIES of the Confederate government with the individual states in the matter of local defense began early in 1861, as has been indicated,[1] and continued until the curtain fell in 1865. Sometimes the activities of the governors took the form of demands upon the Confederate government for more troops and guns for state defense; sometimes they consisted in the organization of "state troops." In either event they made for a policy of dispersion and competition with the central government which was disastrous to the plans of the general staff to weld together the entire fighting force of the Confederacy under one command. The Confederate government was aware of the vital importance of consolidating its forces and tried vainly through conscription, through the organization of local defense troops in 1863 and again in 1864, and through requisition upon Governor Brown in August, 1864, to obtain control. In February, 1865, and again in March the President made his last appeals to Congress for a general militia law, which, however, were unheeded. The governor of Georgia was the chief offender in these particulars. Indeed, other states were slow to take this line of action, particularly in the matter of keeping state troops, until Georgia led the way.[2]

Brown's efforts in 1861 to increase the coast defense, already defended by Confederate forces under General A. R.

---

[1] *Supra*, p. 66.     [2] See Owsley, *State Rights*, pp. 1-75.

LOCAL DEFENSE 163

Lawton, his demands for the return of Georgia troops from Virginia, and his organization of state troops under the negative clause of the constitution, "Nor shall any State keep troops . . . of war in time of peace or engage in war unless actually invaded . . ."[3] have already been noted. In vain the Secretary of War told Brown that it was the Secretary's "solemn public duty" to reinforce the army on the Potomac, that it would be "suicidal" to withdraw troops from that point, and that ten other governors were demanding Enfield rifles from the blockade-runner, "Fingal."[4] Brown's demands continued.[5] By November 19, 1861, there were 5,500 Confederate soldiers and 8,000 state troops on the coast.[6] Although Brown's letters implied willful neglect, the Confederacy seems to have done all it could to reinforce and fortify the Southern coast. Coast defense required batteries rather than rifles, and these the Confederacy did not have in sufficient number.[7] The next few months were filled with the struggle between the Governor and the legislature over the policy to be adopted with reference to the state troops. The Governor wished to retain them, the legislature thought they should be turned over to the Confederacy. When the latter plan prevailed, the Governor attempted to have the Con-

---

[3] Cf. *C. R.*, III, 53-54, 60-61, 63-64, 68-70, 126, 128-30; *ibid.*, II, 131, 139-40, 512-14; Avery, p. 204; *Republican*, Nov. 12, 1861; *Federal Union*, Nov. 10, 1861.

[4] *C. R.*, III, 139-45. This was the famous blockade-runner purchased by Admiral Bulloch in England.—Bulloch, I, 109-27; S. B. Thompson, pp. 19-20, 41.

[5] In Oct., 1861, Gen. Robert E. Lee was sent by the War Department to fortify the coasts of S. C., Ga., and eastern Fla. Lee's work at Savannah and Charleston and on the coast protecting the railroad between them withstood the assaults of the enemy until taken at the end of the war from the landward side. See Freeman, *R. E. Lee*, I, 607.

[6] *C. R.*, II, 142; *ibid.*, III, 169, 170-71. Cf. *O. R.*, Ser. IV, Vol. I, p. 1067.

[7] Brunswick had to be abandoned because of the impossibility of procuring sufficient cannon to fortify it, as Lee himself said. See correspondence between Lee and Brown, *C. R.*, III, 151-53, 163-65. Ordnance Officer W. G. Gill's report on the condition of the Georgia coast defense, made just prior to the fall of Port Royal, may be conveniently found in Derry, p. 183.

federate government accept the troops with their state organization, which meant retaining the general officers whom he had appointed.[8]

Of how much value were the state troops in the defense of the coast in 1861? How much did they interfere with the central government's military program? The answer to either question can of course be but a guess. The troops were not called upon to do any fighting,[9] but they assisted in building the fortifications at Savannah and their presence may have discouraged an attack on Fort Pulaski. Not men, but arms was the need during 1861, and the more immediate danger was on the Tennessee-Virginia front. Arms in the hands of troops on the coast of Georgia were not available for those on the firing line. It is open to question whether the force concentrated at Savannah, in view of its excellent fortifications, was necessary to its defense. That the President thought the number of men held at that point to be detrimental to operations where the danger was more imminent is indicated in correspondence between himself and Governor Brown in May, 1862, when a brigade was badly needed in Chattanooga.[10]

Whether it was a military or a political necessity that impelled the Governor to call out the troops in the fall of 1861, there is no way of knowing. There were savage attacks from the press during the gubernatorial campaign, charging that he had left the coast defenseless, that he had removed all the arms from the arsenal at Savannah to Milledgeville, leaving the citizens of the coast city with "not a gun," and other similar accusations.[11] The charges were no doubt mere campaign material, but as such they may have influenced the

---

[8] Cf. *C. R.*, III, 146, 147; *O. R.*, Ser. IV, Vol. I, pp. 825-26, 909-10, 842-43; *Acts of the General Assembly, 1861*, p. 141.

[9] Jackson's farewell address to the troops, Apr. 16, Avery, p. 329; *Republican*, Apr. 18, 1862.

[10] *C. R.*, III, 203-4, 205-6, 181-83.

[11] *Republican*, Sept. 5, 24, 27, 1861. Cf. *C. R.*, II, 37-38.

LOCAL DEFENSE                               165

Governor's action. There seems little doubt that Brown's efforts to increase the security of the state were important in his reëlection. That the defense of the Confederacy might be jeopardized by such a course was outweighed, even if it were realized, by the more immediate or seeming danger to residents of the state. It must also have been true that service in the state army—where the troops were near their homes and were not called upon to face the enemy—satisfied the instinct of patriotism, frittered away enthusiasm, and dampened the ardor for enlistment when the Confederacy was at last in position to arm the men. The results were evident shortly afterwards in the poor response made to the Governor's proclamation for three-year volunteers for the Confederacy with the added inducement of a fifty-dollar bounty and his threat to conscript them.[12]

One of the bitterest controversies of Brown's controversial career grew out of the raising of troops for the Confederacy in 1863 for purposes of local defense. The plan was a failure and so acrimonious was the correspondence the following year between Brown and the Secretary of War in regard to the matter that each doubted the veracity of the other and plainly said so. The correspondence between the Governor and General Cobb was no less bitter.[13] The bad feeling thus engendered continued throughout the war, and, together with the collapse of the local defense plan of 1863 and that of the following year, contributed no little to the failure of the Confederacy to achieve its independence.

Grant's capture of Jackson, Mississippi, and his continued pressure on Vicksburg, together with other defeats of Confederate forces in the states along the Mississippi, spread alarm throughout the lower South. Brown asked for the return of a certain regiment and legion of Georgia troops

---
[12] *Ibid.*, pp. 213-15.
[13] Gen. Cobb was in command of the organization of the local defense troops.—*O. R.*, Ser. IV, Vol. II, p. 818.

for the state's defense.[14] In this situation the President saw an opportunity to take over local defense, secure control of the various state military organizations, and through uniformity, proper discipline and training, and the centralization of command, increase the efficiency of all the forces of the Confederacy.

Congress had previously provided legislation for such a contingency. An act of August 21, 1861, "to provide for local defense and special service," authorized the President to accept volunteers to serve for such time as he should prescribe, for the defense of exposed places or localities, or such special service as he should deem expedient. Muster rolls were to set forth distinctly the service to be performed, volunteers were not to be considered in actual service until specifically ordered out by the President, and they were to be paid and subsisted only when on duty.[15] An act of October 13, 1862, "to authorize the formation of volunteer companies for local defense," contemplated more limited service. Its object was to provide a means of enabling employees of manufacturing plants or residents of isolated communities to defend themselves against raiding parties and to secure to the men through being in Confederate service the rights of prisoners of war should they be captured in such defense. It permitted any group of not less than twenty persons who were over the age of forty-five years, or otherwise not liable to military duty, to form military companies, elect their officers, and establish rules and regulations for their own government. They were to serve without pay or allowance.[16]

The Confederate troops for local defense which the President contemplated were to be organized under the first act. They were to be composed of the non-conscript population, and were to serve presumably until the end of the war. On

---

[14] *C. R.*, III, 325-26; Rowland, V, 510.
[15] *C. R.*, III, 344-45; *O. R.*, Ser. IV, Vol. I, p. 579.
[16] *Ibid.*, II, 206-7; *C. R.*, III, 345-46.

LOCAL DEFENSE 167

June 6, Seddon, secretary of War, explained the plan to Brown and other governors and it was on the basis of this letter,[17] modified by subsequent correspondence between the two men, that the troops in Georgia were organized. The Secretary pointed out that greater concentration of forces was necessary in order that the Confederacy might meet the numerically superior armies of the enemy and to accomplish this it was necessary to so organize the reserves of the population that they might, while continuing their ordinary pursuits, still be available for local defense in emergencies. He stated reasons why the militia could not well serve this purpose and why local organizations of volunteers "for limited periods and special purposes" organized under the local defense acts would afford more assurance of prompt and efficient service.[18] As a means of securing the volunteer organizations the Secretary proposed to make a requisition on Georgia which the Governor should make known in a proclamation threatening a draft if the men did not volunteer. As between the two alternatives, that of voluntary organizations for special service within the state under officers of their own selection, and with the privilege of remaining at home in the pursuit of their ordinary vocations, "unless when called for a temporary exigency to active duty," and that of "continuous service for an appointed time, under compulsory draft as militiamen," the Secretary thought the preference would be for the former. He accordingly made a formal requisition upon Governor Brown for 8,000 men, for service within the state, for the period of six months from August 1, 1863, "unless in the intermediate time a volunteer force, organized under the law for local defense and special service, of at least an equal number be mustered and reported," subject to the President's call.[19]

---
[17] *Ibid.*, pp. 339-44.
[18] *Ibid.*, pp. 340-41.
[19] *Ibid.*, pp. 342-44. It is interesting to note that the U. S. government one year earlier sought to use the draft as a club to secure volunteers, very much

There was a long correspondence between Governor Brown and the Secretary over the matter,[20] Brown offering to raise the troops under the requisition, the Secretary trying to secure the other type of organization. Brown thus offered the "club" instead of the organization which the "club" was designed to secure. Brown stated that since there was no state or Confederate law subjecting those over forty-five years of age to draft, it would be difficult for him to assist unless his plan was accepted. Finally he agreed to offer both plans and promised success if the Secretary would discontinue other methods of raising troops until he had completed the task. He promised to allude in his proclamation to the possibility of a draft, "without saying whether there is State authority for it or not," and admitted that it might "stimulate the volunteer spirit," [21] quite an admission for Governor Brown to make, since he claimed from the beginning of the war to the end that conscription laws were unnecessary as well as unconstitutional.

The Governor's plan was unwillingly accepted by Seddon,[22] but, as subsequent events proved, several points were not clear. Under what plan were the troops to be raised? What was to be their term of service? What was to be their area of service? What was to be their status—state or Confederate?

It seems clear that Brown had engaged to offer both plans of organization. The records do not show whether in the troops he raised Brown kept the two types separate, or indeed whether he raised any at all under the Secretary's plan. Under Brown's plan the term was for six months, under the Secretary's plan the term was "for an appointed time,"

---

as Seddon was endeavoring to do. The threat was successful, since men preferred to volunteer and obtain federal, state, and local bounties rather than to be drafted without them.—Shannon, I, 271 *et seq.*

[20] *C. R.*, III, 347-58.
[21] *Ibid.*, pp. 349-53.
[22] *Ibid.*, pp. 354-58.

## LOCAL DEFENSE

which, as later stipulated in General Order No. 86, was for the war.²³ The area to be defended, in so far as it had been stated in the correspondence, was that of the vicinity of any one of the organizations, according to Seddon's letter of June 6, or seemingly a wider range, according to Brown's suggestion of June 13. According to General Order No. 86, no authority was given for restricted areas of service within the respective states and no provision was made for the organization of companies with a minimum of twenty, since the order contemplated the raising of troops under the act of 1861 rather than that of 1862. The question of status, involving the appointment of officers, was never agreed upon, and ultimately involved the President, Brown, Seddon, Rains, Cobb, Cooper, and the legislature. The controversy over the point extended from August, 1863, until the end of the war.

In the correspondence between Brown and Seddon in 1864-65, the latter enclosed a copy of General Order No. 86,²⁴ which Brown declared he had no recollection of ever having seen before.²⁵ There is no reason to doubt his word. Indeed, bits of evidence here and there tend to confirm his statement. But even had he received a copy at the time it was issued it could have had no bearing, since Seddon had agreed to special arrangements with Brown at variance with the instructions of the adjutant general. Seddon was at fault in having allowed Brown to wear him down. It was an old trick of the Governor to withhold troops or ammunition from the hard-pressed administration while he bombarded officials with his demands, as in the offer of the brigade in 1861, the closing of the Savannah arsenal to Confederate officers in the same year, the "skeleton regiment" episode, and the question of filling the President's requisition of June, 1861, to mention only a few instances.²⁶

---
²³ *Ibid.*, pp. 686-89; *O. R.*, Ser. IV, Vol. II, pp. 602-3.
²⁴ *C. R.*, III, 682.
²⁵ *Ibid.*, p. 696. ²⁶ See *ibid.*, III, 104-5, 108-10, 112-13.

Brown's energy and thoroughness were never more in evidence than during the period of raising the 8,000 troops for local defense.[27] On June 22 he issued a stirring proclamation in which he adroitly made use of the "club" with which Secretary Seddon had provided him: "If the force is not organized by the first of August, by the tender of volunteers, I am notified that the President then makes a positive requisition for it and requires that such requisition be responded to if need be *by draft*."[28] The call was based upon the "different acts of Congress for local defense," he continued, and the execution of the organization having been confided to him he required that all companies, battalions, and regiments which had lately organized and tendered their services to the President for local defense, as well as all thereafter to be organized, report to him.[29] Militia and civil officers were required to volunteer, for which purpose furloughs of six months were granted to the former. The people were to mark every person who without sufficient excuse should refuse to volunteer.[30] General Order No. 16, issued by the state adjutant and inspector general,[31] gave instructions to militia officers for drafting those between eighteen and forty-five in counties not having filled their quotas.[32] Neither those who had hired substitutes for Confederate service nor unnaturalized foreigners were exempted.[33] The men were authorized to prescribe in their muster

---

[27] See eulogy in *Intelligencer*, June 18, 1863.

[28] *C. R.*, II, 457; *Constitutionalist*, June 24, 1863; instructions of Gen. Wayne, *Southern Confederacy*, June 25, 1863.

[29] *C. R.*, II, 459-60. Here Brown exceeded his authority. The Secretary had not promised the Governor control of troops already tendered.

[30] *Ibid.*, pp. 460-62. A second and third proclamation were issued and the date of the draft was set for Aug. 4.—*Ibid.*, pp. 463-68; *O. R.*, Ser. IV, Vol. II, pp. 614, 639-41.

[31] *C. R.*, III, 374-77.

[32] In July Toombs thought volunteering was not turning out well.—Phillips, *Correspondence*, p. 621.

[33] See Brown's correspondence with the British consul, *supra*, Chap. V, n. 114.

## LOCAL DEFENSE

rolls the limits within which they were to serve, which, however, must include "a reasonable boundary within the State, not more than one-fourth of its territory...." [34] A further provision permitted companies of forty-four men among factory and machine shop employees with service limited to their own localities or counties.[35]

Meanwhile the military situation on the borders of Georgia, with Rosecrans flanking Bragg out of Middle Tennessee, naturally stimulated volunteering, so that by September Brown was able to announce that he would tender to the President 15,000 troops instead of the 8,000 called for. The draft had been necessary in only a few counties.[36] The President complimented Brown upon his "prompt action and gratifying success" and invited him to Richmond to discuss measures to "increase the strength of the army and the security of the State." [37]

Brown had perhaps never been so happy, despite the enemy's near approach. He had vindicated his contention that troops could be raised without conscription.[38] He ignored the contributing factors of the threat of a draft, the attractive terms of service, and the stimulus of the immediate danger to the state. The troops constituted what was evidently to his mind an ideal citizen army: the term was short, the

---
[34] *C. R.*, III, 375-76.
[35] *Ibid.*, pp. 376-77. These were evidently to be organized under the act of Oct. 13, 1862.—See *O. R.*, Ser. IV, Vol. II, pp. 711-12.
[36] *C. R.*, II, 471; *O. R.*, Ser. IV, Vol. II, pp. 789-90. This response was in striking contrast to volunteering in the North. Cf. President Lincoln's call for 100,000 men from four states when Lee invaded Pa., to which only 12,000 responded, one third of whom came from Ind. which had not been included in the call.—Shannon, I, 296.
[37] *C. R.*, III, 415, 416. At this time the utmost cordiality seemed to exist between Brown and the President. When the latter visited Ga. in Oct., he was met by Governor Brown who introduced him to the audience in Atlanta. At the President's invitation Brown accompanied him to Carthage and Marietta, at both of which places the President spoke to large audiences.—Rowland, VI, 57-58, citing *Charleston Daily Courier*, Oct. 9, 1863.
[38] See Avery, p. 263.

men were not to leave the state without their consent, they were to be called out only in emergencies affecting the commonwealth of Georgia and to be kept out of productive labor for the shortest time possible, they had been raised by himself, and he still had hopes of appointing the officers.[39]

When in September the Confederate government telegraphed for the local defense troops to reinforce Bragg's army,[40] Brown issued a proclamation calling out those who had volunteered to defend Atlanta and the territory north to the Tennessee River. He urged those in other parts of the state to volunteer for this particular service and even to go beyond the state if necessary, and exempted the troops in several counties who were considered indispensable at home. Companies organized for the defense of factories, workshops, or ironworks were instructed to remain at work, drill twice a week, and await orders.[41]

At this point the question of the appointment of officers arose. The act of 1861 and General Order No. 86 under which these troops were supposed to be raised[42] prescribed that when regiments were tendered the men should elect their field officers; when companies were tendered the President should commission the company-elected officers, organize the companies into regiments, and appoint all the remaining officers. Vacancies occurring afterwards were to be filled by Confederate authority. The status of the troops was, however, never clear, and in the end the Governor claimed they were state troops, or militia, and denied the right of the Confederacy to appoint the officers. On August 24, 1863,

---

[39] In the meantime misunderstandings were arising over Brown's organizing companies of 44 men when General Order No. 86 called for 64.—Col. Rains to Seddon, and Seddon's reply, *C. R.*, III, 746, 412-13. There was later a dispute over the area which the troops were required to defend. They are important only as bearing upon the later controversy between Brown and Seddon, and Brown and Cobb.

[40] *Ibid.*, II, 470-73.

[41] *Ibid.*, pp. 791-92. Cf. Rowland, VI, 19, 20; *Southern Confederacy*, Sept. 18, 1863; *Republican*, Sept. 18, 1863.

[42] *O. R.*, Ser. IV, Vol. I, p. 579; *ibid.*, II, 602-3.

Colonel Rains had reported to the War Department that Brown was commissioning company officers,⁴³ and when the troops were called out to reinforce Bragg at Chattanooga Brown entered into a correspondence with the President and the War Department in which it would seem that he thought he should appoint the general officers.⁴⁴ In his address to the troops in September Brown said that the President had denied his right to command them, but added: "Whatever may be my opinion of my right or the rights of the State in connection with the command . . . I can have no conflict with the Confederate authorities in the face of the enemy. . . ." ⁴⁵ He stated that he would give to General Cobb all the assistance within his power and would serve in any capacity in which he could be useful. He concluded with a plea for coöperation: "Let . . . us bury all past differences of opinion and personal jealousies till we have driven the wicked invader from the sacred soil of our beloved state." ⁴⁶

The battle of Chickamauga was fought, the "wicked invader" was driven temporarily from the "sacred soil" of the state, and Brown resumed his efforts to secure the appointment of officers for the local defense troops. Cobb asked the War Department for a ruling on the matter. He said that Brown insisted upon filling all vacancies by election according to state law, including those of field officers. He recommended that if possible the concession be made as a lesser evil than a conflict with state authorities.⁴⁷ Although the War Department was compelled to act in accordance with

---
⁴³ *C. R.*, III, 401, 412-13.
⁴⁴ Cf. *ibid.*, pp. 409, 410-11, 415, 416-17.
⁴⁵ *Ibid.*, II, 476-77. The complaint seems surprising in view of Brown's statement in his proclamation of June 22 that "the command of the troops now required of this State will, under the Act of Congress, belong to the President and not to me, so soon as they have been organized and mustered into service."—*Ibid.*, p. 459. That this was the understanding of the state adjutant is evident by the fact that he recommended to Cooper, on Aug. 13, a certain officer as colonel of one of the local defense regiments.—*O. R.*, Ser. IV, Vol. II, p. 711.
⁴⁶ *C. R.*, II, 476-77.  ⁴⁷ *Ibid.*, III, 420.

the law, it expressed a willingness to give weight to the Governor's recommendations in the matter of appointments.[48] The concession did not satisfy the Governor and he declared that he would continue to issue commissions until the legislature should meet and pass upon the question.[49] Cobb, on the other hand, announced his intention to forward notice of vacancies to Richmond for commissions, as it was his duty to do. It is not clear which side won. The six-months term of the troops expired soon afterward and Brown's controversies henceforth were concerned with other matters.

Brown reported the controversy to the legislature in his message of November 5, 1863, saying that the policy of promotion "subjects every man's claim to the President's favoritism, prejudice or caprice. . . ." He reminded that body that its predecessor had by seating members who were Confederate officers virtually decided that Georgia troops in the field were militia and not armies of the Confederacy.[50] On December 14 the legislature met the Governor's wishes in part by passing a joint resolution requesting the Georgia delegation in Congress to use its "zealous efforts" to procure for Georgia troops the necessary change in Confederate law to permit them to elect their regimental, battalion, and company officers.[51] Nothing further came of the matter as far as the general service was concerned.[52]

---

[48] *Ibid.*, p. 421.   [49] *Ibid.*, pp. 423-25. Cf. *ibid.*, pp. 421, 425-26.

[50] *Ibid.*, II, 526 *et seq.* The state constitution forbade anyone who held a military commission or other appointment having emolument or compensation under the state or Confederate States from holding a seat in the legislature, except justices of the inferior court, justices of the peace, and officers of the militia. As a means of evading the provision and seating members who were officers in Georgia regiments in Confederate service and on furlough to attend the 1862-63 session of the legislature, that body ruled that the members in question were officers of the militia. The Governor pointed out at the time that if these members were officers of the militia, the regiments, battalions, and companies commanded by them were militia of the state in Confederate service, and entitled to select their officers, fill vacancies, and have such officers commissioned by the executive of the state.—*Ibid.*, p. 340.

[51] *Ibid.*, III, 446-47.   [52] See *ibid.*, pp. 446, 448-50.

## LOCAL DEFENSE 175

The Union army having been defeated at Chickamauga and having retreated to Chattanooga, the danger was over, in Brown's opinion, and he thought the local defense troops should be allowed to return to their homes. Bragg's army was so short of men and the enemy forces were being so rapidly increased that the Confederate administration could not allow the men in that section of Georgia to be discharged. They were kept in service until the end of their terms of enlistment, although they did not leave the state. Here again it should be noted that the status of the troops may be called into question. If the troops were militia, as Brown contended a part of the time, might not the Confederacy treat them as any other militia "in the service of the Confederate States" and keep them continuously in service for six months? Some writers have taken this view. It must be remembered, however, that Brown had been most explicit in restating Seddon's terms—that the troops should be called out only in an emergency and then be allowed to return to their homes—and that he had acquiesced however unwillingly in the President's appointing the officers, which he certainly would not have done had the troops possessed a clear status of militia. The fact of the matter would seem to be that the troops in question had the same status as any other Confederate troops obtained through requisition, except that they were to serve a shorter term and under special conditions. Whether the Confederacy violated these conditions would, then, depend upon whether an "emergency" existed, and clearly this was a question for the Confederacy to decide. It is the justification Seddon gave when he told Brown that "the situation on the frontier of Georgia for the last six months has all the time been so critical that a judicious administration did not justify the disbanding of any troops under the control of the Department." [53]

Brown either could not or would not understand the Con-

---
[53] *Ibid.*, III, 487.

federacy's desperate need for men. Ever since conscription began in 1862 he had opposed taking men out of production to fill the armies. Five days after the battle of Chickamauga he warned that crops must be gathered and wheat sowed. The provision question was, he insisted, the great question of the struggle.[54] In addition, he told the Secretary, the President, and the legislature that the government must keep faith with the men, else they would not continue to volunteer.[55] Brown next made a definite move to secure the discharge of the troops—at least all circumstances point to its being his work. The lieutenant colonel of the ninth regiment of state guards, stationed at Rome, submitted to the Governor on the part of the regiment a written protest against being held in service, which the Governor in turn submitted to the President. Among other things it contained a passage which might easily have been dictated by the Governor, so nearly did it express his sentiments: "Subjugation by our enemy we have never feared, but let us see to it that in our struggle for independence the Constitution and the laws be not hushed into silence, and thereby the liberty of the citizen hopelessly and irretrievably lost." [56]

In his notation to the Secretary of War for a report from General Cobb on the matter, the President commented: "I expect it will be found that the policy has been to relieve the men from duty as far as circumstances would permit." [57] Certainly this was true. After the battle of Chickamauga on September 19-20 and until November 23 the two armies faced each other at Chattanooga, just across the Georgia border. Ten days after Brown added his plea for discharge to that of the ninth regiment, the Federal army raised the siege and in the battles of Lookout Mountain and Missionary

---

[54] Brown returned to the subject again and again. Cf. *ibid.*, pp. 431-33, 434-38, 452, 458-61, 484-88.
[55] *Ibid.*, pp. 418-19; *ibid.*, II, 504, 507, 524.
[56] *Ibid.*, III, 431-38.
[57] *Ibid.*, p. 433.

LOCAL DEFENSE 177

Ridge defeated Bragg and drove his army into Georgia. Under these circumstances it seems amazing that a patriot such as Brown professed to be, a governor presumably anxious for the safety of his state, could have held that no emergency existed.

The fortunes of the Confederacy becoming even more critical, Seddon suggested on January 13, 1864, that local defense troops be substituted at Savannah and at other points on the Georgia coast to release regular Confederate troops for duty outside the state.[58] Brown told Seddon that the troops could not be used as he had indicated, since the terms of a part of them had already expired and they had been discharged and the others would be discharged in five days. In regard to raising another force for local defense, at which Seddon had hinted, the Governor said that the failure of the government to keep faith with the troops that had been called out early in September and held in service in the field, "when no raid was approaching Georgia and no sudden emergency called for their service," had injured the prospects for a supply of provisions for the coming year and had caused great dissatisfaction among the troops, which would make it difficult to enlist others. He had lately been through portions of the state and had found them "drained of supplies." [59]

Since Brown admitted the necessity for increasing the army, it is interesting to note how he thought it could be

[58] *Ibid.*, p. 452. Brown did not reply until Jan. 29. He explained the delay as being due to the fact that he had been absent from his office. It is conceivable that Brown delayed his reply in order to muster out the troops and prevent the Confederacy's retaining them through requisition.

[59] *Ibid.*, pp. 459-60; cf. Jones, *Diary*, II, 145-46. The report of Maj. Cummings, commissary of subsistence in Ga., on Feb. 13, 1864, does not agree with Brown's observations.—*C. R.*, III, 469. In his correspondence with Cobb in 1864, Brown said: ". . . whether you employed those called to the field 'only when and so long as' the emergency lasted for the kind of service which they were called for to perform . . . or kept them in the field . . . that you might not be left with wreaths upon your shoulders without a command, is a subject upon which those who were then subject to your orders are entitled to and doubtless have their own opinions."—*Ibid.*, p. 555.

done. "Make but little further drafts upon the producing class," he said, "and put the troops whose names are now on the muster rolls, and who are in the pay of the Government, and especially the almost countless swarms of young, able-bodied officers, who are to be seen on all our railroad trains and in our hotels, into the army. . . ." This would increase the armies 25 to 50 per cent, he estimated, and be sufficient to meet any force of the enemy. It was because of these idlers "in brass buttons and gold lace" that drafts had to be made upon the producing class, he told the Secretary. The enemy would still have a numerical superiority of three to one, he admitted, but he thought the disparity in numbers was unimportant.[60]

The Confederacy had from the beginning been doing just that, but with the forces of the enemy constantly increased by new levies upon a larger population than that of the South and by mercenaries brought into the country under the guise of immigrants, it was only a question of time until the armies of the South, unless their ranks could be filled and a decisive victory quickly obtained, must succumb to the overwhelming odds. The Governor's military knowledge was not profound, to say the least, and his aversion to conscription and enrolling officers clouded his judgment.

In 1864, when Cobb was endeavoring to organize the reserves in Georgia under the conscription act of that year, Brown's obstructions led to a bitter correspondence between the two men which brought out the numerous misunderstandings that had arisen with reference to the organization of the local defense troops in 1863. Brown stated that without conscription he had furnished "more than double the number required," to which Cobb replied that the number existed only "on paper," due to Brown's division of the state into territorial districts and that at no time was an adequate number available at threatened points. The correspondence con-

---

[60] *Ibid.*, pp. 461-62. Seddon's reply, *ibid.*, pp. 484-88.

LOCAL DEFENSE 179

tinued until each accused the other of knowingly misrepresenting the facts.[61]

When in August, 1864, Brown refused to honor the President's requisition for 10,000 troops and gave as one reason for his refusal the "bad faith" of the administration in keeping a part of the local defense troops in continuous service for six months,[62] Seddon felt that he should put his side of the matter on record. He told Brown that it had been designed to raise troops for local defense as the general rule throughout the state to constitute a part of the provisional army and that the Governor had instead formed "nondescript organizations, not conforming to the regulations of the provisional army, scant in men and abounding in officers, with every variety of obligation for local service, . . . and for the brief period of only six months." He said that "scarce a decent division of four thousand men could be mustered for the field," and that the danger was too great, the number too limited, to allow of furloughs.[63] Charges and countercharges were made regarding the type of troops, conditions under which they had been organized, term and areas of service, size of companies, and number enrolled. Each accused the other of "garbling" extracts from previous correspondence to prove his point.[64]

The matter was greatly involved and in part it is impossible to determine who was right and who was wrong. Seddon's charge that the units did not conform to the regulations of the provisional army is confirmed by Rains and Cobb,[65] each of whom stated that Brown's companies numbered only forty, rank and file. Cobb stated in his report to Adjutant Cooper, on September 28, 1863, that Brown's call for these troops fixed the size of companies at forty,

---
[61] *Ibid.*, pp. 520-38. Cf. *ibid.*, pp. 554, 564, 571.
[62] *Ibid.*, pp. 618-19.
[63] *Ibid.*, pp. 636-37.
[64] *Ibid.*, pp. 654 *et seq.*, 682 *et seq.*, 695 *et seq.*
[65] *Ibid.*, pp. 401; *O. R.*, Ser. IV, Vol. II, pp. 831-32.

rank and file, and that to have changed it would have caused great dissatisfaction and would have given mortal offense to the Governor "who seemed to be making every effort to respond efficiently to the call of the President." [66] If the companies were "scant in men" the force when organized would necessarily "abound in officers," as Seddon charged. Brown, on the other hand, declared that the companies "had the number of men specified in the statutes and no one of them had a supernumerary officer." [67]

In his report Cobb continually referred to the difficulties he had encountered in organizing the troops because of the "infinite variety of territorial limits which the different companies had selected." [68] The difference of opinion in regard to the term of service and the territorial limitations seems to have been due to Seddon's unfortunate letter of June 6, 1863, which he evidently wrote before he himself clearly understood the type of organization required; to Brown's insistence upon raising the troops in his own way and his final offer of both types of organization which were incompatible; and to the failure of the War Department to send Brown a copy of General Order No. 86.[69]

Who was guilty of "garbling"? Brown had been guilty of "garbling" notoriously in his correspondence with President Davis in regard to the constitutionality of conscription and it was natural, therefore, that Seddon should think him

---

[66] *Ibid.*, pp. 831-33; Rains' report, *C. R.*, III, 746-47.

[67] *Ibid.*, p. 657. No doubt some of the misunderstanding was due to the fact that Brown had organized some of the men under the act of 1862, a copy of which Seddon had enclosed with his letter of June 6, but which the adjutant general's orders had not authorized. Such companies, however, should have been few in number and would not have come under Cobb's observation.

[68] *O. R.*, Ser. IV, Vol. II, pp. 831-33. Although General Order No. 86 made no provision for restricted areas of service, it seems to have been expected by the administration that they would be organized in this manner.—Cf. Seddon to Rains, *C. R.*, III, 412-13; Davis to Brown, *ibid.*, pp. 414-15; Cobb's report, *O. R.*, Ser. IV, Vol. II, pp. 831-33; Cooper to Cobb, *ibid.*, pp. 798-99.

[69] In regard to the last point, Brown wrote Seddon during the quarrel, "Anyway, I obey no *orders* from your Department."—*Ibid.*, p. 696.

## LOCAL DEFENSE 181

guilty in this instance, just as various historians have done since that time. However, each man saw the matter from a different standpoint—Brown from that of the plan under which the troops were actually organized, Seddon from that which the Confederacy had desired and which he thought had been adopted—and in that event neither "garbled." As to how many troops were actually raised or how many were effective, it is difficult to judge. Brown reported to the legislature that 18,000 had volunteered.[70] Cobb's report of September 29, 1863, stated that muster rolls would indicate approximately 15,000, but he thought it "unsafe to rely upon a larger number than 10,000," because one sixth of the companies had been detailed by the Governor which Cobb considered "prudent and wise," because of the large number of infirm men who had to be discharged, and because of the large number who failed to report. He thought there would not be a sufficient number in the field at any one time to require any division organization.[71]

Local defense by volunteers had proved a failure and Congress next resorted to conscription. The law of February 17, 1864,[72] was passed in anticipation of the Union army's invasion of Georgia as soon as winter should break.[73] Cobb was ordered to organize the reserves—those between the ages of seventeen and eighteen and between forty-five and fifty—as a local defense force and for detail service within the state.

---

[70] *C. R.*, II, 524.

[71] *O. R.*, Ser. IV, Vol. II, pp. 831-33. For the remainder of the correspondence between Cobb and Brown, see *C. R.*, III, 538, 553-55, 564-65, 671-72. One of the difficulties in determining the strength of the troops was due to tardy muster rolls. In his letter of June 13, 1863, in which Brown urged the adoption of his plan in raising the troops, one of the advantages he stressed was the speed with which the organization could be effected and muster rolls transmitted.—*Ibid.*, pp. 349-53. This proved to be a delusion, as the state adjutant general's letter to Cooper shows.—*O. R.*, Ser. IV, Vol. II, pp. 800-1.

[72] *Supra*, p. 90.

[73] In an editorial, "Richmond or Atlanta," the *Tri-Weekly Constitutionalist* on May 1 speculated upon whether Atlanta or Richmond was to be the goal of the huge preparations going on in the Union armies, and decided that Atlanta was to be the real point of attack.

It was essential to the safety of Georgia and of the lower South in general that the raw troops be organized and drilled as quickly as possible.[74] Nevertheless Governor Brown managed to exempt probably 15,000 men.[75]

Early in May Sherman's Atlanta campaign began. On May 18, May 21, and June 24 Brown called out a part of his newly organized militia[76] and sent them to Johnston's assistance, asking of the President cavalry and 5,000 guns.[77] The guns were sent but the President telegraphed that he had sent all reinforcements possible, even detaching troops from positions exposed to the enemy, and added that the disparity of forces in North Georgia was less than at any other point in the Confederacy.[78] Brown replied that he did not see how Forrest's operations in Mississippi or Morgan's raids in Kentucky could interfere with Sherman's plans, and suggested that the President's information as to the relative strength of the two armies in North Georgia could not be from reliable sources. He added: "If your mistake should result in loss of Atlanta . . . posterity may have reason to mourn over the error."[79] The President replied rather sharply that he was surprised that official reports and estimates were unreliable but that until Brown's "better knowledge" was communicated he would "have no means of cor-

---

[74] Toombs, who was state adjutant and inspector general, commented upon the fact that the militia in the Atlanta campaign, 12,000 strong, was untrained.—Stovall, p. 277.

[75] *Supra,* pp. 95 *et seq.*

[76] *C. R.,* II, 703-4, 707-9. See editorial in *Weekly Chronicle and Sentinel,* Feb. 3, 1864, with reference to Brown's organization of militia under the recent act of the legislature.

[77] *C. R.,* III, 568, 574, 576-77, 590. Cf. *ibid.,* pp. 601-3. Although Brown was told, in reply to his inquiry, that the enemy did not grant to troops in the service of states the right of prisoners of war, he decided they would be protected by the fact that they were for the time being "in Confederate service."

[78] Rowland, IV, 288-89. At Resaca, Johnston had more than 70,000 men, Sherman 98,325.—Knight, II, 776. Johnston's forces were at all times proportionately greater than Lee's.

[79] Rowland, VI, 280. Cf. Joseph E. Johnston, *Narrative of Military Operations,* pp. 360-62, henceforth cited as Johnston, *Narrative.*

LOCAL DEFENSE 183

recting such errors." He thought that most men in Brown's position "would not assume to decide on the value of the service to be rendered by troops in distant positions." He would be glad also to know the source of Brown's information as to "what the whole country expects, and posterity will judge." [80]

On July 9, 1864, Brown issued a proclamation calling out every man able to bear arms—all the reserve militia from fifty to fifty-five and sixteen to seventeen, and, with a few exceptions, all white persons between seventeen and fifty, including Confederate exempts and details.[81] Although every effort at harmony between state and Confederacy should have been made for its psychological effect, the Governor added in his proclamation: "A late correspondence with the President . . . satisfied my mind that Georgia is to be left to her own resources to supply the reinforcements to General Johnston's army. . . . If the Confederate Government will not send the large cavalry force . . . the people of Georgia, who have already been drawn upon more heavily in proportion to population than those of any other state of the Confederacy, must . . . rush to the front . . . to drive [the enemy] from the soil of the Empire State." [82]

Cobb telegraphed Richmond for a ruling as to "how far this remarkable proclamation" was to be obeyed. He expressed the opinion that Brown's purpose was "to make issues with the President." [83] Cobb was told that while exempts

---

[80] Rowland, VI, 280-81. This is perhaps the only occasion on which the President did not use the utmost deference in dealing with Governor Brown. Johnston had asked for 4,000 cavalry from Ala. and Miss. to destroy the railroad between the enemy and Dalton. A cavalry force had been sent to him but no more could be spared because of impending attacks at Mobile and the necessity of protecting the valuable machinery at Selma and the large supplies in that vicinity.—*Ibid.*, pp. 283, 288-92.

[81] *C. R.*, II, 710 *et seq.* Cf. Johnston, *Narrative*, pp. 348, 369-370. Avery (p. 284) says Brown "infringed pretty nearly on the cradle and the grave" in his call. Brown wrote Stephens that he had armed and placed at the front under his two calls over 10,000 men.—Phillips, *Correspondence*, p. 650.

[82] *C. R.*, II, 710, 715. Cf. *ibid.*, pp. 719-21.     [83] *Ibid.*, III, 591.

might be subject to the call, detailed men being already in Confederate service were not liable to state duty.[84] However, the matter was left to Cobb's discretion with the hint that it would be possible "to tolerate the call . . . as an assignment to temporary duty."[85] Meanwhile Seddon had read the Governor's proclamation the "terms and tendency" of which he "deplored," and he advised Cobb that detailed men might in an emergency join the Confederate reserves, adding, "If Governor Brown insists on forcing conflict, the responsibility must rest on him. . . ."[86] Cobb tactfully worked out a satisfactory solution by means of which it was agreed with Governor Brown that exempts were liable to the Governor's call and that detailed men who were engaged in public service should remain at their post of duty while detailed men not thus engaged should have the choice of going into the militia or having their details suspended and going into Confederate service. Cobb later expressed the opinion that had the detailed men been withheld Brown would have attributed to that fact the fall of Atlanta and would probably have brought on a collision between Confederate and state officers.[87]

That there might be no mistake as to the status of the

---

[84] Later, in the summer of 1864, the inferior court of Clay County, Ga., ruled in the case of *Mandeville* v. *Anthony*, that Confederate detailed agriculturists were liable to do state militia service. Judges Lochrane and Hook, of the superior courts, had previously so ruled.—*Minutes of the Executive Dept.*, pp. 726-27. The supreme court of Georgia made a similar ruling.— *C. R.*, III, 709. In the case of *Barber* v. *Irwin* the court held that the law freed exempts from Confederate service only.—33 Ga. 27. It also ruled in the cases of *Baldwin* v. *West* and *Cobb* v. *Stallings*, that tax assessors and collectors of the Confederacy—public officers—were not liable to militia duty, since neither the state nor the Confederacy might obstruct the machinery of the other, and that in case of conflict, Confederate law was supreme.—34 Ga. 72.

[85] *C. R.*, III, 592.

[86] *Ibid.*, pp. 596-97. Cf. Brown's demand on the President to stop Confederate officers from "throwing obstacles in the way" and the President's notation to Seddon.—*Ibid.*, pp. 593, 594.

[87] *Ibid.*, pp. 639-42.

## LOCAL DEFENSE

troops he had sent to Atlanta, Brown issued an address in which he stated that the troops were under General Hood, who had replaced Johnston on July 18, "until such time as I may choose to assume command, or until I shall order [the force] disbanded when I am satisfied the emergency has passed." [88]

To prevent the Governor's exercising the right to decide "when the emergency has passed," Seddon made a futile effort to bring the Georgia militia into Confederate service. He wrote Brown on August 30, saying that Georgia was faced with a serious invasion and making requisition for 10,000 or more militia "and such further force of militia to repel invasion as you may be able to organize for Confederate service." [89] Brown had ever argued that requisition was the only constitutional method by which the Confederate government could raise and increase its provisional army, but if in view of this fact the Secretary expected a prompt compliance with his requisition, he was mistaken. The Governor waited nearly two weeks before replying, and in the meantime, Atlanta having fallen, withdrew the troops from Hood's command and gave them a furlough of thirty days, "ostensibly for the purpose of gathering the autumnal crops," [90] but in reality to prevent their being enrolled in Confederate service.[91] Included in the furlough were the Con-

---

[88] *Ibid.*, pp. 605-6. *Cf. ibid.*, II, 724-25. Brown had headquarters in Atlanta. —Waddell, p. 278; Phillips, *Correspondence*, p. 644.

[89] *C. R.*, III, 607. The correspondence, which extended from August 30 to Jan. 6, 1865, may be found in *ibid.*, pp. 607, 612-22, 628-38, 643-68, 679-86, 690-701; extracts in Fielder, pp. 319-54. It was also published in the *Chronicle and Sentinel*, in March, 1865, and in pamphlet form, entitled *Correspondence between the Secretary of War and Governor Brown Growing out of a Requisition Made upon the Governor for the Reserve Militia of Georgia to be Turned Over to Confederate Control*, Boughton, Barnes & Moore, State Printers, 1865. On the title page of the pamphlet are the instructions, "Read and Hand on to Your Neighbor." A copy may be found in the Library of Congress and in the De Renne Library at Wormsloe, Ga.

[90] Thomas R. Hay, *Hood's Tennessee Campaign*, p. 21.

[91] William T. Sherman, *Memoirs*, II, 138-39.

federate details whose furloughs were "to remain in force until further orders." [92] In Brown's opinion the emergency was over.

Brown's reply to Seddon and his subsequent letters fairly reeked with venom and with insults to the President. He regretted that the President had been so late in making the discovery that Georgia was faced by a "formidable invasion" and had scattered his forces from Texas to Pennsylvania "while a severe blow was struck at the heart of the Confederacy." Continuing his tirade, he said that it was only after the President had learned that he (Brown) had an organization of gallant, fearless men "ready to defend the state against usurpations of power as well as invasion of the enemy" that he made requisition for the force. Since no other state was called upon to make such a sacrifice, and since the constitution permitted states to keep "troops of war" when actually invaded, he refused to "gratify the President's ambition" and surrender the state's troops when they were "the only remaining protection against the encroachments of centralized power." [93] He would instead order the troops to the front to defend the state, retaining the power to furlough or disband them when they could be spared from the military field. The Governor ended with the demand that the President either send reinforcements to Georgia or that

---

[92] *C. R.*, III, 609-12. Cf. Mrs. D. Giraud Wright, *A Southern Girl in '61*, p. 190, henceforth cited as Mrs. D. Giraud Wright.

[93] The campaign against the "centralization of power in the hands of the President" had been going on for some time in the anti-administration press, particularly in Stephens' organ, the *Chronicle and Sentinel*. While Brown was busy thwarting Cobb's efforts to organize the reserves and fighting the suspension of the writ of habeas corpus, that journal on June 1 published an editorial, "Political Demagogary" defending the Governor and accusing Cobb of "active participation in State politics." (Cobb had helped to thwart the Governor's plans in the spring session of the legislature.—See *infra*, p. 214). Cobb's political policy was said to be that of "lodging despotic power in the hands of the President." The editor thought that the interference of the administration with the politics of the state was "one of the most alarming symptoms . . . of that tendency to centralization and despotism . . . exhibited by the powers at Richmond."

he return the Georgia troops "to rally around her glorious flag . . . and to strike for their wives and their children, their homes and their altars and the 'green graves' of their kindred and sires. . . ." [94]

"It requires forbearance in reply to maintain the respect I would pay to your station, and observe the official propriety you have so transcended," the Secretary wrote to Brown. He pointed out that uncertainty of control and retention would impair the usefulness of the troops to the Confederate officer and "embarrass all calculations for their employment and efficiency in combined operations." Appealing to the Governor's supposedly high regard for constitutionality, the Secretary called attention to the fact that the Confederate government was charged with the common defense and that none of the laws contemplated the fulfillment of this duty by state troops, organized and held by the state in its own service, and under officers responsible only to the state. At this time Sherman's overtures to Brown and Stephens were in progress,[95] and Seddon pointedly compared Brown's action in refusing the President's requisition to that of Massachusetts and Connecticut in the War of 1812, adding: "The impression was not wanting either then or since, that they were even in communication with the enemy, or at least proposed to give them encouragement and moral support."

If the 10,000 militia had been incorporated with veteran regiments prior to May 1, the Secretary said, they would not improbably have "hurled back the invaders," and that they were not ready was due to obstacles which the Governor had himself interposed. Seddon's most scathing rebuke was directed to Brown's statement that it was necessary to retain the men as a defense against centralized power. Seddon preferred to consider the remarks as "inconsiderate utterances" rather than "the foreshadowing of a guilty purpose to array

---
[94] *C. R.*, III, 620-21. Cf. *ibid.*, II, 825 *et seq.*
[95] *Infra*, p. 224.

your State in armed antagonism against the Confederacy, and so to betray the cause of herself and sister States." Continuing in the same vein he said: "Our enemies appear to have conceived you were even prepared to entertain overtures of separate accommodation, and that your state . . . could be seduced or betrayed to treachery. . . ." [96]

The Governor protested against Seddon's intimation that he intended to use the militia against the Confederacy, but his protestation was nullified by the further remark that he would not hesitate to use it to protect all the just rights and constitutional powers against "external assaults and internal usurpations." He pointedly added: "There is scarcely a single provision in the constitution for the protection of life, liberty or property in Georgia that has not been and is not now being constantly violated by the Confederate Government. . . . In this state of things militia is necessary." [97] About this time Sherman's march to the sea drove the Governor out of Milledgeville and interrupted the correspondence. It was resumed afterwards and continued until January 6, 1865, when Brown as usual had the last word.[98]

Uneasy over Hood's failure to hold Atlanta and the "defection of Governor Brown," [99] Davis hurried to Georgia and appointed Beauregard to the command of the Military

---

[96] *C. R.*, III, 628-38.
[97] *Ibid.*, pp. 666-68. Cf. Jones, *Diary*, II, 341.
[98] *C. R.*, III, 690-701. *The Richmond Sentinel*, voicing the opinion of the majority probably, charged that the invasion of Ga. was due to the Governor's exempting 15,000 men for a service which was performed in Va. with 1,400; in Ala. with 1,000; in Miss. with 110.—Quoted by the *Weekly Chronicle and Sentinel*, Dec. 21, 1864. The *Weekly Chronicle and Sentinel* in an editorial, "Wrong, No Matter What He Does," said that the chief executive of Ga. was sure on all occasions to find "snappish, churlish, individuals . . . ready and eager to find fault."—Sept. 28, 1864.
[99] Hay, *Hood's Tennessee Campaign*, p. 22. See *infra*, p. 229. On the floor of the U. S. Senate seventeen years later, Brown, then a member of that body, was taunted by a Virginia senator with disloyalty to the Confederacy in withholding the militia in 1864.—*Cong. Record*, 47th Cong., sp. sess., pp. 93-94. Cf. Wirt A. Cate, *Lucius Q. C. Lamar*, p. 383, henceforth cited as Cate.

Division of the West, embracing the two departments of Generals Hood and Taylor.[100] In furtherance of plans agreed upon with these and other officers, great rallies were held in which the President made impassioned appeals to the people and endeavored to inspire them with his own iron determination. At Macon[101] he replied to the charge that he had abandoned Georgia, saying that the "miserable man" that made such a charge was "a scoundrel" and "not the man to save the country." The pro-Brown press seized upon the President's words as having reference to Brown.[102] "But while Davis was firing the Georgia heart, Vice President Stephens . . . was doing what he could to break down the influence of the administration," aided "by Governor Brown, the fault-finder," [103] and others of like mind, and their newspapers continued to insist that the President had abandoned Georgia to save Virginia.[104]

On November 15, 1864, Sherman set fire to Atlanta and started on his march to the sea. The valuable stores at Macon and the public records of the capital were in danger. Beauregard ordered Taylor to bring troops from the department of Mississippi and Alabama and assume command of all forces in Georgia operating against Sherman. The Confederate administration sent all the guns and troops that could be spared from other points. Governor Brown "loaned" the militia to the Confederate general as he had done in the Atlanta campaign.[105] In compliance with a suggestion from

---

[100] Hay, *Hood's Tennessee Campaign*, p. 29.
[101] Dodd, *Davis*, p. 333.
[102] Cf. *Intelligencer*, Sept. 30, 1864, and *Weekly Chronicle and Sentinel*, Oct. 12, 1864.
[103] Dodd, *Davis*, p. 336.
[104] Cf. *Weekly Chronicle and Sentinel*, Oct. 12, 1864, and the *Intelligencer*, to which the *Constitutionalist* made reply, Sept. 30, 1864.
[105] *C. R.*, III, 675, 678, 688 *et seq.; ibid.*, II, 804-6, 808. Governor Vance was not very much impressed with Brown's "state troops." "Governor Brown is a *humbug* & can do nothing but get in the way," he wrote to D. L. Swain, president of the University of North Carolina.—Zebulon B. Vance Papers, Vol. V.

Toombs[106] he appealed on November 17 to the legislature to authorize him, with the least possible delay, to make a levy en masse of all the male population, with plenary powers to compel obedience. A joint resolution was immediately introduced to call out all able-bodied men, including members of the legislature.[107] Governor Brown then had a taste of what the President had so many times experienced from the Governor's opposition in impending crises. Linton Stephens, the Governor's bosom friend and fellow conspirator in all his schemes against the military measures of the Confederacy, arose in the lower house of the legislature and in an impassioned speech denounced the proposed resolutions as "monstrous," "tyrannical," and "dangerous to liberty." He wanted "no master . . . be he Abe Lincoln, Jeff Davis, or Joe Brown, or anybody else." [108] The resolution, amended to exempt members of the legislature, passed, and on November 19 the Governor issued a proclamation calling out all between sixteen and fifty-five with a few exceptions,[109] and even offered freedom to convicts who should assist in repelling the invader.[110] Organization camps were established at various points, subsisted by the Confederate government.[111]

Naturally Brown's "citizen army" thus suddenly called to the field could be of little value, since before the men could be organized and armed Sherman had swept through the state, fortunately passing Macon by, and on December 10 had begun the siege of Savannah which ended with the surrender of the city eleven days later. On December 19 the Governor furloughed "until further orders" the men in the camps who had not been organized. Those whose organiza-

---

[106] *C. R.*, III, 673.
[107] *Ibid.*, II, 790-91; *H. J., 1864*, p. 122; *S. J., 1864*, p. 78.
[108] Waddell, pp. 287-88.
[109] *C. R.*, II, 799-802; *Acts of the General Assembly, 1864*, pp. 19-20. Linton Stephens voted for the amendment to exempt members of the legislature.—*H. J., 1864*, pp. 128-29. The Governor "invited" the members to report.
[110] Avery, p. 317.
[111] *C. R.*, II, 805.

## LOCAL DEFENSE

tions had been completed were ordered to perform police duty in their respective communities on Friday and Saturday of each week.[112] The levy en masse had turned out to be far less dangerous to liberty than Linton Stephens had feared.

Wheeler's cavalry, Cobb's reserves, and Brown's "troops of war" under General Smith—reassembled after their thirty-days' furlough[113]—valiantly attempted to hinder Sherman's progress but without success.[114] As Sherman's army approached Milledgeville the legislature disbanded and with the executive and judicial departments fled. It was at this time that the story originated with reference to the Governor's "cow and cabbages." [115] It was said that the Governor had fled to the "wire-grass region" of the state, but this was evidently a fabrication of his enemies.[116]

Meanwhile the fortunes of the Confederacy were becoming daily more desperate. Hood's army had been shattered in Tennessee and nothing stood between Sherman and South Carolina and his ultimate junction with Grant in Virginia. On January 11, 1865, the President telegraphed in cipher

---

[112] *Ibid.*, pp. 814-16.
[113] *Ibid.*, p. 774.
[114] Avery, p. 306; Pollard, *Davis*, p. 391.
[115] *Infra*, Chap. X, n. 2.
[116] See letter of Julius Brown, son of the Governor, to the Secretary of War, U. S. A., Apr. 18, 1903, Confederate Archives, Adjutant General's Office, War Dept., Washington. A facetious account of Brown's "army" is given by Gen. Richard Taylor, *Destruction and Reconstruction*, pp. 211 *et seq.* He also relates how with the aid of Toombs its members became "unconstitutional patriots." Troops were needed in S. C. to protect the railroad connecting Savannah and Charleston. Taylor wished to use Brown's "army" which under Taylor's orders had already been sent to Savannah by a roundabout route by railroad to avoid Sherman's army, but the Governor's aversion to having the troops leave the state was an obstacle. Taylor and Toombs accordingly had the cars bearing the men shunted off on a switch and the next morning the men awoke in S. C. just in time to repulse the enemy in the battle of Honey Hill and save the railroad.—*Ibid.*, p. 215. Cf. Brown's report to the legislature, *C. R.*, II, 820; Brown to Gen. R. C. Tyler, *Southern Watchman*, Jan. 18, 1865. Governor Brown's friends denied that he had objected to the troops' leaving the state in the instance referred to.—See Gen. Ira R. Foster's statement, made Jan. 30, 1880, in Fielder, pp. 313-17.

to General Hardee in Charleston to use every effort to obtain men from Georgia, adding, "If your relations to Governor Brown enable you to influence him, that is a means to be employed." To Governor McGrath of South Carolina he sent a similar message.[117] But the situation was urgent and the President, in response to appeals from South Carolina for assistance, telegraphed Brown himself, asking for men and suggesting that Brown and he "must look forward and leave discussions of the past to a more convenient season." The need for men was "not only immediate, but continuing," the President urged.[118] There is no evidence that Brown sent additional men to General Smith at Augusta, as the President urged, but he did order some of the reserve militia to arrest deserters.[119]

On February 1, 1865, Sherman left Savannah, and Beauregard, evidently expecting Augusta to be attacked, telegraphed Governor Brown to send to General Smith all the forces that could possibly be put into the field as "the crisis is again upon your State."[120] Two weeks later Columbia, South Carolina, was burned, the evacuation of Charleston was forced, and Sherman moved northward to join Grant. On February 24 Brown notified Beauregard that he was withdrawing the state troops in order that they might have a furlough "till the State is again threatened by the enemy."[121] Johnston's diminished forces—the remnant of the Army of Tennessee—were contending with Sherman's army in the Carolinas, but the Georgia state troops were safe at home.

In March the Confederate government ordered the detailed agriculturalists out, whereupon Governor Brown issued a countermanding order to the effect that they were a part

---

[117] Rowland, VI, 447, 451.
[118] *Ibid.*, pp. 448; *C. R.*, III, 704-5.
[119] *O. R.*, Ser. I, Vol. XLVIII, Pt. II, p. 168.
[120] *C. R.*, III, 706.
[121] *Ibid.*, p. 707; Jones, *Diary*, II, 428.

## LOCAL DEFENSE 193

of the state troops now on furlough and that they were not to obey any order from a Confederate officer until disbanded by the state.[122] At the moment the siege of Petersburg was nearing an end, the arsenal at Fayetteville, North Carolina, had been captured, and Wilmington had fallen. On the west of Georgia, Wilson's Union cavalry was preparing the raid which within a month and three days was to result in the capture of Selma and Montgomery, Alabama, West Point and Columbus, Georgia, and yet Brown's troops, including the Confederate details, were on furlough.

Shortly after the surrender of Mobile, Brown ordered out the state troops to defend Columbus, the call including all able to bear arms, "whether they belong to the State or Confederate service," [123] but they were too late. Before Brown's citizen army could mobilize—in fact, the next day, April 16, after the call—Columbus was captured and the battle of West Point was fought. These were the last engagements east of the Mississippi. Lee had already surrendered. On April 26 the Army of Tennessee surrendered to Sherman and on May 4 General Richard Taylor surrendered to General Canby the department of Alabama and Mississippi.[124]

On May 3 General James H. Wilson from his headquarters at Macon, Georgia, "requested" the surrender of Brown's troops,[125] and this time there was no defiance on the part of Georgia's governor. It had required the power of the United States government to obtain possession of Brown's "troops of war."

[122] *O. R.*, Ser. IV, Vol. III, pp. 1137-38; *C. R.*, III, 709.
[123] *Ibid.*, p. 712.
[124] Price, Buckner, Trent, from trans-Mississippi, surrendered to Canby at New Orleans, June 2.
[125] *C. R.*, III, 715-22.

## CHAPTER VIII

## HABEAS CORPUS: SECOND MAJOR ASSAULT ON THE RICHMOND GOVERNMENT

THE OPPOSITION to suspension of the writ of habeas corpus was even more disastrous to the Confederate cause than was the conscription controversy. Its heaviest fire came in 1864 when the cumulative effect of criticisms had aroused suspicion and doubts of the government's intentions and when military disasters and skillfully directed peace propaganda[1] had created discontent. While the suspension of the writ met with opposition in practically all the states of the Confederacy[2] it was in Georgia that the opposition was so well organized and so ruthlessly directed as to lead many contemporaries and later historians to question the loyalty of its leaders, if not openly to declare them traitors. Although Governor Brown had been in the forefront of conscription opposition, it was Vice President Stephens who gave leadership to the forces opposing the suspension of the writ of habeas corpus.[3] He was, however, soon joined by the Governor.

Martial law and the suspension of the writ[4] were used with great caution in the South[5] and in no instance did President

---

[1] *Infra,* Chap. IX.
[2] For similar opposition in the North, see Rhodes, III, 486; *ibid.,* IV, 164 *et seq.,* 229, 250 *et seq.,* 417; Schwab, p. 190; Moore, p. 121 *et seq.*
[3] For Stephens' sentiments and activities during the summer of 1862, see Johnston and Browne, pp. 418, 420, 421.
[4] There was confusion in the South as in the North as to the relation between the two.—Owsley, *State Rights,* pp. 169-71.
[5] With reference to its use North and South, cf. Rhodes, V, 471; Owsley, *State Rights,* p. 202.

## HABEAS CORPUS

Davis exercise the power without authority from Congress. Three laws provided limited periods for the suspension of the writ,[6] the aggregate time of suspension amounting to one year, five months, and two days, or less than half of the war's duration.[7] The President did not suspend the writ in Georgia in 1862, but General Bragg declared martial law in Atlanta in August of that year on his own initiative[8] and appointed the mayor as civil governor. Stephens declared that Bragg had no more authority to make the appointment than had a streetwalker,[9] and immediately began a correspondence with Governor Brown regarding the matter. On September 1 Brown wrote in reply that he was gratified to know they felt alike on the subject. He would have called the proceeding into question at once, but he was fearful, since no other

---

[6] Feb. 27, 1862, amended Apr. 19; Oct. 13, 1862; Feb. 15, 1864.—*Journal of C. S. A.*, II, 28, 29, 179, 197, 220, 475, 481; *ibid.*, III, 684, 712, 722, 796. It was upon the law of 1864 that the Stephens-Brown attack was made in force.

[7] Rhodes, V, 471.

[8] *Southern Confederacy*, Aug. 20, 1862. Cf. *Messages and Papers*, I, 219-27; Jones, *Diary*, I, 113, 115, 116, 120.

[9] For Stephens' constitutional arguments against martial law and the suspension of the habeas corpus, cf. *War between the States*, II, Appendix Q; Cleveland, pp. 747-49; Johnston and Browne, pp. 421-23. For the history of martial law in America and the manner in which it operates, see Randall, pp. 142-43, 146, 153-54. Stephens held that "in this country there is no such thing as martial law and cannot be until the Constitution is set aside." With reference to the suspension of the privilege of the writ of habeas corpus, he agreed that Congress had the right under certain circumstances to suspend the privilege, but that this power was limited by the Bill of Rights in the Constitution, and therefore no arrest could be made without a warrant issued by the courts upon probable cause and supported by oath for an offense recognized by existing law. He seems to argue that the prisoner is entitled to a preliminary hearing, and to a "speedy trial by jury."—Cf. Stephens' address to the legislature, Mar. 16, 1864, Cleveland, pp. 761-66; *Tri-Weekly Constitutionalist*, May 1, 1864; Linton Stephens' resolutions, *O. R.*, Ser. IV, Vol. III, pp. 234-35; editorial in *Republican*, Apr. 12, 1864; Senator Johnson to Stephens, Mar. 4, 1864, Flippin, p. 247.

On this subject Randall (p. 153) says that suspension of the privilege allows summary arrest, permits detention without judicial hearing to show cause, and without indictment on the basis of an offense recognized by the civil law. Prisoners are merely held till the emergency is over, when they are either released or tried in the civil courts. In the meantime the writ may still issue on petition, but there is no compulsion to obey its mandate.

governor had raised the question, of being considered "too refractory for the times." [9a] The Governor had conveniently forgotten that in the preceding March he was favorable to General Lee's suggestion of martial law for Augusta and Savannah.[10]

In his message to the legislature Brown referred to Bragg's order as "high-handed usurpation," tending "to the subversion of the government and the sovereignty of the State." He took the same position as Stephens regarding the lack of authority in Congress to proclaim martial law and the privileges that belonged to arrested persons even when the privilege of habeas corpus was suspended.[11] Linton Stephens was convinced that Davis and Lincoln were vying with each other in "usurpations and tyrannies," while their "emissaries and bribed journals" prepared the "sickened and weary hearts of the people for the *coup d'etat*." [12] Toombs, too, was sure that "Davis and his Jannissaries" were availing themselves of the public danger to aid them in their "selfish and infamous schemes." [13]

The furor created in Georgia caused the War Department to repudiate Bragg's order and issue instructions forbidding military commanders to proclaim martial law or suspend the writ without authority from the President.[14] Administration forces in Congress were unable to obtain an extension of the law and it expired by limitation on February 13, 1863, although the necessity continued, particularly with the rise in that year of the so-called "peace societies." [15]

When Grant and Sherman were making preparations for

---

[9a] *Phillips, Correspondence*, p. 605.
[10] *C. R.*, III, 210.
[11] *Ibid.*, II, 305-7.   [12] Waddell, pp. 257-59.
[13] Phillips, *Correspondence*, p. 601.
[14] *Southern Confederacy*, Sept. 24, 1862. Cf. General Orders Nos. 42, 56, 66, *O. R.*, Ser. IV, Vol. I, p. 1149; *ibid.*, II, 39, 83.
[15] Jones, *Diary*, II, 95; *O. R.*, Ser. IV, Vol. III, pp. 393-98. Cf. Stephens' fear of a dictator and of another suspension of the writ, Cleveland, pp. 172-74, 175-77; Johnston and Browne, p. 453.

## HABEAS CORPUS

their great offensives in Virginia and Georgia, President Davis again urged the suspension of the writ of habeas corpus. He anticipated that the law repealing substitution would be tested in the courts and thought that if a single judge declared the repeal to be unconstitutional that judge "would be besieged with applications for the writ and conscripts would be discharged." [16] On February 15, 1864, Congress suspended the writ for the period of three months after the meeting of the next Congress, but in deference to the opposition limited it to specified offenses and in other ways safeguarded civil liberty.[17] Brown was in the midst of his quarrels with, or criticisms of, the administration over conscription, exemptions, the appointment of officers, impressment, and the tithe when the law was passed, and his opposition to the Confederacy, in combination with the Stephens brothers, henceforth became truly formidable. A deeper motive actuated the men than mere opposition to measures, as subsequent events proved.

In his message recommending the suspension of the writ the President said that "conventions were advocated with the real design of accomplishing treason under the form of law." The reference was to peace propaganda advocating state conventions for the purpose of proposing amendments to the constitution. The Confederate constitution provided that upon the demand of three state conventions Congress should summon a convention of all the states to consider the proposals.[18] Ostensibly the purpose of those advocating state conventions was to propose amendments to strengthen the government in the prosecution of the war. In reality the plan was either to carry measures through the convention by

---

[16] For other reasons for the suspension at this time see *Messages and Papers*, I, 395-400. One of the judges who used the writ to discharge conscripts was O. A. Lochrane, an appointee of Governor Brown.—Avery, pp. 456-57.

[17] *Journal of C. S. A.*, IV, 207; Jones, *Diary*, II, 152-53.

[18] Article V, section 1. A copy of the Confederate constitution compared in parallel columns with that of the U. S. may be found in Davis, *Rise and Fall*, I, pp. 648-75.

which President Davis would be set aside, or, by the secession of one or more states from the Confederacy, to start a movement which would force the administration to make peace.[19] It was charged by those behind the movement that the President was opposed to peace. The events that followed cannot be understood without an examination of the previous conduct of the Vice President.

Stephens' antagonism to the central government and his utopian peace proposals began early. Whether he was a "Union man at heart," as a biographer who knew him well asserts,[20] or whether his opposition to the administration was based upon personal pique and thwarted ambition because of his failure to become "the brains of the Confederacy" [21] is not easy to determine. But he early became the "apostle of discontent," the "wet nurse" of the Georgia group, to which state "all the great malcontents seemed to have gravitated." [22] He claimed to have no personal feeling of antago-

---

[19] Governor Vance seemed fearful of the possibility of "separate state action" on Dec. 30, 1863, at which time he wrote to Governor Brown on the subject. His letter is not available but Governor Brown's reply of Jan. 16, 1864, may be found in the Zebulon B. Vance Papers, III, 396. A year later, Jan. 18, 1865, Vance wrote a similar letter to Brown.—*C. R.*, III, 702-4. See *infra*, pp. 229 *et seq.*

[20] Henry W. Cleveland, to Jefferson Davis, Rowland, X, 6. Cf. Tatum, p. 4.

[21] Cleveland, in Rowland, X, 6-10. Cf. Stephens' statement of what he would do if he should become President.—Johnston and Browne, pp. 447-48. After having thought the matter over Stephens seems to have been terrified at the thought that he might have to assume such responsibilities.—*Ibid.*, p. 449. Capers (p. 331) makes the statement that there was a "respectable minority" in Congress in 1861 that thought the capital should remain in Montgomery with the Vice President in charge of the civil government while the President assumed control of the armies with headquarters in Richmond. The author has been unable to substantiate this statement. Capers was chief clerk and disbursing officer of the Treasury in the provisional government, and he should have known the sentiment on the subject. If he is correct, the fact may go far to explain Stephens' disappointment.

[22] Owsley, *State Rights*, p. 184; Edward Chase Kirkland, *The Peacemakers of 1864*, pp. 208-10, henceforth cited as Kirkland.

HABEAS CORPUS 199

nism toward the President,[23] but his correspondence and his actions do not support the claim.[24]

As early as January, 1863, Stephens was discussing the possibilities of peace,[25] and after the battle of Chancellorsville he proposed a plan—which evidently did not deceive President Davis—by which, under the plea of a renewal of the cartel for the exchange of prisoners, a proposition might be made to the Lincoln government for peace on the basis of the "sovereignty of the States, and the right of each in its sovereign capacity to determine its own destiny."[26] Whatever Stephens' academic or doctrinaire views, President Davis was a realist, and he told Stephens that diplomacy and arms must act in conjunction and that a peace commissioner ought to go "with a victorious and threatening army." President Davis permitted Stephens to make the effort in 1863, when Lee invaded Pennsylvania, but he so arranged his instructions as to prevent his compromising the Confederacy.[27]

Giving the excuse that the climate of Richmond did not

---

[23] *O. R.*, Ser. IV, Vol. III, pp. 279-80; Cleveland, pp. 786-90.
[24] Cf. opinion of his close friend, Senator Johnson, in Flippin, pp. 253-54; *O. R.*, Ser. IV, Vol. III, pp. 278-81; Cleveland, pp. 790-95; Rowland, X, 171.
[25] Pendleton, pp. 307-8.
[26] *Messages and Papers*, I, 339-41; Stephens, *War between the States*, II, 558-62; Cleveland, p. 170. Another of Stephens' visionary peace plans he made known to Cobb with the request that he present it to President Davis. He proposed that all Federal prisoners be released unconditionally and supplied with a copy of an address to be made by the President to the effect that the South was not fighting against the Union but for the principles upon which the Union was based. He thought the address would be "read and pondered by thousands" and would affect the presidential election of 1864, since it would produce "momentous results among the friends of Constitutional Liberty." Each released prisoner would thus become a diplomat. Cobb pointed out the danger to Confederate prisoners if the Southern government retained none for retaliatory purposes.—Stephens, *War between the States*, II, 517 et seq.
[27] *Messages and Papers*, I, 341-43; Stephens, *War between the States*, II, 563-67; Kirkland, p. 210; Cleveland, p. 171; Rowland, V, 515-19.

agree with him, Stephens remained in Georgia nearly two years and carried on warfare against the Confederate administration.[28] His close friend, Senator Johnson, pointed out to him in vain the danger to his reputation and to the fortunes of the Confederacy in his remaining away from his post of duty.[29] It seems evident that Stephens' motive in remaining in Georgia was to prepare the ground for, and to take part in, the great offensive against the Confederate administration which culminated in the special session of the legislature in March, 1864. That Stephens was the moving force in the scheme and Brown the "understudy," [30] there seems little doubt.

The technique of the conspirators involved a long and careful preparation in which, through voluminous correspondence and numerous conferences, the control of certain newspapers was assured and the support of various leaders of public opinion was sought. There was to be a special session of the legislature preceded by a careful rehearsal of the parts of the various actors. The Governor was to open the assault. Linton Stephens was to offer resolutions opposing the suspension of the writ of habeas corpus and proposing a peace plan, and Alexander Stephens was to follow with his endorsement. The whole was to be broadcast using state and private funds. The plan worked out with precision except for two flaws that were fatal to its full consummation—certain leaders of public opinion refused to countenance the

---

[28] See *supra,* Chaps. V and VI. One of Stephens' friends has this to say of his ill health: "Mr. Stephens had the advantage which physical weakness recognizes, and he always could retire himself out of difficulties by falling back 'on the state of his health'."—Felton, p. 23.

[29] Flippin, pp. 231, 249, 250-51. Cf. Johnson's letter to Judge Cochran on the danger of building up an opposition party.—*Ibid.,* pp. 233-34.

[30] Owsley, *State Rights,* p. 185. Newspapers held that Brown was the tool of "far shrewder men" with whom to rule or ruin was the great maxim of life.—Moore, p. 271. The statement is borne out by the correspondence which passed between Stephens and Brown and between Stephens and some who did not favor the scheme.

## HABEAS CORPUS

scheme and the legislature was not as tractable as had been anticipated.

Just when the plan was determined upon there is no way of knowing, but that it was well advanced before the laws were passed by Congress in February, 1864, to which the participants pretended to object, is evident from available correspondence. On November 29, 1863, Senator Johnson in commenting upon his recent visit to Georgia said: "I am glad I went. . . . It was too plain, that a purpose existed to inaugurate open hostility to the President. Differing as I do from the President in several particulars, yet I am satisfied that a warfare on his administration will be disastrous. It will discourage the army; divide the people at home and weaken the energies of the country. . . ."[31]

On January 4, 1864, Brown wrote to Stephens: "I expect . . . to get home next Saturday night and will be glad to get your letter and views on the question alluded to in your letter. I would be obliged if you would mark all your letters private across the seal of the envelope, as I often have to leave my mails to be opened by secretaries and prefer that your letters should always be handed to me to open."[32] On January 28 the Governor mentioned having received two letters from Stephens and thanked him for suggestions. He stated that he had not yet written a line of his message but expected to begin soon. He hoped "to be able to do some good by proper state action."[33] The letter is significant as showing the preparation that was being made so far in advance of the meeting of the legislature on March 10, the call for which was not issued until February 27. In all probability the public was not yet aware that a special session was contemplated. Even earlier, Brown had written Governor Vance that it was quite probable he would be "under the necessity

---

[31] Flippin, p. 249.
[32] Phillips, *Correspondence*, p. 631.
[33] *Ibid.*, p. 633.

of convening the legislature . . . in extra session early in the spring." ³⁴ On February 13 the Governor wrote to Stephens: "I will be obliged if . . . you will set a day and meet me at Linton's at Sparta where we can compare notes, etc., on the subject of which we have lately corresponded. I am anxious to have the benefit of your suggestions upon the communication in the shape in which I will soon have it. . . . I wish to call the legislature together in the early part of March and I wish to act with caution and prudence." ³⁵

On February 15 Congress suspended the writ of habeas corpus and five days later Brown wrote to Stephens: "The great wrong which you anticipated has been done by Congress and I confess I contemplate with horror the suspension of the habeas corpus. Every state in the Confederacy should denounce and condemn the wicked act." He promised to meet Stephens at Linton's on Thursday.³⁶ On March 4 Brown thanked Stephens for the copy of the act abolishing the British Star Chamber which he promised should be printed as an appendix to his message. "I have re-written the article on habeas corpus for the message since we parted and have I think made it stronger," he wrote. He suggested that Stephens endeavor to secure the aid of Senator Hill who had voted against the measure, but admitted that he was doubtful of his success in doing so. Brown thought the timidity of the members of the legislature was to be dreaded.³⁷

If further evidence were needed to establish Stephens' part in preparing the Governor's message it may be found in Stephens' own words on the subject: "I advised it from stem to stern and approve it. I don't mean the language, but the policy and the course taken. . . ." ³⁸ It seems equally well established that Stephens assisted his brother in preparing the peace and habeas corpus resolutions, notwithstanding

---

³⁴ Unpublished letter, dated Jan. 16, 1864, Zebulon B. Vance Papers, III, 396.
³⁵ Phillips, *Correspondence*, p. 633.   ³⁶ *Ibid.*, p. 633.   ³⁷ *Ibid.*, p. 634.
³⁸ Letter to Senator Johnson, Apr. 8, 1864, *O. R.*, Ser. IV, Vol. III, p. 281.

HABEAS CORPUS 203

the statement of one of his biographers to the contrary[39] and that of Stephens himself, in his *War between the States*.[40] While the anti-administration party in Georgia—the "anarchists," as they were called[41]—plotted to bring Confederate measures into disrepute, Senator Hill of the "monarchist" group,[42] with Howell Cobb and L. Q. C. Lamar of Mississippi,[43] was in Georgia for the purpose of encouraging the people in support of the war and of neutralizing the efforts of the Brown-Stephens group. Hill spoke at LaGrange on March 1 on the value of the measures recently adopted by Congress. On the suspension of the writ he said that

[39] Cleveland (pp. 183-84, 189) says, "They were drawn up and presented by the Honorable Linton Stephens . . . without any consultation with his more widely known brother."

[40] II, 531. Stephens says he had nothing to do with drawing up the resolutions but that he thoroughly approved of them. But on Apr. 8, 1864, Stephens wrote Senator Johnson, taking responsibility for both sets of resolutions and saying that they were prepared by Linton "after full consultation."—*O. R.*, Ser. IV, Vol. III, p. 279. It seems likely that the latter statement is correct, since the letter was written within three weeks after the adoption of the resolutions by the legislature, while several years had elapsed before the publication of Stephens' book. Nor is it reasonable to suppose that so important a part of a program which had been so carefully prepared by the three men would have been omitted from the various discussions and correspondence which preceded the special session. It is difficult to believe, for instance, that when the three men met at Linton Stephens' home in February the resolutions and their place in the program were not thoroughly discussed. A further reason is the fact of the close intimacy between the brothers and their regular and frequent exchange of letters in which they made known to each other seemingly their every thought. Again, both were in Milledgeville when the legislature met on March 10—Alexander Stephens probably as the guest of the Governor. See Brown's invitation, Mar. 4, Phillips, *Correspondence*, p. 634.

[41] Coulter, *Georgia*, p. 308.

[42] The term was applied by the "anarchists" to supporters of the administration. It would seem that Senator Johnson might with propriety be placed with the "monarchists," since, though he often differed with the administration on policy, he was loyal to it and had no sympathy with the "Wigfalls, and Toombs and Browns," whose course in his judgment "did great injury to our cause, which was calculated to destroy the confidence of the people in the government, and lead to counter-revolution."—"Autobiography," *American Historical Review*, XXX (Jan., 1925), 332. Johnson's friendship for Alexander Stephens probably accounts for his omitting the names of the Stephens brothers.

[43] Cate, pp. 108-10.

while he did not vote for the bill, he felt that the President would use the power wisely. It did not authorize illegal arrest, it created no star chamber court, and it gave license to no *lettres de cachet*, as its enemies claimed. He said that good men need not fear it, but spies would do well to depart and traitors would do equally well to keep silent.[44] In view of Hill's speech, the possibility of securing his assistance in passing the proposed resolutions condemnatory of the habeas corpus act did not look promising; nevertheless Stephens made the effort. Hill refused, but wrote a conciliatory letter on March 14 which a recent writer thinks was intended to appeal to Stephens' well-known vanity and to soften his antagonism to the administration.[45]

Stephens was no more successful in winning Senator Johnson to his scheme. Indeed, the correspondence was characterized by stinging rebukes from Johnson. He said he had not voted for the suspension of the writ, but he thought little harm would grow out of it and he admitted that Richmond was full of spies and traitors.[46] Five days later Johnson wrote: "I will not participate in denouncing Congress and

---

[44] *Chronicle and Sentinel*, March 23, 1864.

[45] Pearce, pp. 90-94. Stephens had asked Hill's opinion of the Governor's message, delivered four days earlier. Hill pointed out in what particulars he agreed or differed from it. For the part of the message on the causes of the war Hill knew Stephens was responsible—"the footprints are *too plain* not to be recognized." Hill saw Stephens' work also in the part devoted to the habeas corpus. He agreed that civilians should not be subject to the military, but "to a certain extent and for proper cases," he thought the public safety *did* demand the suspension of the writ. "But in all this," he added, "I think you will find that Mr. Davis will agree with us. Should this be so we ought not to denounce him in advance." He and Stephens differed, Hill said, in that he had confidence in the President and feared an issue would weaken the Confederacy. On the question of making peace, he thought intercourse with Lincoln ought to be held only under the rules of war and as an enemy. He "utterly and entirely" disagreed with the part of the message relating to finance, secret sessions, etc., and regretted that the Governor had made an issue which was so unjust to the motives of Congress and unsustained by facts. He thought it "horrible that such a lame beginning and such a sublime ending should constitute the same message."—Phillips, *Correspondence*, pp. 634-37.

[46] Mar. 4, Flippin, p. 247.

the President, because my views do not prevail.... If the war cannot be conducted on my plan ... I will fight the war according to the President's plan and policy.... This may be an error, be it so, it is an honest error and accords best with my views of patriotic duty and sound statesmanship." [47] Stephens had said that if the administration would not voluntarily retire "they ought to be made to retire." Johnson dissented from such a course as "wrong in principle & dangerous in policy." He knew of but one constitutional mode of making the administration retire and that was by impeaching the President. He was "unaware that he has done anything that would sustain that process." [48] On the day on which Brown delivered his message Johnson wrote to Stephens: "But for my life, I can see no good to come from a wholesale abuse of Congress and Davis. It will but weaken us greatly.... The assaults are mainly levelled at [the President].... He is the President by choice of the people. He has four years yet to hold office. Hence, we must succeed or fall under his lead. Or else, he must be deposed. ... Are you prepared for that movement? ... It means blood and carnage and anarchy or despotism.... Is it the best mode to resist the enemy, to destroy popular confidence in those, to whom the people have confided this great struggle?" [49]

While the struggle over Linton Stephens' peace and habeas corpus resolutions was at its height Johnson wrote again, lamenting that Stephens as vice president should avow his hostility and advise the legislature to array the states against the government. "Nothing has yet occurred which fills me with so much gloom and sadness," he said. He had expected rashness from Toombs and Brown, but not from Stephens. "Think of our situation," he pleaded. "We are on the eve of decisive and doubtful battles with the enemy.

---

[47] "Autobiography," *American Historical Review*, XXX (Jan., 1925), 333-34.
[48] *Ibid.;* Flippin, pp. 251-52.     [49] *Ibid.*, pp. 252-53.

... It must result in disaster; it can do nothing else. It will wind up the revolution in disgrace & subjugation." [50]

On March 10, 1864, the special session of the legislature met and listened to the Governor's message. He combined fervor for the Southern cause with criticisms of the government, which, whether or not so intended, could not fail to weaken that cause with the people. Neither the one side nor the other could wholly condemn or wholly endorse the message—which was perhaps exactly what was intended. After dealing with the problems of relief for soldiers' families, cotton planting, illegal distilleries, and the currency,[51] the remainder of the message was devoted to the new conscript law,[52] to conflict with the Confederate government, the suspension of the writ of habeas corpus, causes of the war, and how peace should be sought.[53]

On the question of conflict with Confederate authorities the Governor enlarged upon the theme of state sovereignty and affirmed his intention to continue to repel all encroachments of the central government. He expressed "deep mortification" at the action of Congress "in attempting to suspend the writ . . . and confer upon the President powers expressly denied to him by the Constitution" under a "pretext of *necessity*," which he denied existed, and "at the *request* of the Executive." The power to suspend the writ was an implied power and as such must in its exercise yield to the express restrictions found in the Bill of Rights. It was an attempt to revive the odious practice of issuing *lettres de cachet*. He was aware of no instance in British history since 1689 where the king had ordered the arrest of any person in civil life but by judicial warrant, or where he had attempted to suspend the privilege of the writ. To attempt such a thing in 1864 "would cost the present reigning

---

[50] Mar. 19, *ibid.*, p. 253.  [51] *Supra*, p. 142.
[52] *Supra*, pp. 91, 181.
[53] *C. R.*, II, 587-655; *H. J., 1864*, pp. 5-52. Cf. Avery, pp. 268 *et seq.;* Fielder, pp. 281-306.

Queen no less price than her crown." The law of Congress he designated as "an Act to authorize the President to make *illegal and unconstitutional arrests*." Under it any citizen at any moment might be dragged from his home "at midnight by armed force" and "imprisoned at the will of the President" or "examined in the Confederate Star Chamber." When such "bold strides towards military despotism . . . are taken . . . it is the duty of every patriotic citizen to sound the alarm, and of State Legislatures to say in thunder tones . . . that there is a point beyond which freemen will not permit encroachments to go." Independence from the Northern states was of little value if constitutional liberty were lost at home.[54]

The discussion of the causes and conduct of the war led naturally into the question of peace, and the Governor expressed the opinion that the war could not be terminated by force of arms, but must be brought to an end through negotiation. He said that the Northern people had not been permitted to know that on two occasions the South had sought peace,[55] and he thought it was the duty of the Confederate government to keep before the civilized world the fact that the Southern people were willing at any time to make peace whenever the enemy was ready to recognize "the great fundamental principles of the Declaration of Independence, . . ." After each important victory the Confederate government should "make a distinct proposition to the Northern Government for peace upon these terms." If the proposition were declined, let the fact be published in the newspapers, that the Northern people might know it and "hurl from power those who deny the fundamental principles upon which their own liberties rest." He would not stand on the "delicate point of etiquette or diplomatic ceremony," but would make the proposition again and again.[56] This

---
[54] *C. R.*, II, 610-19.
[55] Through commissioners at the beginning of the war and through Stephens' efforts in 1863.   [56] *C. R.*, II, 649-50.

plan he thought should be supplemented by a plebiscite in the Confederate and border slave states, with all armed force withdrawn. "Let both Governments adopt this mode of settlement . . . and the ballot box will soon achieve what the sword cannot accomplish. . . ." True, Lincoln had repudiated the plan in the beginning, but that was no reason why the proposition should not be renewed.[57]

Brown's opposition to the suspension of the writ of habeas corpus and his premature peace proposals must have been received by the enemy as evidence that the solidarity of the Confederacy was breaking. The question of peace was a function of the central government and its discussion by the governor of a "sovereign state" was, therefore, of the utmost significance. Sherman's peace proposals to Brown and Stephens[58] followed a few months later as a matter of course.

Avery states that the influence of the Governor "went out beyond state bounds" and that he was the "acknowledged leader and exponent of the large element of citizens in his way of thinking." [59] Toombs praised Brown's championship of "Southern liberty." [60] The press was divided,[61] though the majority attacked the Governor for criticizing the acts of Congress in the Confederacy's desperate situation and called him "disorganizer," "madman," "marplot." [62] The *Savannah News* feared the Governor's message would prove to be "one of the most dangerous fire-brands yet thrown into the Confederate camp," [63] and the *South Carolinian* predicted

---

[57] *Ibid.*, pp. 651-54.   [58] *Infra*, p. 224.

[59] P. 270. Brown told Stephens with evident satisfaction that his message had been published *"in extenso* in the Northern papers."—Phillips, *Correspondence,* p. 640.

[60] Avery, p. 272. Toombs favored the habeas corpus resolutions.—Phillips, *Correspondence,* pp. 637-39.

[61] The *Southern Confederacy,* Mar. 23, 1864, which approved of the message, published similar views from the *Memphis Appeal* (which was published in Ga.), *Chronicle and Sentinel, Intelligencer,* Milledgeville *Union.* The *Register* gave only qualified approval, and the *Constitutionalist,* though it agreed with the Governor, disapproved of a "vein of indignant temper running through the whole production."

[62] Avery, p. 272.   [63] Quoted by the *Macon Telegraph,* Mar. 17, 1864.

that a Hartford convention odium would attach to the Governor and his compatriots.[64] Commenting at length upon the Governor's message the *Richmond Examiner* said: "There are men unquiet, self-assertive, wrong headed, contentious and troublesome, to whom the plain beaten road of common sense, common feeling and common duty is odious; that are never content unless they are doing something that nobody else is doing—that nobody wants them to do—and we much fear that Governor Brown is one of this kind." [65]

The *Macon Telegraph* thought Brown was patriotic, but "constitutionally arbitrary," and "honestly but morbidly sensitive" on the subject of executive encroachments, while himself exercising greater powers than any previous executive of Georgia had ever exercised or claimed. It expressed the interesting opinion that "if he ever gets to be President . . . State rights will cease to be a favorite topic of his message." [66]

On the same day on which the Governor delivered his message Linton Stephens introduced his resolutions on the suspension of the habeas corpus[67] and on the subject of peace,[68]

---

[64] Quoted by the *Republican*, Mar. 15, 1864, cited by Moore, p. 272, n. 42.
[65] Quoted by the *Macon Telegraph*, Mar. 28, 1864.
[66] Mar. 28, 1864. Other newspapers in opposition to the Governor were the Savannah papers, the Macon papers, the *LaGrange Reporter*, the *Athens Watchman*, the *Marietta Advocate*, the *Columbus Times*.
[67] *H. J., 1864*, pp. 51-52. The habeas corpus resolutions—five in number—repeated the Governor's arguments as to the unconstitutionality of the act of Congress, declared the law "utterly void" and a "dangerous assault upon the constitutional powers of the courts, and upon the liberty of the people," and urged Georgia's representatives in Congress to work for its repeal. Constitutional liberty being the goal of the Confederate army and one of the great elements of its strength, according to the fifth article, faithful adherence to the principle "will inspire the people of the North with a desire and a determination" to put an end to a contest "waged by their government openly against *our* liberty, and as truly, but more covertly, against their own." The resolutions as amended and adopted may be found in *O. R.*, Ser. IV, Vol. III, pp. 234-35; Johnston and Browne, pp. 455-56; Cleveland, pp. 184-86; Stephens, *War between the States*, II, 788-90; Waddell, pp. 269-71. See *Weekly Chronicle and Sentinel*, Mar. 16, 1864.
[68] *H. J., 1864*, pp. 51-52. The peace resolutions, consisting of seven articles —eight as amended—gave the historic reasons for, and justification of, se-

and a few days later Alexander Stephens by invitation addressed the legislature supporting them. One of Stephens' biographers thinks the habeas corpus resolutions occupy the same position in the history of Georgia as the resolutions of 1798-99 occupy in the history of Virginia.[69] There is little doubt that Brown and the Stephens brothers felt that they were playing a great, historic role.

It was known in advance of the meeting of the legislature that an assault was to be made upon Confederate policies. Friends of the administration, of whom Howell Cobb, Benjamin H. Hill, A. H. Kenan, and L. Q. C. Lamar were the leaders, were on hand to neutralize the opposition by matching lobbies with it and by speaking in the evenings before the legislature as the Stephens-Brown forces were preparing to do.[70]

Alexander Stephens' address to the legislature on "The State of the Confederacy,"[71] was, according to a biographer, "one of the great efforts of his life."[72] Stephens described the Southern people as between Scylla and Charybdis—on the one hand perils from without, on the other perils from

---

cession and charged the war to the U. S. government. They recommended that the people "acting through their state organizations and popular assemblies" use their efforts to put an end to the conflict, and that the Confederate government, after each signal victory and on other occasions, whenever none could "impute its action to alarm," make an official offer of peace on the basis of the "principles of 1776." This procedure would "constantly weaken and ultimately break down" the enemy by showing the willingness of the South to make peace and by placing upon the U. S. government the responsibility for continuing the war. Such a course would "be regretted by nobody, . . . except men whose importance and whose gains would be diminished by peace, and men whose ambitious designs would need cover under the ever-recurring plea of the necessities of war." The resolutions as amended and adopted may be found in *O. R.*, Ser. IV, Vol. III, pp. 235-37; Johnston and Browne, pp. 457-59; Waddell, pp. 272-75; Cleveland, pp. 186-89; Stephens, *War between the States*, II, 532-36. Cf. Avery, p. 273; *Weekly Chronicle and Sentinel*, Mar. 16, 1864.

[69] Cleveland, p. 184; *H. J., 1864*, p. 68.
[70] Cate, pp. 108-10; *H. J., 1864*, pp. 57, 60, 69.
[71] The speech may be found in Cleveland, pp. 761-86, and in the *Tri-Weekly Constitutionalist*, May 1, 1864.
[72] Cleveland, p. 181.

## HABEAS CORPUS

within. The latter arose from questions of policy as to the best means of repelling the enemy, achieving independence, and keeping secure the people's rights and liberties. He admitted that conditions were serious but claimed they were not desperate or hopeless, since there was still subsistence for another year. "But how it will be next year, if the policy adopted by Congress, at its late session,[73] is carried out, no one can safely venture to say." He then launched into a review of those acts of Congress to which their attention had been called by the Governor. It was a painful duty to express disapproval, but he did it "in a spirit of friendship and good will." The tax and funding acts were "neither proper, wise, or just," and he suggested that the legislature follow the Governor's recommendations in these matters.[74] He asserted that conscription was not necessary and thought "brains must do something as well as muskets." It was for the legislature to say whether the forces lately conscripted[75] should be turned over to the Confederacy, but he warned that under the conscription law no one between the ages of seventeen and fifty could tan leather, make shoes, grind grain, shoe horses, or repair harness without "permission from the President." [76]

The suspension of the writ of habeas corpus, he asserted, was the important question. It was not only unwise, impolitic, and unconstitutional, but exceedingly dangerous to public liberty. He discussed the origin of the habeas corpus in England, compared the law of Congress to *lettres de cachet,* and in general employed the language of the Gov-

---

[73] Cleveland, p. 764. The reference was to the conscription act which Stephens and Brown contended would take so many men out of production as to end the war by starvation.

[74] *Ibid.,* p. 765. Stephens said little about the tax and currency questions, he later explained to Senator Johnson, "because money, at best, in my estimation, is but trash. Greater and more vital interests were in jeopardy."— O. R., Ser. IV, Vol. III, p. 281.

[75] Those between the ages of seventeen and eighteen, and between forty-five and fifty, conscripted for local defense by the law of Feb. 17, 1864.

[76] Cleveland, pp. 766, 782-83.

ernor's message and of his brother's resolutions. He said that he knew of no reasons of public safety that required the law, nor had he heard of any. He knew only that Congress "had attempted to do just what cannot be done—to authorize illegal and unconstitutional arrests." The gist of the law he claimed lay covered up in the fifth specification which applied to attempts to avoid military service. "Here," he said, "is a plain and indisputable attempt to deny every citizen . . . ordered into service, the right to have the question whether he is liable to military duty under the laws tried and adjudicated by the courts." To show how the law operated he read letters of harrowing experiences of men forced into conscription despite their age,[77] and asserted that the law gave to the President the power to arrest and imprison "every man, woman, and child in the Confederacy." He recommended that the legislature declare the act unconstitutional, in the meantime submitting the matter to the courts.[78] In closing he warned against two fatal delusions—a dictator and "that most insidious enemy which approaches with the syren song, 'independence first and liberty afterwards.' . . . Let [independence and liberty] ever be held and cherished as objects co-ordinate, co-existent, coequal, coeval and forever inseparable." [79]

A part of the press in and out of Georgia intimated very plainly that Stephens was a traitor.[80] The *Charleston Courier*

---

[77] *Ibid.*, pp. 770, 776, 778-79. See Tatum, p. 21, for a wild story told of the misuse of the law.

[78] Cleveland, pp. 782-85. No decision on the constitutionality of the suspension of the writ of habeas corpus was rendered by the supreme court of any Southern state.—Brummer, p. 129.

[79] Cleveland, pp. 785-86. Cf. Avery, p. 272; Johnston and Browne, p. 455; *Republican*, Mar. 21, 1864.

[80] The *Lynchburg Virginian* compared Stephens to Calhoun in opposition to President Jackson's proclamation and force bill.—Quoted by *Weekly Chronicle and Sentinel*, May 18, 1864. The *Raleigh Conservative*, supporter of the Vance element in North Carolina, characterized the speech as "breathing the most unwavering devotion to Southern independence."—*Ibid.* The *Southern Confederacy* and the *Chronicle and Sentinel* also defended him.

## HABEAS CORPUS 213

inquired whether the Vice President had "any constitutional objections against taking his seat in Richmond." [81] Senator Johnson expressed his opinion to Stephens in no uncertain terms. On April 6 he wrote: ". . . You are wrong in view of your official position; you are wrong because the whole movement originated in a mad purpose to make war on Davis and Congress;—You are wrong because the movement is joyous to the enemy, and they are already using it in their press." [82] Four days later he pointed out to Stephens that the army and its officers had confidence in President Davis and intimated how serious would be the consequence to Stephens personally and to the country if, through the death of Davis, Stephens should become President and because of his identification with the anti-administration group fail to secure the army's support.[83]

---

[81] Quoted by the *Chronicle and Sentinel*, May 18, 1864, which replied editorially. Brown also urged Stephens to go to Richmond but for a different reason. He thought his presence there would be valuable "while the policy of the new Congress is forming."—Phillips, *Correspondence*, pp. 642, 643. Stephens did not, however, go to Richmond for some time, but took up his residence in South Carolina.—Dodd, *Davis*, p. 337. He finally returned to his post of duty in Richmond late in the year and used his influence to prevent a bill renewing the suspension of the writ of habeas corpus from passing. He offered the editor of the *Richmond Whig* $200 to republish Taney's decision in the Merryman case (Johnston and Browne, p. 476), cast the deciding vote on a tie in December on an amendment to the bill to suspend the writ (*ibid.*, p. 477), and attempted to address the Senate. When by parliamentary tactics a vote on this privilege was prevented and his own previous ruling on a question was reversed in an appeal to the Senate (*Journal of the C. S. A.*, IV, 385-87), Stephens claimed this was an indignity and threatened to resign. Ultimately Senator Hunter arranged for Stephens to speak in a secret session on Jan. 6. See *infra*, p. 235. Cf. Johnston and Browne, p. 477; *War between the States*, II, 287-88.

[82] Flippin, pp. 253-54.

[83] *Ibid.*, p. 254. For other opinions of Stephens' conduct, cf. Pendleton, p. 307; Stephenson, pp. 172-74; Rhodes, V, 447-48. The charge that the Vice President was in open hostility to the President and was organizing a peace party created quite a scandal, and Stephens made an explanation to the Secretary of War. Cf. *War between the States*, II, 531; Cleveland, pp. 190-91, 786-90. For Stephens' rather lame excuse after the war, see *War between the States*, II, 537. Cf. letter to Senator Johnson, Cleveland, pp. 790-95. A recent historian thinks Stephens had "a witch doctor's nose for smelling out infractions of the constitution, . . . and caused the government more trouble

In the violent struggle in the legislature it was charged that the peace resolutions aimed to censure the President and to prepare the way for separate state action in negotiating peace. Both charges were denied by the Brown-Stephens group, nevertheless the legislature would not pass the resolutions in the form in which they were offered, and amendments failed to carry.[84] Opposition to the habeas corpus resolutions was even more bitter and determined. After a motion to table was lost in the house by a vote of forty-nine to eighty-eight, the resolutions were taken up seriatim and amended. A substitute motion was then offered and debated expressing confidence in the President in the use of the power and leaving the matter to the courts for decision. Linton Stephens opposed the amendment. Avery reports that he "uttered with nervous fire the memorable and ringing expression, 'I am for the cause and not for dynasties!'"[85]

Another subject upon which the legislature could not agree was the Governor's recommendation to withhold from the Confederate government men from seventeen to eighteen years of age and from forty-five to fifty whom the law of February 17 made liable to conscription.[86] Hopelessly deadlocked and bitterly angry, the legislature adopted a resolution to adjourn on the folowing Saturday, March 19. On the morning of that day it received a message from the Governor convening an extra session on Monday, March 21,

---

than all the traitors combined."—H. J. Eckenrode, *Jefferson Davis,* pp. 320-21. One of Stephens' biographers said in 1882, when Stephens was a candidate for governor, that he would not be elected, because "the old soldiers have not forgot 1861-5. . . ."—Wm. M. Browne to Davis, Rowland, IX, 175-76. Browne was mistaken—the Bourbon Democracy of that period (*infra,* Chap. XII, n. 1) put him over. The peculiar physical and mental make-up of the Stephens brothers may explain much in their conduct which would otherwise be puzzling.—Cf. Waddell, pp. 289-90, 292; Cleveland, p. 97 and note.

[84] *H. J., 1864,* pp. 51-52, 58, 97-98; news dispatch from Milledgeville, Mar. 18, *Weekly Chronicle and Sentinel,* Mar. 23, 1864; Cleveland, pp. 189, 792. Cf. Stephens, *War between the States,* II, 532.

[85] P. 272; *H. J., 1864,* pp. 51-52, 76, 91, 98-100, 102, 104-8, 116-19, 120.

[86] *Supra,* p. 91.

unless the peace and habeas corpus resolutions and the conscription law should be acted upon in the meantime.[87] The session was prolonged until midnight, action was taken on the three measures, and in addition a resolution was adopted unanimously expressing confidence in the President.[88] The habeas corpus resolutions, as amended, were passed by a majority of three in the lower house and eight in the Senate.[89] Friends of the administration succeeded in amending the peace resolutions by adding section eight, which pledged the resources of Georgia to the prosecution of the war until the independence of the Confederate States should be established, and thus practically destroyed the effect which their author had intended.[90]

Pro- and anti-administration forces had clashed in the press and in the halls of the legislature in lobbying for their respective sides.[91] A correspondent — supposedly Howell Cobb— writing under the pseudonym "Senex" in the *Republican* on March 26,[92] charged that the Governor lobbied

---

[87] *C. R.*, II, 673-76; *H. J., 1864*, pp. 60, 76, 106-8, 109-11, 116-18, 123.

[88] *Acts of the General Assembly, 1864*, p. 154; *Weekly Chronicle and Sentinel*, Mar. 23, 1864; Avery, p. 273. It seems that even up to the middle of June the Governor had not sent copies of the resolutions to Richmond, except those dealing with the conscript act, and it was said to be due to the inclusion of the resolution expressing undiminished confidence in the President. See Cleveland, pp. 790-95.

[89] *Acts of the General Assembly, 1864*, pp. 152-54; Avery, p. 272. Cf. *Weekly Chronicle and Sentinel*, Mar. 30, 1864. A protest, holding that the suspension of the civil authority was within the powers of Congress and that the courts should decide its constitutionality, was signed by 43 members.—*H. J., 1864*, pp. 118-19.

[90] *Acts of the General Assembly, 1864*, pp. 156-59; Johnston and Browne, p. 459; Cleveland, p. 189; Avery, p. 273. Cf. *Weekly Chronicle and Sentinel*, Mar. 23, 1864. Stephens claimed that he saw the amendment before it was introduced and had no objections to it; also that it was offered by one who was in favor of Linton's resolutions, and that it passed without a dissenting vote.—Cleveland, p. 792. This may well have been true, since without it the resolutions obviously would not have been adopted.

[91] Moore, pp. 272-73; Avery, p. 272.

[92] Cobb wrote to the *Macon Telegraph* under the pseudonym "Troup," according to the *Chronicle and Sentinel*. See editorial on "Political Demagogary," June 1, 1864.

publicly and privately and that he sat in the houses while the resolutions were being discussed and voted upon. He further charged that on Friday before the vote was taken the Governor sold cotton cards to members of the legislature for $10 when they were not available to the public and were worth $40 to $60, and that he exchanged state for Confederate notes to the extent of $200 with each member of the legislature, dollar for dollar, when the former were worth twice as much as the latter. In this way, the correspondent said, Brown obtained the votes of thirty-six members, although two resigned before the vote was taken.[93]

That there was foundation for the charge is evident from Brown's letter to Stephens on April 5 in which he says he has sent Steele of the *Confederate Union* "a line of argument," suggested by Linton Stephens, with which to meet the charge.[94] The "line" evidently was to the effect that since the state constitution forbade members to increase their own compensation, the Governor had resorted to this method of enabling the members to meet the high cost of living, and that he had never at any time asked anyone more than $10 for cotton cards. In reply the *Republican* stated that no one could get cards, other than the Governor's favorites, unless in exchange for skins, and that, if the Governor's own explanation were true, he had violated the constitution "at a time when a cherished purpose was suspended by a hair." The *Republican* did not mince words—"He did it to get votes as he regarded everybody as purchasable." [95]

With his usual thoroughness Governor Brown set about the task of spreading propaganda. He sent copies of his message and of Linton Stephens' resolutions to the captain of each company in Georgia regiments in Confederate service and copies to the clerk of the court of every county in the Confederacy—at the expense of the taxpayers. Since Alex-

---
[93] Reported by Moore, p. 272, n. 43.
[94] Phillips, *Correspondence,* pp. 639-40.     [95] Apr. 8, 1864.

ander Stephens was not a member of the legislature, the printing and sending out of his speech must needs be paid for by private funds. The Governor accordingly arranged with the "Messrs. Wartzfielder" [96] to pay the $200 necessary for 1,500 copies while he himself, Jonas Thweatt, and Philip M. Russell, political boss of Chatham County and member of the legislature,[97] paid for an equal number. He sent a copy to the lieutenant of each company to whose captain he had sent his own message, so that "if the captain is against us and does not let the company have the one, the lieutenant may let them have the other." On the same principle he sent a copy to the sheriff of each county in the Confederacy, his message having gone to the clerks of the courts. The Waitzfelders did not wish their names known, "but they are ardently with us," Brown told Stephens.[98]

In view of his former popularity with Georgia soldiers, Brown's chagrin must have been great when some of the organizations reacted unfavorably to his propaganda and passed condemnatory resolutions, as did the Twenty-fourth Georgia Regiment, the Rose Dew Battery, and General George T. Anderson's Brigade.[99]

[96] Evidently Leopold and Solomon Waitzfelder, who were proprietors of the Milledgeville Manufacturing Co. They were trusted friends and agents of the Governor. See *C. R.*, II, 240, 879-81.

[97] Avery, pp. 33, 262, 351.

[98] Phillips, *Correspondence*, pp. 639-40, 640-41.

[99] The regiment viewed with "alarm and indignation" the untimely attempt of the governor of Georgia to cripple the legislation of Congress, condemned his recommendation in regard to peace, and declared that Congress was the "true exponent of the feelings of the people and the soldiery."—*Richmond Sentinel*, quoted by the *Republican*, Apr. 5, 1864. The Rose Dew Battery condemned the Governor's message and both sets of resolutions.—*Columbus Times*, Mar. 30, 1864. The most severe were the resolutions of the brigade. It condemned the Governor for calling a special session of the legislature for an "unhallowed purpose," for his willingness to sacrifice everything to "self-aggrandizement and personal ambition," and for "prostituting the dignity of high office to the accomplishment of unholy ends." The action of the legislature in following the Governor's recommendations it characterized as "unwise and unpatriotic" and intended "to subserve partisan interests."
[The resolutions are not available, the above being taken from the Gov-

Brown left nothing undone that would aid in carrying out his plans, whether it was a matter of securing newspaper support[100] or the appointment of judges who were "right" on the "great questions of the day." He offered a judgeship to Linton Stephens but was not displeased when he refused it. He thought Linton's services would be needed in the next session of the legislature when he expected the "Consolidationists" with Cobb as "high priest" to make a desperate effort to carry measures "favorable to their purpose." [101]

The passions aroused in the legislature were reflected in the press during the spring, summer, and fall,[102] and in the discussions of the participants. Howell Cobb was supposed to have denounced Brown as a traitor and expressed a willingness to go some distance to see him hung, and Ben Hill to have called both the Governor and Stephens traitors.[103]

The immediate effect of the agitation was to render null

---

ernor's reply of May 2, 1864, which may be found in the *Weekly Chronicle and Sentinel*, May 18, 1864; the *Daily Constitutionalist*, May 15, 1864; *C. R.*, III, 509-14; *O. R.*, Ser. IV, Vol. III, p. 374. Cf. references to soldiers' resolutions in Brown's letters to Stephens, in Phillips, *Correspondence*, pp. 640-42].

[100] See Brown's letter to Stephens with reference to purchasing stock in the *Constitutionalist*, Phillips, *Correspondence*, p. 644.

[101] Toombs was discussed for the judgeship. Brown promised to appoint whomever Stephens, Toombs, and Linton should agree upon. — *Ibid.*, pp. 642-43.

[102] The *Richmond Whig* felt that the peace resolutions showed "too much anxiety to proffer what was not wanted."—Quoted by the *Macon Telegraph*, Mar. 23, 1864. The *Republican* (Apr. 12, 1864) thought the Confederacy could win the war if not deprived of men by state and court interference. The *Constitutionalist* in an editorial, "Nil Desperandum," (May 15, 1864) thought the peace resolutions "rather absurd" but probably "harmless." The *Weekly Chronicle and Sentinel* carried a series of editorials favorable to the whole movement which expressed not only Stephens' sentiments but employed his style as well. It would be interesting to know whether they were written at "Liberty Hall." Cf. issues of Mar. 23, 30, May 18, June 1, 1864. Among other things the *Chronicle and Sentinel* charged that the government was in the hands of a "grasping Executive and a cringing Congress."—Quoted by the *Macon Telegraph*, Mar. 23, 1864. The editorials finally became so offensive that the government lost patience, withdrew its patronage, and threatened to arrest the editor.—See issue of June 22, 1864.

[103] Brown's letter to Stephens, in Phillips, *Correspondence*, p. 641.

## HABEAS CORPUS 219

the suspension of the writ of habeas corpus in Georgia,[104] and to influence the legislatures of Mississippi, Alabama, and North Carolina to make protest to Congress against the act,[105] as did the conference of governors at their meeting in Augusta.[106] It also caused a movement in Congress to repeal suspension. When that action failed[107] and the law expired on August 1, 1864, Congress refused to renew it despite the President's protest and the fact that the sieges of Petersburg and Atlanta were just beginning.[108] While a bill to renew suspension was being debated in the winter session of Congress, Governor Brown on February 15, 1865, added his voice to the opposition in a list of indictments against the Confederacy by saying: "Citizens who belong neither to the land nor naval forces of the Government . . . are arrested by provost guards and Government detectives, under charges of treason or other indictable offenses, or disloyalty, without warrants or other processes from the courts, and imprisoned at the pleasure of the Government in open disregard of the Constitution. . . . Good and loyal citizens . . . are arrested if they fail to carry passes, while Federal spies procure or force passes, and travel over our thoroughfares at their pleasure. . . ."[109]

[104] See report of J. L. M. Curry who had been appointed commissioner in connection with the execution of the act in that state, *O. R.*, Ser. I, Vol. LII, Pt. II, p. 648.
[105] *Journal of C. S. A.*, IV, 729; Avery, p. 272; Rhodes, V, 456.
[106] *C. R.*, II, 778-79.
[107] Because of the President's report on May 20 of the value of the law and his earnest admonition that "to repeal it would be perilous if not calamitous" (*Messages and Papers*, I, 452-53; *O. R.*, Ser. IV, Vol. III, pp. 429-30), no action was taken.
[108] See Owsley, *State Rights*, pp. 193-202, for conditions at this time. In a confidential message of Nov. 9, 1864, the President laid before Congress a report from the Secretary of War showing dangerous conspiracies in certain sections with which the civil authorities were unable to cope.—*Messages and Papers*, I, 498; *Journal of C. S. A.*, IV, 263; *O. R.*, Ser. IV, Vol. III, p. 819. A bill was introduced and debated during the entire session but was not enacted.—*Journal of C. S. A.*, IV, 387.
[109] *C. R.*, II, 838. In a secret session on Mar. 13, 1865, the President in his last message asked for the suspension of the writ as "not simply advisable

The peace propaganda if not immediate[110] in its results was none the less insidious and effective. To suggest to the North a peace plan based upon anything so vague as "the great principles of 1776" was of course an absurdity, as the three men were well aware. Pearce goes to the heart of the matter when he says: ". . . Despite fine words and elastic phrases couched in glittering generalities, it is plain enough that the advocates of peace were preparing the Southern mind for a peace without victory and for a very probable reunion with the North, with just so much guarantee of state sovereignty and control over 'domestic institutions' as could be wrung from the Lincoln Government." [111] He is of the opinion that the agitation left the Confederacy appreciably weaker. Ben Hill expressed the same opinion in a speech after the war when, referring to Brown's propaganda, he said that malcontents, "many of them, too, who had done all in their power to hurry our people into secession," made "brazen assertions that the laws of the Confederate Government, enacted to carry on the war, were unconstitutional and void," and "scattered these documents of twin falsehood and treachery among our people . . . and through the army . . . and among our enemies to prove to them that our

---

and expedient but almost indispensable."—*Journal of C. S. A.*, IV, 704-5; *Messages and Papers*, I, 548-49. A bill was introduced but it was defeated two days before the session ended and one month before Lee surrendered his army.—*Journal of C. S. A.*, IV, 723; Rhodes, V, 456-57; Jones, *Diary*, II, 450. Stephens, who had returned to Richmond, aided in defeating both bills.—See Johnston and Browne, p. 476.

[110] One immediate result was the introduction by Senator Orr of South Carolina in the Confederate Senate, on June 2, 1864, of a joint resolution "in relation to opening negotiations for peace between the Confederate States and the United States." To head off Orr's resolution, Hill four days later introduced a resolution declaring the disposition, principles, and purposes of the Confederacy in relation to the existing war. Hill's resolution passed 12 to 7; Orr's failed by a vote of 5 to 14.—*Journal of C. S. A.*, IV, 143, 164, 197, 211.

[111] Pp. 93-94.

people were dividing, that our armies were weakening, and that they had only to take courage and keep up the struggle, and surrender was inevitable." [112]

[112] Address before the Southern Historical Society, Atlanta, Feb. 18, 1874.—Benjamin H. Hill, Jr., pp. 399-401. The Hon. J. C. C. Black expressed a similar opinion when he said that "weakened by stabs from behind, inflicted by hands that should have upheld," the Confederate cause went down.—Address at the unveiling of a monument to B. H. Hill, *Atlanta Constitution*, May 2, 1896.

## CHAPTER IX

## PEACE PROPAGANDA[1]

IF THE Southern cause was weakening because of war weariness and continued attacks upon the administration, the situation was no less critical in the Lincoln government, where in 1864 Northern morale reached its nadir.[2] The Emancipation Proclamation, issued under pressure of the Radicals, had alienated the Conservatives, and in his efforts to win them back President Lincoln had lost the support of the Radicals[3] who called a Republican convention in May and nominated Fremont for president. This action compelled the President's followers to appeal to "war Democrats" for support and to name him as the candidate of the Union party. In the last days of August the Democratic National Convention enthusiastically adopted a platform declaring the war a failure and demanding peace, with General McClellan as the nominee.[4]

Meanwhile Grant's on-to-Richmond campaign had been anything but a success. From May 3 to June 10 he lost in killed, wounded, and missing more men than Lee had in his army.[5] A large part of the population called him "Butcher

---

[1] Peace propaganda through the spring and summer of 1864 was discussed in Chap. VIII.

[2] In July, 1864, gold reached 285, the highest point of the war.—Rhodes, IV, 509.

[3] Cf. Kirkland, pp. 26 *et seq.*, 36 *et seq.*, 108-12, 124 *et seq.*

[4] *Ibid.*, pp. 129 *et seq.;* Stanwood, pp. 304 *et seq.*

[5] The number of killed, wounded, and missing was 62,551, which included 3,000 officers.—Swinton, *Campaigns of the Army of the Potomac,* p. 491, cited by Rowland, X, 5.

Grant" and demanded peace.⁶ In July the Davis bill, setting forth the Radical conception of war aims and of reconstruction, received a pocket veto and was followed by the Wade-Davis Manifesto expressing the Radicals' opinion of their president. In the Middle West disaffection over the President's earlier yielding to the Radicals and the consequent reversing of war aims⁷ had resulted in the formation of powerful peace societies which now threatened counter-revolution.⁸ Well might President Lincoln write in August, 1864, that he did not expect to be reëlected.⁹

Under these conditions Southern hope rose high. If the South could present a solid front to convince the discouraged Northern people that peace was possible only through negotiation, and if Southern arms could hold Sherman in check until after the presidential election, the Southern cause might yet triumph. Both conditions were seriously jeopardized by Governor Brown, the Vice President, and their supporters by the assault they made on administration measures in the March session of the legislature,¹⁰ only two months before Sherman invaded Georgia; by their continued warfare on the suspension of the writ of habeas corpus and advocacy of the peace resolutions throughout the summer and fall; by the Governor's nullification of the February conscript law in defiance of the action of the legislature; and

---

⁶ Peace efforts on the part of the North in 1864, having more or less the support of President Lincoln, included Horace Greeley's conference with Confederate commissioners at Niagara, the Jacques-Gilmore visit to Richmond, the Black mission, Lincoln's draft of a peace offer, made at the suggestion of the National Executive Committee of the party, and the Blair proposals.—Cf. Kirkland, Chap. II and pp. 94-124; Davis, *Rise and Fall*, Chap. L.

⁷ Kirkland, pp. 29-36.

⁸ *Ibid.*, pp. 124 *et seq.;* John W. Headley, *Confederate Operations in Canada and New York,* Chaps. XXII-XLVI.

⁹ Greeley feared an insurrection in the North, and both he and Thurlow Weed thought if the elections were held in August, New York and Pennsylvania would go Democratic by 100,000.—Milton, *The Eve of Conflict,* pp. 127-28.

¹⁰ *Supra,* pp. 201 *et seq.*

by his refusal in August to honor the President's requisition.[11]

Early in May Sherman began the Atlanta campaign; in July his army crossed the Chattahoochee; and on September 2 Atlanta fell, the victory assuring Lincoln's reëlection and putting an end to peace proposals in the North. With Georgia thrown open to the enemy, with the Governor's furloughing the state troops,[12] and with existing conditions as above described, it is little wonder that Sherman thought it would be easy to detach Georgia from the Confederacy through a separate peace.[13] He accordingly sent verbal messages to Brown and Stephens,[14] inviting them to a conference with himself. "It would be a magnificent stroke of policy

---

[11] *Supra,* p. 179.

[12] Sherman thought the Governor's action was significant and sent a copy of Brown's letter to Hood to his government with the statement that he had reason to believe that Governor Brown and Vice President Stephens wished to visit him. On Sept. 17 President Lincoln telegraphed Sherman expressing his interest in the Governor's furloughing the troops.—Sherman, *Memoirs,* II, 137 *et seq.*

[13] Cf. Avery, p. 301; Flippin, p. 259; Pearce, p. 95. Shortly after the fall of Atlanta Stephens published a letter favoring the suspension of hostilities and the election of delegates to a convention of all the states, the convention to formulate a peace plan to be binding upon those states which ratified it.—Johnston and Browne, pp. 469-71; Cleveland, pp. 191-96; Avery, p. 286. His letter "attracted much attention, and gave occasion for much misrepresentation," his friendly biographers remark.—Johnston and Browne, p. 469. Stephens' thinking on the subject of peace "seems somewhat akin to Horace Greeley's in its confusion."—Kirkland, p. 233.

In reply to an inquiry for his views on a peace movement to influence the presidential election, Senator Johnson in a published letter took the position that such a move would be construed in the North as a confession of weakness and would intensify the war spirit there. As the party assailed, the South could not, in his opinion, initiate an honorable peace.—Flippin, pp. 260-62; *Weekly Chronicle and Sentinel,* Oct. 12, 1864.

[14] William King and Joshua Hill were the bearers of Sherman's messages. After Sherman's efforts with Brown and Stephens had failed, he sent Judge A. R. Wright, a Union man, to Washington to act in peace negotiations between Lincoln and Davis, but Wright informed Lincoln and his cabinet that Georgia would not accept their terms. He did not approach Davis, knowing that he, too, would refuse the terms offered. On the peace efforts of King, Hill, and Wright, cf. *O. R.,* Ser. I, Vol. XXXIX, Pt. II, p. 381; Avery, pp. 302, 304; Fielder, p. 310; Flippin, p. 260.

## PEACE PROPAGANDA 225

if we could, without surrendering principle or a foot of ground, arouse the latent enmity of Georgia against Davis," Sherman wrote to Lincoln.[15] He stated that the people did not hesitate to say that "Stephens was and is a Union man at heart," in consequence of which Davis would not trust him nor let him have a share in the government.[16]

According to his *Memoirs*, Sherman's offer to Governor Brown was to spare Georgia, confine his troops to roads in crossing the state, and pay for all supplies for his army if Brown would withdraw the state troops from the armies of the Confederacy.[17] Brown stated in his official report that Sherman had offered him the opportunity to view the section which the Union army had already devastated and had expressed the hope that it might not be necessary to lay waste any more of the state's territory.[18] Brown refused to meet the General, but his reply was ominous for Confederate unity. Neither he nor General Sherman had authority to make peace, he pointed out, for while Georgia was "as sovereign as when she seceded from the Union" and could "through a convention negotiate treaties and declare peace," [19] she had "conferred no such power upon the Governor." But Georgia would never make separate terms with the enemy. "Whatever may be the opinion of her people as to the injustice done her by the Confederate Administration," he said, "she will triumph with her Confederate sisters, or she will sink with them in one common ruin. The intelligent people of Georgia already understand, and our enemy will soon learn, that the independent expression of condemnation of the errors, to

---

[15] Sherman, *Memoirs*, II, 137 *et seq*.
[16] *Ibid*.
[17] *Ibid*., pp. 138-42.
[18] Official report of Governor Brown in *Confederate Union*, published in *Constitutionalist*, Sept. 29, 1864.
[19] This statement was, of course, not true. Georgia could not negotiate treaties nor declare peace as long as she was a member of the Confederate States of America. She could do so only by seceding. It seems evident from subsequent events that this was the Governor's thought.

use no stronger term, of the Administration is one thing, and disloyalty to our sacred cause is another, and quite a different thing." [20] If Lincoln wished to stop the war, Brown continued, let him plant himself upon the principles of 1776 and let President Lincoln and President Davis agree to transfer the issue to the ballot box where each sovereign state could decide where its allegiance should lie.[21]

That the Governor intended by his published reply to Sherman to create sentiment for a state convention to share responsibility for separate state action seems evident from his convening the legislature shortly afterwards, his recommendations for a convention, and from Linton Stephens' and Joshua Hill's efforts[22] to carry out the Governor's recommendations. The conclusion is strengthened by Brown's comments to Stephens, his efforts to secure the endorsement of the Governors' Conference for a convention, and by Sherman's opinion.

On September 30 Brown wrote to Stephens that he had expected the administration press to attack his reply to Sherman as looking to a possible contingency in which Davis would not be recognized as supreme. On October 12 he made a similar allusion, saying that he expected to be

---

[20] Official report of Governor Brown, *loc. cit.*

[21] *Ibid.* Cf. Fielder, p. 311; Avery, p. 303; Stephenson, p. 174. In other words, Governor Brown proposed to let the people decide the matter over the heads of the two governments. Cf. letter of Stephens to his brother Linton, Oct. 18, 1864, Johnston and Browne, p. 475. An editorial, no doubt Stephens-inspired, on the subject of a convention of all the states of the old Union appeared in the *Weekly Chronicle and Sentinel,* Sept. 28, 1864. Opponents of the Confederate administration persisted in such a possibility until the Hampton Roads Conference disposed of the myth.

[22] Joshua Hill had been a Union man from the beginning, although he had somewhat hedged on the question for purposes of the gubernatorial campaign in 1863. Brown wrote to Stephens on Sept. 30, 1864, that Joshua Hill "agrees fully with us on the line of policy we have acted upon in Confederate politics." He stated further that since there was a vacancy in the state senate from Hill's district and "we need a leader in the senate," where Hill would "render a public service," he had written Hill asking him to run. Brown asked Stephens to endeavor to secure Hill's consent.—Phillips, *Correspondence,* p. 653.

PEACE PROPAGANDA 227

attacked by the ultra-administration men on the point Stephens had mentioned. Referring to the approaching Governors' Conference he said: "I intend to sound them a little upon their feelings in reference to a convention of states. I wish I could see you but will not have time." [23] Sherman was of the opinion that Brown seriously entertained the thought of peace[24] but that he "hardly felt ready to act, and simply gave a furlough to the militia and called a special session of the legislature. . . ." [25]

Sherman's communications with the Governor and the Vice President were known before Brown's statement was published, and Toombs, thoroughly alarmed for his friend's reputation, wrote to Stephens: "Do not by any means go to see Sherman, whatever may be the form of his invitation. It will place you in a wrong, a very wrong position. . . . If Sherman means anything he means to detach Georgia from the Confederacy. Better any fate than that. Davis is impregnable upon the peace issue. In every shape and form and at all times he has professed to seek peace, and in truth up to this time his actions have conformed to his professions. The fundamental law commits it to his hands, and nothing could be of more evil tendency than for other officers of the Confederacy, or state governments, to meet any person, and much less a general of the army, to discuss the question." [26]

Stephens' reply to Sherman's proposal was in the form of

---

[23] *Ibid.* The conference of governors from Confederate states east of the Mississippi met in Augusta, Ga., on Oct. 17 and adopted a set of resolutions, but Brown did not succeed in including one for a convention of all the states. —*C. R.*, III, 625-26, 628, 777-80; *O. R.*, Ser. IV, Vol. III, p. 685.

[24] Cf. opinion of Senator Mahone, *Cong. Record,* 47th Cong., sp. sess., pp. 106 *et seq.;* Fielder, p. 633.

[25] *Memoirs,* II, 140.

[26] Phillips, *Correspondence,* pp. 652-53. Pollard, in agreement with Toombs in regard to President Davis' willingness to make peace, states that he was always hasty to send peace messages to Washington on every possible occasion, "but in convenient disguise, so that they might not convey any confession of weakness or of over-anxiety for the termination of hostilities."— *Davis,* p. 238.

a letter dated October 1 and addressed to William King. Doubtless because of Toombs' warning, it was more restrained than was Brown's reply. He said that peace was very dear to him if it could be obtained without sacrifice of principle and honor, but neither General Sherman nor himself had authority in the matter. If, however, Sherman thought that the two could agree upon terms to be submitted to their respective governments and would make known the fact in some formal manner, he would with the consent of the Confederate authorities meet Sherman in an attempt to restore peace and harmony upon principles of honor, right, and justice to all parties.[27] Brown wrote to Stephens: "I am glad you made the proposition . . . for an interview on the terms mentioned by you. It keeps the door open. . . ."[28]

Sherman's communications with Brown and Stephens alarmed the Confederate administration and the President went immediately to Georgia.[29] In a dispatch to Sherman on

---

[27] Cleveland, pp. 196-97; Johnston and Browne, p. 472; Avery, p. 302.

[28] Phillips, *Correspondence,* p. 654. Stephenson (p. 174, n. 1) comments: "It is still to be discovered what 'door' Stephens was supposed to have kept open." With reference to the Governor he inquires, "What was the motive of Brown in withdrawing the Georgia militia from Hood's army? Was there something afoot which has never quite revealed itself in history?"

So persistent were rumors that Brown favored a reconstruction of the old Union that the Governor's aide-de-camp published a reply to a citizen's inquiry upon the subject. He said the Governor felt that his position on the conditions under which he would favor a reconstruction of the old Union "and go into fraternal embrace with the foul invaders of our homes and rights, the murderers of our brave men, and the abusers and insulters of our women—in a word, the base and fiendish uncivilizers of the age"—had so often been given to the country in official form he thought it unnecessary to spend time in further explanation.—*Weekly Chronicle and Sentinel,* Oct. 12, 1864.

[29] Avery (p. 302) states that there is no ground for believing that Davis' visit was in any way connected with distrust of Stephens and Brown, but all the facts point the other way—even though the military situation in Georgia was of itself sufficiently grave to call for the President's presence there. Jones, who as a clerk in the War Department was in a position to know, states on Sept. 20 that there is a rumor that Sherman has invited the Vice-President, Brown, and H. V. Johnson to confer with him on the question of the return of Georgia to the Union, and that the government in consequence had called for a list of all Georgians who had sailed from Confederate ports

September 27, President Lincoln commented on Davis' visit adding, "I suppose that Brown and Stephens are the objects of his visit."[30] Davis visited Hood's army, made plans for cutting Sherman's communications with Chattanooga, held war rallies, and expressed his contempt for "croakers" whom he challenged to go to the front. He urged the people to rise en masse and deal with Sherman as the Russians had dealt with Napoleon at Moscow. "Let men not ask what the law requires," he exhorted, "but give whatever freedom demands."[31]

On the day following the President's departure from Georgia, Stephens addressed the people of Augusta, saying that the resources of the South were exhausted and that peace ought to be made.[32] On November 1 he told his audience at Crawfordsville that the South left the Union to rescue the Constitution, and "it is our high duty to keep it, and hold it and preserve it forever." Away with the idea of getting independence first and liberty afterwards, he exclaimed, for "Liberties once lost may be lost forever!"[33] "If ever a man of mature years and high reputation talked and behaved like a child, it was Stephens in the autumn of 1864...."[34]

Brown's recommendations to the legislature from this time on called for plebiscites in each state for a convention to amend the Confederate constitution or for action looking

---

during the summer. Two days later he reports the rumor that the President has gone to Georgia to prevent the consummation of the plan.—*Diary*, II, 287.

[30] William T. Sherman Papers, Vol. XIV.
[31] Dodd, *Davis*, pp. 333-36; Rowland, II, 361.
[32] Dodd, *Davis*, p. 336.
[33] Cleveland, p. 760.
[34] Dodd, *Davis*, pp. 336-37. For correspondence between President Davis and Stephens in regard to the latter's publishing a letter charging that Davis preferred the election of Lincoln to that of McClellan—in other words that Davis preferred war to peace, cf. *O. R.*, Ser. IV, Vol. III, pp. 840, 934, 1000; Rhodes, V, 477. Eckenrode (pp. 320-21) expresses the opinion that the government would have been justified in imprisoning Stephens.

to a convention of all the states composing the old Union.[35] He of course knew that a convention of the states of the old Union was impossible, particularly after Sherman had taken Atlanta, but it served his purpose as propaganda by creating the impression that President Davis was the only obstacle to a negotiated and honorable peace.[36]

When the Georgia legislature met on November 3, 1864, Lee was being besieged in Richmond, Hood had started on his Tennessee campaign, Sherman was in Atlanta soon to start on his devastating march to the sea. Exactly three years, ten months, and two days had elapsed since the seizure of Fort Pulaski when Governor Brown delivered to the legislature a message which was evidently intended to be utterly devastating in its effect upon the Confederate government. He castigated the administration for permitting the loss of Atlanta, the Governor showing to his own satisfaction exactly how the authorities could have prevented it. But "the misfortunes following the misguided judgment of our rulers must not have the effect of relaxing our zeal or chilling our love for the cause," he added. While many may deplore the government's "errors and mismanagement" and others "attempt to justify all its mistakes and defend all its errors," all, as one man, would, he felt, "remain true to our sacred cause and be prepared, if necessary, to expend our last dollar and shed our last drop of blood in its defense." [37]

Since the administration and the "cause" were by virtue of necessity identical, any loss of confidence in the one, certainly and surely hindered the success of the other. Did or did not the opponents of the administration realize this

---

[35] *C. R.*, II, 649-50, 743 *et seq.*, 851-53, 867.

[36] See Dodd, *Davis*, p. 345. In the weeks preceding the meeting of the Georgia legislature in Nov., 1864, the Stephens brothers had a lengthy correspondence on the subject of the "despotism" of the Confederate government, a general convention, and the right of states to secede from the Confederacy.— Cf. Johnston and Browne, pp. 473-75; Waddell, pp. 285-86; Stovall, pp. 273-74.

[37] *C. R.*, II, 735-38; *S. J., 1864*, pp. 5-31.

fact? It was recognized fully by Cobb, Ben Hill, and Johnson, who, though they frequently differed from the administration, nevertheless refrained from public criticism and gave the government their wholehearted support. [38]

As a preliminary to his recommendations for peace, Brown, in his message, discussed the despotic power which he saw in the administration. "Confederate independence with centralized power, without State sovereignty and Constitutional and religious liberty," [39] would be "very little better than subjugation." He thought it could not be denied that the Confederate government had made "fearful strides towards a centralized government with unlimited powers," and that the longer the war lasted the less probability there was that at its termination there would be "a return to the Constitutional forms of republican simplicity. . . ." [40] But how

---
[38] Cf. Cobb's letter to Seddon, Feb. 4, 1864, *O. R.*, Ser. IV, Vol. III, p. 75; "From the Autobiography of Herschel V. Johnson," *American Historical Review*, XXX (Jan., 1925), 332.

[39] Brown professed to believe that the administration was ready to deny religious liberty.

[40] *C. R.*, II, 738-40. As a matter of course the necessities of war had led to a centralization of power, otherwise the Confederacy would never have been able to maintain itself four years. The same charges were made against Lincoln and Wilson, and will probably always be made against the executive in wartime. Probably no historian today would deny that the exercise by President Lincoln of war powers not delegated to him by the Constitution nor authorized by Congress had much to do with the success of the Federal government in winning the war. In the matter of the habeas corpus, for instance, Attorney General Bates prevented a case from going to the Supreme Court lest that body should declare the President's suspending power unconstitutional, as Taney had ruled in chambers in circuit court in the Merryman case (17 Fed. Cases 144). Bates thought that a decision pronouncing the President's arbitrary arrests illegal would "do more to paralyze the Executive . . . than the worst defeat our armies have yet sustained." —Stanton Papers, No. 52,223, cited by Randall, p. 132.

In 1861 Congress ratified President Lincoln's acts in enlarging the army and navy without authority.—William A. Dunning, *Essays on the Civil War and Reconstruction and Related Topics*, pp. 20-21. Probably because a formula could not be agreed upon that would not censure the President, the act legalizing his suspension of the writ of habeas corpus was not passed until Mar. 3, 1863, and then it was "irrelevantly tucked away in an act to increase the pay of privates in the army," and put through the Senate by "a piece of sharp practice on the part of the presiding officer."—Randall, pp. 128-30.

could the war be terminated? Not by the sword, he told a war-weary people, for the prospects were that the war would continue until "both sides were exhausted"; till debts were accumulated which posterity could never pay; till hundreds of thousands more men were slain and millions of women and children reduced to widowhood, orphanage, and poverty; till taxes had become unbearable; till the civil laws had ceased to be respected and highway robbery and murder were everyday occurrences; and the Federal and Confederate governments had usurped all the powers claimed by the most absolute despots. He feared President Lincoln and President Davis would never agree upon terms for negotiation and that war must rage till there was a change of administration—unless the people of both countries "in their aggregate capacity as sovereign States" should require both governments to stop fighting and negotiate a settlement "upon the principles of 1776, as laid down in the Georgia resolutions." [41]

The proposed plan necessitated the secession of all states from their respective central governments if they were to be represented in the convention as "sovereign, equal, and independent states." On this point the Governor said: "While I am satisfied that separate State action may, and most probably will, be a necessary preliminary to a treaty of peace, I do not wish to be misunderstood upon this point." [42] The sovereign states of the Confederacy seceded separately from the old Union and each had the same right to secede from the Confederacy, but he thought they were pledged to stand by and aid each other against the enemy till the end of the struggle, and that no one of them could honorably withdraw

---

Even in the World War, when the need for the exercise of arbitrary power was perhaps much less in the United States than in any civil war in any country, such measures as the Espionage Act, the Sabotage Act, the Selective Service Act, the Sedition Law, and the Threats-against-the-President Act were deemed necessary in the United States. These statutes took the place of martial law and the suspension of the writ of habeas corpus.

[41] *C. R.*, II, 740-41.
[42] *Ibid.*, p. 748.

## PEACE PROPAGANDA 233

from the contest and make a separate treaty of peace. However, the people of the Confederate States could "meet in Convention and abolish the Confederate Government whenever its usurpations and abuses of power have reached a point where the sovereignty of the States and the rights and liberties of the people are no longer secure under it," he said. The people of the North had "the same right in their own government." [43]

Stripped of its verbiage and evidently insincere professions of the practicability of a "convention of all the states of the old Union," Brown's plan was for conventions in three states, necessitating a convention of all the Southern states, and a vote in that convention to abolish the Confederate States of America. The Governor's message created a sensation in the North where it was predicted that he would take Georgia out of the Confederacy and that other states would follow. The Governor's message was a "delicious morsel for the enemy," the *Republican* angrily commented.[44]

Linton Stephens promptly introduced into the legislature resolutions calling a state convention to consider peace negotiations along the lines recommended by the Governor, while friends of the Confederate administration introduced resolutions pledging anew the fidelity of the state to the Confederacy.[45] The *Constitutionalist* published the latter resolutions on November 19 and made a plea to all the state leaders—Brown, Stephens, Toombs, Cobb, Hill, Johnson—to present to the enemy a solid front. The *Republican* urged Linton Stephens to withdraw his peace resolutions and the legislature to pass the others, as had been done at two previous sessions. The *Constitutionalist* thought that unless Stephens was sufficiently patriotic to do this, the legislature should by vote consign his resolutions to oblivion "and so ease and settle the public mind." [46]

---
[43] *Ibid.* [44] Quoted by the *Constitutionalist*, Nov. 16, 1864.
[45] Avery, p. 304; *S. J., 1864*, pp. 34, 44; *H. J., 1864*, p. 60.
[46] Nov. 16, 1864.

In the meantime those supporting Stephens' resolutions were spreading the idea that President Davis favored the resolutions and wanted Georgia to take the lead in calling a state convention. This was an old trick of opponents of the President, which Brown had played successfully in his gubernatorial campaigns of 1861 and 1863. Members of the legislature, however, wrote to the President asking for an expression of his opinion. The President replied on November 17 and referred them to his recent message[47] as proof that he had "not contemplated the use of any other agency in treating for peace than that established by the Constitution of the Confederate States." He feared the resolutions would lead the enemy to the false idea that some of the states were about to abandon their sister states and make a separate peace. The fallacies in the general convention plan he exposed by showing that to call such a meeting preliminary negotiations would be required, not only to determine the time and place and number of delegates, but also to agree upon certain other questions—whether the states were or were not to be bound by the action of the convention; whether Virginia would sit in a convention with the so-called state of West Virginia as her equal, or whether the United States would deprive West Virginia of its rights; what authority was to represent Louisiana, Tennessee, Kentucky, and Missouri which were now in the hands of the enemy. He thought it would be much simpler to negotiate for peace at once rather than to "negotiate for the appointment of negotiators who are to meet without power to do anything but make proposals." He said that the author of the resolutions as-

---

[47] In the message of Nov. 7 to which he referred, the President said: "Whenever there shall be on the part of our enemies a desire for peace there will be no difficulty in finding means by which negotiations can be opened, but it is obvious that no agency can be called into action until that desire shall be mutual. When that contingency shall happen the Government to which is confided the treaty-making power, can be at no loss for means adapted to accomplish so desirable an end."—*O. R.*, Ser. IV, Vol. III, p. 800; *Messages and Papers*, I, 497; *Journal of C. S. A.*, IV, 252 *et seq.*

sumed that the obstacle to making peace lay in the difficulty in finding proper agencies, "whereas the whole and only obstacle is that the enemy will not treat at all or entertain any other proposition than that we should submit to their yoke, acknowledging that we are criminals and appeal to their mercy for pardon." [48]

The President's letter was effective. Despite the Governor's wishes, Linton Stephens' eloquence, and Joshua Hill's lobbying, the resolutions calling a convention to consider peace did not pass. Instead, a resolution was adopted on November 12 expressing confidence in the wisdom, patriotism, and virtue of President Davis in carrying on the military and civil affairs of the government during the past difficult year.[49]

The Georgia legislature having refused to take the lead in the peace plans of the Governor and the Stephens brothers, Alexander Stephens returned to his post of duty in Richmond and started a campaign of attack along another line—that of securing the President's removal through congressional action or of negotiating directly with Washington over the President's head. Having by a ruse obtained permission to address the Senate,[50] Stephens in a closed session of that body on January 6, 1865, delivered a two-hour arraignment of the administration in which he charged it with incompetence, bad judgment, and despotism, and demanded an entire reversal of all its policies, domestic, foreign, and military.[51] Stephens next assisted in preparing peace resolutions proposing a convention of all the states, the de-

---

[48] Rowland, VI, 403-6.
[49] *S. J., 1864*, pp. 34-44, 62-63; *H. J., 1864*, p. 60. While the struggle was in progress in the Georgia legislature an echo was heard in the Confederate Senate, where on Nov. 17 a resolution was passed asking the President whether any state of the United States had expressed a willingness to go into a convention with the Confederate States for the purpose of negotiating peace.—*Journal of C. S. A.*, IV, 269.
[50] *Supra*, Chap. VIII, n. 81.
[51] The speech was not, of course, reported.—See Stephens' account in the *War between the States*, II, 287-89,

tails of which were to be arranged by three commissioners to the Lincoln government who were to be selected by the House and provided with passports by President Davis.[52]

There was every indication that the resolutions would pass when the situation was fortunately relieved by the visit of Francis P. Blair and the resulting Hampton Roads Conference. Stephens later expressed the opinion that the whole arrangement with Blair was planned—by Davis, presumably—to forestall his peace resolutions.[53] Doubtless he was right, for Blair's fantastic proposal with reference to Mexico would otherwise no doubt have received scarcely the respect of a hearing from President Davis. Indeed, Blair's visit was little short of a godsend to the administration, since it enabled President Davis not only to halt the progress of the Stephens resolutions in Congress,[54] but also, by appointing Stephens on the peace commission,[55] to put the Vice President in a position where henceforth he could do the administration little harm.[56]

---

[52] *Journal of C. S. A.*, VII, 451-52; Johnston and Browne, pp. 480-82.

[53] *Ibid.*, p. 486; Cleveland, pp. 187-98. Cleveland later expressed the opinion that it was a scheme of Seward's who thought, by making impossible conditions which he knew the South would refuse, to crush the anti-war party in the North.—Cleveland to Davis, Nov. 25, 1887, Rowland, X, 11.

[54] In a letter to James M. Mason, June 11, 1870, ex-President Davis stated that he had not intended to put Stephens on the peace commission, but that others convinced him it would be best to do so, since Stephens had been speaking in the Senate on the practicability of arranging a peace by conference, and his appointment would at least "check his evil doing in the Senate. . . ."—Mason, pp. 539 *et seq.*

[55] Stephens was unwilling to accept the appointment and made the excuse that his absence from the Senate would be remarked upon. He especially wanted Davis to go, which, with the inevitable failure of the conference, would of course have given the Stephens-Brown group new ammunition to be used against the administration. Upon his return, Stephens opposed making a written report, which, however, President Davis very astutely insisted upon.—See Stephens, *War between the States*, II, 590 *et seq.*

[56] So little does Professor Smith, author of *The Francis Preston Blair Family in Politics*, take account of the situation in Richmond at this time that (p. 309) he says of Blair's visit: "President Davis was impressed and somewhat misled." He pictures Davis as deciding "after a night of reflection" to participate in the reconquest of Mexico!

President Davis had all along insisted that stubborn resistance was the only alternative to unconditional surrender, and that diplomacy, to be successful in wartime, as he told the Vice President in 1863, required a victorious and threatening army. If, therefore, Stephens as peace delegate failed in negotiating a settlement, he could no longer oppose the President's policy. If he accepted the condition which the United States government had already announced, that of unconditional surrender, he would be thoroughly discredited, for the South was by no means ready to accept such terms. Nor would Stephens be the only one silenced. Governor Brown and others who with Stephens had insisted that President Davis was the only obstacle to a negotiated and honorable peace would no longer be able to obtain a hearing. And so it proved. The Hampton Roads Conference with its demand for unconditional surrender[57] ended the propaganda for negotiations with the United States.

While Stephens was endeavoring in Richmond to carry peace proposals over the President's head, Governor Brown called a special session of the legislature to meet on February 15, 1865,[58] for the purpose, it was freely said, of pro-

[57] Report of commissioners, sent to the Confederate Congress by the President, *Messages and Papers*, I, 519 *et seq.*; Stephens' account of the conference, *War between the States*, II, 576-622; official documents and reports, *ibid.*, Appendix R; Kirkland, Chaps. IV-V; Mason, pp. 601-2. Stephens had no doubt promised himself, as one of his friends suggests, to play the role of a great Pacificator at the conference.—Felton, p. 34. For side light on Stephens' part, cf. letter of Henry W. Cleveland to Davis, June 4, 1888, Rowland, X, 20. The conference also ended the hope that any one governor may have entertained for negotiating peace for his state alone, since the official report of the commissioners stated that Lincoln had said he would entertain no proposals from the Confederate States as such, since that would be a recognition of their existence as a separate power, and, "for like reasons, that no such terms would be entertained by him from States separately. . . ."
Davis thought the severe terms demanded at the peace conference were decided upon after Blair had reported to Lincoln what he had heard in Richmond.—*Rise and Fall*, II, 618-19. This may well have been true since Blair mingled freely with the Stephens group and must have been made acquainted with the facts of the pending peace resolutions and the cabal against the President.
[58] *C. R.*, II, 817.

posing a state convention to depose the President or to take Georgia out of the Confederacy.[59]

In a letter which has all the earmarks of sincerity, Governor Vance urged Brown on January 18, 1865, to prevent such a move. He saw many indications in Georgia, as in his own state, of a desire to call a convention "for vague and indefinable purposes," which he felt if accomplished would lead to counter-revolution and bloodshed. He besought Brown to prevent this as he felt sure North Carolina would follow in whichever direction Georgia led. He thought that governors and legislatures "will have all the necessary moral weight [to end the war?] and can accomplish every desired object short of [without] revolution." He understood President Davis was inclined to make earnest efforts toward peace and he thought this "legitimate and proper channel" should be exhausted "before we take matters into our own hands or inaugurate revolutionary measures." [60]

On February 1 a two-and-one-half-column editorial from the pen of the Connecticut[61] editor of the *Chronicle and Sentinel* aided Brown's plans by quoting the children of Israel as demanding a king and God's reply warning them against such an institution. It stated that the air was

---

[59] Editorial in *Memphis Appeal*, quoted by the *Southern Banner*, Jan. 18, 1865. Cf. Stephens, *War between the States*, II, 656.

[60] *C. R.*, III, 702-4. Brown did not reply until Feb. 6, and then only through an aide-de-camp, who stated that the Governor had left the capital for a week's absence and that his views would be made known to the legislature on the fifteenth.—*Ibid.*, p. 706.

[61] Cf. Senator Hill's letter to Augusta Evans, the novelist, in which he spoke of "native traitors" and "immigrant spies" as holding high office or editing papers and "adroitly, earnestly sowing the seeds of disaffection and disunion." The letter in some way reached the press and was published in the *Columbus Sun*. It was commented upon by a correspondent, "Georgia," in the *Macon Confederacy,* and editorially by the *Chronicle and Sentinel* on Mar. 31, 1865. N. S. Morse purchased the *Chronicle and Sentinel* during the war, became intensely loyal to the Federal government as the fortunes of the Confederacy waned, and at the end of the war burned or secreted the files of the paper for 1861-65. He was later manager of the New York *Evening News*.—Rabun L. Brantley, *Georgia Journalism of the Civil War Period*, p. 17.

PEACE PROPAGANDA          239

"heavy with treason to the dearest rights of freemen," and exhorted all freemen of Georgia and other states of the South to congregate "in sovereign conventions."

On the fifteenth the Governor delivered to the legislature a philippic against the administration in which he charged that the whole body politic was diseased and called for the deposition of the President through the appointment of a commander in chief of the armies.[62] This was to be brought about by three states' calling conventions and recommending an amendment to the Confederate constitution. He also recommended that commissioners be appointed to all Confederate states to exhort them to assemble in conventions.[63] Although the Vice President,[64] from Richmond, and Linton Stephens exerted their influence for a convention such as the Governor recommended, there were only two affirmative votes in the lower house on the direct issue. In the senate a strong resolution for a vigorous prosecution of the war passed with only two opposing votes.[65]

The loyalty of the Georgia legislature under the circumstances was extraordinary. Judge John A. Campbell, assistant secretary of War, reported less than a month later: "Georgia is in a state that may properly be called insurrectionary against Confederate authority. Her public men of greatest influence have cast reproach upon the laws of the

---

[62] Lee had been appointed general in chief on Jan. 31, under the act of Jan. 23.—*Journal of the C. S. A.*, IV, 510.

[63] *C. R.*, II, 851-53; *S. J., 1865*, pp. 7-29. Cf. Jones, *Diary*, II, 436.

[64] H. J. Eckenrode thinks Stephens is an "excellent illustration of the evil a good man may do when he becomes divorced from sanity."—*Jefferson Davis*, p. 324.

[65] *Acts of the General Assembly, 1865*, p. 84; B. H. Hill to Davis, Mar. 25, 1865, "Georgia and the Confederacy," *American Historical Review*, I (Oct., 1895), 100-2. Cf. *C. R.*, II, 867. While the senate resolution was pending, a substitute amendment was offered, providing for the election of delegates to a convention to meet Apr. 15. The substitute was lost 4 to 16, the original resolution passing 25 to 2.—*Chronicle and Sentinel*, Mar. 10, 1865. "Troup" (supposed to be Howell Cobb), writing in the *LaGrange Reporter* on Mar. 17, 1865, suggested that Brown had despaired of the success of Southern arms and desired to make "fair weather" with Lincoln.

Confederacy and the Confederate authorities, and have made the execution of the laws nearly impossible." [66] Cobb had made a similar report on January 20, saying that disloyalty "could not be worse," and predicted that if a convention should be called it would be "an unconditional submission concern." [67]

No doubt the influence of Senator Hill, who addressed the legislature in opposition to the Governor's recommendation and "paid his respects to original secessionists now turned peace advocates," was responsible for the overwhelming defeat of the Governor's plan. Hill wrote to President Davis that he was satisfied that Brown's message was the "first step in a concerted movement to inaugurate another revolution" which he felt had now been defeated.[68] In his speech at LaGrange on March 11—the last made in the South for the continuance of the war—Hill reviewed Brown's message, pointing out its misstatements, and charged that it had discouraged Southern troops and encouraged the enemy.[69] He reviewed the Hampton Roads Conference and the terms offered to the South, painted the horrors of reconstruction should the South surrender, and replied to critics of the administration who relied upon disaffection to the President and sought in that way to destroy the Confederate government.[70] The *Chronicle and Sentinel* accused Hill of "exhausting the vocabulary of Billingsgate in his villification of Governor Brown" and charged that Hill had not scrupled to accuse Brown of "treason most foul and damning," nor to insinuate that he was "little better than . . . Cataline or Benedict Arnold." [71]

---

[66] *O. R.*, Ser. I, Vol. LI, Pt. II, p. 1066.

[67] Cobb to Davis, "Georgia and the Confederacy," *loc. cit.*, pp. 99-100.

[68] *Ibid.*, pp. 100-2; Pearce, pp. 107-8.

[69] *Weekly Chronicle and Sentinel,* Apr. 19, 1865, quoting the *Confederate Union.*

[70] The entire speech is in the *LaGrange Reporter,* Mar. 24, 1865, and in Benjamin H. Hill, Jr., pp. 373-93. Extracts in the *LaGrange Reporter,* Mar. 17, 1865.   [71] Apr. 12, 1865.

## PEACE PROPAGANDA 241

The *Confederate Union,* organ of the state administration, was bitterly disappointed that the legislature had not ordered a convention. In an editorial headed "The Contrast" it compared Brown's recommendations to the legislature with Davis' to Congress. It said that Brown's remedy was a convention in which the people should decide the question of war or peace, while Davis asked for the suspension of the writ of habeas corpus, the abolition of class exemptions, and authority vested in himself "to decide who shall publish a newspaper, preach a sermon, doctor the sick, teach the young." As between the Governor's "reasonable recommendation" and the President's proposal to be made a "dictator," the editor favored the former.[72]

Brown had failed in his efforts to secure a convention, but he continued his opposition to the administration. On March 30 he told the state troops: "We have nothing to fear so much as the breaking of the spirits of our people by unwise laws, unjust taxation, and a departure from principles which are dear to them and for which they are willing to fight. . . . The people of Georgia . . . regard him as most disloyal, who does most to break down the barriers which uphold constitutional liberty, and to trample under foot the great principle for which they took up arms. . . ."[73]

Within a few days Lee had surrendered and the fall of the Confederacy was imminent. Notwithstanding, Stephens' newspaper, the *Chronicle and Sentinel,* was carrying on the campaign against the administration as late as April 19. On that date it published an editorial of one and one-half columns, entitled "Subjugation," in which it sarcastically referred to the "dish of horrors" which it said administration supporters handed out regarding the treatment of the South in the event of defeat. The editor was confident that even if defeated, the Southern people would not be subjugated or

---

[72] Apr. 1, 1865.
[73] News dispatch from Atlanta, dated Mar. 30, published in the *Weekly Chronicle and Sentinel,* Apr. 19, 1865.

degraded or their property confiscated. It even thought that success might yet be possible for the Southern Confederacy —provided Brown, Toombs, and Stephens were allowed a voice in the councils of the Danville government.[74]

---

[74] The capital was at Danville, Va., for a short time after the fall of Richmond.

## CHAPTER X

## THE FALL OF THE CONFEDERACY

THE SESSION of the legislature which was disrupted by Sherman's army in November, 1864, resumed its work on February 15 of the following year. Because of the damaged condition in which the Union troops had left the capitol, the meetings had to be held in the City Hall in Macon. The fact was doubtless uppermost in the Governor's mind as he prepared his vitriolic message.[1]

Doubtless, too, the irate Governor's disposition was not improved by the stories bandied about with reference to the removal of his "cabbages and cow" at the time of the flight of his family from Milledgeville.[2] The story is important not because it was true—it probably was not true—but as showing the animosity toward the Governor which existed at the time. Another story of about the same date which the *Chronicle and Sentinel* hotly denied was that Brown claimed the right of a refugee in the payment of taxes on a home that escaped the fire which destroyed the one the family had left.[3]

---

[1] The message has already been noticed in so far as it pertained to peace.—*Supra*, p. 231.

[2] The story and its refutation had many variations, but the main lines were to the effect that as Sherman's army approached the capital Brown and his family fled from the executive mansion carrying with them on a freight train all their private effects, even to "cabbages and a cow," and leaving ammunition and the state archives to fall into the hands of the enemy.—Cf. Avery, pp. 310-11; Sherman, *Memoirs*, II, 188; Phillips, *Correspondence*, p. 657; *Weekly Chronicle and Sentinel*, May 3, 1865; Taylor, p. 212; Gen. Ira R. Foster's version, Fielder, pp. 313-17.

[3] May 3, 1865.

The Governor was doubtless annoyed by the stories, but he was furious over the invasion of Georgia, which he charged the Confederacy had with criminal negligence permitted. His message enumerated all the hardships of war—the enormous burdens of direct taxes, impressment of private property, disregard of the habeas corpus, the use of spies who arrested "good and loyal citizens," the failure of the government to give protection to lives and property of citizens in many parts of the Confederacy, the exemption of "favorites" from military service, the "legalized robbery" which the government's new financial policy would entail, the policy of conscription, "adapted to European serfs but repugnant to the spirit of a free people," secret sessions of Congress,[4] the appointment of officers "contrary to the constitution," the policy of dispersion.[5] All these things were contributing causes for the state of affairs in which the Confederacy found itself, according to the Governor. He said that the time had come for a change, for the President's policy was such as to result in reconstruction either with or without subjugation. The achievement of independence seemed to be the great and only good aimed at by those who held power at Richmond, and "we have been told from the halls of Congress that courts must be closed, and *state lines obliterated,*

---

[4] Brown frequently excoriated secret sessions regardless of the obvious fact that oftentimes the fate of a battle depended upon secrecy and that it was vital to the life of the Confederacy that some actions of Congress should not be known to the enemy. The *Chronicle and Sentinel,* which reflected the views of the Governor and the Vice President, published an editorial from the *Athens Watchman* which declared that the "abominable custom" had "changed our form of Government and subverted the constitution," and that by "a bold *coup d'état*" the "servants" had become the masters of the "patient, taxpaying, loyal people . . . who have poured out their life-blood like water . . . to be cheated and enslaved by a set of miserable political mountebanks and jugglers, as corrupt and contemptible as the Illinois rail-splitter himself."—Dec. 21, 1864.

[5] Brown had himself contributed no little to the policy of dispersion. To Brown's frantic appeals for men and arms during 1861 and 1862, for instance, the Secretary of War at one time replied that the Confederacy could not scatter its armies into fragments at the request of each governor who might be alarmed for the safety of his people.—*C. R.,* III, 142-43.

## FALL OF THE CONFEDERACY 245

if necessary, to accomplish this object." If this were so, then he thought the struggle was vain, for Southern independence was but a means to an end, the end being the preservation of the people's rights and liberties. He did not want the freedom and plainness of his speech misconstrued—he was actuated only by the desire to promote the cause "so dear to every patriotic heart." [6]

Brown's message aroused bitter passions and a duel was narrowly averted between the editors of the *Southern Confederacy* and the *Macon Telegraph*. It was charged and denied that Brown was faithless to the Confederacy, that he had speculated in corn, salt, and cotton, building up a fortune out of the necessities of the people, that he was inordinately ambitious and insanely jealous of the President.[7] The legislature as usual refused to be swayed by the Governor and remained loyal to the administration. It heard addresses of encouragement from Senator Hill, Toombs, Cobb, and others and refused to call a convention. It passed a resolution for a vigorous prosecution of the war and instructed the Governor to send a copy to each brigade commander from Georgia. It also took action against one of its members who was charged with treason for raising a "tory company" and saluting the United States flag.[8]

That Brown would be a gubernatorial candidate for reelection in 1865 seems to have been a foregone conclusion. Senator Hill writing President Davis of Brown's recent efforts to discredit the Confederate administration said he thought that Brown had jeopardized his success by his actions, and added: "I now look confidently to his defeat in October next." [9] The *Southern Recorder* in March promised

---
[6] *Ibid.*, II, 835 *et seq.*
[7] Avery, p. 319 *et passim.*
[8] *Acts of the General Assembly, 1865*, p. 84; Avery, p. 319 *et passim.* Cf. *H. J., 1864*, pp. 35, 36, 40. Allred (or Elrod) was arrested but was released on a writ of habeas corpus by Brown's friend, Judge Lochrane.
[9] "Georgia and the Confederacy," *American Historical Review*, I (Oct., 1895), pp. 100-1.

to bring out a candidate, saying that Brown had held the office long enough. It also wanted to have an accounting of state funds, to know the size of the state debt, and the number of exemptions from conscription.[10] The *Columbus Times* was confident the Governor would not again be a candidate, but the *Confederate Union* felt there were no grounds for such a view and that a large majority of the people wanted Brown's services continued.[11] "Orion" in the *Macon Confederacy* stated that there was "a fixed purpose if not a foregone conclusion" to require Governor Brown to serve another term. The writer thought that the "frequent and emphatic endorsements of the sovereign people" would compensate "our noble Governor" for the scurrilous abuse heaped upon him "by the partisans of the President." [12] In an editorial three and one-half columns in length the *Chronicle and Sentinel* on May 3, 1865, reviewed the public life of its candidate and approved him for a fifth term. It claimed that in the prosecution of the war Governor Brown had accomplished more "than any other ten men, without exception, including General Lee and President Davis in the number."

While the gubernatorial campaign was thus in preparation Richmond was evacuated, the armies of the Confederacy were surrendered, and seemingly the calendar was rolled back four years.[13] Brown surrendered the state troops to General James H. Wilson[14] and received his parole on May 8. He had previously issued a proclamation[15] convening the legislature in special session for May 22 "to consider the existing state

---

[10] Quoted by the *Chronicle and Sentinel,* Apr. 1, 1865.
[11] *Ibid.*
[12] Quoted by *Weekly Chronicle and Sentinel,* Apr. 19, 1865.
[13] The *Chronicle and Sentinel* was very much pleased and sought to curry favor with the U. S. authorities by saying that the Federal soldiers had done no more wicked things than the "rulers of the late so-called Confederacy."— May 24, 26, 1865. It must be remembered that the editor was a Northern man.
[14] *Supra,* p. 193.
[15] May 3, 1865.

# FALL OF THE CONFEDERACY 247

of things, and to provide the best means . . . for meeting the exigencies of the times."[16] With thousands of women, children, and wounded soldiers without food and shelter and the civil government in chaos, the necessity for convening the legislature seemed obvious. Stanton took another view of the matter[17] and on May 9 Brown was arrested, despite his parole, and taken to Washington.[18] On June 3 he telegraphed his wife that he was returning home by way of New York and Savannah and would arrive on June 20.[19] According to Brown's account, he was imprisoned nine days and was then paroled a week in Washington, after which he was released, it having been made known to President Johnson that his arrest had been in violation of his parole.[20] Brown was in Washington and free from prison from May 20 to June 3, at which time he presumably left for New York. There is no doubt that he utilized the time in endeavoring to ascertain the sentiment toward the South and incidentally toward himself. Stanton made "a decided im-

---

[16] *C. R.*, II, 878-79; *Federal Union*, May 9, 1865. (The Milledgeville *Confederate Union* had resumed its former name.)

[17] Gen. "Dick" Taylor, who was in charge of the Alabama-Mississippi Military Division at the time of the surrender, relates that he discussed with Federal Gen. Canby the question of calling the legislatures in those states for the purpose of repealing secession and abolishing slavery. The governors followed their advice and were imprisoned "for abetting a new rebellion." Taylor (p. 227) comments: "The North had been declaring for four years that the war was for the preservation of the Union, and Canby and I, in the innocence of our hearts, believed it."

[18] *C. R.*, II, 884-85; *ibid.*, III, 717-26. Cf. attitude of Stanton and Grant, *ibid.*, pp. 727-28. Others arrested in Georgia were Vice President Stephens, Gen. Howell Cobb, and Senator Hill. Toombs escaped to Europe.

[19] *Ibid.*, pp. 729-30; Fielder, p. 311.

[20] *C. R.*, II, 864-65. Published material relative to Brown's arrest and imprisonment may be found in *O. R.*, Ser. I, Vol. XLIX, Pt. II, pp. 630, 646-48, 680, 681, 706, 753, 836, 847, 1060, 1064, and Special Orders Nos. 73 and 74, *ibid.*, pp. 683, 703; *C. R.*, III, 717-26. In the Confederate archives are three unpublished documents in connection with Brown's release. Two are letters from Brown to President Johnson, dated May 20, and the other is from the President to Stanton, dated June 3. The letters disclose that Brown had at least one interview with the President and presumably one or more with Stanton. On June 3 Stanton and Brown signed the latter's parole.

pression" upon him, but in what way we are not told.[21] On June 18 the *Daily Chronicle and Sentinel* carried an editorial headed "Governor Brown" which stated that Brown's release was not relished in the North. Presumably as a means of ingratiating the Governor with the powers-that-be, it charged that the organs of the late Richmond powers in Georgia "have treated Governor Brown in the most shameful manner" and have told untruths "times without number."

On June 17 President Johnson appointed James Johnson of Muscogee County provisional governor of Georgia.[22] On the twenty-ninth Brown issued "An Address to the People of Georgia" in which he resigned his office into their hands, expressed his appreciation for the honors they had bestowed upon him, and advised their acceptance of the President's reconstruction program. He stated that he was included in one of the exceptions in the President's amnesty proclamation, that he had received no pardon, he had taken no oath, and he was not permitted to continue as governor of the state.[23] In the following September Brown took the oath of amnesty and moved to Atlanta where he afterwards made his home.[24] When the President's reconstruction program permitted the election of a governor in the following November, Judge Charles J. Jenkins was unanimously elected. Avery states that Brown refused to be a candidate.[25]

One phase of Brown's career had ended and another was about to begin, the bitterness and animosities of which were to dwarf into insignificance those of the war period. But

---

[21] President Johnson to Stanton, *ibid.*

[22] *C. R.*, IV, 8-12; *U. S. Statutes at Large*, XIII, 764.

[23] *C. R.*, III, 884-92. Gen. Wilson was quite perturbed over the "Address" and recommended that the Governor be arrested and removed to a Northern prison.—*Ibid.*, III, 730.

[24] Avery, p. 339.

[25] P. 351. Brown wrote Stephens in November that when he returned from prison and found Jenkins nominated for governor "in the special care of Kenan, Cabaniss & Co.," he met Jenkins and received his assurance that he would bury all past party divisions in his appointments, otherwise he (Brown) would have run against him.—Phillips, *Correspondence*, pp. 670-71.

though his new role aroused the bitterest passions and promised to him greater political and material success, his influence on state and nation was in reality in no way comparable to that which he exerted from 1861 to 1865.

What were Brown's motives, especially throughout 1864 and 1865, in his fight on the Confederate administration? Was he influenced by his adherence per se to the theory and practice of state rights, as he conceived them, or were there other motives? To what extent, if any, was Brown responsible for the failure of the Confederacy to establish its independence? Were his opinions independent of or subservient to those of Stephens and Toombs? Was there coöperative action between Georgia opponents of the Confederate administration and opponents outside the state? What of the various charges of graft and speculation which constantly pursued the Governor? These are questions which any student of the life of Joseph E. Brown seeks to answer.

In reply to the accusations made against Brown's honesty it may be said that none was ever sustained. He built up a considerable fortune during the war—though in no way comparable to that which he amassed during reconstruction—and purchased two plantations, which led to charges that his money had been acquired in large part from handling state cotton and salt and in speculating in food. In the quarrel between Brown and Cobb in the spring of 1864,[26] in which each accused the other of profiteering, Brown told Cobb that after the war began Mrs. Brown had inherited over $20,000 "in gold or its equivalent" which he had invested.[27] Although the state convention of 1865 provided for a commission to investigate the state's finances through the war period with special reference to cotton, nothing was found to substantiate the rumors against the Governor.[28]

---

[26] *Supra,* pp. 90, 92.
[27] *C. R.,* III, 557.
[28] *Report of the Committee . . . on the Financial Operations . . . During the War; C. R.,* IV, 333-34; Avery, pp, 319, 350; Knight, II, 802. The commission

Brown's motives in opposing the Confederate administration in the latter part of the war are open to several explanations. First, as the fortunes of the Confederacy waned and he realized that Southern independence could not be achieved, his well-known proclivity for being on the winning side asserted itself. The quickest way to end the war was to discredit the President, whom he had grown to dislike personally. This was the opinion expressed by Mahone in the United States Senate several years later when he said that Brown was "earnest for the cause till its fortunes began to wane" and then "with his militia he abandoned the starry cross to its fate." [29] Another explanation is that he was firmly convinced that the administration had destroyed civil liberty for all time. He saw nothing, therefore, to be gained by Southern independence and nothing to be lost by reëstablishing the old Union.

There was also the necessity, in the event of the failure of Southern arms, to curry favor with the enemy—to make "fair weather" with Lincoln, as "Troup" suggested[30]—in order to save himself from punishment for the active part he had taken in secession.[31] There is no doubt that when the end came Brown was fearful of his fate. Writing Stephens on April 25, 1865, he said: "If I am arrested and carried off I have prepared my mind to meet my fate with calmness." [32] General R. W. Carswell, whom Brown appointed brigadier general of state troops,[33] is quoted as saying that shortly before the surrender of the Confederate armies Brown visited him at his headquarters in Augusta where he ex-

---

was appointed by the Provisional Governor and received compensation.—*C. R.*, IV, 333-34. A resolution to appoint on the commission ex-Governor Brown and Provisional Governor Johnson was indefinitely postponed.—*Ibid.*, p. 352. Brown's letter of Oct. 30, 1865, to the Provisional Governor with reference to state cotton, *ibid.*, pp. 62-73.

[29] *Cong. Record*, 47th Cong., sp. sess., pp. 93-94.
[30] *Supra*, Chap. IX, n. 65.
[31] See "Notes on the Situation," No. 7, Benjamin H. Hill, Jr., p. 750.
[32] Phillips, *Correspondence*, p. 662.
[33] Northen, III, 417.

pressed the fear that he might be prosecuted for treason, and that he threw himself on a bed and wept.[34] If this theory be true, Brown was successful in his technique, for although he was arrested and imprisoned, he was promptly released, while other leaders were held for longer terms. This theory is also compatible with Brown's career in reconstruction.[35]

Another possible explanation is that Brown was himself aiming at supreme power, feeling, no doubt sincerely, that if he could supplant President Davis, his policies—civil and military—would rally the people to greater effort and thus secure the independence of the Confederacy "with the civil and religious liberties and constitutional rights of the people" unimpaired. There is much to be said in favor of this motive as an explanation of Brown's conduct. He had talked so much about "military despotism" and "constitutional rights" that he had no doubt hypnotized himself into believing that a war could be won with peacetime methods and that soldiers would be invincible in battle if military discipline were relaxed and the soldiers convinced that they were fighting for "liberty." These were Stephens' opinions also, but Stephens is more open to the suspicion of using his doctrinaire views for the purpose of discrediting the administration and of securing a reconstruction of the old Union. That Brown's ambition was insatiable is evident throughout his entire career. On several occasions he was either suggested for, or was thought to be aiming at, higher political honors. Henry S. Cleveland —biographer of Stephens—in a letter to Davis in 1888 expressed the opinion that Brown's conduct in 1864-65 was based upon his hope of becoming president himself.[36] Brown's ardor in the secession movement and his promptness in seizing Fort Pulaski, the Federal arsenals, and New York ships in the Savannah harbor in 1861, led to much discussion at

---

[34] Information given by a distinguished jurist of Georgia in a private letter dated Feb. 28, 1928. The writer states that Gen. Carswell related the story to him.
[35] *Infra,* Chap. XI.    [36] Rowland, X, 22.

the time and later to the effect that he was bidding for election to the presidency in November of that year.[37] The *Constitutionalist* of February 16, 1861, was enthusiastic and quoted a congressman as saying that Brown might as well be nominated for president "for he is bound to go through." [38]

The theory is strengthened by the fact that Brown, in common with the vast majority of the Southern people including the leaders, did not at any time publicly acknowledge that the Confederacy might not succeed in establishing its independence.[39] In none of Brown's messages or correspondence is there anything but assurance of success, provided of course that the policies of the administration were changed and Davis removed. As late as March, 1865, one month before the fall of Richmond, he was in correspondence with the military commander of the Florida district regarding the clearing out of Moccasin Slough to permit boats belonging to Georgia to pass out and run the blockade with cotton.[40] It

---

[37] Cf. Avery, pp. 178, 193; Mahone's charge in the U. S. Senate, Mar. 28, 1888, *Cong. Record,* 47th Cong., sp. sess., pp. 93-94; Underwood to Cobb, Apr. 11, 1861, Phillips, *Correspondence,* p. 560; Frank Moore, *Rebellion Record,* Vol. I, Pt. 3, pp. 22-23, quoting *Savannah Republican.* Hill probably had Brown, Toombs, and Stephens in mind when he referred in his "Notes on the Situation" to "disappointed politicians."—Benjamin H. Hill, Jr., p. 755.

[38] The Eufaula *Spirit of the South,* cited by the *Southern Recorder,* Feb. 5, 1861, thought Brown was full of "Jacksonian will and courage" and "better fitted for President of a Southern Confederacy than any man in the South." We have Avery's statement that Brown refused a position in the Confederate cabinet in 1862 (*supra,* Chap. IV, n. 2) and Brown's reply to Mahone to the effect that he had refused to allow his name to be used for any Confederate position whatever (*Cong. Record,* 47th Cong., sp. sess., pp. 106 *et seq.*).

[39] Cf. Pollard, *Davis,* pp. 116-17, and *idem, The . . . Campaigns . . . of Robert E. Lee . . . and Heroic Deeds of his Companions in Arms,* pp. 238-39. Evidence of the fact is seen in the market price of slaves throughout 1864 and the spring of 1865, which continued to be exceedingly high, even when the depreciated value of the currency is taken into consideration.—Cf. lists in *Chronicle and Sentinel,* Sept. 28, Oct. 12, 1864, and Mar. 10, 1865. There is the further fact that when Senator Wigfall's family received $1,000 in gold from relatives in the North in the last months of the war they promptly converted it into Confederate banknotes.—Mrs. D. Giraud Wright (Louise Wigfall), p. 221.

[40] *C. R.,* III, 710-12.

is not unreasonable to suppose that Brown—possessed as he always was of the most supreme self-confidence—felt that he was the Moses to lead the Confederacy out of the wilderness, and that if Davis could be discredited and removed, his own prestige as the governor of Georgia, his vote-getting ability, and his uncompromising stand on "constitutionalism" would sweep him into the office. But what if Davis and the Southern cause were inextricably bound together? Then he was willing to see the whole structure fall.

A final explanation, not by any means without merit, is that his opposition to the Confederate administration was due to his temperament. He was incapable of coöperating with his peers or his superiors, as his difficulties with the various legislatures show. His placid countenance and mild manner concealed an iron will, which, coupled with a supreme self-confidence, drove him on to rule or to ruin. If Confederate measures were not such as he approved, then those measures were wrong and must be defeated even if such a course involved destruction of the whole edifice. Probably this unfortunate temperament and mixed motives spurred the Governor on in his destructive course.

It is frequently said that the failure of the Confederacy was inevitable, that it never had a chance to succeed. The statement as an explanation suffers from over-simplification. The fact still remains that there is nowhere in history a record of the failure of a revolt of such magnitude as that of 1861-65. That the Confederacy was able to maintain the contest for four years, that it developed a fighting force of such power as to amaze the world, that its people throughout poured out their lifeblood and treasures unstintedly, are facts which are not disputed and which make the ultimate failure of the cause difficult of explanation. The matter is still more puzzling in view of the fact that in the beginning there was little Union sentiment, and what existed was for the most part driven to cover. There are, in consequence, as many explanations as there are writers—the opposing forces were too strong; the excessive use of paper money; neglect of cavalry; the policy of dispersion; lack of industrialization in the South; the policy of conscription; the inability of the people to endure for a sufficient time the hardships of war; lack of munitions, arms, men; lack of transportation; Union sentiment; departure from constitutional principles; and many other arguments.

Yancey, insisting that the adoption of a permanent constitution was the chief difficulty, said that what the country needed was a provisional war government, "restricted only by the nature and extent of its necessities." [41] Pollard was of the same opinion. He thought that the fetters of a "fixed and inelastic . . . constitution, stiffly copied from the United States," created the factions which so bedeviled the President and embarrassed his administration.[42] Schwab comments on the "striking fact" that with the opportunity freely to amend the Federal constitution and with the prospect of a war before them the framers of the Confederate constitution, though they made improvements for peacetime purposes, did not enlarge the President's power by including in his authority as commander in chief the right to suspend the writ of habeas corpus nor make clear and definite the right of Congress to conscript, to call out the state militia, and to impress goods for the army.[43] Taylor refers ironically to the "haste to manufacture a paper constitution in which the powers of different departments were as carefully weighed as are dangerous drugs by dispensing chemists" and to the arrangement for a bicameral legislature which he thought was only "a refuge for mischievous twaddlers to worry the executive and embarrass the armies." [44]

---

[41] DuBose, p. 704.
[42] *Davis,* pp. 200-10. Cf. White, *Rhett,* p. 198.
[43] Pp. 211 *et seq.*
[44] P. 234.

Ben Hill declared that the South was crushed by ideas rather than by bayonets, and that the ideas were two, "neither of which had the slightest foundation in truth"—that the Confederate government had become a military despotism, and that the Southern people had but to lay down their arms and they would be restored at once to all the rights of the old Union. He charged that these ideas were industriously spread by the United States government, but more particularly by "malcontents at home and in high places," who had "done all in their power to hurry our people into secession," and having been "most active in destroying the Union" were later "most active in destroying the Confederacy." [45] The same thought was expressed by President Davis in an address before the Southern Historical Society in Richmond in 1873 when he said: "We were more cheated than conquered into surrender." [46] Owsley insists that the failure of the South to establish its independence was due, not to the lack of resources nor yet to the lack of men, but to internal political conditions—state rights and local patriotism. He is convinced that if the South had allowed the Confederate government the same freedom which the people of the North allowed their government, it would have been almost an impossibility for the South to suffer defeat. But the Stephenses, the Toombs, the Browns, and the Vances could not wait till the war was over to try out their theories and air their differences, he adds.[47]

In the last analysis all these opinions agree. The successful prosecution of the war was no doubt hindered by a rigid, permanent constitution of confederated states, which, thanks to Alexander Stephens, copied the worst features of the

---

[45] "Notes on the Situation," No. 9, Benjamin Hill, Jr., p. 401; address before the Southern Historical Society in Atlanta, Feb. 18, 1874, *ibid.*, pp. 398 *et seq.*
[46] *Ibid.*, p. 401.
[47] *State Rights*, p. 2 *et passim.*

United States Constitution—checks and balances and division of powers[48]—and, also like the United States Constitution, failed to give the President and Congress adequate, clear-cut war powers. The Confederate government as inferior in numbers, in area, and in resources, and as the active party in the move for independence, had greater need for freedom of action than did the United States government.

But of more importance than the type of constitution—indeed, perhaps the reason for that type of constitution—was the fact that Southern nationalism had not fully come to maturity.[49] True the South had always possessed a unity that made it more than a geographical expression. Its immigration had been more homogeneous than other sections, and this fact, together with occupation, slave labor, and the race question, made for a unity of interests, traditions, aspirations, problems, and dangers that set it apart from the rest of the country.[50] But the unity was not complete in 1861 and the fact made for two factions in the Confederacy: those who were section-conscious and who accordingly supported the Confederate administration, and those who were state-conscious and formed the state rights group.[51] To the latter group Southern nationalism never became emotionally a reality, and this fact constitutes the tragedy of the Con-

---

[48] A jealousy for congressional prerogatives often led the Confederate Congress into aggressive opposition to the President, as a similar jealousy led U. S. Congresses to oppose Andrew Johnson and Woodrow Wilson.

[49] Except in South Carolina where it was ripe as early as 1851. Cf. N. W. Stephenson, "Southern Nationalism in South Carolina in 1851," *American Historical Review*, XXXVI (Jan., 1931), 314 *et seq;* White, *Rhett,* pp. 146, 155, 162, 188 *et seq.*

[50] See Carpenter, p. 17 *et passim.*

[51] See Stephenson, p. 27. There were also individuals who used the shibboleth of state rights as an excuse—those whose ambitions were not gratified in the setup of the new government. Schwab is no doubt right when he says (pp. 352-53) that the abundance of able and ambitious leaders, civil and military, proved to be a liability rather than an asset to the Confederate cause. Ben Hill declared that the internal dissensions among distinguished men did more to bring on Southern defeat and humiliation than did the armies of Grant and Sherman.—Benjamin H. Hill, Jr., p. 364.

FALL OF THE CONFEDERACY 257

federacy. Not until the hardships of war and the suffering and humiliation of the reconstruction period had done their work was there a unity "which even today, after the operation of powerful opposing forces, defies destruction and puzzles outsiders," and which a recent historian mistakenly thinks existed fully at the beginning of the war.[52] Southern nationalism was strong, and against an outside foe it would have presented a solid front, but toward the American foe the weakness in the Achilles heel—state rights—was naturally in evidence.

The pattern of thinking of the state rights group had been set by the struggles of the South as a minority in the old Union, when its leaders were compelled to depend upon the principle of constitutional guarantees to maintain Southern rights in the Union on an equal footing with the more populous Northern states. In that period Southern statesmen had used constitutional guarantees—state rights—as a means to an end.[53] But lesser men, mistaking the means for the end and being unable to see that because of homogeneity of population and similarity of climate and occupation no reason existed for their use in the Confederacy, transformed a weapon into an abstract principle and themselves into doctrinaires. To this group Brown belonged. He never grasped the fact that the reason for the great constitutional arguments in the halls of Congress for the past thirty years which had so profoundly influenced his thinking lay in a dissimilarity of social and economic conditions which did not, to any appreciable extent, exist in the Confederacy, and that

---

[52] Carpenter, p. 17.
[53] See *Supra,* p. 47. "No state and no section . . . has found any difficulty in adopting or opposing the State-Rights theory, whenever its interests lay that way. . . . That the Eastern States did not become the stronghold of the State-Rights party was due, not to their attachment to Federal political doctrines, but rather to the fact that, upon the whole, Congressional legislation (other than the Embargo) and a broad judicial construction of the Constitution favored their economic and social interests."—Charles Warren, *The Supreme Court in United States History,* I, 388, henceforth cited as Warren.

there were, therefore, no conflicting interests between Georgia and other Southern states. He was "so intensely patriotic to Georgia that he never could grasp completely nor understand the problems and purposes of the Confederacy as a whole. . . . The length to which the quarrel went threatened at times to provide a bigger problem for President Davis than meeting the Federal armies." [54] The same thought is expressed by another historian who says that Brown saw the military situation only from the point of view of a citizen of an invaded state, never from that of the general staff, and that this view prevented "that unity of command that was the only basis for any hope of ultimate Confederate success." [55]

Davis, on the other hand, being a statesman, having the responsibility of the Confederacy, and coming as he did from one of the newer states where the feeling of Southern nationalism existed in place of the local patriotism of the older states, was a stanch advocate of Southern independence. Only a Southern nationalist could have given the ringing reply that he gave to Jacques and Gilmore: "We will go on [fighting] unless you acknowledge our right to self-government. We are not fighting for slavery. We are fighting for independence, and that, or extermination, we will have. . . . You may emancipate the rest [of the slaves], you may emancipate every negro in the Confederacy, . . . but we will be free! We will govern ourselves! We will do it, if we have to see every Southern plantation sacked, and every Southern city in flames." [56]

Secession meant to Brown only slavery and state sovereignty and when conscription or other centralizing measures violated the principle of state sovereignty as he conceived it,

---

[54] Coulter, *Georgia*, p. 307.
[55] Hay, *Hood's Tennessee Campaign*, pp. x-xi.
[56] Quoted by Kirkland, pp. 94-95. Cf. Davis, *Rise and Fall*, II, 610-11; editorial, "Is it Peace?" in *Constitutionalist*, July 30, 1864; *supra*, Chap. IX, n. 6.

he felt that the Southern people were losing precisely what they had started in to fight for.⁵⁷ Brown stated his position on numerous occasions, one of which was in an interview with a correspondent of the Charleston *South Carolinian,* in which he denied that he was in opposition to the Confederacy. He said that Georgia in common with her sisters as a sovereign state had delegated to the general government, as an agent, certain powers; and only when these were transcended or usurped by Davis or by Congress had he stepped forward to enter his protest. The encroachment of "centralized power" had been the "curse of the continent," and it "behooved every statesman in the South to see to it that while yielding to our own general government all proper support, every attempt by it to interfere with the action of the state authorities should be promptly met and checked." He would be the "last man in the Confederacy to throw obstacles in the way of the President," under any other conditions.⁵⁸

Pollard also thought that the conscription law was unconstitutional, but being a Southern nationalist he justified it as a revolutionary measure. "The true distinction as to the assumption of irregular and extraordinary powers in a state of war is a moral one," he said during the war, "to be decided by good or bad effects; and as this law certainly did save the Confederacy, we must consider it as a beneficent stretch of power, and account opposition to it, as a single measure, untenable, unwise, and unpatriotic." ⁵⁹

Brown's apologists usually stress the fact that he was "sincere." Avery speaks of him as the man "fated to bear the colors" in the struggle against Confederate encroachment.⁶⁰ Fielder says that Brown did not oppose Davis "except in the vital and important matters wherein they differed in

---

⁵⁷ See interview which Brown gave to *Cincinnati Commercial Appeal,* May 7, 1867. Brown favored a union on the order of the German Confederation.—*C. R.,* II, 638.
⁵⁸ Quoted by Avery, pp. 290-91.
⁵⁹ *Davis,* p. 213.   ⁶⁰ P. 225.

judgment," and that Brown never failed to coöperate in all matters "wherein they agreed" [61]—which is exactly no justification whatever. That Congress, the legislature of his own state, the Georgia supreme court, and other men who were upholders of the principle of state rights often differed with him was of no consequence to Governor Brown.

Aside from the attempts of Avery, Fielder, and Stephens to justify Brown's conduct toward the Confederate administration, he stands undefended in history so far as the author can ascertain. Dodd says Brown "put every obstacle in the way of the administration," [62] and Freeman calls him "the chief malcontent in the southeastern states." [63] Eckenrode thinks that he ventured upon a degree of opposition "that bordered on treason," and that he was a "popularity hunter, imbued with a hatred for Davis." [64] Hay is less severe in his estimate, but he admits that Brown "was always in conflict with something or somebody," that he daily became more independent, and that he and Stephens "acted as the spearhead of the peace movement." [65]

Owsley, whose *State Rights* is a study devoted to political conditions in the Confederacy, is one of Brown's severest critics. He thinks he "never ceased night or day . . . to throw obstacles in the path of the Confederacy," and that his "patriotism reached very little further than the borders of his own political opportunities which coincided with the boundaries of the State of Georgia." He accuses Brown of "engaging in frequent, numerous, and far-fetched quarrels with the sorely beset Richmond government" and "spoiling at all times for a quarrel with President Davis" in at least one of which he "enforced his arguments by a garbled quotation from Davis himself." He thinks Brown's conduct in

---

[61] P. 261.
[62] *Davis*, pp. 283, 300.  [63] *R. E. Lee*, I, 607.
[64] P. 300.
[65] See "Joseph Emerson Brown, Governor of Georgia, 1857-1865," *Georgia Historical Quarterly*, XIII (June, 1929), 89-109.

# FALL OF THE CONFEDERACY

furloughing the troops "during the most critical moments of the campaign around Atlanta" was little short of treasonable.[66]

Miss Thompson is of like opinion with reference to Brown's furloughing the troops. She thinks his actions in the matter are "inexplicable" unless they be taken as "preliminary moves toward peace," that his own explanation—that the crops needed to be gathered—is entirely inadequate, and that if he could have acted upon his own responsibility he would have accepted Sherman's peace offer.[67] Stephenson finds the Governor of Georgia one of the puzzling figures of Confederate history: "With the whole fabric of Southern life toppling about him, Brown argued, quibbled, evaded, and became the rallying point for disaffection. . . . He never seemed conscious of the war as a whole or of the Confederacy as a whole. To defend Georgia and if that could not be done to make peace for Georgia—such in the mind of Brown was the aim of the war." [68]

Moore, who calls Brown "a strong-willed martinet," holds a similar opinion: "So far as he was concerned the war had primarily been a Georgia problem. . . . The plan of the Chief of Staff, the President, to have one unified and harmonized military force to move at his behest, hither and thither, according to the rules of strategy against the invaders, was of no consequence to him." He was never deterred by considerations of expediency from "ventilating his political obsessions. . . ." [69] Writing of Brown and Vance the same author says: "They made life uncomfortable for President Davis. Controversial in character, anti-Davis in feeling, particularistic by nature and training, supinely self-confident by endowment and because of a spectacular rise in life, and unbending

---

[66] Pp. 15, 28, 35, 50, 68, 91, *et passim;* Owsley, *King Cotton Diplomacy,* pp. 19, 50.
[67] C. M. Thompson, pp. 37-38.
[68] Pp. 145-47.
[69] Pp. 230, 275.

States' rightist in principle, they were admirably equipped to torment the souls of the military strategists at Richmond. Their patriotism was essentially local. They could not think consistently in terms of the whole Confederacy. They were simply allies of the other States, and often puny allies at that...." [70]

Rhodes compares Lincoln's difficulties with Governor Seymour of New York to those of Davis with Brown and Vance and concludes that Seymour was far more considerate of his president. While there was some friction over the arrest of Vallandigham and over the draft riots, Rhodes feels that in the dangers of Lee's invasion of Pennsylvania, Seymour "displayed a patriotic zeal and a well-directed energy which could not have been excelled by a Republican in his position." [71] He thinks that Brown and Vance had the "itch for disputation," and that they "trumped up differences with the President," while other Southern governors gave loyal support.[72]

It would of course have been an advantage to the Confederacy to have had in the governor's chair in Georgia a different type of man, but this was not possible to accomplish by ballot, as friends of the administration found in 1861 and 1863. The only other method of getting rid of Brown in this office was to entice him into the army. Several governors, North and South, went into the army and there was a time in 1863 when Brown seemed inclined that way. When the local defense troops were called out in 1863 he expressed a willingness to serve in any capacity, seemingly showing a preference for that of aide to General Cobb, though the matter was not pressed.[73] In 1862 President Davis received a letter from one L. E. Bleckley of Atlanta, dated May 2,

---

[70] P. 296.
[71] IV, 331.
[72] V, 475-77.
[73] *C. R.*, II, 476-77; *ibid.*, III, 526, 531, 545, 561, 565, 572.

# FALL OF THE CONFEDERACY          263

which seems sufficiently important in this connection to quote almost in its entirety:

> ... My opinion is that Gov. Brown has military ability, and that he is willing to use it for the defense of the country, especially for the defense of Georgia. At this crisis, when the State is menaced at so many points, he might (I think he would) vacate the Ex. chair for a Major General's commission. He has such tact and energy, is so vigilant and persevering, that our people would feel very great confidence in his management.
>
> Since the passage of the Conscription Law and the introduction of other changes, the Executive Officers of the several states have lost much of their relative importance, and Gov. Brown could do more good now in the field than at Milledgeville. Such I think would be his own view of the matter, and it is upon that idea that I rest my hope of his accepting military command if it were tendered.
>
> I write without his prompting or that of any other person, and if my suggestion is of any value, I know you will not the less esteem it because it comes from an unpretending citizen and one who has not the good fortune to be known to you.[74]

The letter was submitted to Lee, whose comment reads: "Respectfully returned. I have no knowledge of the military capacity of Gv. Brown or of his wishes. R. E. Lee." [75]

This letter may or may not have been written with the Governor's consent. At any rate the army probably felt that it had trouble enough with civilian officers and did not care to multiply those troubles by including one so contentious as the Georgia governor.

The power behind the throne in opposition to the Confederate administration was Alexander Stephens, who throughout the war, one suspects, waited and hoped for reunion with the United States. State rights formed a convenient camouflage for this desire. Realizing this, President

---
[74] Personal Papers of Joseph E. Brown.
[75] Ibid.

Davis neutralized as far as possible Stephens' opportunities for mischief.[76] Linton Stephens also wished reunion, but one has the feeling somehow that his devotion to "state rights" and "liberty" was more sincere. Brown was more than a mere satellite of Alexander Stephens, although he was tremendously flattered by Stephens' friendship and went further in his opposition to the President than he would have done without Stephens' support. The two men trod so near the line separating treason from loyalty as to make it difficult oftentimes to determine on which side they were moving. Brown and Toombs had little in common during the war; they had less than nothing in common after the war. Toombs, with his individualistic philosophy, cared little for state rights. His coöperation with the group was due to other reasons. It was a tragedy to Toombs and to the South that circumstances made his great talents unavailable to the Confederacy.

The author has been unable to find evidence of collusion between the Georgia malcontents and those of other states. But it would be difficult to see how the influence of the Georgia group could have been enhanced. Stephens as vice president of the Confederate States of America was a national figure. Brown as four times governor of one of the most important states in the Confederacy was in a position of influence and power. Toombs before the war and in the period of secession was the greatest statesman in the South. Linton Stephens was generally recognized as the echo of his brother, but as a member of the Georgia legislature he was able through his various resolutions to command the attention of the entire Confederacy. There was no need for secret coöperation with opponents of the administration in other

---

[76] Eckenrode (p. 324) thinks Stephens did much against the Southern cause, "not from want of patriotism, but from lack of common sense," that "an idealism incurable by fact, grief over the separation of the South from the Union and the horrors of war distracted his impressionable mind and made him a liability to his country and one of the causes of its overthrow."

states. Georgia and Richmond, the legislature and the press, offered a forum and a medium from and through which adherents and opponents alike might take their cues.

That Brown was important in the failure of the South to achieve independence seems obvious. His attitude toward conscription and the matter of local defense; his furloughing the troops in 1864 and 1865; his undignified correspondence with Cobb, the secretary of War, and even with the President himself; his opposition to the habeas corpus; his premature peace efforts; his various messages to the legislature, beginning in 1861, filled with criticisms of Congress and of the President, with reference to practically every war measure—all these of necessity weakened the Confederacy by decimating its armies, by breaking down the morale of both soldiers and civilians, by encouraging disloyalty, and by encouraging the enemy.

Whether or not Governor Brown was "sincere," the records seem to justify the conclusion that he was one of the chief actors in the great drama upon which the curtain fell at Appomattox. He played a leading role in 1860-61; he played a different but no less important one in the three years that followed. In the one he aided materially in creating a Southern Confederacy; in the other he helped to destroy it.

## CHAPTER XI

## RECONSTRUCTION

SINCE BROWN's career after 1865 gives the key to his character, an examination of his conduct in the fifteen years following the close of the war is necessary to an understanding of his relations with the Confederacy.

Under President Johnson's reconstruction plan—somewhat less liberal than Lincoln's—Georgia adopted a new constitution, repealed secession, abolished slavery, and in November, 1865, elected state officers and congressmen. The new legislature ratified the Thirteenth Amendment, passed a law to authorize Negroes to testify in courts, adopted a mild labor code,[1] and elected United States senators. In April, 1866, the President declared peace restored. But Radical Republicans, denying the right of the President to reconstruct the Southern states, refused to seat the elected representatives, passed the civil rights bill over the President's veto, and by the necessary two-thirds vote proposed to the states the Fourteenth Amendment. On November 9, 1866, the Georgia legislature refused to ratify the amendment. If, said the legislature, Georgia is a state, then the amendment has been proposed in an unconstitutional manner, since she was not represented in Congress. If she is not a state, then she has no right to ratify and her action would have no binding force.[2] There was also the additional reason,

---

[1] Edwin C. Woolley, *The Reconstruction of Georgia*, pp. 18-21, henceforth cited as Woolley.

[2] The point was met by applying to it the theory of "relation," an operation known to private law. It had been previously applied in constitutional

though not formally expressed, of the alternative of Negro suffrage or a reduction in the state's congressional representation.[3] The controlling reason in Georgia as in all other Southern states for rejecting the Fourteenth Amendment was the dishonor of which the people felt they would be guilty if they should thus assist in placing their former leaders under political disability, for whatever guilt attached to their leaders was shared by themselves.[4]

The Radicals had never intended the adoption of the Fourteenth Amendment to end requirements for readmission of the Southern states. It is believed that, in fact, they did not mean for the amendment to be adopted at the time and included the clause disfranchising all Southern leaders to insure its rejection and so make opportunity for outright Negro suffrage, that the Radicals might be assured of political control in the section lately "in rebellion."[5] As a matter of campaign strategy, the congressional guarantee bill, promising admission as soon as the Fourteenth Amendment should be ratified, was tabled instead of being defeated, and the idea was allowed to prevail that only the ratification of

---

law in giving to acts of territorial legislatures the same effect as though they had been done after statehood was obtained. The body ratifying the Fourteenth Amendment need not be the legislature, the argument ran, but since it will become the legislature the ratification will, by relation, be imputed to the state legislature.—See *Cong. Globe*, 41st Cong., 2nd sess., pp. 1710, 2062, cited by Woolley, p. 71.

[3] In Southern opinion the South had never had adequate representation, because of the compromise in the Constitution by which only three fifths of its slaves were counted, while unnaturalized persons, chiefly resident in the North, were included in the population for determining the basis of representation.

[4] *S. J., 1866*, pp. 39, 42, 44, 65-72; *H. J., 1866*, pp. 68-69. Cf. Johnston and Browne, p. 604; Pearce, pp. 136 *et seq*. In petitioning for the pardon of Jefferson Davis, the Georgia legislature said that if Davis were guilty then "so are we; we were the principals, he was our agent. Let not the retribution of a mighty nation be visited upon his head, while we who urged him to his destiny are suffered to escape."—Quoted by George F. Milton, *The Age of Hate*, pp. 254-55.

[5] Howard K. Beale, *The Critical Year: A Study of Andrew Johnson and Reconstruction*, pp. 202-10, henceforth cited as Beale. During the debate on the amendment Thad Stevens said he trusted the Almighty would "never permit the Democratic party to gain the ascendency."—Rhodes, VI, 176.

the amendment was required. The strategy of the Radicals was successful, the Southern states rejected the amendment and on March 2, 1867, Congress passed over the President's veto the military reconstruction act providing for the abolition of the Johnson state governments, the division of the South into five military districts in which military governors should have complete civil and military power, and the calling in each of these states of a constitutional convention. Delegates to the convention were to be chosen by all citizens, regardless of race or color, except those disfranchised for rebellion. The revised constitutions were required to accept the franchise provided in the act and to be ratified by a majority of those who had been allowed to register. When Congress had accepted the constitutions, and when the legislatures elected under them had adopted the Fourteenth Amendment and it had become a part of the Constitution of the United States,[6] then the states would be admitted into the Union and military government would cease.

During 1865-66 Governor Brown was in correspondence with President Johnson, doing what he could for the restoration of normal conditions. He advised with members of the legislature, defended a client in the United States district court to determine the constitutionality of the test oath, and in a county convention said with reference to the race question: "While we cannot accord to the negro race social and political equality, I believe it is the fixed purpose of nineteen twentieths of the people of Georgia to see that they have legal equality and that justice and equity be constantly administered." [7] In a published letter of February 14, 1866, Brown declared that "madness alone could dream of political equality" between the two races and that the United States government would not permit the enforcement of such a law.[8]

After the Fourteenth Amendment had been voted down

---

[6] *U. S. Statutes at Large,* XIV, 428; XV, 2, 14.

[7] Avery, pp. 358-60; Fielder, pp. 756 *et seq.; C. R.,* III, 730-31.

[8] *Atlanta Intelligencer,* Feb. 18, 1866; Knight, II, 816.

and while the first military reconstruction bill was pending in Congress, Brown went to Washington to sound out the situation and gauge public opinion.[9] Whether he was "influenced by motives of ambition, excited by temptations offered him on the 'High Mountain' to which he was carried in Washington," whether he was dominated by fear for himself for his zeal in secession, or whether he was moved to sacrifice himself for the good of the Southern people, historians, like the people of his time, are not agreed. He returned from Washington a Radical Republican and in a letter published in the *Atlanta New Era* of February 26, 1867, advised the people to acquiesce in the Congressional program of reconstruction.[10] Taking the position that the people of the South were a conquered people and subject to the will of the conqueror, he advised the full acceptance and enforcement of the Fourteenth Amendment, Negro suffrage, and the military reconstruction bill which he predicted Congress would pass.[11] At a banquet given in Atlanta in April in honor of General Pope, who had come to assume command of the "third district" under congressional reconstruction, none other than ex-Governor Brown responded to the toast, "Reconstruction—Let it proceed under the Sherman bill without appealing to the Supreme Court of the United States, the arbiter of our civil rights, and not of political issues." [12]

Avery states that the press "poured hot shot" on Brown. He was called "scalawag," "renegade," "the betrayer of the honor and interest of the state," "Judas Iscariot" and

---
[9] Avery, p. 363.
[10] See Phillips, *Correspondence*, p. 703, n. 3.
[11] In view of Brown's opposition to the suspension of the writ of habeas corpus in wartime it is amazing that he should accept without a struggle a measure in peacetime which, as President Johnson said in his veto, placed the people of ten states "under the absolute domination of military rulers." See Edward McPherson (comp.), *Political History of the United States of America during the Period of Reconstruction*, pp. 166-75, henceforth cited as McPherson.
[12] *Atlanta New Era*, Apr. 14, 1867.

"Benedict Arnold." [13] Brown's friends were stunned, his enemies thought that he was running true to form. As told by a recent writer, when Toombs returned from Europe and was told of Brown's apostasy he denounced it as a lie and when it was verified took to his bed.[14] When Sherman introduced a bill exempting Brown from the provisions of the military reconstruction act[15] the press screamed "collusion." From the status of a popular idol Brown suffered, in the words of his friend Avery, an "alteration in public favor, so sudden, so complete, so overwhelming and savage as to constitute the most extraordinary personal vicissitude of the extraordinary period. . . . It was a frightful struggle, . . . it battered and ostracised him. . . ." [16] Horace Greeley was delighted with the new convert to the party and declared that Governor Brown deserved the thanks of his neighbors.[17] Brown immediately began a vigorous campaign in favor of congressional reconstruction, speaking in Savannah on April 18, in Augusta on April 27, in Milledgeville on June 6.[18] In the capital city he declared that he belonged to no party organization "except the Reconstruction party of Georgia." In an interview in the *Cincinnati Commercial Appeal* on May 7 he repeated that he was in favor of accepting whatever terms were offered and of "living up to them like men that have been beaten." He was bitter against those who were unwilling to reconstruct under the Sherman act and fearful that their conduct might lead to something like the Brownlow regime in Tennessee where "only negroes and Union Southerners could vote."

---

[13] Avery, p. 364; Fielder, p. 425; Pearce, p. 153. The press in general expressed this view.

[14] Claude G. Bowers, *The Tragic Era—the Revolution after Lincoln,* p. 208, henceforth cited as Bowers.

[15] See James G. Blaine, *Twenty Years of Congress,* II, 211-12, henceforth cited as Blaine.

[16] P. 336.

[17] *New York Tribune,* May 20, 1867.

[18] Reported in *Atlanta New Era,* Apr. 24, 1867; *Augusta Daily Press,* Apr. 25, 1867; *Federal Union,* June 11, 1867.

## RECONSTRUCTION 271

On April 10, 1867, Governor Jenkins issued from Washington, where he had gone to test the constitutionality of the reconstruction act, an address to the people of Georgia. He said there yet remained a third department of government "whose decrees, unlike the executive veto, cannot be overridden by Congress," [19] and advised "a firm but temperate refusal" to acquiesce in the act and "a patient, manly endurance of military government until . . . better counsels shall prevail at the Federal capital." [20]

While Governor Jenkins and governors of other Southern states sought in vain through the nation's highest tribunal for relief for their states from the enforcement of Radical reconstruction, Ben Hill employed his voice and his pen to arouse the despairing people to action. In his Davis Hall speech and his "Notes on the Situation" in the summer of 1867 he called upon the people to present a solid front against the unconstitutional program of the Radicals. The effect of his exhortations was felt throughout the South. When Hill arose to speak in Davis Hall, Atlanta, feeling in the crowded house was tense. General Pope's military staff occupied front seats and the General himself had just sent an order to Hill forbidding a controversial speech. Disregarding the possible consequences to himself, Hill made the speech he had intended. He denounced the Radicals, declared their military acts unconstitutional, and advised voters to defeat their program by registering and refusing to vote for a convention,[21] or, if the convention were held, to vote against

---
[19] Rhodes, VI, 184.
[20] Avery, p. 367. Cf. *Georgia* v. *Stanton,* 6 Wallace 50; *Georgia* v. *Meade, Grant, et al.,* 6 Wallace 241. The next year Governor Jenkins was removed by order of the military commander of the district, whereupon he took the state's seal and money out of reach of the Radicals.
[21] The act of March 23, 1867, provided for ratification by a majority of the registered voters, hence the strategy of registering and by inaction causing the convention plan to fail of adoption. This strategy gave such promise of success in 1868, and the need of Radicals for Republican electors in that year was so great, that on March 11, 1868, Congress amended the reconstruction acts so as to provide that elections under them should be decided

the adoption of the constitution which they would offer. In this way, he pointed out, the South could at least refrain from being a party to its own dishonor. He spoke for two hours and "when he had done Georgia was once more on her feet, and Georgians were organized for the protest of 1868 and the victories of 1870." [22]

Hill's "Notes on the Situation," which have been characterized as the "Federalist of Southern rights," [23] consisted of twenty-two letters published in the *Chronicle and Sentinel* between June 19 and August 1, 1867.[24] Hill believed that relief from Radical measures could be secured by appeals to the courts and by solidarity in political action. "Sue in damages for every injury; indict for every crime," he urged, and offered his services as a lawyer free, "for the written constitution is my client, and the preservation of its protection the only fee I ask." [25] In reply to Brown's argument that the South must submit to any terms its conquerers chose to impose, Hill answered with scorn: "None but a barbarous people, Northern radicals and Southern renegades, ever said so —a conquered people are subject to the terms of the conquest, made known and demanded before, or at the time of the conquest . . . and to no other terms or will whatever . . . and none but a treacherous conqueror would demand more." [26] He argued that if the South consented to the reconstruction measures, then they would become valid and

---

by a majority of the votes cast.—*U. S. Statutes at Large,* XV (Public Laws), 41.

[22] Benjamin H. Hill, Jr., p. 294, quoting from "one who was present." The entire speech may be found in *ibid.,* pp. 294-307.

[23] Bowers, p. 212.

[24] The "Notes on the Situation" may be found also in Benjamin H. Hill, Jr., pp. 730-811. Henry Grady said of them: "In my opinion they stand alone as the profoundest and most eloquent political essays ever penned by an American. They were accepted as the voice of the South, uttering her protest and her plea, and as such were discussed on the streets of London and the Boulevards of Paris, no less than in the cities of the North. Even now they stir the blood and kindle the pulse of the most phlegmatic reader. . . ." —*Ibid.,* pp. 51-52.

[25] "Notes on the Situation," Nos. 12 and 13.   [26] *Ibid.,* No. 6.

the Southern people would be the authors of their own shame. "Therefore it is that emissaries come, and renegades labor, and original secessionists become orthodox loyalists, and by persuasion and by threats, by bribing some and alarming others and deceiving all, seek to get the *people to consent*." [27] What made the reconstruction acts so nauseating, Hill wrote, was that they were commended and urged

by some who were born among us—who have been often trusted and honored by us; nay, by those who hurried us into secession to get our rights, to save our honor, and to "avoid equality with the negro"; who assured us secession would be peaceable, and who, after secession, did all they could to provoke a war; who pledged us the "last man and the last dollar" if the war should come, and who employed their talents in discouraging the men, in quarreling with ourselves and making money when the war did come; who bravely promised us that no enemy should invade our soil without "marching over their dead bodies," but who, when the enemy came, only betrayed us to subjugation; who now inform us of their confidential receptions into the counsels of our oppressors, and can bring from those counsels only the assurance that unless we drink of this cup, one more bitter shall be provided.[28]

Replying to the argument that if the South did not accept the military bills a more odious plan would be provided and property confiscated, Hill inquired how, if this plan failed through being found unconstitutional, a worse one could succeed? Disfranchisement, confiscation, and far worse evils cannot come through the existing state governments, he said, but they can come and they will come through the government which this plan of reconstruction proposes to establish. Taking a fling at Brown, whose accumulated wealth during the war had led to ugly rumors, Hill said that a few of the Radicals were rich, having prospered while their

---
[27] *Ibid.*, No. 4.
[28] Benjamin H. Hill, Jr., p. 753.

victims were sacrificed and having shown a talent to make money while their dupes showed a will to lose blood. It may be reasonable that they should make great sacrifices to keep what they have made, for what is honor worth to such men? he inquired. "If anything can be baser than degradation, it is such a motive for sinking to it." [29]

Brown replied to Hill with a "Review of the Notes on the Situation," [30] in which he alleged the inconsistency of Hill's political career and charged him with opposing reconstruction only because the measures in question disfranchised him and prevented his holding office. After replying to Brown[31] Hill continued in his "Notes on the Situation" to kindle "the fires of hope in Georgia and elsewhere" and to lead the people "to remember that their cause was not lost." [32]

Until December, 1867, only Hill of the old leaders engaged in the task of arousing the people and leading them to see what might be accomplished by presenting a solid front through organization.[33] Stephens, in retirement at "Liberty Hall," differed widely from Brown on reconstruction. "If Governor Brown and others see fit 'to take to lifeboats' in our stranded position," he said, "I have no quarrel to make with him or them, for pursuing that course," but he thought they would be "swamped in the surf." [34] Stephens was firmly convinced that the two races could not exist on a basis of equality and was fearful that the country was on the verge of a "consolidated, centralized, Despotic Empire." [35]

On July 11 Herschel V. Johnson published a reply to citizens of Atlanta who had asked his views on reconstruc-

---

[29] "Notes on the Situation," No. 5. Cf. Bowers, pp. 314 *et seq.*

[30] Published in the *Chronicle and Sentinel,* Aug. 1 to Aug. 9, 1867, and also as a 32-page pamphlet.

[31] "Notes on the Situation," Nos. 15-17.

[32] President Davis speaking at the unveiling of a statue of Hill, *Atlanta Constitution,* May 2, 1886.

[33] Pearce, *passim.*    [34] *War between the States,* II, 653 *et seq.*

[35] Letter to J. Barrett Cohan, May 25, 1867, Alexander H. Stephens Papers, 1844-1886; Stephens, *War between the States,* II, 655.

tion. He stated that he would "never approve, consent to or accept the poison chalice, . . . nor advise our fellow-citizens to do so." Like Hill, he proposed that all register with a view to "defeating the scheme for our degradation and the overthrow of the Republican government." [36] In December Johnson coöperated with Hill in the "Conservative Convention of the People of Georgia," which was held in Macon on the fifth, and wrote the "Address to the People of Georgia and of the United States," setting forth the "true sentiments of the white race of the State." [37]

Toombs had refused to apply for amnesty[38] and took no part in public life until the campaign of the following year, when he was one of the speakers at the Bush Arbor mass meeting. In a speech a month after that meeting he gave again his opinion of Brown: "He has betrayed his natural and foster mother. . . . He is false to nature. What more can I say to commend this wretch to your detestation? He has fatigued public indignation; it is no longer equal to his crimes! Ignoble villain! Buoyant solely with corruption, he only rises as he rots!" [39]

The registration of voters and elections to the Radical constitutional convention went through under the supervision of the military before the Conservatives had organized. The convention met in Atlanta and sat from December 13, 1867, to March 11 of the following year. Its membership, 169 in all, was composed of a large number of scalawags, about 35 or 40 Negroes, 9 carpetbaggers, and 12 Conservatives.[40] It seemed to many that a "menagerie had been ransacked for its stock of puppets and harlequins and the

---
[36] *Savannah News,* July 18, 1867; Flippin, pp. 281-82.
[37] *Ibid.,* pp. 284-87.
[38] Like President Davis, Toombs never applied for amnesty.
[39] Toombs helped to bring the Bullock regime to an inglorious end and devoted years to the task of supplanting the Radical constitution, which he accomplished in 1877.—Phillips, *Toombs,* pp. 254 *et seq.,* 265, 269-72; Avery, pp. 494-99.
[40] Pearce, p. 162; C. M. Thompson, p. 189. Cf. Blaine, II, 304.

mongrel cullings converted into the travesty of a convention. . . ."[41] Although Governor Brown was not a member of the convention, as head of the Radical party in Georgia he directed its proceedings from the side lines. The members accepted, "almost without challenge, any dictum coming from him."[42] He advised the convention to go no further with reference to the Negroes than the military acts required and to avoid political proscription. He also secured the provision against prosecution for debts contracted prior to June 1, 1865,[43] which Hill charged was "hypocritical and unconstitutional," and intended only to catch votes, and which Linton Stephens declared that no United States court would sustain.[44] When the adopted constitution was submitted to Congress that body struck out the provision.[45] Although the Radical constitution was bitterly opposed by the Conservatives, it was in reality very moderate. Three factors had contributed to its moderation: there were fewer Negroes in proportion to whites in Georgia than in some of the other states, there were a number of respectable white men in the convention, and Brown had exerted his influence to prevent extreme measures.[46]

In the campaign for ratification no quarter was given. Brown led the Radicals for adoption, Hill the Conservatives in opposition. The attitude of the white people toward Brown may well be imagined. Avery states that "the people battered their old idol fearfully," that many "would not listen to his speeches; others insulted; all denounced and ostracized him."[47] On the question of the eligibility of Negroes to hold office, the constitution was not clear.[48] It is thought that Brown's was the master mind in the arrange-

---

[41] Avery, p. 376.   [42] Pearce, p. 163.
[43] *Atlanta New Era*, Jan. 11, 1868.   [44] *Chronicle and Sentinel*, Apr. 5, 1868.
[45] Cf. *Cong. Globe*, 40th Cong., 2nd sess., Appendix, p. 510; *ibid.*, pp. 285-89; *H. J., 1868*, p. 52.
[46] C. M. Thompson, pp. 197-98.   [47] P. 384. Cf. C. M. Thompson, pp. 202-8.
[48] Pearce, p. 167, citing *Journal of the Constitutional Convention of 1867-68*, pp. 148-50.

ment, so that he might "carry the Cherokee section of the state on the anti-negro-office-holding quality of the constitution,"[49] and enable Radical speakers to assure white audiences that Negroes were not eligible to office, and black audiences that they were. Hill brought out the fact in the campaign and contended that the constitution provided for both social and political equality of the races. Brown denied the charge.[50] Later when Negro members were expelled from the legislature[51] and the case went before the state supreme court, Brown, who was then chief justice, and Associate Justice McCay in a two-to-one decision upheld the right of Negroes to hold office.[52]

The "mulatto-tinkered constitution," as the Conservatives called it,[53] made, as Hill said, by "criminals who sprang at one bound from the State prisons of the north into the convention,"[54] was adopted by more than seventeen thousand majority and the Radical, Rufus B. Bullock, was elected governor over General John B. Gordon.[55] How the

[49] C. M. Thompson, p. 197.

[50] Brown's speeches, Mar. 18, 19, in *Atlanta New Era*, Mar. 20, 1868, and *Atlanta Constitution*, Aug. 11, 1868; Avery, p. 401. Brown's speech at Marietta on Mar. 18, 1868, may be found in pamphlet form in the Georgia Dept. of Archives and History, Atlanta.

[51] The resolution to expel the Negroes from the Senate quoted Brown's statement as authority.—*S. J., 1868*, p. 84. The resolution was laid on the table and the Negro members were later expelled individually.—*S. J., 1868*, pp. 13, 121-27, 129, 130, 134-35, 137, 243-44, 273, 277-78. The resolution to expel Negro members from the House passed on Sept. 3.—*H. J., 1868*, pp. 242-43. When Governor Bullock objected, the House informed him that the houses of the General Assembly are the "keepers of their own consciences, and not his Excellency."—*Ibid.*, pp. 296, 302-3. Cf. *S. J., 1868*, p. 326.

[52] *White* v. *Clements*, 39 Ga. 232; Knight, II, 842; C. M. Thompson, pp. 215-16; Avery, p. 415; McPherson, pp. 466 *et seq.* It is interesting to note that the opinion was that of two scalawags, appointed by Radical Governor Bullock, while a Northern man, Hiram Warner, who had lived long in the South, dissented.

[53] Pearce, p. 168; C. M. Thompson, p. 203.

[54] John C. Reed, "Reminiscences of Ben Hill,"*South Atlantic Quarterly*, V (Apr., 1906), 142.

[55] Avery, pp. 384-85; C. M. Thompson, pp. 204 *et seq.;* Davis, *Rise and Fall*, II, 747-48; Knight, II, 827 *et seq.;* Ellis P. Oberholtzer, *History of the United States Since the Civil War*, II, 57, henceforth cited as Oberholtzer.

Radical program was put through is described by Avery: "Hulbert,[56] as fine a master of political opportunism as the world ever saw, had the handling of registration and election returns. . . . The transfer of the unidentifiable colored voter to weak points, enabled a 'sharp and quick' manager . . . to produce any required result." [57]

In May Brown with other delegates from Georgia, including Foster Blodgett who was to become one of the chief beneficiaries of the reconstruction period in Georgia, went to the Republican National Convention which nominated Grant and Colfax on a platform approving the entire reconstruction program. "The press of the state exhausted its vocabulary in damning him." [58] Carl Schurz as temporary chairman named Brown one of a committee of two to escort the permanent chairman to the platform, whereupon the convention gave three cheers for Joe Brown. While the convention was waiting for the committee on credentials to report, a delegate called attention to the presence "in full heart and in full fellowship" of one of the former governors "in the days of the rebellion" who had since "become reconstructed" and had "proved himself as true as steel, a genuine convert." He thereupon moved that ex-Governor Joseph E. Brown of Georgia be invited to address the convention. Brown advanced to the platform amid "thunderous applause" and made a lengthy speech.[59] Laughter and applause greeted his opening statement that he came as a "reconstructed rebel," born in "Mr. Calhoun's district of South Carolina." He "supposed" that he had "religiously believed" Calhoun's doctrines to be correct. He went into secession as a state rights man, "and stood by it as long as there was a chance to sustain it." But when the President of the Confederate

---

[56] Col. Hulbert was later appointed superintendent of the State Road.
[57] P. 384.
[58] Pearce, p. 174, n. 10; Avery, p. 385.
[59] *Proceedings of the National Union Republican Convention, 1868*, pp. 25, 33-36, henceforth cited as *Proceedings*.

States abandoned the great state rights doctrine and adopted conscription which gave him the appointment of officers, he took issue with the President. When the South was defeated he asked himself what was his interest and his duty and having determined upon his course he had "advocated every measure from that time to this, for reconstruction." (Applause) "When Congress, which had the legitimate control of this question (Cheers and prolonged applause) proposed the constitutional amendment . . . I advised . . . that it was better to accept it. . . . I did not then suppose [the South] would get better terms. I am satisfied we must submit to worse ones." He had advised also that the reconstruction acts be accepted though he might have "courted popularity by a different course." He thought his course was "more honorable" than that of the man who having received the same protection as himself from the government yet "stays in its bosom its enemy, prepared to sting it when opportunity offers." ("Good! Good!" and applause) The Hamiltonian and Websterian construction of the constitution having been established by the sword, and that being the platform of the Republican party, his oath of allegiance naturally led him into that party. It was a "very unpopular doctrine" in the South, but he thought it the "true doctrine." [60] He assured the convention that there were "many original secessionists in the South who are Republicans." In closing he begged the Republican party to permit Governor-elect Bullock to convene the legislature on ten days' notice, to receive promptly into Congress the senators whom the legislature would elect, and to give "us" control of the state government and its patronage, "which we fought for and won, and which we must have if we are to succeed in this contest." (Great applause) [61]

Some historians have claimed that at the Chicago conven-

---

[60] "The operation of the conscience and the intellect through the guidance of the sword was widely acclaimed."—Bowers, p. 225.
[61] *Proceedings,* pp. 33-36; Oberholtzer, II, 155.

tion Brown opposed Negro suffrage, doubtless basing their opinion upon Avery,[62] who gives that impression, but the *Proceedings* of the convention show instead that Brown justified the clause of the Fourteenth Amendment which gives a state the alternative of Negro suffrage or a reduction in representation and said of Negro suffrage: "While we grant to the colored people all their rights, civil and political, we do not expect them to be our masters." He also said that in Georgia the majority of the people were white and that in those states where conditions were otherwise Negro domination could be avoided "if our white race act properly." [63]

Upon his return from Chicago Brown began a vigorous campaign for the election of the party nominees. Mrs. Felton, who in 1922 was an ad interim appointee to the United States Senate, and whose scrapbooks for more than a quarter of a century were the "dread and terror of politicians," [64] says that Brown was the author of the address which was adopted on June 25 by the Republican executive committee in Georgia exhorting the Negroes to political activity. "Why should you longer bend the knee to the pretended aristocracy of this State?" it asked. "The God of nature made you their equal. Arise and assert your equality. . . ." [65] Mrs. Felton also relates that in August after Brown was appointed chief justice he made an incendiary speech in the City Hall in Atlanta to a mixed audience of whites and blacks in which he said:

---

[62] P. 385.
[63] *Proceedings*, pp. 33-36.
[64] Knight, II, 876.
[65] Felton, pp. 51-53. Mrs. Rebecca Felton's husband was a member of Congress from 1875 to 1881, and a reformer in state politics, serving in the legislature from 1884 to 1890. She was beside him throughout his political career —practically his campaign manager—and was one of the best informed persons in the state on public issues. "Her marvelous brain was a dynamo of intellectual energy."—Knight, II, 876. Cf. Robert P. Brooks' account in *Dictionary of American Biography; Who's Who in the South, 1927;* obituary, *Atlanta Journal*, Jan. 26, 1930.

When, in the history of the past, did you ever know four
millions of people with the ballot in their hands, to surrender
it without bloodshed? It cost a revolution to give it to them,
nothing short of bloody revolution can take it away from them.
. . . If there are any outbreaks and disturbances, they, I
predict, will grow out of the attempts of the white race to
deprive the colored race of this right, or to interfere with its
free exercise. . . . The colored people have but little, except
their lives, to risk in the fight. . . . The white race have the
same risk, and in addition . . . they have property to lose.
. . . There are 30,000 white Republicans in Georgia—there are
90,000 of you, my colored friends. . . .[66]

Probably nothing during the period of reconstruction
gave such satisfaction to the vast majority of the white
people of Georgia as the defeat a few months later of ex-
Governor Brown for the United States Senate. Governor
Bullock favored his appointment but was unable to control
the legislature. It will be recalled that the Conservatives had
organized in December, 1867, and had begun a vigorous
campaign against the Radical program. General Gordon
was defeated for governor, it is true, and the Radical constitution was adopted, but the sweeping victories which the
Radicals had expected did not materialize. The two parties
were rather evenly divided in the two branches of the
legislature,[67] and the Conservatives, in alliance with a few
Republicans, determined to defeat Brown at whatever cost.
They attempted to elect Alexander Stephens but failing in
this they combined on Joshua Hill who, although a Republican, was not a Radical. When the election of Hill was announced, with one hundred ten votes to Brown's ninety-four,
there was such wild applause that the galleries had to be
cleared. In Atlanta buildings were illuminated, bonfires

---

[66] Pp. 56-57; Avery, p. 389. For Brown's explanation of this speech, see
his De Gives' Opera House speech in 1880, Fielder, pp. 556-57.

[67] For different estimates, cf. C. M. Thompson, p. 208, and Woolley,
pp. 48, 99-100. The Conservatives also elected three of the seven congressmen.

lighted, and congratulatory speeches made.[68] Toombs wrote Stephens on August 9 giving his opinion of the election: "... I preferred that Brown should be beaten by Joshua Hill to almost any other man. ... There was political justice in making the earliest traitor defeat the worst one and break down his party. ... [Brown's] special knowledge, especially of all rogues in the State, is prodigious, and I think it was about worth the State to beat him. ... Hill is a poor devil ... I did my utmost to elect him, and ask of him no other favour than not to join us or speak to me." [69] Brown's political services were not long without reward, however, for Governor Bullock appointed him chief justice of the state supreme court, demoting Hiram Warner from that position to associate justice.[70]

Meantime the Democratic National Convention had nominated Seymour and Blair on a platform calling for the immediate restoration to all the states of their rights in the Union and of civil government to the American people, amnesty for all past political offenses, and the regulation of the elective franchise in the states by their citizens. The reconstruction acts it characterized as "usurpations, and unconstitutional, revolutionary, and void." [71] This was the position which Ben Hill had assumed from the first. Conservatives took on new hope and bent their efforts to carry the state for the Democrats, hoping that the Johnson state government might be restored, as the platform and Blair's

---

[68] *S. J., 1868,* p. 91; *H. J., 1868,* pp. 100-8; Avery, p. 398; C. M. Thompson, p. 210; Flippin, pp. 293-94. Dr. H. V. Miller was elected over Foster Blodgett.

[69] Phillips, *Correspondence,* pp. 702-3. Hill proved to be useful to the Conservatives in that he spoke in the Senate against Foster Blodgett whom the Radical legislature later endeavored to send to that body and he exposed the corrupt methods of the Bullock regime.—Avery, pp. 457.

[70] Knight, II, 841. Cf. Flippin, p. 94; Avery, p. 399.

[71] *Official Proceedings of the Democratic National Convention 1868;* Stanwood, pp. 322, 324.

"Brodhead letter" [72] promised. The Democratic state convention met in Atlanta in July and displayed the greatest enthusiasm, notwithstanding the fact that the ratification of the Fourteenth Amendment was pending in the reconstruction legislature only a few blocks away. Among the more than one thousand delegates from one hundred and eight counties was every important leader of public opinion except Brown. During the sessions "public passion . . . beat piteously upon Joe Brown." [73] The convention adopted the national Democratic platform, declaring the reconstruction acts "unconstitutional, revolutionary, and void," nominated presidential electors and other officers, and arranged an enormous rally to inaugurate the campaign.

The Bush Arbor mass meeting of July 23, 1868, stands out as one of the most important events in the history of the period. Railroads ran excursion trains and brought twenty thousand people to hear the discussion of the question which was uppermost in the minds of the people—Southern restoration and white supremacy.[74] Transparencies of various kinds called attention to Brown, one reading "Joe Brown—a traitor to his section and an outcast from society—Judas Escabes Brown." [75] Hill, Toombs, and Cobb[76] spoke. Never before in the history of the state had three such orators appeared on the same rostrum, and for five hours the crowd

---

[72] Rhodes, VI, 303; John S. Bassett, *A Short History of the United States, 1492-1929*, p. 642.

[73] Avery, p. 390. During the previous month the *Atlanta Constitution* carried a series of articles, "A Prophet Foretelling His Own Infamy," quoting Brown's speeches of 1860 in which he pictured the horrors of Black Republican rule.

[74] The legislature had just two days before ratified the Fourteenth Amendment.

[75] See C. M. Thompson, p. 224.

[76] Cobb's speech may be found in pamphlet form in the Georgia Dept. of Archives and History, Atlanta. This was Cobb's last public speech. He died suddenly in New York in 1870.

listened and wildly applauded. "The pelting given Gov. Brown was simply savage." [77] The hero of the occasion was Hill. His Davis Hall speech, his "Notes on the Situation," his leadership in the reorganization of the Democratic party in the interest of white supremacy, had given him a sure place in the hearts of the people.[78] When he arose the crowd "went wild with enthusiasm." It is generally agreed that he made the most eloquent and masterful speech of his life, a "fierce philippic, deserving to rank with those of Demosthenes." The story is told that while Hill was denouncing the scalawags someone in the audience called out, "He means Joe Brown." Fixing his eyes upon the man Hill said, "You forget, my friend, where you are. That name is too indecent to be mentioned in the presence of ladies." [79] At the close of the speech Toombs threw his hat in the air and embraced Hill. The Democrats carried the state for Seymour and Blair by a majority of 45,688.[80]

The event of reconstruction which, according to Avery, wounded Brown most deeply in the estimation of the people and followed him most relentlessly through later years was Brown's part in the prosecution of the Ashburn murderers. Because of it Colonel R. J. Moses, one of the counsel for the defense, refused to practice in the state supreme court while Brown was chief justice.[81] On the night of March 31, 1868,

---

[77] Avery, p. 392.

[78] *Ibid.*, p. 385; Benjamin H. Hill, Jr., p. 52.

[79] Reed, "Reminiscences of Ben Hill," *loc. cit.*, pp. 141-42. Accounts of the Bush Arbor meeting may be found in Avery, pp. 391-92; Phillips, *Toombs*, p. 260; Pearce, pp. 173-81; William E. Brewton, *The Life of Thomas E. Watson*, p. 126, henceforth cited as Brewton; Knight, II, 836-37; Benjamin H. Hill, Jr., pp. 52-53. Hill's speech, *ibid.*, pp. 308-19.

[80] Stanwood, p. 328. For the manner in which Georgia's electoral vote was handled in Washington, see *ibid.*, pp. 329-32. It is estimated that of the white vote in the United States, Grant received 2,562,000, Seymour 2,653,000.—Charles H. Coleman, *The Election of 1868*, pp. 369-70, henceforth cited as Coleman. Georgia had been restored to her former position in the Union under the "Omnibus Bill" of June 25, 1868, which was designed to secure for Grant the electoral vote of the admitted states.—Rhodes, VI, 285.

[81] Avery, p. 388.

RECONSTRUCTION 285

G. W. Ashburn, an extreme Radical, was killed in Columbus by masked men, supposed to be members of the Ku Klux Klan. As a member of the Radical constitutional convention Ashburn had been "an incendiary and a demagogue" and at the time of his death was living with a Negro woman. General Meade removed the civil authorities, proclaimed martial law, and arrested a large number of persons, some of whom were leading citizens. The prisoners were confined in "sweat boxes," an "improvised prison of planks in an open field under the hot sun," [82] while other third degree methods were employed and Negro testimony obtained.[83] Brown was employed by General Meade to assist the prosecution and, it was said, received a fee of $5,000. Counsel for the defense included some of the best known men in the state, among whom were Alexander Stephens and James M. Smith who a few years later was elected governor. The trial continued from June 29 until July 20, when, the Fourteenth Amendment having been ratified and Governor Bullock inaugurated, General Meade suspended the case until further notice.[84] The prisoners were admitted to bail, their bonds being signed by more than four hundred citizens of Columbus, and later the cases were dismissed. The political nature of the trial seems to have been pretty well established by affidavits from government detectives who testified to that effect. Mrs. Felton comments upon the "vindictive, ungenerous and unmanly conduct" of Brown in the prosecution,[85] and a Georgia historian states that Brown's part in the trial "served to increase the obloquy in which he was held." [86]

Brown's defense of himself was that he sought to protect the prisoners by taking the case with the understanding that he was to control it and that as soon as the civil government

---

[82] Oberholtzer, II, 361.
[83] See *Columbus Sun*, July 25, 1868, containing statement from Dr. Kirksey, Chipley, Bedell, Wood, and fifty others in regard to their treatment.
[84] Avery, pp. 386-89; Knight, II, 837 *et seq.*
[85] Pp. 55, 57.
[86] Knight, II, 838.

of the state began to function, the military should relinquish the case. Avery thinks Brown rendered a service to the prisoners in that he prevented the employment of more extreme men as prosecutors. Others pointed out that Brown's explanation was not made until after General Meade's death when it could neither be verified nor denied.[87] The question of the "Columbus prisoners" arose a number of times in Brown's later career, particularly in 1879 in connection with the scandal of convict leasing and the attempted removal of Captain John W. Nelms, keeper of the penitentiary. By that time Brown was an impressive figure in the industrial life of the state and the "hidden power" in the Democratic party[88] to which he had returned, and he took steps to vindicate himself.[89]

The failure of the legislature to adopt the Fifteenth Amendment,[90] in view of the fact that Negro suffrage already existed by virtue of the reconstruction acts and the newly adopted state constitution, seems at first glance a paradox. Two reasons are given, both of which were doubtless operative. Although the legislature had been elected under the Radical's own constitution and with themselves conducting the election which insured the exclusion of old leaders, a number of younger and less prominent Democrats had nevertheless been returned through the efforts of the Conservatives. Voting with them oftentimes and particularly on all questions pertaining to the Negro were many North Georgia Republicans—originally the stanchest of all Democrats—

---

[87] Avery, pp. 386-89, 550-55. Cf. Knight, II, 837 *et seq.*

[88] Alexander M. Arnett, *The Populist Movement in Georgia*, p. 25, henceforth cited as Arnett.

[89] Avery, pp. 388, 551. Pamphlets published in the later controversy, not consulted by the author, are *Governor Brown and the Columbus Prisoners, Governor Brown and the Columbus Prisoners Again,* and L. F. Garrard's *A Reply to Governor Brown's Pamphlet on the Columbus Prisoners,* all of which may be found in the De Renne Library, Wormsloe, Ga. See Brown's speech on the eve of his election to the U. S. Senate in Nov., 1880, Fielder, p. 555.

[90] *S. J., 1869,* p. 806; Avery, pp. 411, 415 *et seq.*

representing a part of the state where there had been few slaves and where there was strong race prejudice. The combination made up in large part the majority that expelled the Negro members of the legislature in September, 1868.[91] The North Georgia Republicans were the more easily led to this action by the fact that in the campaign for ratification Brown had specifically declared that the constitution did not make provision for Negroes to hold office.[92] The other reason seems to have been that Bullock wanted military intervention in order to reseat the Negroes and secure a legislature more amenable to his recommendations. He had accordingly vetoed the resolution to refer the matter of Negro eligibility to the courts.[93] Not having been able to get Congress to act, he hit upon the plan of defeating the amendment.[94] The Governor's plan worked and in December, 1869, the military again took charge of the "district of Georgia," [95] the legislature was "purged" of some of its Conservative members, the expelled Negroes were reseated, and on February 2, 1870, the amendment was ratified.[96]

Bullock's next move was in the interest of "prolongation." [97] Failing in this scheme both in Congress and in the legislature[98] and facing the certainty of an investigation and impeachment for the mismanagement of the State Road and the misuse of state funds when the Democratic legislature,

---

[91] *House Misc. Doc.*, No. 2, p. 6, 40th Cong., 3rd sess.; Woolley, pp. 56-57; Avery, p. 401.
[92] See C. M. Thompson, pp. 211 *et seq.*
[93] *S. J., 1869*, p. 263; *H. J., 1869*, pp. 228 *et seq.*
[94] *H. J., 1869*, p. 575; Avery, p. 411; C. M. Thompson, p. 261.
[95] *H. J., 1869*, p. 618; *S. J., 1869*, p. 806; *Cong. Globe*, 41st Cong., 2nd sess., pp. 232, 292; McPherson, pp. 609-10.
[96] *Acts of the General Assembly, 1870*, pp. 492-93. Cf. *H. J., 1870*, p. 3; Avery, p. 424; C. M. Thompson, pp. 262 *et seq.;* Blaine, II, 464-65; Hugh McCulloch, *Men and Measures of Half a Century*, pp. 514-18, henceforth cited as McCulloch.
[97] To prolong the life of the "purged" legislature two years. See Avery, p. 440.
[98] *U. S. Statutes at Large*, XVI (Public Laws), 363-64; *H. J., 1870*, pp. 342-43.

elected in December, 1870,[99] should meet, Bullock secretly resigned in October, 1871, and fled from the state.[100] Georgia was now ready to begin a fourth reconstruction—this time her own—which may be said to have ended with the disfranchisement of the Negroes in 1908.[101]

The exact point at which Brown broke with Bullock is not known. Brown had established a law firm in partnership with O. A. Lochrane[102] and H. I. Kimball[103] and the three scalawags had all along been close to the heart of affairs in the Bullock administration. The Radical party had, however, split on patronage, the policy of military interven-

[99] *Tribune Almanac, 1871,* p. 75; *Federal Union,* Mar. 14, 1871.

[100] Woolley, pp. 97, 105-8; C. M. Thompson, pp. 238-45; Avery, pp. 433 *et seq.,* 458-59, 461; Rhodes, VI, 403. The *Atlanta Constitution* was bitterly opposed to Bullock and refused to publish his proclamations. Bullock sued it for libel, but the suit "only excited derision."—Avery, p. 452. Avery was editor of the *Constitution* from 1869 to 1874.—*Ibid.,* p. 614.

[101] Georgia's three previous reconstructions were: 1865, 1867-68, 1869-70. With reference to Negro disfranchisement, see Edward M. Sait, *American Parties and Elections,* pp. 30-31, 37, 41-43, 52, 55.

[102] Lochrane had been appointed judge of the superior court of Macon by Governor Brown in 1861 and again in 1865. His decisions on conscription, on the state's right to a writ of possession for arms loaned to the Confederacy, and on the suspension of the writ of habeas corpus were in full accord with the Governor's views. He was a member of the legislative committee in the Johnson government just after the war which investigated Brown's handling of state cotton. Later he moved to Atlanta, went over to the Radicals, and when Brown resigned from the state supreme court in 1870, Governor Bullock appointed him chief justice ad interim where he served until Governor Smith restored Hiram Warner to that office in Jan., 1872. He was attorney for the creditors of the fraudulent bonds issued by Bullock and rejected by a later Democratic legislature at which time he came to grips with Toombs. He was implicated in the Mitchell heirs deal and other controversies of the Radical period.—Avery, pp. 73, 108, 221, 319, 350, 426, 456-57, 493, 499.

[103] Kimball was supposed to be "Bullock's man Friday," though Pearce (p. 291, n. 14) thinks the relation might well have been reversed. He was implicated in several crooked deals with Bullock, including the sale of the opera house and state aid to railroads. The agent of Henry Clews told Avery (p. 457) that more than $300,000 of the money advanced on state-endorsed bonds to build the Brunswick & Albany Railroad had been used to build the Kimball House.—Fielder, pp. 467-68, 473-74, 484; Avery, pp. 412-14, 418, 444-48, 461; C. M. Thompson, pp. 218-21. For a racy description of Kimball's methods, see Bowers, pp. 300-1.

tion in 1869-70, the purging of the legislature, and the prolongation scheme. In addition, the Kimball opera house scandal, that of the fraudulent railroad bonds, and other irregularities were coming to light.[104] Brown was known to be in the anti-Bullock group, though seemingly he was not very active. Avery states that in the controversy "Brown kept firmly aloof." [105] He did, however, advise the ratification of the Fifteenth Amendment, saying that Negro suffrage already existed in the South and that the amendment would put it upon the North. In the same letter, which was a reply to members of the legislature who had asked his opinion, he said: "Many patriotic citizens believe they see in the present movement schemes of personal ambition and personal gain at the expense of the State. If they are right, it is all important that every friend of Georgia, who is in a position to serve her, should be at his post, to protect the public property, the public credit, and the public interest." [106] On January 24, 1870, Toombs wrote Stephens of a recent visit he had made to Atlanta "in the interest of the present coup d'etat of Bullock and his conspirators," in which he and Brown had worked together to elect an anti-Bullock speaker of the house. "Rather a strange conjunction," he admitted, "but you know my rule is to use the devil if I can do [no] better to save the country." [107] After another visit to Atlanta two weeks later Toombs wrote that Brown seemed really in earnest to defeat the schemes of Bullock.[108]

At the inauguration of the Democratic governor, Colonel James M. Smith, in January, 1872, Brown was among the

[104] *H. J., 1869*, pp. 260, 618; Avery, pp. 418, 457-58, 462, 494-99; C. M. Thompson, *passim*.
[105] P. 417.
[106] Avery, p. 425. A few days earlier Brown had shown disaffection toward Bullock by giving a personal opinion contrary to an official opinion of Bullock's attorney general.—*H. J., 1870*, pp. 10-16; *Atlanta Constitution*, Jan. 19, 1870.
[107] Phillips, *Correspondence*, p. 707. Cf. C. M. Thompson, p. 264; Woolley, pp. 95-96.
[108] Phillips, *Toombs*, p. 264.

leading men who accompanied the governor to the rostrum, and in the elections of that year he supported Greeley for president and Smith for governor.[109] Brown had "turned a double somersault" and landed back in the Democratic fold.

---

[109] Avery, pp. 251, 468-69. Governor Smith had been selected in the special election in Dec., 1871, to fill Bullock's unexpired term, and was elected for a full term the following year.

## CHAPTER XII

## REHABILITATION

THE STIGMA of Brown's career in reconstruction may be said to have continued until the year 1880, when, upon receiving the highest political honor within the power of the state to bestow, he felt that the wisdom of his course and the motives which he had professed were acknowledged and himself completely vindicated.

Brown's rehabilitation in the Democratic party did not come by chance. It was shrewdly and skillfully accomplished. No move on a chess board was ever more carefully calculated. The political acumen which the unknown gubernatorial candidate displayed in 1857 had grown and ripened with the years. It had made possible the victory of that year, and the succeeding victories of 1859, 1861, 1863. It had enabled him to calculate accurately which way the cat would jump in 1867 and what the stars decreed in 1870. True it had failed him once in 1868, but the humiliation was wiped out in the same year when a chief justice was demoted for his special benefit. If a popular statesman made an ambiguous statement under circumstances which were themselves suspicious, the opportunity was seized to show that the erstwhile idol and himself were advocating the same policy. If the Democratic party, grasping at a straw, seized upon a "new departure," [1] the people were repeatedly told that the party had come over to Brown's platform. If an aristocrat of the old regime—accustomed to conduct public affairs as

---

[1] The "new departure" was the fusion of Democrats with Liberal Republicans in 1872 in support of Horace Greeley for president.

a public trust requiring the highest sense of honor and integrity—allowed his indignation to overcome his discretion and proposed "the code" as a remedy in a quarrel, the incident was made to reflect upon the old gentleman. When the people of the state—reduced to poverty through four years of war, the confiscation of their slaves, and the rapacity of the carpetbag-scalawag-Negro regime—expressed doubt of the future, certain newspapers were quick to point out the necessity of utilizing the infallible judgment and extraordinary business ability of the ex-Governor.

Thad Stevens' desire to make the South over in the image of New England would have become a reality in Georgia during the seventies and eighties if some of the leaders of that period could have had their way. Reconstruction philosophy and methods had left their indelible marks. In business life the Babbitts were in the forefront shouting for the "New South" and the "new order of things," which meant the industrialization of the state in the interest of so-called "progress." In politics the former Bullock supporters under the leadership of Brown went over to the Democratic party in 1870, or two years later in the Greeley campaign. "There was a feeling among the old timers like Toombs and independents like Felton that the coalition of this 'Bullock Democracy' with the rising business-minded conservatives was inimical to popular interests." [1a]

---

[1a] Arnett, p. 29. The term Bourbon Democracy is applied to the politics of this period, but it is a misnomer in that it connotes the leadership of the planter aristocracy, while as a matter of fact few of the old leaders were in evidence. Indeed, they looked on in scorn. Toombs and Stephens, for instance, opposed fusion with the Liberal Republicans in 1872, in part because the movement was a compromise with the scalawag element in the state which in particular was inoculated with the "progress" virus. Stephens was accordingly defeated for the U. S. Senate the next year.—Arnett, pp. 22, and n. 4, 23; Avery, p. 58.

Toombs was convinced of the necessity of curbing capitalism and devoted the remaining years of his life to bringing corporations under public control.—Phillips, *Toombs*, pp. 269-72; Knight, II, 884-88; Avery, pp. 499, 530. When in 1882 the Bourbon Democracy prevailed upon Stephens to be its candidate for governor to prevent the Independents from nominating him,

## REHABILITATION

One of the incidents which aided Brown's rehabilitation, at least negatively, was the unpopularity of Benjamin H. Hill which followed Hill's speech at the Delano banquet on December 28, 1870, and Brown's claim that Hill had come over to his position on reconstruction. The incident had to do with the leasing of the State Road by a company of which Hill was a member and Brown was president.[2] The road had been looted by Foster Blodgett who had been appointed superintendent by Governor Bullock,[3] but the Radicals were intent upon obtaining a more permanent hold on this valuable property, which under normal conditions produced a monthly income of $50,000. Others felt that it would be better to lease or sell the road rather than to run the risk of an annual deficit such as Blodgett's administration had shown.[4] On October 24, 1870, the "purged" legislature gave the Governor authority to lease the road. But when in the following December, Governor Bullock awarded a twenty-year lease at a rental of $25,000 a month,[5] under circumstances

---

Toombs declared Stephens was in his dotage.—Felton, pp. 371-81; Knight, II, 920; Arnett, pp. 44-45. Upon being told during his last illness that the legislature was still in session, Toombs exclaimed, "Lord, send for Cromwell!"—Phillips, *Toombs*, p. 273.

For a portrayal of Bourbon Democracy, cf. John Ransom, "Reconstructed but Unregenerate," Frank Owsley, "The Irrepressible Conflict," and H. Clarence Nixon, "Whither Southern Economy," in *I'll Take My Stand*, pp. 1-27, 61-91, 176-200; sketch of life of William H. Felton, by Robert P. Brooks, in *Dictionary of American Biography*; obituary of William H. Felton, in *Atlanta Journal*, Sept. 25, 1909; Felton, pp. 48, 541, 630; H. Clarence Nixon, "The New South and the Old Crop," *Essays in Honor of William E. Dodd*, Chap. XI.

[2] As a condition of Brown's becoming president, Hill stipulated that Brown should resign from the state supreme court.—Benjamin H. Hill, Jr., pp. 60-61. For Brown's resignation see *Atlanta New Era*, Dec. 28, 1870, and *Savannah News*, Dec. 31, 1870.

[3] *Minutes of the Executive Dept., 1870-71*, p. 449. Cf. Johnston, *W. & A. R. R.*, p. 62; Fielder, p. 481; Avery, p. 449; Phillips, "An American State-Owned Railroad," *Yale Review*, XV (Nov., 1906), 281.

[4] C. M. Thompson, pp. 238 et seq.; Fielder, p. 480; Woodward, *Meet General Grant*, p. 433. The act of the General Assembly and the lease may be conveniently found in Johnston, *W. & A. R. R.*, Appendix A.

[5] *Acts of the General Assembly, 1870*, pp. 423-27.

which to say the least were suspicious,[6] to a company of which Brown was president and H. I. Kimball a member,[7] there was general indignation.[8] Toombs, who considered the lessees "a lot of the greatest rogues on the continent," [9] made an effort to break the lease.[10]

Hill's connection with the leasing company as told by himself and corroborated by Miss Thompson, historian of reconstruction in Georgia, was due to his employment by certain railroads of the state to organize a competing company to bid for the lease. The president of the Georgia Railroad was acting with ex-Governor Brown in organizing a company, and other railroads of the state were afraid the State Road would discriminate against them in favor of the Georgia Railroad. Being unable to get representation in Brown's company, they very astutely brought into their company Simon Cameron, John S. Delano, secretary of the Interior, and other friends of President Grant. These two rather hostile groups finally combined and secured the lease.[11]

---

[6] A historian who has made a careful study of the subject states that the lease was unfairly obtained and that the legislature in 1872 voted to sustain it against the majority report of the investigating committee.—C. M. Thompson, pp. 253-54. Testimony was given to the effect that Brown had stated that $50,000 had to be raised "to be distributed to outsiders."—*Report of Joint Committee on Lease of the W. & A. R. R., 1872.*

[7] Avery, p. 479. Cf. C. M. Thompson, pp. 218-21.

[8] Avery, p. 479; C. M. Thompson, pp. 172-73, 229-35, 245 *et seq.*; *Atlanta Constitution,* Jan. 12, 14, 30, 1871. For opposing views as to corruption, see C. M. Thompson, p. 246, and Pearce, pp. 218-22; also letter of James P. Simmons in *Atlanta Constitution,* Aug. 9, 1872, and speech of Dunlap Scott in lower house, Aug. 8, 1872, in *Atlanta Constitution,* Aug. 16, 1872.

[9] Phillips, *Correspondence,* p. 711.

[10] Fielder, p. 482; Benjamin H. Hill, Jr., p. 61; *Chronicle and Sentinel,* May 12, 13, 1871. For testimony before the joint committee on the lease, 1871, cf. C. M. Thompson, pp. 251 *et seq.*; Fielder, p. 501.

[11] Benjamin H. Hill, Jr., p. 59; C. M. Thompson, pp. 247-48; *Atlanta New Era,* Dec. 29, 1870. Stephens was a member of the leasing company, but because of Toombs' warning letters (Phillips, *Correspondence,* pp. 711-12) and the storm of indignation which followed the announcement of the personnel of the leasing company, he withdrew and transferred his interest to the state.—Stephens' letter to editor of the *Constitutionalist* reprinted in *Republican,* Jan. 10, 1871; Johnston and Browne, p. 502. Brown replied to Stephens through the press.—*Republican,* Jan. 13, 14, 1871.

In honor of Secretary Delano and other capitalists from the North, Governor Bullock gave a banquet at the Kimball House on the day after the lease was awarded. Hill was one of the invited guests. This, together with the fact that he entered into a business deal with Northern capitalists, carpetbaggers, and scalawags[12] (although some of the members of the leasing company were Georgians untinted with scalawagary), and the fact that the reason for his actions were not then clear, gave rise to criticism. In addition, Hill, during the campaign for the election of the legislature, had published three weeks previously an "Address to the People of Georgia" in which he had said that reconstruction was now an accomplished fact, the three amendments having become a part of the Constitution of the United States and beyond the reach of the Supreme Court. He felt the North would make no move to repeal any of the amendments, since that section preferred a national to a federal form of government. He thought, therefore, that the duty of citizens under the circumstances was to elect honest men to office and endeavor to bring back prosperity and good will. In this connection he said that "a black man who cannot be bought is better than a white man who can be, and a Republican who cannot be bought is better than a Democrat who can." [13]

At the banquet Delano gave a toast to Georgia in which he referred to it as a state. Hill replied that he was glad to know Georgia was at last a state, and since the word came from the lips of a cabinet official he felt it meant that reconstruction was indeed over. He said that he had been accused of being a Radical but that he was not and never could be. As times and events and circumstances change he thought it necessary that "we should adapt ourselves to them if we expect to prosper. . . ." Referring to his membership in the Democratic party he said that he "did not go to be a Demo-

---
[12] Woodward, *Meet General Grant*, p. 433.
[13] Benjamin H. Hill, Jr., pp. 55-59.

crat," but had become one from necessity. He asked Delano to say to the administration at Washington that the people of Georgia had three ideas—to resist wrong, to resent insult, and to submit to the law.[14]

By his reference to the reason for his having become a Democrat Hill meant to imply that reconstruction measures had forced Georgians into one party, former Whigs having joined with Democrats for their common protection.[15] His words were misunderstood and, taken in conjunction with his previous "Address," gave deep offense to his friends and followers.[16] It was said that Hill had joined Brown in his reconstruction program and that, like Brown, he had been attracted by the loaves and the fishes. Hill was under the necessity of making explanations for a number of years.[17] When asked the difference between his present position and that of Brown in 1867, Hill replied: "It is just the same as that between two sons, one of whom helps assassins to slay his father and the other, after exposing his life and all to prevent the slaughter and fails, simply and sadly recognizes the fact that he is dead, and decently buries him, and honestly goes to work for the family. Is there no difference between parricide and filial love?" [18]

There was of course a vast difference between the positions of the two men. Hill had opposed reconstruction as long as there was a chance that through the action of the Supreme Court the reconstruction acts might be declared unconstitutional, or through political action they might be repealed, or because of the refusal of the Southern states to ratify, the Fourteenth and Fifteenth Amendments might fail. Several

---

[14] *Ibid.*, pp. 62-63; Pearce, pp. 230 *et seq.*
[15] Benjamin H. Hill, Jr., p. 64.
[16] Pearce, p. 208; Phillips, *Toombs*, p. 265.
[17] See Hill's explanation to Henry Grady ten years later, Benjamin H. Hill, Jr., p. 64; letter to the legislature, *Chronicle and Sentinel*, Sept. 30, 1871; addresses to the legislature, 1875 and 1877, Benjamin H. Hill, Jr., pp. 429 *et seq.*, 473 *et seq.*
[18] *Ibid.*, p. 60; Pearce, p. 214 citing *Columbus Sun and Times*, Jan. 21, 1871.

suits in the United States Supreme Court[19] gave hope for a brief time, and the platform of the Democratic party in 1868 seemed to offer a way out. But the court was intimidated,[20] the amendments were ratified, the Democrats were defeated,[21] and it was evident that the national platform of the party on the Southern question would be quite different in the next presidential election.

But aside from these considerations there was to Hill and other Southern leaders a great principle at stake involving the honor of the Southern people, which Hill had stressed so vehemently in his "Notes on the Situation" and which Johnson had in mind when he said: "Our oppressors can put chains upon us if they will, . . . but let us consent to it *never*. . . . They can rob us of *freedom*, but let us never *agree* to be slaves. They may overthrow *constitutional liberty;* but let us never *embrace* their *despotism*."[22] By December, 1870, when Hill counselled obedience to the Constitution and the laws, reconstruction was an accomplished fact, though without the consent of the Southern people, and no alternative remained but obedience or emigration. Nevertheless Brown and his friends persisted in the myth that in 1870 Hill came

---

[19] Cf. *Ex-parte Milligan,* 4 Wallace 2; Warren, III, 145-76; Milton, *The Age of Hate,* pp. 541-45; *Mississippi* v. *Johnson,* 4 Wallace 478; Warren, III, 178-79, 185-86; *Georgia* v. *Stanton,* 6 Wallace 50; Warren, III, 179 *et seq.; Ex-parte McCardle,* 6 Wallace 618 and 7 Wallace 506; John Bassett Moore, *Four Phases of American Development,* p. 132, n. 1.

[20] Warren, III, 179 *et seq.;* Milton, *The Age of Hate,* pp. 438-39.

[21] Grant's popular majority in 1868 was only 309,584 (Stanwood, p. 328), showing that Hill's judgment was not so far wrong as far as public opinion in the nation was concerned.

[22] Flippin, p. 282. Jonathan Worth of North Carolina expressed the same thought when he wrote: "If we are to be degraded we will retain some self-esteem by not making it self-abasement . . . If we were voluntarily to adopt [the Fourteenth Amendment] I think we should be the meanest and most despicable people on earth."—Bowers, p. 140, citing J. G. deR. Hamilton, *The Correspondence of Jonathan Worth,* II, 665. John Forsyth, editor of the *Mobile Register,* expressed a similar view: "It is one thing to be oppressed, wronged, and outraged by overwhelming force; it is quite another to submit to voluntary abasement."—Walter L. Fleming, *Civil War and Reconstruction in Alabama,* p. 394.

over to the position which Brown had taken in 1867, and so overwhelming is the power of reiteration that many were half or wholly convinced, and even reputable historians have in some instances adopted this view.

Brown had moved to Atlanta shortly after the close of the war, his practical mind sensing the business possibilities in the struggling little town destined to grow into a great city. He dealt in Atlanta real estate, owned three large farms in the state, accumulated large mineral interests, and became president of several large corporations.[23] So extensive were Brown's interests in Dade County that Mrs. Felton refers to it as "Brown's State of Dade." [24] The Dade Coal Company, with its holdings of iron ore in Bartow County, was said to be worth $1,000,000. The company used convict labor, leased from the state,[25] a custom which began with the reconstruction government.[26] In 1874 the law permitted leasing for five years, in 1876 for twenty years.[27] Mrs. Felton, whose husband made a fight against the barbarous

---

[23] Brown was president of the Western & Atlantic R. R. Co., the Southern Railway and Steamship Co., the Dade Coal Co., the Walker Coal and Iron Co. He was for a time the sole proprietor of the Dade Coal Co., later a half-owner. He was also part owner of the Rising Fawn Iron Works. His mineral interests covered the greater part of several counties. In addition, he had large real estate holdings in Atlanta.—Fielder, pp. 405, 488-89, 503; Avery, p. 606; Arnett, p. 27.

[24] P. 162.

[25] Fielder, pp. 488, 503; Felton, pp. 516 *et seq.;* Walter Wilson, "Georgia Suppresses Insurrection," *The Nation,* CXXXIX (Aug. 1, 1934), 127; proposal submitted to Governor James M. Smith of Georgia March 24, 1874, by Joseph E. Brown, president of Dade Coal Co., to lease 100 convicts for 5 years at $10 a year (Georgia Dept. of Archives and History, Atlanta); letter from Senator Joseph E. Brown, Washington, to Governor Colquitt, Dec. 13, 1881. stating that he had appointed Captain W. O. Reese to inflict all punishment necessary to discipline convicts employed by the Dade Coal Co. (Joseph E. Brown Correspondence, Georgia Dept. of Archives and History, Atlanta).

[26] Knight, II, 865-66. After Sherman's army destroyed the penitentiary Brown recommended that the penitentiary system be abolished and other modes of punishment substituted—hanging for robbery, burglary, and horse stealing; whipping and branding for lesser offenses.—*C. R.,* II, 830-32.

[27] Knight, II, 865, citing Governor Gordon's message of Dec. 10, 1886, *H. J., 1886,* pp. 412 *et seq.* Mrs. Felton says (pp. 516-18) that through some technicality in the last-named law, "Ex-Governor Brown was guaranteed three

system, says that in 1880 the three larger companies having convict leases, which included Brown's, paid to the state only $22,061.40 for the hire of 1,200 and that all but $2,000 was expended by the state in paying for guards, chaplains, and physicians for the leased convicts. The amount which Brown paid to the state in that year she gives as $6,464.28,[28] or less than seven cents per working day, the hours for which were not limited.[29] It seems, however, that Brown's convict camps were well managed. Dr. Felton, referring to the fact on the floor of the legislature in 1885, stated that there was at least "one humane man in charge of Georgia's miserable convicts, or a portion of them." [30]

But if Brown was one of the richest men in the state he was also one of the most generous in the use of his money. He contributed liberally to the various Baptist churches of Atlanta, giving to one $800 for repairs, to another $500 toward the organ fund. He gave $1,000 to the Baptist Orphans' Home; he contributed to Mercer University and the Southern Baptist Convention; and in 1880 he made a donation of $50,000 to the Southern Baptist Theological Seminary.[31] In 1883 he gave to the University of Georgia $50,000 to establish a scholarship fund for the education of poor boys.[32] "Such liberality tended to stifle rumors that he had accumulated his riches through questionable means."

---

hundred long-term, able bodied slaves" for twenty-three years instead of twenty.

[28] P. 518.

[29] Previous to 1876 the day was limited to ten to twelve hours.—*Ibid.*

[30] *Ibid.,* p. 591. The Feltons did not succeed in reforming the system except in part. Not until the administrations of Governors Atkinson and Hoke Smith, in 1897 and 1907, were adequate reforms in the prison system instituted.—Knight, II, 1001-5, 1085. Cf. George H. Clarke, "Georgia and the Chain-Gang," *Outlook,* LXXXII (Jan. 13, 1906), 73-79; A. J. McKelway, "The Convict Lease System of Georgia," *Outlook,* XC (Sept. 12, 1908), 67-72; Editorial, "The End of the Convict Lease System in Georgia," *Outlook,* XC (Oct. 3, 1908), 238-39.

[31] *History of the Baptist Denomination in Georgia,* pp. 67-68; Avery, pp. 5-8, 605-6.

[32] Knight, II, 918; *Constitution,* June 24, 1934, article by Ralph T. Jones.

Despite Brown's absorbing business and political interests he found time to labor for civic betterment and public education. He continued as president of the Board of Education of Fulton County to which he had been appointed in 1868, and for twenty years he served as a member of the Board of Trustees of the University of Georgia.[33]

An aftermath of the Bullock investigating committee was the controversy between Brown and Toombs in 1872 with reference to the Mitchell heirs' case, which came near resulting in a duel between the two men. In 1842 Samuel Mitchell donated five acres of land in Atlanta as a terminus for the State Road then under construction. A part of the gift was used and in 1859 the legislature authorized the city to utilize the remainder as a public park. The location of the park property was such as to excite the interest of parties engaged in real estate and in 1867 Brown brought suit for the Mitchell heirs to recover the park property from the city on the ground that it was not being used for the purpose for which it was donated. While the suit was pending Brown became a member of the state supreme court and turned the case over to Lochrane, his law partner, who in 1868 attempted unsuccessfully to secure a reconveyance from the legislature. Lochrane not having accomplished his purpose, H. I. Kimball,[34] Brown's other partner, came into the picture as agent for the Mitchell heirs with an offer of compromise, the city's claim having in the meantime been extinguished. Lochrane prepared a memorial to the "purged" legislature which Kimball managed and in July, 1870, Kimball offered the state $35,000 to relinquish its claim. According to Toombs, the deal was put through the legislature in a most extraordinary manner, several better offers from Atlanta citizens being turned down in short order, with Brown, Lochrane, Kimball, and Foster Blodgett on the floor at the time. Within a few days the property was sold for

---

[33] Fielder, p. 488.   [34] See C. M. Thompson, pp. 218-21.

more than $200,000, Brown and his New York partner, E. Waitzfelder & Company, purchasing a part for more than $50,000 and erecting on it a building at a cost of more than $27,000.[35]

Brown stated that as chief justice he had taken no active part in the matter, but that he had "felt at perfect liberty to confer with the heirs or their counsel" and that he knew of "no unfair or illegal means used by anyone to carry the bill through the legislature." He expressed the opinion that the propositions submitted by other Atlanta citizens were "not made in good faith."[36] He thought the state had made a good deal since now it would receive taxes from the property. Indeed, the state might well have made the reconveyance without compensation, he said, since it had no use for the property. He denied the charge that the Mitchell "orphans" had received none of the benefit of the recovered property and thought the compromise had benefited both the heirs and the state.

Before Toombs' and Brown's statements appeared in the press, a private letter written by Toombs was published in the *Griffin News*[37] insinuating that Brown and his law partners had lobbied the bill through the legislature and defrauded the state. Brown replied through the *Constitution* that the charge was false and its author an infamous liar.[38] Brown was a deacon in the Baptist Church and state law forbade dueling, nevertheless Toombs sent to inquire whether Brown would "give satisfaction under the Code," to which Brown seems to have replied that he would give his answer whenever the challenge was received. The conversation was

---
[35] Brown's statement of the case appeared in the *Constitution*, Aug. 5, 1872, and is quoted by Avery, pp. 486-92. See also Brown's statement in *Constitution*, Aug. 22, 1872. Toombs' version, more complete in detail, appeared in the *Atlanta Sun*, July 16, 1872, and is quoted by Avery, pp. 479-82. Brown's statement, as far as it goes, agrees with that of Toombs.
[36] Avery, p. 490.
[37] On June 27, 1872, quoted by Avery, p. 477. See Knight, II, 866.
[38] July 3, 1872, quoted by Avery, p. 477.

not put into writing and Toombs' messenger and Brown later disagreed as to what had passed between them, but it seems that Brown prepared to meet Toombs, writing his resignation as deacon and selecting James Gardner as his second.[39] The matter of the duel was allowed to drop and the two men carried on the quarrel through the press, Toombs saying in the *Atlanta Sun* that he did not think it probable that Brown *personally* engaged in the bribery, being too cunning and skillful as a lobbyist to run such a risk, especially when he had three such experts as Lochrane, Kimball, and Blodgett to engineer the bill through the legislature.[40] A contemporary biographer of Toombs states that the prospect of a duel "between these two old men" [41] shocked the public sense of propriety, and that "Toombs was censured for provoking Brown into an attitude of expecting a challenge and then declining to send it." He thinks the episode gave Brown the opportunity "to appear in a better light than he had done for a long time." [42]

During reconstruction Brown had of course been supported by the Radical press. Later the *Atlanta Constitution* was his champion, especially after Henry Grady bought a fourth interest in 1880.[43] In 1876 that journal said editorially: "No man stands higher today in the estimation of the people of Georgia than does Governor Brown. . . . If he desired political preferment, there is no one they would more delight to honor—no one whom they would more implicity trust," [44] which was probably a trial balloon rather than a statement of fact.

In 1874 a novel was published[45] in which one of the charac-

---

[39] Stovall, p. 335; Avery, p. 477; Brewton, p. 131. Brown's and Nicholl's letters were published in the *Constitution*, July 17, 18, 20, 1872, quoted by Avery, pp. 483-84.
[40] July 16, 1872.  [41] Brown was fifty-one, Toombs sixty-two.
[42] Stovall, pp. 335-36. Cf. Phillips, *Toombs*, pp. 266-67.
[43] Cf. Felton, p. 266; Avery, p. 614. It is not known who supplied Grady with the funds.
[44] Dec. 31, 1876.  [45] William Dugas Trammell, *Ça Ira—A Novel*.

ters without doubt portrayed the ex-Governor, even to his peculiar pronunciation of judgMENT.[46] The author evidently intended through exaggerating and mildly ridiculing the attitude of the people toward Brown to aid him in recovering public esteem:

> Mr. Malcomb was a lawyer and a political leader. Before the war he had been a politician, after the war he had risen to the dignity of a statesman. He was now engaged in the profession of money getting. He was not an aristocrat—he was "the representative native Southern statesman of the new order of things." He was a strict Baptist and many people said that he had, on many occasions, led the whole church to vote for him for high political offices and thought his great success mainly attributable to this fact. He gave liberally to institutions of his church. It was charged that he never did anything but from the deepest policy—that whatever he gave he was absolutely sure of a return vastly larger than ordinary money-lenders could reasonably hope even to get. In short, it was said this man never made a miscalculation—that he never failed to put his money "where it would do the most good." [47]
>
> It was also said that he could beat any man in Georgia at "covering up his tracks." . . . It was currently believed by some, that he was always engaged with governors, legislatures, city councils, railroad officials, and great speculators, in certain mysteries; and many people seemed to have a vague feeling . . . that these mysterious transactions . . . were of the very darkest character, enormously swindling at all points; and that if the mask could only be torn off this saint of the church, . . . this man, with his honeyed words and gracious smile, . . . would be found to be the wiliest hypocrite, the most hardened, skilful, practiced, unconscionable knave on the face of the earth. . . . If he was on speaking terms with the Governor, some people were duly qualified to swear that . . . *he* was the real Governor; . . . that the man in the executive mansion was a mere puppet in his hands; . . . that . . . said puppet was put where he was by the influence of this man himself, in order that he might . . . make his "raids on the treasury." If his carriage was seen in

---
[46] *Supra,* Chap. I, n. 56.
[47] Pp. 30-31.

front of a printing-office, it was positively asserted that that paper had been paid a round sum to publish two columns of lies editorially, for him at an early day; for which he was sure, somewhere, at some time, to receive at least ten times what he paid the paper. If he was seen to whisper in the ear of a member of the legislature, the member was bribed beyond a shadow of a doubt; if he took him by the hand . . . you could get the glimpse of a greenback sticking to the clumsy legislator's hand when he withdrew it. If the City Council had a contract to let out, or city property to sell, and his name appeared anywhere in the transaction, said council was denounced for having "sold out" to him. If a newspaper said a good word for him, no doubt it was paid to say it; but if it was consistently friendly towards him, manifestly he either owned the whole thing or a large interest in it. Finally, when he deemed it necessary to reply, through the public print, to his accusers, and did so, to all appearances positively unanswerably, this was only another evidence of his wonderful astuteness in "covering up his tracks." . . . But the clearer his case the worse it was for him—clearly there was something dark behind; nay, for that matter, he could make black white, or white black, with the utmost precision and despatch.[48]

There was, however, a change in public opinion, after which Mr. Malcomb was "universally beloved":

> He was put up as a candidate for Mayor, because of his "splendid executive and financial abilities, and rare judgment in all practical matters, as well as his great influence as a business man." This fact indicated "the decay of strong party animosities," for if three years earlier any man had dared suggest him "as a suitable man for democrats to vote into an office of honor or trust, he would not only have been politically outlawed, but a strong effort, and probably a successful one, would have been made for his social outlawry." His candidacy showed also that "the business men were taking matters of importance into their own hands; that . . . questions of material wealth and progress should enter as the important elements into the management of their municipal affairs."[49]

---

[48] Pp. 32-33.    [49] Pp. 219-20.

It seems that Mr. Malcomb was not elected mayor. The author makes him say in advance of the election that in his judgment he would be defeated but that he could bring such influences to bear as would cut down the majority. Mr. Malcomb seems to have been a member of the city council and to have worked for the establishment of public schools for both whites and blacks.[50]

During these years Brown never relaxed his political activity in the Democratic party. He had never lost control of North Georgia, having in large part taken that section into the Radical party with him in 1867 and out again in 1870-72. Both "Bullock Democrats" and "Bullock Republicans" belonged to him, "because he knew their inside complications." [51]

In the Hayes-Tilden contested election Brown was greatly exercised over the rumor that Hayes was to be fraudulently counted in and inaugurated by military force. If this should be done, he said in a published letter in the *Atlanta Constitution*, and the people of the United States should "submit patiently and peaceably to military usurpation, . . . it is mere mockery to talk of the peaceful remedy of the ballot box in the future." He urged Southern Democrats to remain firm, seat Tilden, and restore local government "to those states where it had been taken from them by fraud and military usurpation." [52] In Florida, where at the request of the Democratic party he went to make the argument before the court in the interest of Tilden,[53] he was the "cynosure of the nation's gaze, . . . the unpaid advocate of public welfare and political honesty." [54] After Hayes was inaugurated Brown wrote two letters to the *Atlanta Constitution* under the non

---

[50] P. 253.
[51] Felton, pp. 69-70, 162. Cf. Avery, pp. 521, 526; Arnett, p. 29.
[52] Dec. 31, 1876.
[53] Brown's argument may be found in Fielder, pp. 507-19. Cf. Oberholtzer, III, 285-86; Brown's De Gives Opera House speech, Fielder, pp. 543-44.
[54] *Ibid.*, p. 506.

de plume, "Citizen," bitterly attacking the Democrats, particularly Senator John B. Gordon and John Young Brown, for the "bargain" with Hayes. He said that the price of the loss of a Democratic administration was too much to pay for "something that rightfully belonged to us." He thought that "too much publicity" and too much credit were given to Gordon's supposed services as senator.[55] Brown pronounced Hayes' election "the grandest fraud ever perpetrated on the American people," in answer to which, Mrs. Felton's remark about Brown's previous activities is apropos: "In 1868 his 'Radicalism' was oozing out in every pore. In 1874 his Democracy was burning him up with its fire and fury." [56]

A few leaders controlled the Bourbon Democracy of the time and named candidates throughout the state. Discontent with this state of affairs resulted in the insurgent movement on the part of the agrarian interests—forerunner of Populism[57]—in the seventh and ninth congressional districts, under the leadership of Dr. William H. Felton and Emory Speer. It threatened for a few years to become serious to the ruling oligarchy. The movement started in 1874 when Dr. Felton ran as an Independent against the regular nominee, L. N. Trammell, Brown's candidate. He forced the "Bullock Democrat" out of the race by exposing his connection with the "suppressed" testimony in the legislative committee which investigated the fraudulent bond transactions of Bullock's administration.[58] Felton continued to carry the "bloody seventh" until the formation of the "triumvirate" in 1880.[59]

---

[55] Apr. 7, 15, 1877.
[56] P. 66.
[57] Arnett, *passim;* Brewton, Chaps. XXXI, XXXII.
[58] Arnett, p. 34. With reference to the bonds in question cf. Woolley, pp. 105-8; C. M. Thompson, pp. 229-35. A part of the bonds were repudiated and to make the action of the legislature binding, the constitution of 1877 prohibited their payment.—Phillips, *Toombs,* pp. 269-72; Avery, pp. 494-99.
[59] Avery, pp. 513-14; Fielder, pp. 521 *et seq.;* Felton, p. 162; Knight, II, 875, 923. For election tactics of Brown in the use of the State Road which traversed the seventh district, see Felton, p. 193.

## REHABILITATION

About this time an editorial, "The Wisest Man," appeared in an Atlanta newspaper, indicating that Brown himself would sooner or later be a candidate for office:

> Who is the wisest man in Georgia? The moment the question is asked the minds of all intelligent men in the State will be turned in one direction and to one person. He is so well known to the people of Georgia, he is so conspicuous for his clear-headedness and level-headedness, that it is not necessary to name him. His name has already suggested itself to the mind of the reader. Some think of him with dislike. Some, on reading these lines, will indulge in severe animadversions, and will have harsh things to say of him; some may even use terms that are denunciatory; but the very fact that they know who is meant when the wisest man in the State is spoken of without being named, is proof that whatever their feelings may be, they pay intellectual homage to a great mind, and their very protest against this article is their endorsement of it. No two names will suggest themselves to any intelligent Georgian in answer to the question, "Who is the wisest man in the State?" The man stands, in this respect at least, peerless and unrivaled; there will be no debate in one's own mind, nor with his neighbor, as to who this man is; nor will there be a dissenting voice; everybody knows who is meant, as well as if his name were announced. Now, so long as this man is alive, can we afford to do without him?[60]

One of Georgia's United States senators during the seventies was General John B. Gordon, "the Chevalier Bayard of the Confederate Army," who had been with Lee at Chancellorsville and Gettysburg, in the Wilderness Campaign, and at Appomattox. He was immensely popular and when in 1873 the term of Joshua Hill expired, Gordon was elected over Alexander Stephens and Benjamin H. Hill. Six years later he was reëlected.[61]

The Forty-sixth Congress, in which Gordon's second term

---
[60] Published in the *History of the Baptist Denomination in Georgia*, p. 67, in the sketch of Joseph E. Brown.
[61] Knight, II, 872.

commenced on March 4, 1879, held three sessions, the second of which began on December 1, 1879, and ended on June 16 of the following year. On May 19, 1880, three weeks before the end of the second session, the country was startled by the press announcement of the resignation of Senator John B. Gordon of Georgia and the appointment to the vacancy by Governor Alfred H. Colquitt of ex-Governor Joseph E. Brown. Mrs. Felton, who was in Washington where her husband was a member of the House of Representatives, saw the Georgia members of Congress just after they had read the morning papers "standing around in groups, like they had just come from a funeral." [62] A seat in the United States Senate "vacated and filled between dark and daylight," the highest office in the state given to "Bullock's ex-Chief Justice by a *Simon-pure*[63] Democratic governor," struck Georgia like a "bolt from the blue," [64] and shook it "from center to circumference." [65] The fury of the people knew no bounds. In Columbus, where the treatment of the "Columbus prisoners" was fresh in memory, the telegraphic announcement of Brown's appointment aroused violent indignation and a procession bearing crape-covered drums summoned to a mass meeting one of the largest crowds ever gathered at the county's courthouse. Brown was denounced in the strongest possible terms, not an unpopular act of his career or a charge proved or unproved against him being omitted. The state had been "disgraced" and "brought to shame" by the appointment of a man, the adopted resolutions stated, "who betrayed the State of Georgia into the hands of her enemies in her darkest hours of trial and counselled and instigated measures which had they prevailed would have incarcerated

---

[62] P. 305.
[63] The term always designated those who were untainted with scalawaggery. See Arnett, pp. 30-31.
[64] Felton, pp. 9, 85, 289, 302; Fielder, p. 523.
[65] Avery, p. 583.

many of her best citizens within the walls of a dungeon." [66]

The reasons for Brown's appointment were explained at length by Colquitt and Gordon. Colquitt pointed out Brown's services to the Democratic party in denouncing Bullock, supporting James M. Smith for governor, and laboring in Florida for Tilden. Without Brown's assistance in reclaiming North Georgia, he felt that the Democratic party, "upon the supremacy of which seems to depend all that is valuable to us as a people," would be disrupted. Believing these things and feeling that the state needed in the Senate a man of Brown's type — temperate, cautious, conservative, farsighted—he had appointed him and was "prepared to take the consequences." [67]

In a speech in Atlanta Gordon said that "as a matter of sentiment most of us would have preferred some other Georgian than Brown," but that thousands of people in and out of the state were beginning to agree with General Joseph E. Johnston that Joseph E. Brown was the best selection that could have been made.[68]

He hinted that Northern Democrats thought the success of the party required that the "olive branch" be extended to those who had "differed with us in the transition stage." He referred to Brown as "a man of large property, deeply interested in material progress," a lifelong Democrat, "who though denounced by us for voting for Grant and reconstruction in 1868, was joined by us in voting for Greeley and reconstruction in 1872." He read from Governor Colquitt's letter to himself announcing Brown's appointment in which Colquitt said that two of the strongest Democratic districts

---

[66] *Columbus Times,* May 21, 1880; *Constitution,* May 22, 1880; Felton, p. 85. Cf. Mahone's taunt in the U. S. Senate on Mar. 28, 1881, *Cong. Record,* 47th Cong., sp. sess., pp. 93-94; Brown's reply the following day, *ibid.,* pp. 106 *et seq.,* and Fielder, pp. 630-42.
[67] Knight, II, 902-4, 908.
[68] Brown had espoused the cause of Johnston in the latter's quarrel with President Davis.

in the state were lost to the Democratic party, a third and a fourth were threatened, and the party was apparently on the verge of dissolution; that friends and lifelong followers of ex-Governor Brown among the hardy yeomanry of the mountains were dissatisfied and ready to break with the organization; and that he felt by the appointment of Brown he might "recall them to their allegiance, recapture these Democratic strongholds, harmonize former differences, assuage bitterness, and assure the future of Democratic supremacy." For ten or twelve years, Gordon continued, Brown had been "unfaltering in his devotion to the Democratic party," and "it is due our manhood that we either cease hostility to [him], or cease to ask his time and talents and money for the benefit of our party." [69]

The press of Georgia and of the nation was filled with inquiries—and answers—of why Gordon had resigned. Curiosity was intensified by the suddenness of his resignation so near the end of the session. In explanation it was said that he had accepted a lucrative business offer in Oregon which would permit of no delay, but when he returned to Georgia instead of going to the Pacific coast other explanations were given. It was said that he was to be president of the Western & Atlantic Railroad Company, but Brown authorized the *Atlanta Constitution* to say that he had no intention of resigning the office.[70] Gordon seems to have made conflicting statements regarding his future plans, as did the *Constitution*.[71] Ex-Governor James M. Smith in an address in Columbus said the people had a right to know why Gordon "so suddenly resigned and clandestinely," and why Governor Colquitt "condoned the political sins and iniquities of Joseph E. Brown." [72] In a speech in Atlanta on

---

[69] *Savannah News,* June 5, 1880; *Chronicle and Sentinel,* June 6, 1880; Avery, pp. 562-63.

[70] May 22, 1880; Fielder, p. 523; Avery, p. 553.

[71] Cf. sketch of John Brown Gordon, Northen, III, 508-15; Felton, pp. 266, 303-4, 306-8, 527-37.   [72] *Ibid.,* pp. 266 *et seq.*

June 4 and another in Augusta on the following day, Gordon stated that for "months and months" he had been making arrangements to retire from public life for financial reasons and when an old Confederate friend in Oregon made him a flattering business proposition which required his immediate presence on the Pacific coast, he had sent his resignation on May 14 to Governor Colquitt. Later, however, Victor Newcomb, president of the Louisville & Nashville Railroad, had offered him a position which he had accepted "because it would enable him to remain in Georgia." [73] Gordon's explanation did little to allay the feeling that a "trade" had been entered into by the three men which, however, each denied.[74]

Probably the true explanation is that Governor Colquitt, whose administration had begun under propitious circumstances and had ended under dark clouds,[75] could not be reelected without Brown's support. The price of that support was appointment to the United States Senate, which Brown passionately desired as a "vindication." [76] A lucrative business connection was, therefore, found for Gordon to induce him to resign, or pressure, the nature of which has never been ascertained, was in some way applied. The fact that six

---

[73] *Savannah News,* June 5, 7, 1880; *Chronicle and Sentinel,* June 6, 1880. Cf. letter from Gordon's father to editors of *Constitution,* May 26, 1880, and *Savannah News,* May 27, 1880; Gordon's interview with Washington correspondent of *Constitution,* May 27, 1880; Avery, pp. 562-63.

[74] Interview with Brown and Colquitt, *Constitution,* May 23, 1880; Colquitt's address in Atlanta, *ibid.,* May 29, 1880; telegraphic news item from Atlanta, *Savannah Morning News,* May 29, 1880; Gordon's interview with Washington correspondent, *Constitution,* May 27, 1880. Cf. letter from "Seneca" to editors of the *Chronicle and Sentinel* and the *Constitution,* in *Savannah News,* May 31, 1880; dispatch from Washington correspondent, *Constitution,* June 2, 1880; editorial in *Savannah News,* May 27, 1880; Avery, p. 553.

[75] Avery, pp. 545 *et seq.;* Fielder, p. 500; Felton, pp. 286, 288-89, 311; Arnett, pp. 38-39; Knight, II, 889-98; sketch of life of Colquitt, Northen, III, 67-71; Clark, *Memoirs,* pp. 339-48.

[76] Avery (pp. 563-64) naïvely remarks, "To Governor Brown this unsolicited tender of this peculiar trust was an event of unspeakable importance."

years later Gordon was elected governor for two terms and served as United States senator for another six years would indicate that he had no aversion to public life and that he had recouped his fortune in a remarkably short time. Whether Brown, with whom Gordon was not very friendly,[77] made possible the business connection for Gordon with the Louisville & Nashville Railroad there is no way of knowing. For the next few years Gordon was engaged in promoting railroads in Georgia and Florida,[78] and a recent historian thinks it was significant that "Gordon's ambitions were chiefly in the field of railroad construction and management in which Brown held a commanding position." [79]

Another possibility is that Brown's policy as president of the Western & Atlantic Railroad Company may have indirectly been the controlling factor in Gordon's appointment. It was a time of cutthroat competition in railroad building and the Louisville & Nashville, particularly active at this time in extending its connections to Mobile, Pensacola, New Orleans, and the Atlantic,[80] was casting longing eyes on the State Road,[81] the policies of which under Brown were said to be more favorable to Louisville & Nashville competitors.[82] President Newcomb may have expected, or have been led to expect, that Brown's appointment to the Senate would

---

[77] Avery, p. 553; Knight, II, 903.

[78] Avery, pp. 561-62; Knight, II, 903; Felton, pp. 288-311. For expansion of the L. & N. R. R. in this section at this period, see John Leeds Kerr, *The Story of a Southern Carrier,* pp. 37-46, henceforth cited as Kerr.

[79] Arnett, p. 39. It may or may not be significant that Brown was in Nashville where a part of the offices of the L. & N. and those of its soon-to-be-acquired connecting line, the N. C. & St. L., are located when he received Governor Colquitt's telegraphic appointment.—Fielder, pp. 522-23. Fielder states that Brown had previously refused the appointment.—*Ibid.* The L. & N. acquired the N. C. & St. L. through stock control before June 30, 1880.—Kerr, p. 41.

[80] *Ibid.,* pp. 37-46.

[81] It was rumored at this time that President Newcomb had said that "contingencies might arise that would make an independent line into Atlanta a necessity."—Felton, p. 302, citing *Constitution,* Mar. 26, 1880.

[82] Cf. Felton, p. 307, citing editorial in *New Orleans Times,* date not given.

# REHABILITATION 313

result in his resignation from the presidency of the company operating the State Road, with a consequent change in policy and perhaps even the sale of the road.[83] Ten years later the Louisville & Nashville Railroad gained direct access to the Atlanta gateway through the leasing of the State Road by the Nashville, Chattanooga & St. Louis Railroad, which it controlled.[84] In any event the feeling persisted that there was a Colquitt-Gordon-Brown arrangement in 1880, carefully worked out and agreed to by each.[85]

Another explanation for Gordon's precipitate resignation within three weeks of the end of the session, other than the one he himself gave, is that he wished to give his successor the advantage of a *fait accompli* when the successor should go before the legislature in the following November as a candidate for election to the unexpired term. The fact that Brown, though a new member, made three speeches[86] during the three weeks[87] in which he sat in the second session of the Forty-sixth Congress, one of which was a defense of secession, would seem to be proof that he was given the period in which to make an impression on Georgians and that he very skillfully availed himself of the opportunity.[88] Brown's

---

[83] See Felton, p. 304. Mrs. Felton states (pp. 570-71) that by 1885 the L. & N. owned 13 shares and controlled 7 more of the 23 shares in the company operating the State Road, but that it later discovered the holding of shares did not carry with it the right to vote and that control remained with the original lessees. Cf. act to lease the W. & A. R. R., *Acts of the General Assembly, 1870*, p. 423.

[84] Kerr, pp. 47-48.

[85] Knight (II, 903), who doubtless bases his statement upon Avery and Fielder, says that Gordon was surprised when Brown's appointment was announced.

[86] Fielder, p. 524.

[87] From May 26 to June 16, 1880.—Knight, II, 911.

[88] Brown's services in this period, duly chronicled by the Brown-Colquitt press, consisted in securing an appropriation of $10,000 for the harbor of Brunswick over the adverse report of the committee; the passage of a bill to allow the Savannah, Florida & Western R. R. to build a bridge over St. Mary's River; and the defeat of a provision in the reapportionment bill which would have lost to Georgia a representative in Congress. He made an unsuccessful fight to have the appropriation of $65,000 for Savannah

314    JOSEPH E. BROWN

speech on June 12 on the Mexican War pension bill was a vigorous defense of secession, a reminder of the hard terms imposed upon the South in reconstruction, a denial that Southerners held seats in Congress by the grace of any political party or government or power other than by their guaranteed rights under the Constitution, and a plea for generosity in the matter of pensioning ex-Confederates who were Mexican War veterans.[89] In Fielder's estimation it was the most effective rebuke that had been given since the war to the policy of "waving the bloody shirt." [90]

Brown's Fourth of July address, "Our Country," [91] in the city hall, Atlanta, was in part an attempt to justify his reconstruction record, an adroit appeal to the acquisitive instincts of his audience, and a bid for the Negro vote in the forthcoming election.

We differed among ourselves [he said] about the best means of meeting the emergency. Some of us thought we saw no chance but to acquiesce. . . . If we could not succeed when we had 500,000 of the gallant sons of the South in the field . . . how could we resist further, when we had surrendered our armies and the conquerors stood with 1,200,000 bayonets over

---

harbor increased to $100,000.—Avery, p. 565; Fielder, p. 524; *Savannah News,* May 29, June 2, 1880; Knight, II, 911; Brown's speech on the Savannah harbor bill, *Savannah News,* June 18, 1880. Toombs remarked that Brown at once "scented the treasury." See Brown's reply in his De Gives Opera House speech, Fielder, p. 553.

[89] *Cong. Record,* 46th Cong., 2nd sess., pp. 4479 *et seq.* Brown's speech may also be found in *Savannah News,* June 28, 1880, and in Fielder, pp. 593-604. Cf. Avery, pp. 565-66.

[90] P. 525. Fielder was biased in his judgment, or had forgotten that four years earlier, on Jan. 11, 1876, in the House of Representatives, Ben Hill had delivered his masterful speech on the "Andersonville Atrocities" (Benjamin H. Hill, Jr., pp. 440-62), following which the *London Times* congratulated the South on having a man like Hill who had the "ability and courage to defend his section and establish the truth of history."—Quoted by Pearce, p. 281. Hill had made two other speeches of the same nature before Brown's —"The Union and Its Enemies," delivered in the Senate on May 10, 1879, and "The Union under the Constitution Knows No Section," June 11, 1879.—Benjamin H. Hill, Jr., pp. 561 *et seq.;* 594 *et seq.*

[91] Fielder, pp. 772-80.

us? Others thought . . . we might get rid of these measures by means of the Democratic party. We differed . . . in angry spirit sometimes, but honestly on both sides. . . . We were finally obliged to come to the point of acquiescing in all the reconstruction acts . . . and of adopting the three constitutional amendments. . . . Today, whatever may have been our differences of opinion in the past, we are a unit on that point: We have all acquiesced.[92]

He saw no reason why the South might not henceforth "move forward in a grand and glorious program to wealth, to power, and to greatness." [93] In regard to Negro suffrage he said that it was a source of power to the South since if the Fourteenth Amendment were not enforced that section would lose thirty votes in Congress and in the electoral college. If the people of the North should propose an amendment to take the ballot from the Negro he felt sure the democracy of the whole South would rally to the colored man. "He gives us power and he shall ever exercise the elective franchise," he said.[94] He made a plea for the education of all children, white and black. It costs money to educate people, he admitted. "But . . . you will never find an enlightened, educated people who do not make money." [95]

The first meeting of the party after Brown's appointment was at the Democratic state convention in Atlanta on June 9, where the object of the meeting—the selection of delegates to the Democratic National Convention—was completely overshadowed by the interest of the delegates in the gubernatorial race in which it was evident the appointment of Brown would be the issue.[96] The Colquitt forces effected a strong organization with Henry Grady of the *Atlanta Constitution* as chairman of the campaign committee. The opposition did not unite upon a candidate, but it was a unit in

---
[92] *Ibid.*, p. 776.    [93] *Ibid.*, p. 777.
[94] *Ibid.*, p. 778.
[95] *Ibid.*, p. 779. The address appeared in the *Constitution*, July 7, 1880.
[96] Avery, p. 564; Fielder, p. 527; Brewton, p. 141.

its determination to prevent the renomination of Colquitt and to prevent the election of a legislature favorable to the selection of Brown to fill Gordon's unexpired term.[97]

Of the state nominating convention which met in Atlanta on Wednesday, August 4, 1880, Avery says, "There never has been in the history of Georgia, and there never probably will be such another Convention. During war days no such fever had been aroused. . . ."[98] In the campaign for the election of delegates the struggle had been ferocious—nothing was left unsaid or undone. There were, in all, five candidates for the gubernatorial nomination, but it was Colquitt against the field. The Colquitt forces, however, presented a solid and disciplined phalanx, the result of the formation of the triumvirate—Colquitt, Brown, and Gordon—which was destined from this time to rule the state for a number of years. Colquitt, a planter-business man, major general in the Confederate army, and heir to his distinguished father's prestige, had a large following despite the scandals of his administration. He was able to appeal even to the planter aristocracy, although Bourbon Democracy was anything but agrarian in its philosophy and benefits. Gordon, who was perhaps Colquitt's greatest asset,[99] was popular with the Confederate soldiers and with the business and commercial classes of the "New South" type. Brown led the "Bullock Democrats."[100] The convention was composed of 549 delegates with 350 votes, the majority pledged to Colquitt. L. N. Trammell, a Colquitt man, was elected president, he who had made Brown the "dark horse" nominee in 1857 and had been forced out of the race for Congress by Dr. Felton in the "bloody seventh" in 1874. There was precedent for nominating by majority vote, but the anti-Colquitt forces,

---

[97] Avery, pp. 564, 568-69, 572.  [98] *Ibid.*, p. 572.
[99] Arnett, pp. 29-31, 42; Felton, pp. 48, 541, 630.
[100] *Ibid.*, pp. 163, 288. Arnett (p. 42) is doubtful whether Brown was a help or a hindrance. For Mrs. Felton's picturesque description of the triumvirate, see pp. 163, 168, 288-89.

# REHABILITATION 317

threatening to bolt the convention, compelled the adoption of the two-thirds rule.[101] The Colquitt majority, however, forced the adoption of such rules as would prevent the nomination of a "dark horse." [102]

On the first ballot Colquitt received 208⅔ votes while his nearest competitor received 58½, the remaining votes being distributed among the three other candidates.[103] By the ninth ballot Colquitt had gained one vote, but the convention was deadlocked and various unsuccessful attempts were made by the opposition at this time and throughout the remaining days for some other form of nomination. One of the more drastic proposals was that primaries be held in all counties on the same day for delegates to a convention to be held in September.[104] The Colquitt forces were determined not to accept any overtures from the opposition, and the opposition was equally as determined not to permit Colquitt's nomination.[105] Colquitt's manager, Patrick Walsh, editor of the *Chronicle*, sent a dispatch to his paper at midnight, Saturday, August 7, saying: ". . . There will be no nomination for Governor unless the minority unite upon Colquitt. . . . There are but two ways of relieving the deadlock. One is to rescind the two-thirds rule . . . and the other is to refer the matter back to the people without a nomination." [106] In all, thirty-two ballots were taken, and the convention adjourned at the end of its seventh day without a nomination, Colquitt lacking nine votes of the necessary two thirds. Colquitt forces recommended their candidate to the

---

[101] Avery, pp. 32, 512, 572; *Savannah News*, Aug. 5, 1880; Knight, II, 908.
[102] Avery, pp. 572-76; Knight, II, 908; Brewton, pp. 143-48.
[103] *Savannah News*, Aug. 6, 1880.
[104] Avery, pp. 577-86; Northen, III, 76 *et seq*. When it became evident that the Colquitt forces meant to nominate their man or disrupt the convention, Thomas W. Watson, then only twenty-three years of age, made an eloquent speech which "swept the opposition into delirium" and launched young Watson on his political career. His speech may be found in Brewton, pp. 144-46 and in Avery, pp. 579-80; extracts in Knight, II, 909.
[105] *Savannah News*, Aug. 7, 1880.
[106] Quoted by *ibid.*, Aug. 9, 1880.

voters[107] while the minority remained in the hall and selected as their standard bearer Thomas N. Norwood, former United States senator.[108] General Alexander R. Lawton, who under Brown's orders had taken Fort Pulaski in 1861 and who had been quartermaster general of the Confederate government, was selected as candidate for the United States Senate.[109]

The campaign that followed—the bitterest in the history of the state—was a continuation of the convention struggle.[110] "Slanders were unearthed afresh. The mills of vituperation began once more to grind."[111] In Macon at a joint debate between the gubernatorial candidates, Colquitt tried for two hours to make himself heard "amid a storm of catcalls, cheers, hisses, groans, cries, jeers, insults."[112] The Colquitt forces made it appear that a vote against their candidate was a vote for the Radical party, although the Republicans had nominated no candidate for governor.[113] Each side accused the other of appealing to the Negro vote which held the balance of power. As a matter of fact both sides appealed to the Negroes, although the Colquitt forces seem to have been more successful in this respect.[114] The scandals

---

[107] *Ibid.,* Aug. 11, 12, 1880. Letter of notification of action of convention and letter of acceptance from Governor Colquitt, *ibid.,* Aug. 16, 1880.

[108] Because the opposition had not united on a candidate before the campaign to elect delegates it was not as effective as the Colquitt forces who were pledged to their candidate. Dr. William H. Felton could have united the opposition and probably have drawn some support from the Colquitt forces as the convention dragged on without a nomination, but though invited at the end to become their candidate, he felt obligated to his district in which he was making the race for reëlection to Congress—in which, however, he was defeated.—Felton, pp. 288-311, 340; Knight, II, 910.

[109] Fielder, p. 528; Knight, II, 912.

[110] Avery, p. 586; Fielder, p. 527.

[111] Knight, II, 909.

[112] Avery, p. 592.

[113] *Savannah News,* Aug. 18, 1880; Avery, pp. 595-96.

[114] Avery, pp. 568 *et seq.;* Felton, p. 264; Arnett, pp. 40 *et seq.* Arnett thinks reconstruction had familiarized the people with unfair election tactics which they now employed. Mrs. Felton says that Brown, having been a Radical at one time, "understood the business." In the seventies the Negro

REHABILITATION 319

of Colquitt's administration,[115] including the leasing of convicts,[116] and, in general, Colquitt's "fatal mistakes and food appointments"[117] formed the theme of the opposition. The appointment of Brown was, however, the real issue of the campaign.[118] Toombs was opposed to Colquitt, but reserved his choicest epithets for Brown.[119] The plea for party regularity was of great value to Colquitt, since he was without question the majority candidate. The *Savannah News* in a series of editorials stressed the point and reminded its readers that the "science of politics is not a game of personalities." [120] The smoothly oiled political machine of the triumvirate won the day. Colquitt received 118,349 votes, and Norwood 64,004,[121] Colquitt's majority being 54,345 as compared with his majority of 80,000 in 1876.

On the evening before the legislature was to select a United States senator, Brown spoke before an immense audience in the De Gives Opera House.[122] It was without question the greatest effort of his life. Prepared with the utmost care, his speech showed to a greater extent than any other of his public utterances his uncanny understanding of the psychology of the masses and his ability to reach them

---

vote had largely been eliminated, but with such contests as that of 1880 and with the growth of insurgency in the Democratic party, each faction sought to obtain it. Such conditions ultimately led by general consent of the whites to the disfranchisement of the colored race.

[115] Editorial in refutation, *Savannah News*, Aug. 21, 1880.

[116] Letter from John W. Nelms to the *Constitution,* published in the *Savannah News*, Aug. 21, 1880; editorial in reply to Norwood, *ibid.*

[117] Brewton, p. 149.

[118] See ex-Governor James M. Smith's review of Brown's political career, as given by Felton, pp. 61-62.

[119] Avery, p. 599. Avery's list of supporters of Norwood and Colquitt respectively (pp. 592-93, 595) would seem to indicate that the majority of the well-known public men supported Norwood. It is interesting to note that among those supporting Colquitt and Brown was Col. R. J. Moses who had refused to practice in the supreme court while Brown was chief justice.

[120] Aug. 14-18, 1880.

[121] *H. J., 1880,* p. 37; Avery, p. 601.

[122] Brown's speech may be found in Fielder, pp. 531-59; *Constitution*, Nov. 16, 1880.

without at the same time resorting to demagoguery which would have alienated many. Plausible, free of rancor, and delivered with the calm assurance so characteristic of the man, it made a profound impression. The logic of events was seemingly on his side and he made the most of it. Toombs and Stephens must have winced when, in replying to his opponent's charge that he had been untrue to the Confederacy, Brown said that his course during the war had had their unqualified support. Were they untrue to the Confederate cause, he inquired. The soldiers had voted for him, showing that they believed in his patriotism. He justified his policy in reconstruction by saying that he had deliberately chosen his course with the full knowledge that his motives would be misunderstood and that he would become the most unpopular man from the Potomac to the Rio Grande. But he had been honored by the people of Georgia, he felt he owed a debt to them, and so "forgetful of self-interest" he had labored for their welfare. If he were a traitor in 1868 when he supported Grant, then the whole South was a traitor in 1872 when the Democratic party came over to his platform. He intimated that Hill had adopted a course similar to his own and had expressed regret for the bitter things he had said and written. He read an old letter from Lee, in reply to an inquiry from one of his officers, in which he claimed Lee had given advice similar to his own.

General Lawton had said that by resisting Brown's policy Georgia had freed herself from the oppressor sooner than South Carolina, Florida, and Louisiana, which had taken Brown's advice. Brown replied that those states had taken Lawton's advice and Georgia had taken his. Brown accused his opponent of dragging out dead issues which had separated and embittered the people in bygone years. He predicted that if Lawton should be sent to the United States Senate he would be unable to promote the interests of the state since his colleagues would believe that Georgia was still opposed

REHABILITATION 321

to the Federal government. Lawton had said also that Georgia should send to the Senate a man who represented the opinion of the state. Very skillfully Brown made it appear that Lawton represented only the kid-glove aristocracy while he, a poor boy who had had to make his own way in life, understood the needs of the masses. He said that the people had always elected him to office because they knew he was one of them and represented their interests. Lawton and the aristocracy were living in the past, the masses were looking to the future. Brown told his audience what he had accomplished in the three weeks he had sat in the Senate and what he would endeavor to accomplish for the state if he were returned to that body. He took his audience to the mountaintop and painted for agriculture, business, and the financial interests a glowing picture of the possibilities of material development for the state. As he concluded, a telegram was handed to him which he asked a friend to read to the audience. It was from General Henry R. Jackson who corroborated Brown's statement of having discussed with him in 1867 the motives which impelled the ex-Governor to his reconstruction course.[123]

Brown was elected to the United States Senate by a vote of 146 to Lawton's 64.[124] Four years later Brown was reelected without opposition and with only one vote against him. He served until the end of the term, March 4, 1891, when he retired and General John B. Gordon was elected. Brown died November 30, 1894.[125]

Why did Brown espouse the cause of the Radicals? What influence did he exert? Why did he return to the Democratic party?

---

[123] For an interesting contrast of the two candidates, Brown and Lawton—plebeian and aristocrat—written by a "New South" man signing himself John Temple, see Avery, pp. 602-3, citing the *Athens Sunday Banner*, date not given.
[124] *H. J., 1880*, p. 120; *S. J., 1880*, p. 78; Fielder, p. 561; Avery, p. 602.
[125] Northen, III, 99; Knight, II, 933-34.

His own explanations have been given. Avery did not question his sincerity of purpose[126] and Fielder thought Brown exercised a bold and fearless mind and judgment "in advance of his own people" and indicated the "wisest and best course." [127] Three present-day Georgia historians agree with Fielder. Knight says Brown's course was "prompted by motives of patriotism and was justified by the logic of events." [128] Whether Hill or Brown contributed most to the rescue of Georgia from Radical misrule Pearce thinks "will probably remain problematical." [129] He seemingly accepts the motives Brown professed and comments that "after all the state came over to Brown's viewpoint on reconstruction issues." [130] Brooks seems surprised that a half century after the event "the older people of Georgia and even recent historians" should question the wisdom of Brown's course and characterize him as an opportunist. He thinks the ultimate verdict of history will "probably be otherwise." [131]

Alexander Stephens differed with the opinion so prevalent at the time that Brown had been influenced by motives of ambition, "excited by the temptations offered to him on the 'High Mountain' to which he was carried in Washington." He thought that Brown's course had been determined "more from apprehensions awakened by threats of attainder, of confiscation, and the thousands of other ills that might be expected to attend the rejection of the proposed measure. . . ." [132] The Honorable J. C. C. Black had Brown in mind when in describing reconstruction he spoke of those who

---

[126] P. 454.
[127] P. 267.     [128] II, 989.
[129] Pp. 307-8.
[130] Review of E. M. Coulter's *A Short History of Georgia*, in the *Journal of Southern History*, I (Feb., 1935), 82.
[131] "Joseph Emerson Brown," *Dictionary of Modern Biography*.
[132] *War between the States*, II, 655. Rhodes (VI, 185) thinks Brown understood the revolutionary mood of the North better than did the majority of Southern leaders.

# REHABILITATION 323

"basely bartered themselves for the spoils of office" and "aligned themselves with the enemies of the people and their liberties until the battle was fought," after which they returned to their former allegiance "and fixed upon their own ignoble brows the stigma of a double treachery by proclaiming that they had joined our enemies to betray them." [133] That Brown was an out-and-out opportunist is the opinion of the historian of reconstruction in Georgia: "He was first in secession, first in reconstruction, and very nearly first in the restoration of Democratic home rule. Consequently he came up on top at every revolution of the wheel of destiny." [134] A similar opinion is expressed by a prominent jurist and contemporary of Brown who says that after the war "Brown's opportunism continued to chart his course and to condition his action," [135] and by a recent writer who refers to the ex-Governor as "the chameleon of Georgia politics." [136] Professor E. Merton Coulter, a Georgia historian, agrees with these unfavorable estimates.[137]

If one accepts at their face value the motives which Brown professed, it is yet difficult to see what he could have hoped to accomplish by his course. The Radicals wanted the disfranchisement of leading Confederates and the enfranchisement of the Negro in order to perpetuate the power of the Republican party. They wanted also the sweet revenge of compelling Southerners themselves to proscribe their own leaders and consent to their own dishonor. Compliance constituted acknowledgment that the war was a rebellion and its participants traitors.. This was the view taken by Hill, Herschel V. Johnson, and Stephens in Georgia and by other leaders throughout the South who refused to sacrifice princi-

---

[133] Address at the unveiling of a monument to Ben Hill, in Atlanta, May 1, 1886, *Constitution*, May 2, 1886; Benjamin H. Hill, Jr., pp. 220 *et seq.*
[134] C. M. Thompson, p. 223.
[135] Private letter, 1933.
[136] T. R. Hay, in review of Pearce's *Ben. H. Hill*, in *Georgia Historical Quarterly* (June, 1929).
[137] *Georgia*, pp. 304-11.

ple to expediency.[138] To agree with their adversaries quickly, as Brown counseled, meant not a mitigation of the Radical program but its consummation.[139] In the end, a part of this program was embedded in the federal Constitution and had to be accepted, it is true, but not with the consent of the Southern white population. That Brown's course contributed in any way to mitigate or shorten the reconstruction period in Georgia, other than to secure some degree of moderation in the Radical constitutional convention, is not in evidence. That Georgia's reconstruction was both short and mild in comparison with that of some of the other states in the lower South was due in large part to the fact that her Negro population was proportionately smaller and her Conservative party more able and aggressive.[140] In the matter of the eligibility of Negroes to hold office, where he might have aided the Conservative element, Brown made a decision contrary to his previously stated views. Though he was in this period the power behind the throne,[141] there is no evidence of his having prevented in Georgia any of the corruption which characterized the reconstruction regime everywhere. One must conclude that Brown's services to the people of

---

[138] Stephens, *War between the States*, II, 665; Coleman, p. 15.

[139] The *Federal Union* (Mar. 5, 1867) expressed the general opinion of the Conservatives when it said that Brown's advice simply meant sending Radical representatives to Washington and probably getting a governor like Brownlow of Tenn., in comparison with which military government was preferable. Cf. Stephens, *War between the States*, II, 665; Herschel V. Johnson, in *Savannah News*, July 18, 1867. For economic reasons behind the reconstruction program, see Beale, p. 2 and Chap. X.

[140] See Woolley, pp. 99-100. The strength of the Conservatives is seen in the fact that they carried Georgia in the presidential election of 1868 by a majority of 55,688.—Stanwood, p. 328.

[141] C. M. Thompson, p. 223; Felton, p. 25. When in 1872 the legislature decided to close the investigation of the lease of the State Road and allow it to remain in the hands of the original lessees, the Atlanta correspondent of the *Augusta Constitutionalist* reported to his paper that a "most intelligent gentleman" sitting beside him in the gallery remarked when the vote was announced, "Joe Brown has been governor ever since 1857, and is likely to be governor for the next twenty years."—*Constitutionalist*, Aug. 24, 1872. The opinion seems to have been rather generally held.

REHABILITATION 325

Georgia in the matter of reconstruction consisted in the fact that his course solidified the opposition and made possible an aggressive Conservative party which through its protests and pleas helped to inform the nation of the true state of affairs in the South, and at the polls in 1870 gained control of the state government.

If Brown had not himself benefited to such a degree in the Bullock regime one might more easily accept his professed motives for joining the Radicals. But the fact that he aimed at a seat in the United States Senate—logical it is true from the standpoint that it were better for himself to hold the office than for another more radical, but creating suspicion as to his motives, nevertheless—tended to destroy his usefulness with the Conservatives. It is impossible to say to what extent Brown was implicated in the corruption of the period. His close association with Bullock, Kimball, Blodgett, and others who were beneficiaries of the Bullock regime and his rapid rise to wealth and power naturally made him suspect. His business and financial dealings, in so far as they involved the state government, were investigated by various legislative committees. These exonerated the ex-Governor, but his foes claimed that they merely whitewashed him. Kimball, his law partner, was considered the chief spoilsman of the Bullock administration,[142] but both he and Bullock were later exonerated by the courts.

Brown's claim that Hill in 1870 came over to his position on reconstuction has been discussed and refuted.[143] His claim that the Democratic party in 1872 adopted his platform[144] is untenable for the same reasons.[145] Brown returned to the

---

[142] C. M. Thompson, pp. 230-40; Bowers, pp. 300 et seq.
[143] Supra, pp. 296 et seq.
[144] Fielder, pp. 542-43, 633; Cong. Record, 47th Cong. sp. sess., pp. 106 et seq.; Gordon's statement, Avery, pp. 562-63, Savannah News, June 5, 1880, Chronicle and Sentinel, June 6, 1880.
[145] In the U. S. Senate in 1881 Mahone of Virginia, whose Democracy Brown had questioned, referred sarcastically to Brown's charge when, after reviewing Brown's variable career, he said: "His explanation of all this is

Democratic party because there was no longer any reason for his remaining in the Republican camp. His person and property were now safe, thanks to the fight of the Conservatives of Georgia, and the Republican party was so thoroughly discredited there that no future political honors could be expected from it. When the Bullock regime began to totter, Brown read the handwriting on the wall. There was no danger to be incurred at this point by opposing Bullock—Brown's position as chief justice was secure if he cared to continue in that capacity and by the end of 1870 the lease of the State Road was in his pocket. Georgia was restored to the Union, which according to his oft repeated statements was the goal toward which he had aimed. Brown accordingly readjusted himself to the new political conditions in his state. "By veering with the weather he had escaped its inclemency." Many must have doubted with Senator Mahone whether the "world had produced a man who could so readily readjust himself to all conditions and to all circumstances." [146] Henceforth Brown was a power in the Democratic party—at first a hidden power[147] and then, with "a million in money," the control of the State Road, patronage as United States senator, and not being as "controlled by scruples as may be thought desirable," he more or less openly assumed the "rôle of a Warwick." [148]

Brown's advice in 1867 might with equal force have been given in 1861. In either case it meant submission without a struggle. But between 1861 and 1867 much water had gone under the bridge. Brown's activities in secession and

---

that the Democratic party erred and abandoned him, and now it has righted itself and rallied upon his undying and unchangeable principles. . . . This probably accounts for my anomalous position. When the Democratic party went in search of the Senator from Georgia it left me."—*Cong. Record,* 47th Cong., sp. sess., p. 93.

[146] *Ibid.*

[147] See Felton, pp. 25, 65-69.

[148] Prof. William M. Browne to Jefferson Davis, July 1, 1882, Rowland, IX, 175-76.

REHABILITATION 327

his seizure of Fort Pulaski before Georgia seceded[149] had placed him in a position where a double charge of treason might easily be preferred against him by the Radicals in Washington, with the possibility of imprisonment and the confiscation of his property.[150] His moral courage was not equal to the contingency. With the breakdown of Radical rule in Georgia he made new opportunities for himself in the dominant party which carried him to yet greater heights.

Thus the course of the ex-governor of Georgia from 1867 to 1870 and from that date to 1880 throws light on his course as governor in the last year of the Confederacy's existence. Politically Brown had been "vindicated." But the fact remains that although ". . . some twenty new counties have been created in Georgia in the last twenty years, the name of Brown was never even suggested for any of them. The State has ordered oil paintings of many distinguished sons to adorn the walls of the State House, but the Journals carry no suggestions of one of Brown. Every other monument of marble, stone, or brass that stands on the streets of Atlanta, in her parks, or on the capitol grounds, was erected either by popular subscription or from public funds; but the one to Governor Brown recently placed was done by members of his own family." [151]

---

[149] Governor T. O. Moore of Louisiana had also seized Federal property before the secession of his state.—John Rose Ficklen, *History of Reconstruction in Louisiana*, p. 24.

[150] See Fielder, pp. 425-26. Brown's visit to Washington in the early part of 1867 had familiarized him with the revolutionary mood of the Radicals. Probably no one today will dispute Rhodes' statement (VI, 185) that "the Republican majority in Congress and among the Northern people was determined to have its way, and would no more be stopped by legal principles and technicalities than it had been by the President's vetoes."

[151] Personal letter in possession of the author, from a well-known Georgia lawyer, dated Nov. 24, 1930.

# BIBLIOGRAPHY

### I. Bibliographical Aids

Arnett, Alex Mathews. *The Populist Movement in Georgia.* . . . New York, 1922. Bibliography covers post-bellum period.

Boyd, William Kenneth, and Robert Preston Brooks, comps. *A Selected Bibliography and Syllabus of the History of the South, 1854-1876.* Athens (Ga.), 1918.

Brooks, Robert Preston. "A Preliminary Bibliography of Georgia History," University of Georgia *Bulletin,* X, No. 10A. Athens (Ga.), 1910.

*Catalog of the Wymberly Jones De Renne Georgia Library at Wormsloe, Isle of Hope, near Savannah, Georgia.* 3 vols. Wormsloe (Ga.), 1931.

Dailey, Carrie L. *List of Georgia State Publications.* Atlanta, 1909.

Freeman, Douglas Southall. *A Calendar of Confederate Papers with a Bibliography of Some Confederate Publications.* Richmond, 1908. Preliminary report of the Southern Historical Manuscript Commission.

Jameson, John Franklin, Chairman, Historical Manuscript Commission of the American Historical Association. "Items Respecting Historical Manuscripts," including public and private collections. Third annual report of the Commission, in American Historical Association *Annual Report* for 1898, pp. 565-708.

Morrison, Hugh A. "A Bibliography of the Official Publications of the Confederate States of America," Bibliographical Society of America *Proceedings and Papers,* III (1909), 92-132.

Pearce, Haywood Jefferson. *Benjamin H. Hill.* . . . Chicago, 1928. Bibliography covers secession and reconstruction.

Phillips, Ulrich Bonnell. *Georgia and State Rights.* Washington, 1902. Bibliography covers the ante-bellum period.

———. "The Public Archives of Georgia," American Historical Association *Annual Report* for 1903, I, 439-74. Washington, 1904.

———. "Georgia Local Archives," American Historical Association *Annual Report* for 1904, pp. 555-96. Washington, 1905.

# BIBLIOGRAPHY

Poore, Benjamin P. *Descriptive Catalogue of the Government Publications of the United States . . . 1774-1881.* Washington, 1885. May also be found in *Sen. Misc. Doc. No. 67,* 48th Congress, 2nd session.

Shryock, Richard Harrison. *Georgia and the Union in 1850.* Durham (N. C.), 1926. Excellent bibliography for the decade previous to the War for Southern Independence.

Thompson, Clara Mildred. *Reconstruction in Georgia . . . 1865-1872* ("Columbia University Studies in History, Economics and Public Law," Vol. LXIV, No. I). New York, 1915. Seventeen pages of bibliography for reconstruction period.

United States, Library of Congress. *Publications Issued . . . since 1897.* Washington, 1929.

———. Division of Manuscripts. *Checklist of Collections of Personal Papers in Historical Societies, University and Public Libraries, and Other Learned Institutions of the United States.* Washington, 1918.

———. Division of Manuscripts. *Handbook of Manuscripts in the Library of Congress.* Washington, 1918. New manuscripts are listed in the supplementary list in American Historical Association *Annual Report* for 1930; in the *American Historical Review;* and in *Annual Reports* of the Librarian.

Van Tyne, Claude Halstead, and Walter G. Leland, comps. *Guide to the Archives of the Government of the United States in Washington.* Rev. ed., Washington, 1907.

Virginia State Library. "A List of the Official Publications of the Confederate States Government in the Virginia State Library, and the Library of the Confederate Memorial Literary Society," Virginia State Library *Bulletin,* IV, No. 1 (Jan., 1911), 1-72.

Woolley, Edwin C. *The Reconstruction of Georgia* ("Columbia University Studies in History, Economics and Public Law," Vol. XIII, No. 3). New York, 1901. Bibliography for the reconstruction period.

## II. Manuscripts

Joseph E. Brown Correspondence. Manuscripts Division, Library of Congress, Washington. Consists of one letter to Governor John Letcher of Virginia, two letters to Governor Zebulon B. Vance of North Carolina, and one letter from Julius Brown to the Secretary of War, dated Apr. 18, 1903.

Joseph E. Brown Correspondence. Georgia Department of Archives and History, Atlanta. Consists of 120 letters or copies of

# BIBLIOGRAPHY 331

letters to and from Governor Brown, some of which are also in the *Governor's Letter Book, 1861-1865.*

Personal Papers of Joseph E. Brown. Confederate Archives, Adjutant General's Office, War Department, Washington. These consist of two letters to President Andrew Johnson, and one letter from President Johnson to Secretary of State Edward M. Stanton.

Joseph E. Brown to an unknown correspondent, January 18, 1858. Library of the Historical Society of Pennsylvania, Philadelphia.

William M. Burwell Papers. Manuscripts Division, Library of Congress, Washington.

Samuel W. Crawford Papers, 1860-1873. Manuscripts Division, Library of Congress, Washington.

Jefferson Davis Papers. Confederate Archives, Adjutant General's Office, War Department, Washington.

Miscellaneous Papers of Governors A. B. Moore and John Gill Shorter. Alabama Department of History and Archives, Montgomery.

William T. Sherman Papers. Manuscripts Division, Library of Congress, Washington.

Alexander H. Stephens Papers, 1844-1886. Manuscripts Division, Library of Congress, Washington.

Zebulon B. Vance Correspondence. Confederate Archives, Adjutant General's Office, War Department, Washington.

Zebulon B. Vance Papers. North Carolina Historical Commission, Raleigh.

### III. GEORGIA PUBLIC DOCUMENTS

*Senate Journal.*
*House Journal.*
*Acts of the General Assembly.* Also listed as *Georgia Laws.*
*Minutes of the Executive Department.*
*Governors' Letter Books.*
Salt Account Books:
 *Abstract of Salt Received and Issued.* 2 vols.
 *Salt Distribution under the Governor's Order of July 31, 1862.*
 *Record of Names to Whom Salt Was Distributed.*
*Code of the State of Georgia, 1865,* compiled by D. Irwin, 1865, rev., 1867. *Code of 1868,* compiled by D. Irwin, G. M. Lester, and W. B. Hill, 1873.
*Georgia Reports. Decisions of the Supreme Court of Georgia.*
*The Confederate Records of the State of Georgia,* Vols. I, II, III

IV, VI. Compiled and published under authority of the legislature by Allen D. Candler. Atlanta, 1909-11.

*Report of the Committee Appointed under Resolution of the Convention, on the Financial Operations of the State of Georgia During the War.* Milledgeville (Ga.), 1866.

*Report of the Majority of the Joint Committee Appointed by the General Assembly to Investigate the Fairness or Unfairness of the Contract Known as the Lease of the Western & Atlantic Railroad Made December 27, 1870, by Rufus B. Bullock, Late Governor, and to Investigate the Question of Fraud in Said Contract, if Any Exists.* Atlanta, 1872.

Conventions:

*Journal of the State Convention . . . 1850.* Milledgeville (Ga.), 1850.

*Journal of the Public and Secret Proceedings of the Convention of the People of Georgia Held in Milledgeville and Savannah, in 1861, together with the Ordinances Adopted.* Milledgeville (Ga.), 1861. To be found also in *The Confederate Records of the State of Georgia*, I, 212-751.

*Journal of the Proceedings of the Convention . . . Held . . . in Milledgeville, October and November, 1865.* Milledgeville (Ga.), 1865. To be found also in *The Confederate Records of the State of Georgia*, IV, 130-442.

*Journal of the Proceedings of the Constitutional Convention of the People of Georgia . . . in the Months of December, 1867, and January, February, and March, 1868. . . .* Augusta (Ga.), 1868. To be found also in *The Confederate Records of the State of Georgia*, VI, 199 et seq.

### IV. Confederate Public Documents

*Journal of the Congress of the Confederate States of America, 1861-1865.* 7 vols. Washington, 1904-5. To be found also in *Sen. Doc. No. 234*, 58th Congress, 2nd session.

*A Compilation of the Messages and Papers of the Confederacy, including the Diplomatic Correspondence 1861-1865.* 2 vols. Compiled by James D. Richardson. Nashville, 1905.

*The Statutes at Large of the Provisional Government of the Confederate States of America . . . 1861 to 1862. . . . the Constitution of the Provisional Government and Permanent Constitution. . . .* Edited by James Muscoe Matthews. Richmond, 1864.

# BIBLIOGRAPHY 333

*The Statutes at Large of the Confederate States of America, 1862-1864.* Edited by James Muscoe Matthews. Richmond, 1862-64.

## V. UNITED STATES PUBLIC DOCUMENTS

*Biographical Directory of the American Congress, 1774-1927.* Washington, 1928.

*Charters and Constitutions.* 7 vols. Compiled by F. N. Thorpe. Washington, 1909.

*Congressional Globe* for the 36th, 38th, 40th, 41st Congresses.

*Congressional Record* for the 44th, 45th, 46th, 47th Congresses.

*House Miscellaneous Document, No. 2,* 40th Congress, 3rd session.

United States Census 1860:
 *Population of the United States in 1860, Compiled from the Original Returns of the Eighth Census . . . by Joseph C. G. Kennedy.* Washington, 1864.
 *Agriculture of the United States in 1860, Compiled from the Original Returns of the Eighth Census . . . by Joseph C. G. Kennedy.* Washington, 1864.

*United States Statutes at Large.* Vols. XIII, XIV, XV.

*United States Supreme Court Reports.* Vols. LXVI-LXVII.

*The War of the Rebellion: A Compilation of the Official Records of the Union and Confederate Armies.* 130 vols. Washington, 1880-1901.

*Official Records of the Union and Confederate Navies in the War of the Rebellion.* 31 vols. Washington, 1894-1927.

## VI. CONTEMPORARY WRITINGS

Alfriend, Frank H. *Life of Jefferson Davis.* Cincinnati and Philadelphia, 1868.

Andrews, Eliza F. *The War-Time Journal of a Georgia Girl, 1864-1865.* New York, 1908.

Andrews, Garnett. *Reminiscences of an Old Georgia Lawyer.* Atlanta, 1870.

Avery, Isaac Wheeler. *History of the State of Georgia from 1850 to 1881. . . .* New York, 1881.

Beers, Fannie A. *Memories: A Record of Personal Experience and Adventure during Four Years of War.* Philadelphia, 1888.

Blaine, James G. *Twenty Years of Congress: From Lincoln to Garfield.* 2 vols. Norwich (Conn.), 1884-86.

Brooks, Robert Preston, ed. "Howell Cobb Papers," *Georgia His-*

*torical Quarterly,* V, No. 1 (Mar., 1921), 50-61, No. 2 (June, 1921), 29-52, No. 3 (Sept., 1921), 35-55, No. 4 (Dec., 1921), 43-64; VI, No. 1 (Mar., 1922), 35-84, No. 2 (June, 1922), 147-73, No. 3 (Sept., 1922), 233-64, No. 4 (Dec., 1922), 355-94.

Bulloch, James D. *The Secret Service of the Confederate States in Europe; or How the Confederate Cruisers were Equipped.* 2 vols. London, 1883.

Burge, Dolly Sumner Lunt. *A Woman's Wartime Journal.* New York, 1918.

Calhoun, John Caldwell. *The Works of John C. Calhoun,* edited by Richard K. Crallé. 6 vols. New York, 1854-60. "A Disquisition on Government," I, 1; "A Discourse on the Constitution and Government of the United States," I, 111; "Reply to Webster, 1833," II, 262.

Capers, Henry D. *The Life and Times of C. G. Memminger.* Richmond, 1893.

Chesnut, Mary Boykin (Miller). *A Diary from Dixie,* edited by Isabella Martin and Myrta Lockett Avary. New York, 1905.

Clark, Richard H. *Memoirs of Judge Richard H. Clark,* edited by L. B. Wylie. Atlanta, 1898.

Cleveland, Henry. *Alexander H. Stephens in Public and Private. With Letters and Speeches before, during, and since the War.* Philadelphia, 1866.

Cobb, Howell. See R. P. Brooks and U. B. Phillips; also "Georgia and the Confederacy."

———. *Great Speech of General Howell Cobb Delivered in Atlanta, Georgia, July 23, 1868.* Augusta, 1868. Pamphlet in the Georgia Department of Archives and History, Atlanta.

Cobb, T. R. R. "Correspondence," edited by A. L. Hull, *Southern Historical Society Papers,* XXVIII (1900), 280-301, and *Publications of the Southern History Association,* XI (1907), 147-85, 233-60, 312-28.

Davis, Jefferson. *The Rise and Fall of the Confederate Government.* 2 vols. New York, 1881. See also Dunbar Rowland.

Davis, Varina (Howell). *Jefferson Davis . . . A Memoir by His Wife.* 2 vols. New York, 1890.

DeLeon, Thomas C. *Four Years in Rebel Capitals: An Inside View of Life in the Southern Confederacy, from Birth to Death. From Original Notes, collated in the Years 1861 to 1865.* Mobile, 1890.

DuBose, John Witherspoon. *The Life and Times of William Lowndes Yancey.* Birmingham, 1892.

Dumond, Dwight Lowell, ed. *Southern Editorials on Secession.* New York, 1931.

Felton, Mrs. William H. (Rebecca Latimer). *My Memoirs of Georgia Politics.* Atlanta, 1911.

Fielder, Herbert. *A Sketch of the Life and Times and Speeches of Joseph E. Brown.* Springfield (Mass.), 1883.

Fleming, Walter L., ed. *Documentary History of Reconstruction. Political, Military, Social, Religious, Educational, and Industrial, 1865 to the Present Time.* 2 vols. Cleveland, 1906-7.

"Georgia and the Confederacy," edited by John Osborne Sumner, *American Historical Review,* I (Oct., 1895), 97-102.

Gordon, John B. *Reminiscences of the Civil War.* New York, 1903.

Headley, John W. *Confederate Operations in Canada and New York.* New York, 1906.

Hill, Benjamin H., Jr., comp. *Senator Benjamin H. Hill of Georgia, His Life, Speeches and Writings.* Written and Compiled by His Son. Atlanta, 1891.

Hodgson, Joseph. *The Cradle of the Confederacy: or, The Times of Troup, Quitman and Yancey.* Mobile, 1876.

Hood, John Bell. *Advance and Retreat. Personal Experiences in the United States and Confederate States Armies.* New Orleans, 1880.

Johnson, Herschel V. "From the Autobiography of Herschel V. Johnson, 1856-1867," edited by Percy Scott Flippin, *American Historical Review,* XXX (Jan., 1925), 311-36.

Johnston, Joseph E. *Narrative of Military Operations.* New York, 1874.

Johnston, Richard M., and William Hand Browne. *Life of Alexander H. Stephens.* Philadelphia, 1878.

Jones, John Beauchamp. *A Rebel War Clerk's Diary at the Confederate States' Capital.* 2 vols. Philadelphia, 1866.

LaBree, Benjamin. *The Confederate Soldier in the Civil War, 1861-1865.* Louisville, 1895.

McCulloch, Hugh. *Men and Measures of Half a Century.* New York, 1888.

McPherson, Edward, comp. *Political History of the United States of America During the Period of Reconstruction.* Washington, 1875.

——. *Political History of the United States of America during the Great Rebellion.* Washington, 1865.

Mason, Virginia. *The Public Life and Diplomatic Correspondence of James M. Mason.* . . . New York, 1906.

Miller, S. F. *The Bench and Bar of Georgia: Memoirs and Sketches.* 2 vols. Philadelphia, 1858.

Moore, Frank, ed. *The Rebellion Record.* . . . 11 vols. New York, 1861-68.

Northen, William J., ed. *Men of Mark in Georgia.* 6 vols. Atlanta, 1907-12.

*Official Proceedings of the Democratic National Convention, 1868.* Boston, 1868.

Phillips, Ulrich Bonnell, ed. *The Correspondence of Robert Toombs, Alexander H. Stephens, and Howell Cobb.* American Historical Association *Annual Report, 1911,* Vol. II. Washington, 1913.

Pollard, Edward A. *Life of Jefferson Davis, with a Secret History of the Southern Confederacy.* Atlanta, [1869].

———. *The Early Life, Campaigns, and Public Services of Robert E. Lee . . . and Heroic Deeds of His Companions in Arms.* New Orleans, 1870.

*Proceedings of the National Union Republican Convention, 1868.* Chicago, 1868.

Reed, John C. *The Brothers' War.* Boston, 1905.

———. "Reminiscences of Ben Hill," *South Atlantic Quarterly,* V (Apr., 1906), 141-42.

———. "Joseph E. Brown," *The South in the Building of the Nation,* XI, 128-29. 13 Vols. Richmond, 1909-13.

Rowland, Dunbar, ed. *Jefferson Davis, Constitutionalist: His Letters, Papers and Speeches.* 10 vols. Jackson (Miss.), 1923.

Russell, Sir William H. *My Diary North and South.* 2 vols. London, 1863.

Scharf, John Thomas. *History of the Confederate States Navy from Its Organization to the Surrender of Its Last Vessel.* . . . New York, 1887.

Semmes, Admiral Raphael. *Service Afloat; or, The Remarkable Career of the Confederate Cruisers, Sumter and Alabama, during the War between the States.* New York, 1900.

Sherman, William T. *Memoirs of General William T. Sherman.* 2 vols. Rev. and cor., New York, 1886.

*The Sherman Letters. Correspondence between General and Senator Sherman from 1837 to 1891,* edited by Rachel Sherman Thorndike. New York, 1894.

Sparks, William H. *The Memories of Fifty Years.* Philadelphia, 1870.

Stephens, Alexander Hamilton. *A Constitutional View of the Late*

# BIBLIOGRAPHY

*War between the States: Its Causes, Character, Conduct, and Results.* 2 vols. Philadelphia and Chicago, 1868-70.

Stephens, Linton. *See* J. D. Waddell.

Stovall, Pleasant A. *Robert Toombs: Statesman, Speaker, Soldier, Sage.* New York, 1892.

Sumner, John Osborne, ed. "Georgia and the Confederacy," *American Historical Review,* I (Oct., 1895), 97-102.

Taylor, Richard. *Destruction and Reconstruction.* New York, 1879.

Taylor, Thomas E. *Running the Blockade.* London, 1897.

Toombs, Robert. *See* P. A. Stovall and U. B. Phillips.

Trammell, William Dugas. *Ça Ira—A Novel.* New York, 1874.

Waddell, James D., ed. *Biographical Sketch of Linton Stephens, Containing a Selection of His Letters, Speeches, State Papers, etc.* Atlanta, 1877.

White, Laura A. "The South in the 1850's as Seen by British Consuls," *Journal of Southern History,* I (Feb., 1935), 29-48.

"Why the Confederacy Failed: Opinions of Generals S. D. Lee, Joseph Wheeler, E. P. Alexandar, E. M. Law, Don Carlos Buell, O. O. Howard, and Jacob D. Cox," *Century Magazine,* LIII (Feb., 1897), 626-33. A reply to Duncan Rose, *Century,* LIII (Nov., 1896), 33-38.

Wright, Mrs. D. Giraud (Louise Wigfall). *A Southern Girl in '61.* New York, 1905.

## VII. Non-Contemporary Writings

Adams, Ephraim Douglass. *Great Britain and the American Civil War.* 2 vols. New York, 1923-25.

Arnett, Alex Mathews. *The Populist Movement in Georgia.* New York, 1922.

Bassett, John Spencer. *A Short History of the United States, 1492-1929.* Rev. ed., New York, 1934.

Beale, Howard K. *The Critical Year: A Study of Andrew Johnson and Reconstruction.* New York, 1930.

Beard, Charles A. and Mary R. *The Rise of American Civilization.* 2 vols. New York, 1927.

Bowers, Claude G. *The Tragic Era: The Revolution after Lincoln.* Cambridge, 1929.

Brewton, William E. *The Life of Thomas E. Watson.* Atlanta, 1926.

Brooks, Robert Preston. "The Agrarian Revolution in Georgia, 1865-1912," *University of Wisconsin History Series,* III, No. 3, 393-524. Madison, 1914.

——. "Conscription in the Confederate States of America, 1862-1865," *University of Georgia Bulletin*, XVII, No. 4 (1917), 419-42.

——. "Howell Cobb and the Crisis of 1850," *University of Georgia Bulletin*, XVIII, Ser. 285 (Jan., 1918), 279-98.

Brown, William Garrott. *The Lower South in American History.* New York, 1903.

Brummer, Sidney D. "The Judicial Interpretation of the Confederate Constitution," *Studies in Southern History and Politics Inscribed to William Archibald Dunning . . . By His Former Pupils, the Authors*, Chap. V. New York, 1914.

Burgess, John W. *The Civil War and the Constitution.* 2 vols. New York, 1901.

——. *Reconstruction and the Constitution, 1866-1876.* New York, 1902.

Butler, Pierce. *Judah P. Benjamin.* Philadelphia, 1906.

Callahan, James Morton. *The Diplomatic History of the Southern Confederacy.* Baltimore, 1901.

Carpenter, Jesse Thomas. *The South as a Conscious Minority 1789-1861. A Study in Political Thought.* New York, 1930.

Cate, Wirt Armistead. *Lucius Q. C. Lamar, Secession and Reunion.* Chapel Hill (N. C.), 1935.

Cole, Arthur Charles. *The Whig Party in the South.* Washington, 1913.

Coleman, Charles H. *The Election of 1868. The Democratic Effort to Regain Control.* New York, 1933.

Coulter, Ellis Merton. *The Civil War and Readjustment in Kentucky.* Chapel Hill (N. C.), 1926.

——. *A Short History of Georgia.* Chapel Hill (N. C.), 1933.

Craven, Avery, ed. *Essays in Honor of William E. Dodd.* Chicago, 1935.

Curtis, Frances. *The Republican Party 1854-1904.* 2 vols. New York, 1904.

Cutting, Elizabeth. *Jefferson Davis, Political Soldier.* New York, 1930.

Davis, William Watson. *The Civil War and Reconstruction in Florida* ("Columbia University Studies in History, Economics and Public Law," Vol. LIII, No. 131). New York, 1913.

Derry, Joseph T. "Georgia in the Confederacy, 1861-1865," *The South in the Building of the Nation*, II, 171-218: 13 vols. Richmond, 1909-13.

# BIBLIOGRAPHY 339

Dodd, William E. *Jefferson Davis* ("American Crisis Biographies," edited by Ellis Paxson Oberholtzer). Philadelphia, 1907.

Dorman, Lewy. *Party Politics in Alabama from 1850 through 1860.* Montgomery, 1935.

Dowd, Clement. *Life of Zebulon B. Vance.* Charlotte (N. C.), 1897.

Dumond, Dwight Lowell. *The Secession Movement 1860-61.* New York, 1931.

Dunning, William A. *Reconstruction, Political and Economic, 1865-1877* ("The American Nation," Vol. XXII, edited by A. B. Hart). New York, 1907.

———. *Essays on the Civil War and Reconstruction and Related Topics.* Rev. ed., New York, 1910.

Eckenrode, Hamilton James. *The Political History of Virginia during the Reconstruction* ("Johns Hopkins University Studies in History and Political Science," Ser. XXII, Nos. 6, 7, 8). Baltimore, 1904.

———. *Jefferson Davis, President of the South.* New York, 1923.

*Essays in Honor of William E. Dodd.* By His Former Students, edited by Avery Craven. Chicago, 1935.

Ficklen, John Rose. *History of Reconstruction in Louisiana* ("Johns Hopkins University Studies in History and Political Science," Ser. XXVIII, No. 1). Baltimore, 1910. This study carries the subject through 1868. The author died before the work was completed and it was edited by Professor Pierce Butler.

Fite, Emerson David. *The Presidential Campaign of 1860.* New York, 1911.

Flack, Horace Edgar. *The Adoption of the Fourteenth Amendment* ("Johns Hopkins University Studies in History and Political Science," Ser. XXVI). Baltimore, 1908.

Fleming, Walter L. *Civil War and Reconstruction in Alabama.* New York, 1905.

———. *The Sequel of Appomattox* ("The Chronicles of America," Vol. XXXIII, edited by Allen Johnson). New Haven, 1919.

Flippin, Percy Scott. *Herschel V. Johnson of Georgia, State Rights Unionist.* Richmond, 1931.

Freeman, Douglas S. *R. E. Lee: A Biography.* 4 vols. New York, 1934-35.

Garner, James Wilford. *Reconstruction in Mississippi.* New York, 1901.

Gettell, Raymond G. *History of American Political Thought.* New York, 1928.

Greeley, Horace. *The American Conflict: A History of the Great Rebellion in the United States of America 1860-1866.* 2 vols. Hartford (Conn.), 1864-67.

Hall, Clifton Rumery. *Andrew Johnson, Military Governor of Tennessee.* Princeton, 1916.

Hamilton, Joseph Gregoire deRoulhac. *Reconstruction in North Carolina* ("Columbia University Studies in History, Economics and Public Law," Vol. LVIII, No. 141). New York, 1914.

Haworth, Paul Leland. *The Hayes-Tilden Disputed Presidential Election, 1876.* New York, 1906.

Hay, Thomas Robson. "The Davis-Hood-Johnston Controversy of 1864," *Mississippi Valley Historical Review,* XI (June, 1924), 54-84.

———. "Joseph Emerson Brown, Governor of Georgia, 1857-1865," *Georgia Historical Quarterly,* XIII (June, 1929), 89-109.

———. *Hood's Tennessee Campaign.* New York, 1929.

Henry, Robert Selph. *The Story of the Confederacy.* Indianapolis, 1931.

Hill, Louise Biles. *State Socialism in the Confederate States of America* (No. 9 in "Southern Sketches," edited by J. D. Eggleston). Charlottesville (Va.), 1936.

*History of the Baptist Denomination in Georgia, with Biographical Compendium and Portrait Gallery of Baptist Ministers and Other Georgia Baptists.* Compiled for the *Christian Index.* Atlanta, 1881.

Hollis, John Porter. *The Early Period of Reconstruction in South Carolina* ("Johns Hopkins University Studies in History and Political Science," Ser. XXIII, Nos. 1, 2). Baltimore, 1905.

———. *The Great American Myth.* New York, 1930.

Hosmer, James Kendall. *The Appeal to Arms* ("The American Nation," Vol. XX, edited by A. B. Hart). New York, 1907.

———. *Outcome of the Civil War* ("The American Nation," Vol. XXI, edited by A. B. Hart). New York, 1907.

Howell, Clark. *History of Georgia.* 4 vols. Atlanta, 1926.

*I'll Take My Stand. The South and the Agrarian Tradition.* By Twelve Southerners. New York, 1930.

Johnston, James Houston, comp. *Western & Atlantic Railroad of the State of Georgia. . . . Compiled . . . in Pursuance of Legislative Action 1925. . . .* Atlanta, 1932.

Kendrick, Benjamin B. *Journal of the Joint Committee of Fifteen on Reconstruction* ("Columbia University Studies in History, Eco-

## BIBLIOGRAPHY

nomics and Public Law," Vol. LXII, No. 150). New York, 1914.
Kent, Frank A. *A History of the Democratic Party*. New York, 1928.
Kerr, John Leeds. *The Story of A Southern Carrier: The Louisville & Nashville. An Outline History*. New York, 1933.
Kirkland, Edward Chase. *The Peacemakers of 1864*. New York, 1927.
Knight, Lucius Lamar. *A Standard History of Georgia and Georgians*. 6 vols. New York, 1917.
Latane, John Holladay. *A History of American Foreign Policy*. New York, 1927.
Lee, Fitzhugh. "Failure of the Hampton Roads Conference," *Century Magazine*, LII (July, 1896), 476-78.
Lonn, Ella. *Reconstruction in Louisiana*. New York, 1918. Begins with 1869, supplementing the work of Professor Ficklen.
———. *Desertion during the Civil War*. New York [c1928].
———. *Salt as a Factor in the Confederacy*. New York, 1933.
McCormac, Eugene I. *James K. Polk: A Political Biography*. Berkeley, 1922.
McDonald, R. L. "The Reconstruction Period in Tennessee," *American Historical Magazine* (Nashville), I, No. 4 (Oct., 1896), 305-28.
Milton, George Fort. *The Age of Hate: Andrew Johnson and the Radicals*. New York, 1930.
———. *The Eve of Conflict. Stephen A. Douglas and the Needless War*. New York, 1934.
Minor, Henry A. *The Story of the Democratic Party*. New York, 1928.
Moore, Albert Burton. *Conscription and Conflict in the Confederacy*. New York, 1924.
Moore, John Bassett. *Digest of International Law as Embodied . . . in Documents . . . of the United States*. 8 vols. Washington, 1906. Published also as *House Doc. No. 551*, 56th Congress, 2nd session.
———. *Four Phases of American Development: Federalism—Democracy—Imperialism—Expansion*. Baltimore, 1912.
Myers, William Starr. *The Self-Reconstruction of Maryland, 1864-1867* ("Johns Hopkins University Studies in History and Political Science," Ser. XXVII, Nos. 1, 2). Baltimore, 1905.
Oberholtzer, Ellis Paxson. *History of the United States Since the Civil War*. 5 vols. New York, 1917-37.
Owsley, Frank Lawrence. *State Rights in the Confederacy*. 2nd ed., Chicago, 1931.

———. "Defeatism in the Confederacy," *North Carolina Historical Review*, III (July, 1926), 446-56.

———. *King Cotton Diplomacy: Foreign Relations of the Confederate States of America*. Chicago, 1931.

Parrington, Vernon Louis. *Main Currents in American Thought*. . . . 3 vols. New York, 1927-31.

Patton, James W. *Unionism and Reconstruction of Tennessee, 1860-1869*. Chapel Hill (N. C.), 1934.

Pearce, Haywood Jefferson. *Benjamin H. Hill, Secession and Reconstruction*. Chicago, 1928.

Pendleton, Louis. *Alexander H. Stephens* ("American Crisis Biographies," edited by Ellis Paxson Oberholtzer). Philadelphia, 1908.

Phillips, Ulrich Bonnell. *Georgia and State Rights*. Washington, 1902. American Historical Association *Annual Report* for 1901, Vol. II.

———. "Transportation in the Ante-Bellum South: An Economic Analysis," *The Quarterly Journal of Economics*, XIX (May, 1905), 434-51.

———. "An American State-Owned Railroad: The Western and Atlantic," *Yale Review*, XV (Nov., 1906), 260-82.

———. "Georgia in the Federal Union, 1776-1861," *The South in the Building of the Nation*, II, 146-70. 13 vols. Richmond, 1909-13.

———. *Life of Robert Toombs*. New York, 1913.

———. *Life and Labor in the Old South*. Boston, 1929.

Pike, James Shepherd. *The Prostrate State: South Carolina Under Negro Government*. New York, 1874.

Ramsdell, Charles William. *Reconstruction in Texas* ("Columbia University Studies in History, Economics and Public Law," Vol. XXXVI, No. 1). New York, 1910.

———. "The Control of Manufacturing by the Confederate Government," *Mississippi Valley Historical Review*, VIII (Dec., 1921), 231-63.

Randall, James G. *Constitutional Problems under Lincoln*. New York, 1926.

Reynolds, John S. *Reconstruction in South Carolina, 1865-1877*. Columbia (S. C.), 1905.

Rhodes, James Ford. *History of the United States from the Compromise of 1850*. 9 vols. New ed., New York, 1928.

Robinson, William Morrison, Jr. *The Confederate Privateers*. New Haven, 1928.

Rose, Duncan. "Why the Confederacy Failed: The Excessive Issue of

# BIBLIOGRAPHY 343

Paper Money—The Policy of Dispersion—The Neglect of the Cavalry. By the Son of a Confederate Officer," *Century Magazine*, LIII (Nov., 1896), 33-38. Reply, *Century*, LIII (Feb., 1897), 626-33.

Rowland, Dunbar, ed. *Reviews of Jefferson Davis, Constitutionalist.* Jackson (Miss.), 1924.

Sait, Edward M. *American Parties and Elections.* New York, 1927.

Schwab, J. C. *The Confederate States of America 1861-1865. A Financial and Industrial History of the South during the Civil War.* New York, 1901.

Scrugham, Mary. *The Peaceable Americans of 1860-1861. A Study in Public Opinion* ("Columbia University Studies in History, Economics and Public Law," Vol. XCVI, No. 3). New York, 1921.

Shannon, Fred Albert. *The Organization and Administration of the Union Army 1861-1865.* 2 vols. Cleveland, 1928.

Shryock, Richard Harrison. *Georgia and the Union in 1850.* Durham (N. C.), 1926.

Simkins, Francis B., and Robert H. Woody. *South Carolina during Reconstruction.* Chapel Hill (N. C.), 1932.

Smith, Ernest A. "History of the Confederate Treasury," *Publications of the Southern History Association,* V, Nos. 1, 2, 3 (1901), 1-34, 99-150, 188-227.

Smith, William Ernest. *The Francis Preston Blair Family in Politics.* 2 vols. New York, 1933.

Soley, James Russell. *The Blockade and the Cruisers.* New York, 1885.

*Southern Historical Society Papers.* 47 vols. Richmond, 1876-1930.

*Southern History Association Publications.* 11 vols. Washington, 1897-1907.

*The South in the Building of the Nation....* edited by Julian A. C. Chandler *et al.* 13 vols. Richmond, 1909-13.

Stanwood, Edward. *History of the Presidency, 1788 to 1897.* New York, 1898.

Staples, Thomas Starling. *Reconstruction in Arkansas, 1862-1874* ("Columbia University Studies in History, Economics and Public Law," Vol. CIX, No. 245). New York, 1923.

Stephenson, Nathaniel W. *The Day of the Confederacy* ("The Chronicles of America," Vol. XXX, edited by Allen Johnson). New Haven, 1919.

———. "Southern Nationalism in South Carolina in 1851," *American Historical Review*, XXXVI (Jan., 1931), 314-35.

## BIBLIOGRAPHY

Stryker, Lloyd Paul. *Andrew Johnson, Champion of Lincoln's Cause.* 2 vols. New York, 1929.

*Studies in Southern History and Politics, Inscribed to William Archibald Dunning. . . . By His Former Pupils, the Authors.* New York, 1914.

Tatum, Georgia Lee. *Disloyalty in the Confederacy.* Chapel Hill (N. C.), 1934.

Thompson, Clara Mildred. *Reconstruction in Georgia, Economic, Social, Political, 1865-1872* ("Columbia University Studies in History, Economics and Public Law," Vol. LXIV, No. 1). New York, 1915.

Thompson, Holland. *The New South* ("The Chronicles of America," Vol. XLII, edited by Allen Johnson). New Haven, 1919.

Thompson, Samuel Bernard. *Confederate Purchasing Operations Abroad.* Chapel Hill (N. C.), 1935.

Warren, Charles. *The Supreme Court in United States History.* 3 vols. Boston, 1922.

White, Laura A. *Robert Barnwell Rhett: Father of Secession.* New York, 1931.

Wilson, Walter. "Georgia Suppresses Insurrection," *The Nation,* CXXXIX (Aug. 1, 1934), 127-28.

Wilson, Woodrow. *Division and Reunion* ("Epochs of American History," edited by A. B. Hart). New York, 1893.

Winston, Robert W. *Andrew Johnson, Plebeian and Patriot.* New York, 1928.

Woodward, W. E. *Meet General Grant.* New York, 1928.

―――. *An Enemy of Lincoln—The Life of Thad Stevens.* New York, 1930.

Woolley, Edwin C. *The Reconstruction of Georgia* ("Columbia University Studies in History, Economics and Public Law," Vol. XIII, No. 3). New York, 1901.

### VIII. NEWSPAPERS AND PERIODICALS

Guides to Newspaper Collections:

Brantley, Rabun Lee. *Georgia Journalism of the Civil War Period.* Nashville, 1929.

*Checklist of Newspapers and Official Gazettes in the New York Public Library.* New York, 1915.

Hardin, William, comp. "List of Newspaper Files in the Library of the Georgia Historical Society, Savannah," *Gulf States Historical Magazine,* May, 1903.

Owen, Thomas M., comp. "List of Newspaper Files in the Carnegie Library, Atlanta," *Gulf States Historical Magazine,* May, 1903.
Phillips, Ulrich B. *Georgia and State Rights.* Washington, 1902. List and location of Georgia newspapers for the ante-bellum period.
Shryock, Richard H. *Georgia and the Union in 1850.* Durham (N. C.), 1926. List and location of Georgia newspapers for the period immediately preceding the War for Southern Independence.
Slauson, A. B., comp. *Checklist of American Newspapers in the Library of Congress.* . . . Washington, 1901. Now undergoing revision.
Thompson, C. Mildred. *Reconstruction in Georgia, 1865-1872* ("Columbia University Studies in History, Economics and Public Law," Vol. LXIV, No. 1). New York, 1915. List and location of Georgia newspapers for the reconstruction period.

Newspapers Cited:

Atlanta
*Constitution*
*Evening Telegram*
*Examiner*
*Intelligencer*
*Journal*
*New Era*
*Southern Confederacy*

Athens
*Southern Banner*
*Southern Watchman*

Augusta
*Constitutionalist*
*Chronicle and Sentinel*
*Daily Press*

Columbus
*Sun*
*Times*

LaGrange
*Reporter*

Macon
*Telegraph*

Milledgeville
*Confederate Union,* or *Federal Union*
*Southern Recorder*

Rome
*Southerner*

Savannah
*Daily News*
*Georgian*
*Morning News*
*Republican*

Outside the State
*Cincinnati Commercial Appeal*
*New York Evening Post*
*New York Herald*
*New York Tribune*
*Richmond Enquirer*

## IX. Miscellaneous—Compilations, Encyclopedias, Almanacs, Gazetteers

*American Almanac and Repository of Useful Knowledge* for the years 1857, 1858, 1859, 1860. Boston.

*American Annual Cyclopaedia and Register of Important Events.* 42 vols. New York, 1862-1903. First Series, 1861-1875, Vols. I-XV; New Series, *Appleton's Annual Cyclopedia,* 1876-1895, Vols. I-XX or XVI-XXXV; Third-Series, 1896-1902, Vols. I-VII or XXXVI-XLII.

Ames, Herman V., comp. *American Documents on Federal Relations: The States and the United States.* Philadelphia, 1906.

*Appleton's Cyclopedia of American Biography.* 8 vols. New York, 1887.

Campbell, R. A., comp. *Rebellion Register.* Indianapolis, 1867.

*Confederate States Almanac.* Nashville, 1862.

*Dictionary of American Biography,* edited by Allen Johnson. 20 vols. New York, 1928-36.

*Encyclopedia Americana.* . . . 30 vols. New York, 1926.

Kettleborough, Charles, ed. *The State Constitutions.* Indianapolis, 1918.

*New International Encyclopedia.* 25 vols. 2nd ed., New York, 1927.

Sherwood, Adiel. *A Gazetteer of the State of Georgia.* Nashville, 1860.

*Tribune Almanac Comprehending the Politician's Register and the Whig Almanac.* Published annually 1838-68 by the *New York Tribune.*

White, George. *Statistics of the State of Georgia.* Savannah, 1849.

*Who's Who in the South, 1927.* Biennial. Washington, 1927.

Wood, Robert C. *Confederate Hand-Book.* New Orleans, 1900.

# INDEX

Adams, A. A., refuses to support Joshua Hill for governor, 133
Agents, Confederate, in Europe, 154; state, appointed in large numbers by Governor Brown, 90 n. 59
Akin, Warren, nominated for governor, 31
Aliens, in Union army, 80 n. 3, 178; included in Governor Brown's call for troops, 1863, 136 n. 114, 170
Amendments in Georgia to Federal Constitution, 13th, 266; 14th, 266, 283; 15th, 286, 289, 296
American party, in gubernatorial campaign, 14-19; dissolved in Georgia, 31
Amnesty, Oath of, taken by ex-Governor Brown, 248
Appointment of officers, controversies over. *See* Brown, Joseph E.
Arms, lack of in Confederacy, 49; controversy. *See* Brown, Joseph E.
Army, Confederate, provisional, organized, 50-52; Governor Brown's theory of constitutionality, 55, 73; regular, never organized, 73 n. 110; surrenders, 103, 193, 241, 246; question of Governor Brown's entering, 262-63. *See also* Appointment of officers, Conscription, Military laws, Militia, Local defense, Requisitions
Arsenal, Federal. at Augusta, seized by Governor Brown, 42 n. 100
Ashburn case, ex-Governor Brown's connection with, 284 *et seq.*
Atlanta, Georgia, falls, 184, 185, 188; martial law, 195; residence of ex-Governor Brown, 298

Bank controversy, between Governor Brown and legislature, 20-24
Bartow, Francis S., joins American party, 6; favors immediate secession, 44 n. 105; controversy with Governor Brown, 59
Bayne, Colonel Thomas L., Confederate agent, 156
Beauregard, General P. G. T., appointed to Military Division of West, 188; opposes Sherman, 189
Berrien, John M., opposes Georgia platform, 4 n. 13; joins American party, 6
Billups, J. A., Benjamin Hill's letter to, 136
Blair, Francis P., visits Richmond, 236
Bleckley, L. E., urges officer's commission for Governor Brown, 263
Blockade, Federal, ineffectiveness of, 152
Blockade-running, government control opposed by Governor Brown, 139, 157-61; laws governing, 151-56; repeal, 160-61
Blockade-running, British, 153 and n. 77
Blodgett, Foster, delegate to Republican National Convention, 278; superintendent of State Road, 293; association with ex-Governor Brown, 300, 325
"Bloody Seventh," congressional district, reform movement in, 7 n. 28, 306, 316
Bonds, Confederate, issued in 1861, 39; state endorsement, 141-44; compulsory funding act, 144-45; paid in Europe with cotton shipments, 154, 156, 161
Bonds, Georgia, outstanding at end

of war, 138 n. 1; issued by Radicals, 288 nn. 102 and 103, 289, 306
Bourbon Democracy, definition, 292 n. 1ª, 316; controls party, 306, 216
Boyce, James P., of South Carolina, addresses Georgia legislature on state endorsement, 143
Bragg, General Braxton E., battles, 172, 173, 176-77; proclaims martial law in Atlanta, 195, 196
Breckinridge, John C., supporters oppose fusion in Georgia, 34
Brigade controversy, between Governor Brown and Confederate government, 61-63, 169
Brown, John. *See* John Brown raid
Brown, John Young, in Hayes-Tilden "bargain," 306
Brown, Joseph E., leader of Southern Rights Democrats, 8, 9, 11-12; birth, 11; physical appearance, 13; elected governor, 1857, 19; 1859, 32; 1861, 66-72; 1863, 124-37; moral habits, 30 n. 54; early preparations for defense, 32 *et seq.*, 48, 65-66; influence on secession, 33, 36-41, 44, 47; seizes Fort Pulaski, 41-43; applies policy of reprisal, 43; definition of militia, 55, 64 n. 71, 86; controversy over appointment of officers, 51-57, 61-64, 73, 101, 102, 172-74; over arms, 57-61; over State Road, 64 n. 72; over powder, 65; theory of state rights, 55-56, 72-74, 79-81, 83-87, 91, 101-3, 124, 130, 142 and n. 19, 151, 158, 160, 183-85, 192-93, 206, 209, 225, 231-33, 239, 257-59; friendship with Alexander Stephens, 77, 264; opposes conscription, 79-106; exemptions, 89-90, 92-95, 96, 182; arrest, 103, 247; efficiency as war governor, 107-22; opposition to Confederate financial measures, 142-44, 146, 147-51, 157-61; controversy over local defense, 162-93; refuses to honor requisition, 179; surrenders troops to U. S., 193; opposes martial law and suspension of habeas corpus, 195 *et seq.;* conspires with Stephens against Confederate measures, 200 *et seq.;* sends propaganda to civil and military officers, 216; philippics against the administration, 229, 239, 244; investigated by legislature, 249; motives, 249 *et seq.;* opinions of historians, 260 *et seq.;* joins Radicals, 268 *et seq.*, 278-79, 280; decision on eligibility of Negroes to hold office, 277, 324; appointed chief justice, 280; defeated for U. S. Senate, 281; counsel in Ashburn case, 284 *et seq.;* returns to Democratic party, 288 *et seq.*, 325-26; political rehabilitation, 291 *et seq.;* secures lease of State Road, 293; business connections, 298 n. 23; leases convicts, 298; contributions to church and education, 299-300; connection with Mitchell heirs' case, 300-2; goes to Florida in Hayes-Tilden contest, 301, 309; appointed to U. S. Senate, 308, 315 *et seq.;* explains his course in reconstruction, 314, 319; member of triumvirate, 316, 319; elected to U. S. Senate, 321; death, 321; opinions of contemporaries and historians, 103-6, 224 n. 12, 250 *et seq.*, 321-27
Brown, Julius, writes letter to U. S. Secretary of War, 191
Browne, Colonel William M., Commandant of Conscripts in Georgia, seeks coöperation of Governor Brown, 94
Buchanan, President James A., receives vote of Georgia, 6; policy in Kansas, 7
Bulloch, Captain James D., purchases "Fingal," 163 n. 4
Bullock, Rufus B., Radical governor of Georgia, 277, 287, 288; relations with ex-Governor Brown, 280, 288, 325; host at Delano banquet, 295
Bullock Democrats and Republicans, led by ex-Governor Brown, 305, 316
Bunch, Robert, British consul, 35 n. 75
Bush Arbor mass meeting, 283

Cameron, Simon, member of leasing company, 294
Campaign, gubernatorial, 1857, 15 *et seq.;* 1859, 30 *et seq.;* 1861, 66 *et seq.;* 1863, 122 *et seq.;* 1865, 245-

46, 266; 1868, 276 et seq.; 1871-72, 289, 290 n. 190; 1880, 315 et seq.
Campaign, presidential, 1852, 5, 12; 1856, 6, 14; 1860, 34, 35, 36, 38, 40 and n. 92; 1864, 222, 223 and n. 9, 224 and n. 13, 229 n. 34; 1868, 278, 282-83, 284; 1872, 291 n. 1, 292; 1876, 305-6
Campbell, Judge John A., report on conditions in Georgia, 239
"Camp McDonald Experiment." See Brigade controversy
Carpetbaggers, in state convention, 275; in leasing company, 295
Carswell, General R. W., tells story regarding Joseph E. Brown, 250
Chattanooga, battle of, 173, 176
Chickamauga, battle of, 173, 175, 176
Clark, Judge Richard, seconds nomination of Joseph E. Brown, 8
Cleveland, Henry S., opinion of Governor Brown, 251
Coast defense, Georgia. See Local defense
Cobb, Howell, opposes secession, 1850, 3-4; elected governor, 4; guest of secession convention, 44; member of Provisional Congress, 45; considered for Confederate president, 75; controversies with Governor Brown, 92-94, 174, 177 n. 59, 178, 181 n. 71; organizes reserves in Georgia, 92, 178, 183, 184; commands local defense troops in Georgia, 165, 173; opposes Brown-Stephens conspiracy, 203, 210; charges Governor Brown with lobbying, 215; charges Governor Brown with seeking favor of Lincoln government, 239 n. 65; speaks at Bush Arbor mass meeting, 283
Cobb, T. R. R., addresses legislature on secession, 35, 39; favors immediate secession, 44 n. 105; comment on arms taken by Governor Brown, 57 n. 38
Cobb-Brown controversy, over exemptions, 92-94; over local defense troops of 1863, 178-79
Collusion, question of, among opponents of Confederate administration, 264

Colquitt, Alfred H., candidate for gubernatorial nomination, 8; appoints ex-Governor Brown to U. S. Senate, 308-9; reëlected governor 315 et seq.
Columbia, South Carolina, burned, 192
Columbus, Georgia, captured, 193
Committees of public safety, proposed by W. L. Yancey, 34 n. 73
Commutation. See Substitution
Compromise of 1850, Georgia's reaction to, 2-7; acquiesced in by Joseph E. Brown, 8, 33
Confederate States of America, assured by secession of Georgia, 45, 46; organized, 45, 46, 47, 75; fall of, 246, 253 et seq., 265
Conscription, first act, 79; opposition of Governor Brown, 79 et seq., 183, 206; opposition of Alexander and Linton Stephens, 82, 83-84, 96 n. 88; opposition of Robert Toombs, 83-84, 96, 105, 106, 135; second act, 84; constitutionality established, 85, 87; in North, 97 n. 90; fourth act, 101 n. 108; third act, 181, 214
Constitution, Confederate, provisional, 139 n. 3; permanent, 140, 197 and n. 18, 254, 255-56
Constitutional, Radical Republican, for Georgia, 277
Constitutional guarantees. See State Rights
Constitutional Union party, Southern, 3, 5; national, 31, 34
Convention, advocated by opponents of Confederate administration, 197, 224 n. 13, 226 and n. 21, 229-30, 232-36, 238, 239
Convention, constituent, in Georgia, 1850, 3; 1861, 39, 41, 44, 53 n. 22; 1865, 266; 1867-68, 275-76
Convention, National, Democratic, 1861, 34; 1864, 222; 1868, 282; Republican, 1864, 222; 1868, 278; Union, 1864, 222
Convention, party, in Georgia, Democratic, 1857, 1-2, 6-8; 1861, 67-70; 1868, 283; 1880, 315, 316; American, 15; Opposition, 31; Conservative, 275
Convicts, offered freedom, 190; pun-

## 350 INDEX

ishment recommended, 298 n. 26; leasing, 298-99

Coöperationists, definition of, 36; in Georgia secession convention, 44 and n. 105

Cotton, exported by Georgia, 119; restriction in cultivation, 121-22; price in Europe, 153; amount shipped, 1863, 154; 1864, 156

Cotton cards, appropriations for manufacture of, 116; accusation of bribery in use of, 216

"Cow and Cabbages," story of, 191, 243 and n. 2

Crittenden compromise, failure of, 35

Currency. See Fiscal system

Curry, J. L. M., Confederate commissioner in Georgia, 219 n. 104

Dade Coal Company, employs convict labor, 298 and n. 25

Danville, Virginia, Confederate capital following fall of Richmond, 242

Davis, Jefferson, estimates guns in South at beginning of War, 49; elected president, 76; appoints Toombs to cabinet, 77; corresponds with Governor Brown on constitutionality of conscription, 80-83; estimates Governor Brown's exemptions, 95; recommends repeal of exemption law, 97; opposes substitution, 99 n. 103; congratulates Governor Brown on restricting cultivation of cotton, 122; reported as opposing Toombs for governor, 125; recommends state endorsement of Confederate bonds, 141; and compulsory reduction of currency, 144; reports on value of impressment, 147; seeks from Governor Brown specific instances of illegal impressment, 148; asks removal of restrictions on impressment, 150; issues regulations to control commerce, 155; makes plea for retention of shipping laws, 160-61; on cordial terms with Governor Brown, 1863, 171 n. 37; exchanges telegrams with Governor Brown regarding defense of Atlanta, 1864, 182-83 and n. 80; appoints General Beauregard to command of Military Division of West, 188; hurries to Georgia, 188, 229; addresses Mass Meeting at Macon, 189, 229; seeks to obtain troops from Georgia, 1865, 191-92; uses caution in exercise of martial law and habeas corpus, 194-95; recommends suspension of habeas corpus, 1864, 197; accused of opposing peace, 1864, 198, 229 n. 34; allows Alexander Stephens to attempt peace, 1863, 199; writes letter in opposition to peace resolutions in Georgia legislature, Nov., 1864, 234-35; appoints Alexander Stephens to Hampton Roads Conference, 236-37; address in Richmond, 1873, 255; reply to Jacques and Gilmore, 1864, 258

Davis-Brown correspondence regarding constitutionality of conscription, 80-83

Declaration of Paris, adherence of Confederacy to, 152

De Gives Opera House address, of Senator Joseph E. Brown, 319

Delano, John S., banquet in honor of, 293, 295; member of company leasing State Road, 294-95

Democratic party, in Georgia, split, 1850, 3-5; profits by disintegration of Whig and American parties, 6, 32; nominates Joseph E. Brown for governor, 1857, 8; becomes coalition party during war, 67, 70, 128-30, 132-34; becomes Conservative party during reconstruction, 275, 276, 277, 281, 282, 283, 286, 295-96; defeats Radical Republicans, 1870, 288; joined by ex-Governor Brown and followers, 288-92, 325-26; ruled by "triumvirate," 305, 306, 316, 326; split over appointment of ex-Governor Brown to U. S. Senate, 308 et seq., 316-19

Desertions, in Georgia, 105

Dickinson, Reverend E. A., publishes campaign letter of Governor Brown, 135 n. 111

Disloyalty, in Georgia, 50 n. 14, 240; accusations against Governor

Brown and Vice President Stephens, 264
Dispersion, policy attributed to Confederacy, 244; contribution of Governor Brown to, 244 n. 5
Distilleries, in Georgia, closed by governor, 107 et seq.
Douglas, Stephen A., party of in Georgia, 1860, 34
Draft, threat of in Georgia, 167; in North, 167 n. 19, 170-71
Dred Scott decision, endorsed by Opposition party in Georgia, 1859, 31; recommendation of Governor Brown, 34; refusal of Republican party to accept, 35
Duel, challenge sent by Alexander H. Stephens to Benjamin H. Hill, 15; averted between two editors, 245; proposed between Robert Toombs and Joseph E. Brown, 291-92, 301

Election, of military officers, effect of, North and South, 55 n. 27
Emancipation Proclamation, alienates conservatives, 222
Embargo on cotton, maintained by public opinion, 152 n. 67
Evans, Augusta, novelist, Benjamin Hill's letter to, 238 n. 61
Exemptions, Confederate, law of 1862, 81 n. 8; laws of 1863 and 1864, 89, 99 n. 103; President Davis recommends repeal of laws, 97; Governor Brown's reaction, 98-99; bonded exempts, 99 n. 103, 147 n. 46; called out and furloughed by Governor Brown, 183-84, 185-86; Confederate order countermanded by Governor Brown, 192
Exemptions, in Georgia, civil and military officers, 89-90, 92-93, 94-96, 182

Fayetteville, North Carolina, arsenal captured, 193
Felton, Mrs. Rebecca, campaign manager for husband, 280 n. 65
Felton, Dr. William H., leads reform movement in Democratic party, 7 n. 28, 306; opposes leasing of convicts, 298; offered nomination for governor by opponents of Senator Joseph E. Brown, 318 n. 108
"Fingal," blockade-runner, 163
First Manassas, arms taken in battle of, 57 n. 39; fought without Governor Brown's brigade, 57, 62-63
Fiscal system, Confederate, based upon theory of peace, 139-40; effect of Federal blockade on, 140; opposition of Governor Brown and Alexander Stephens to state endorsement of Confederate bonds, 141-44; Governor Brown's reaction to compulsory funding, 144-45; his opposition to tax law of 1863, 146; to impressment, 147-51; to Confederate control of exports and imports, 151-61
Floyd Sharpshooters, take state arms to Virginia, 59
Forsyth, John, editor, Mobile Register, opposes Radical reconstruction, 297 n. 22
Fort Pulaski, seized by order of Governor Brown, 41-42, 230, 251, 327; delay in sending troops to, 53; seizure condemned by Joshua Hill, 132; fortifications of, 164
Fort Sumter, Federal garrison moved to, 42; attempt of U. S. government to reinforce, 53
Franco-Confederate bank, proposed by European financiers, 156
Freight rates, increased by competition of seaboard states with Confederacy, 154
Fullarton, A., acting British consul at Savannah, correspondence with Governor Brown, 136 n. 114
Funding, compulsory, opposed by Governor Brown, 145
Furlow, Timothy M., candidate for governor, 1863, 133-37
Fusion, attempted in 1860, 34 and n. 72; in "new departure" policy, 291

Gardner, James, candidate for nomination for governor, 2; supports candidacy of Governor

Brown, 1863, 128; aids Alexander Stephens in propaganda against state endorsement, 141 n. 15; serves as second to ex-Governor Brown in proposed duel with Robert Toombs, 302

Georgia, State of, saviour of the Union, 1850, 4 n. 15; secedes, 45; importance to Confederacy, 45-47; de facto independent republic, 48 n. 2; soldiers furnished to Confederate armies, 107 n. 1; charters steamers, 119; debt at end of war, 138 n. 1; undertakes her own reconstruction, 288

Georgia Military Institute, strengthened by Governor Brown, 32

Georgia platform, adopted by state convention, 3; basis of Constitutional Union party, 3; author of, 5

Georgia rifle, commented on by Governor Brown, 33 n. 67

Goose Creek, Kentucky, salt mines, 113

Gordon, General John B., Captain of "Raccoon Roughs," 50 n. 14; defeated for governor, 277, 281; resigns from U. S. Senate, 307 *et seq.;* promotes railroads, 312; serves two terms as governor, 312; member of "triumvirate," 316; elected to U. S. Senate, 321

Governors' Conference, adopts resolution against Confederate regulation of blockade-running, 159; opposes suspension of habeas corpus, 219; fails to adopt resolution for convention of all states, 227 and n. 23

Grady, Henry W., purchases interest in *Constitution,* and supports ex-Governor Brown, 302; chairman of campaign committee for reelection of Alfred H. Colquitt, 315

Grant, General U. S., preparations for offensive in Virginia, 197; casualties, 222

Gray, P. W., Confederate agent in Trans-Mississippi Department, 156

Great Kanawha River, salt mines on, 113

Greeley, Horace, supported for president by ex-Governor Brown, 290

Habeas corpus, suspension of privilege of, opposition led by Alexander Stephens, 192, 235; exercised by President Davis under authority from Congress, 195; Confederate laws, 195 n. 6; conspiracy of Stephens brothers and Governor Brown, 200 *et seq.;* Benjamin Hill and Herschel V. Johnson refuse to join conspiracy, 200, 204-6, 213; Linton Stephens' resolutions, 209 n. 67, 215; effect of Governor Brown's propaganda, 216-17, 219, 239-40; President Lincoln's use of, 231 n. 40

Hampton Roads Conference, Alexander Stephens member of commission, 236-37

Harris, Governor Isham G., elected for third term in Tennessee, 68, 70

Hartridge resolution, 157, 159

Hayes-Tilden contest, ex-Governor Brown's part in, 305, 309

Hill, Benjamin H., joins American party, 6; nominated for governor, 1857, 14-19; attempts fusion, 1860, 34; addresses legislature opposing immediate secession, 39, 47 n. 116; member of secession convention, 44-45; elected to Provisional Congress, 45; addresses legislature on conscription, 58 n. 44, 87-88; defeats Robert Toombs for Confederate Senate, 123 n. 72; opposes Governor Brown's reëlection, 1863, 136; goes to Georgia to neutralize efforts of Stephens-Brown group, 1864, 202-3, 204 n. 45; addresses legislature, 210, 245; letter to Augusta Evans, 238 n. 61; leads opposition to Radical reconstruction, 255, 271 *et seq.,* 283, 289, 323; speaks at Delano banquet, 293 *et seq.;* member of company leasing State Road, 294 *et seq.;* speech in Congress on "Andersonville atrocities," 314 n. 90

Hill, Joshua, sends resignation to speaker of U. S. House of Representatives, 132; candidate for governor, 132-34, 136, 137; carries Sherman's messages to Governor Brown and Vice President Stephens, 224 n. 14; a Union man,

INDEX 353

226 n. 22; lobbies in legislature for peace convention, 235; defeats ex-Governor Brown for U. S. Senate, 281
Honey Hill, battle of, Governor Brown's state troops take part in, 191 n. 116
Hood, General John B., replaces Johnston, 185; receives reinforcements from Governor Brown, 185; fails to hold Atlanta, 188; army shattered in Tennessee, 191
Hunter, Senator R. M. T., arranges for Vice President Stephens to address Senate, 213 n. 81

Impressment, Confederate laws and amendments, 147, 149, 150, 151; opposition of Governor Brown to, 147-51; constitutionality of, 149; opposition of Robert Toombs to, 149 n. 52; recommended by President Davis, 150; value of, 151
Impressment, in Georgia, tanneries, factories, block tin, salt, agricultural products, railroad equipment, slaves, 116, 119, 138, 147 and n. 46
Iverson, Senator Alfred, fails of reelection to U. S. Senate, 35; favors secession, 35; withdraws from race for Confederate Senate, 35 n. 77, 123 n. 72

Jenkins, Governor Charles J., author of Georgia platform, candidate for governor, 5; guest of secession convention, 44; elected governor, 1865, 238; tests constitutionality of congressional reconstruction, 271; removed from office, 271 n. 20
"Joe Brown's Pets," exempted militia officers, 83, 124
"Joe Brown's pikes," description of, 49 n. 6
John Brown raid, resolution adopted by legislature, 33
Johnson, President Andrew, releases Governor Brown from prison, 247; appoints provisional governor of Georgia, 248; reconstruction plan in Georgia, 266; vetoes military reconstruction, 268
Johnson, Herschel V., Southern Rights leader, 5; elected governor, 5, 6, 20-21, 25, 27-28; leads opposition to immediate secession, 44, 45 n. 107; elected to Confederate Senate, 123 and n. 72; refuses to join Stephens-Brown conspiracy, 200, 204-5; loyal to Confederate administration, 201, 204-5, 205-6, 213, 224 n. 13, 231; opposes Radical reconstruction, 274-75, 297, 323
Johnson, James, Provisional Governor of Georgia, 248; appoints commission of investigation, 249 n. 28
Johnston, General Albert Sydney, retreats from lack of arms, 61
Johnston, General Joseph E., orders whiskey for army at Dalton, 110; receives militia from Governor Brown, 182; size of army at Resaca, 182 n. 78; replaced by Hood, 185; opposes Sherman in the Carolinas, 192; surrenders army, 193

Kansas, issue in gubernatorial campaign in Georgia, 7, 15, 16, 31; attitude of Governor Brown on admission of, 33
Kansas-Nebraska Act, wrecks Whig party, 5
Kenan, A. H., coöperationist, 44 n. 105; member of Provisional Congress, 45; bearer of alleged offer to Governor Brown of cabinet position, 79 n. 2
Kimball, H. I., law partner of ex-Governor Brown, 288, 300; beneficiary of Bullock regime, 288 n. 103, 325; member of company leasing State Road, 294; connected with Mitchell heirs' case, 300, 302
King, William, carries Sherman's messages to Governor Brown and Vice President Stephens, 224 n. 14, 228
"King Cotton," theory advanced in Governor Brown's address to legislature, 38; policy adopted and

abandoned by Confederacy, 121-22, 152 et seq.

"Know-Nothings." *See* American party

Ku Klux Klan, alleged connection with Ashburn case, 285

Lamar, H. G., candidate for gubernatorial nomination, 2, 7

Lamar, L. Q. C., opposes Stephens-Brown conspiracy, 203, 210

Lawton, General Alexander R., seizes Fort Pulaski under orders of Governor Brown, 42, 318; receives Georgia state troops, 61; in charge of Georgia coast defense, 162-63; candidate against ex-Governor Brown for U. S. Senate, 318, 320-21

Lee, General Robert E., pleads with Governor Brown for arms, 58; opinion on President Davis, 76 n. 122; favors conscription of slaves, 100; quells rebellion in North Georgia, 105; fortifies Georgia coast, 163 n. 5; proposes martial law for Augusta and Savannah, 196; becomes general in chief, 239 n. 62; surrenders army, 241; comments on proposal of Brown's joining army, 263

Levy en masse, in Georgia, 190-91

Lewis, Dr. John W., lends money to Joseph E. Brown, 11, 13; appointed superintendent of State Road, 28 *et seq.;* makes arrangements for state salt operations, 115; resigns from Confederate Senate, 123 n. 72

"Liberty Hall," residence of Alexander H. Stephens, 218 n. 102, 274

Lincoln, President Abraham, elected, 34, 36, 38, 40; corresponds with Alexander Stephens, 39 n. 88; adopts policy of coercion, 50, 51, 53, 54; referred to by Linton Stephens, 190, 196; referred to by Governor Brown, 208, 226, 232; alienates Conservatives and Radicals, 222, 223; favors peace efforts, 223 n. 6; comments on Governor Brown's furloughing state troops, 224 n. 12; referred to by Alexander Stephens, 229 n. 34, 236; suspends habeas corpus without authority, 231 n. 40; at Hampton Roads Peace Conference, 237 n. 57

"Little Ada," blockade-runner, used by Governor Brown in attempt to evade Confederate regulations, 157, 160, 189

Local defense, in 1861-62, in Georgia, 39, 48, 61, 66, 72, 88, 162-65; acts of Congress 166, 181; controversy between Governor Brown and Confederate officers, 1863, 165-81, 172-74; controversy during Sherman's invasion, 181-93; Governor Brown refuses to honor Confederate requisition, 185 *et seq.;* levy en masse, 190 *et seq. See also* State troops

Lochrane, Judge O. A., discharges conscripts through habeas corpus, 197 n. 16; law partner of ex-Governor Brown, 288 and n. 102; connection with Mitchell heirs' case, 300, 302

*London Index,* comments on cotton shipped, 154

Lookout Mountain, battle of, 176

Louisville & Nashville Railroad, controls State Road, 27 n. 42, 312 n. 79; possible connection with Senator Gordon, 311, 312 and n. 79, 313

Lumpkin, John H., candidate for nomination for governor, 2; Unionist, 1850-51, 7

Luxuries, imported by blockade-runners, 153

McClellan, General George B., nominated for president, 222, 229 n. 34

McGrath, Judge A. G., gives opinion on constitutionality of conscription, 85; asked to intercede with Governor Brown, 192

Macon, Georgia, endangered by Sherman, 189, 190; meeting of adjourned legislature in, 243

Mahone, Senator William, accuses ex-Governor Brown of disloyalty to Confederacy, 188 n. 99, 250, 252 n. 38; refers to ex-Governor

# INDEX

Brown's course in reconstruction, 325 n. 145, 326
Malcomb, Mr., character in novel portraying ex-Governor Brown, 303-4
March to the sea, Sherman's, 99, 189 *et seq.*
Martial law, in Atlanta, 195; opposed by Governor Brown, Alexander and Linton Stephens, 195-96
Means, Dr. Alexander, opposes immediate secession, 44 n. 105; votes for secession, 45
Memminger, C. G., Secretary of Treasury, blames Governor Brown for failure of state endorsement, 144
Mercer University, beneficiary of ex-Governor Brown's contributions, 299
Military laws of C. S. A., 49, 50, 54, 63, 64 n. 71, 73 n. 110, 79, 81, 84, 89-90, 92, 99 n. 103, 101 n. 108, 166, 195 n. 6
Militia, appointment of officers, 54-55; Governor Brown, Alexander and Linton Stephens give definition of, 55, 64 n. 71, 73, 81 and n. 11; President Davis' definition of, 81-82; Georgia law, 90; recommendations of President Davis for Confederate law, 162. *See* State troops
Milledgeville, capital of Georgia, meeting of Democratic convention in, 1; pillaged by Sherman's army, 188, 191
Milton, Governor John, of Florida, loyal to Confederate administration, 127 n. 85, 158
Missionary Ridge, battle of, 176-77
Mitchell heirs' case, controversy between ex-Governor Brown and Robert Toombs with reference to, 300-2; connection of O. A. Lochrane and H. I. Kimball with, 300
Montgomery, Alabama, meeting of Provisional Congress, 45, 47; captured by Union forces, 193; question of the capital's remaining in, 198 n. 21
Moore, Governor A. B., of Alabama, Governor Brown's telegram to, 42

Morgan, Governor Edwin D., of New York, refuses to release shipment of arms, 43
Morse, N. S., owner of *Chronicle and Sentinel*, called "immigrant spy" by Benjamin Hill, 238 n. 61
Moses, Colonel A. J., counsel for defense in Ashburn case, 284

Nashville, Chattanooga & St. Louis Railroad. *See* Louisville & Nashville Railroad.
National Guard Status Act, 1933, 102 n. 114
Nassau, Georgia imports at, 119; port for blockade-runners, 153; value of British blockade-runners at, 153 n. 77
Navy, Confederate, building thwarted, 139
Negroes, in Radical state convention, 275-76; expelled from legislature, 276-77; decision of Chief Justice Brown, 277
Negro suffrage, strategy of Radicals, 267-68; endorsed by ex-Governor Brown, 269; accepted by him at Chicago convention, 280; opposed by Democratic National Convention, 282; repealed in Georgia, 318 n. 114
Nelms, Captain John W., keeper of state penitentiary, 286
Newcomb, Victor, president L. & N. R. R., 311, 312
"New departure," political policy in Georgia, 291. *See* Fusion
New Iberia, Louisiana, salt mine, 115
"New South," definition of, 292, 316
Nisbet, Eugenius A., joins American party, 6; favors immediate secession, 44 n. 105; candidate for governor, 70-72, 128
North Georgia, the "white belt," stronghold of Democratic party, 2, 3 n. 9; insurgency in, 7 n. 28, 306; residence and influence of Joseph E. Brown in, 7, 11, 14 n. 57, 47, 305, 309; traversed by State Road, 26-27; products of, 45; desolated by contending armies, 118; representatives oppose Negro members of legislature, 286

Norwood, Senator Thomas W., nominated for governor, 1880, 318, 319 n. 119
"Notes on the Situation," written by Benjamin H. Hill, 271, 272-74, 297

Oglethorpe Light Infantry, takes state arms to Virginia, 59
Opinions of historians on Governor Brown, 260 et seq.
Opposition Convention, Whig-American, 31
Opposition party in Georgia, opposes Confederate administration, 126, 130, 131, 200 n. 29, 201, 203
Ordinance of Secession in Georgia, adoption, 45; author, 70
Orne, R. M. & Son, promotes gubernatorial candidacy of Timothy M. Furlow, 134; proprietors of *Southern Recorder*, 134 n. 106
Orr, Senator James Lawrence, of South Carolina, introduces resolution for peace, 220 n. 110

Panic in 1857, 20 et seq., 29 n. 51, 30
Peace, General Sherman's efforts for, 187, 224-25, 226, 227, 228; proposals for conventions in the interest of, 194, 197-98, 224 n. 13, 226 and n. 21, 229-30, 232-36, 237-38, 239-40, 241, 245; Alexander Stephens' efforts for, 198, 199 and n. 26, 224 n. 13, 228, 229 n. 34, 235-37; Linton Stephens' resolutions for, 200, 202-3, 205, 209 n. 68, 214, 215, 216; Governor Brown's proposals and propaganda for, 207-8, 216-17, 217 n. 99, 220, 223, 226, 227, 229-30, 232-33, 237-38, 239-40, 241; demands in North and West for, 222-23, 224; President Lincoln's efforts for, 223 n. 6; Hampton Roads Conference on, 236-37, 240
Pensacola, Governor Brown's anxiety with respect to, 42; requisition of troops for, 51, 52
Petersburg, siege of, 97, 193
Polk, President James K., erroneous impression of, 18

Pollard, Edward A., accuses Governor Brown of betraying Confederacy, 103-4
Powder, controversy between Governor Brown and Confederacy, 65
Presidential election, Confederate, 75-76
"Produce loan," Confederate, 139
Provisional Congress, elections in Georgia, 45; meets in Montgomery, 47; consent necessary to appointment of officers, 50; elects president, 76
Provisional Constitution, *See* Constitution

Quitman, Governor John A., of Mississippi, early advocate of secession, 47

Rebellion in mountain counties of Georgia, Governor Brown accused of responsibility for, 105, 126
Reconstruction, in Georgia, President Johnson's plan in operation, 248, 266-67, 268; supplanted by plan of Radicals, 226 et seq., 323; ex-Governor Brown's conversion and leadership, 269-70, 274, 276-81, 284-86; opposition of Robert Toombs, 270, 275 n. 39, 282, 283, 284, 289; of Governor Jenkins, 271; of Benjamin Hill, 271-74, 276, 277, 282, 283, 284, 323; of Alexander Stephens, 274, 285, 323; of Herschel V. Johnson, 274-75, 323; of Howell Cobb, 283; Rufus B. Bullock elected governor, 277, 287-88; ex-Governor Brown breaks with Radicals, 288-90
Rehabilitation, political, of ex-Governor Brown, 291 et seq.
Relief, state, for needy, 107, 113-18, 120, 121
Reprisals, policy advocated and applied by Governor Brown, 36-37, 43
Republican party, composition of, 6. *See* Reconstruction
Requisition, for troops for provisional army, leads to "skeleton regiment" controversy, 51-54; Governor Brown's theory of, 55-

# INDEX

56; his refusal to honor, 179, 185-86, 224

Rhett, Robert Barnwell, opposes compromise with North, 34, 47; in line for Confederate president, 75

Richmond, Virginia, proposed as army headquarters rather than capital, 198 n. 21; Vice President Stephens' absence from, 199-200, 213 and n. 81; necessity for suspension of habeas corpus in, 204; Grant's campaign against, 222-23; Vice President Stephens returns to, 233, 237, 239; visit of Francis P. Blair to, 236, 237 n. 57; fall of, 242 n. 74, 246

Russell, Philip M., contributes to Governor Brown's propaganda fund, 217

Salt, Governor Brown's efforts to obtain, 112-16

Saltpeter, sale by Governor Brown to Confederate government, 71

Savannah, siege of, 190

Scalawag, term applied to ex-Governor Brown and other Southern Radical Republicans, 269, 275, 277 n. 52, 284, 295

Secession, threatened in 1850, 2-4; influence of Governor Brown on, 9, 11, 32-34, 36-37, 39-43, 250, 251; adoption of ordinance, 44-45; Governor Brown's conception of, 79-80, 101, 103, 186, 231, 241, 244, 245, 258-59, 261-62. *See also* State Rights

Secret sessions in Confederate Congress, charged by Governor Brown, 145, 244 and n. 4

Seddon, James A., Secretary of War, controversy with Governor Brown over local defense troops of 1863, 165-81; over requisition of 1864, 185-88

Senate, Confederate, addressed by Vice President Stephens, 213 n. 81, 235

Senate, United States, ex-Governor Brown defeated for, 281; appointed to, 308 *et seq.;* services in, 313 n. 88, 314; elected to, 321

Seymour, Governor Horatio, of New York, in comparison with Governors Brown and Vance, 262; nominated for president, 282, 284 and n. 80

Sherman, General W. T., invades Georgia, 92, 95, 97, 99, 104, 182, 185, 188, 189, 223, 224, 320; forces adjournment of legislature, 99, 188; overtures to Governor Brown and Vice President Stephens, 187, 208, 224, 225, 227, 228; marches to the sea, 188, 189, 190, 191; besieges Savannah, 190, 192; receives surrender of Johnston, 193

Shorter, John Gill, commissioner from Alabama to Georgia, 41 n. 96

Slaves, fugitive, 34 n. 74, 35; Governor Brown's reference to, 36, 40, 74; in Union army, 100 n. 104; conscripted by Confederate Congress, 100-1 and n. 108; opposition of Governor Brown to freeing, 101, 258-59; reference of President Davis to, 258

Smith, Governor James M., of Georgia, counsel for defense in Ashburn case, 285; elected governor, 289, 290 n. 109, 309; demands to know why ex-Governor Brown was appointed to U. S. Senate, 310

Smith, Governor William, of Virginia, refuses to join Governor Brown in shipping controversy, 158

Specie, in Confederacy, 139, 140 n. 10

Speer, Emory, insurgent in Democratic party, 306

South, The, as a minority in the Union, 47 and n. 117, 257

Southern nationalism, strength and weakness of, 256-58, 259

Southern Rights party, in 1849-50, 3 n. 10, 4, 7, 8

State endorsement of Confederate bonds, opposed by Governor Brown and Alexander Stephens, 141-44

State Rights, opinion of William L. Yancey on Governor Brown's conception of, 83; used as subter-

fuge, 256 n. 51, 263, 264. *See* Brown, Joseph E.
State Road, built, owned, and operated by State of Georgia, 10, 16, 26-28, 27 n. 42, 312 n. 79; factor in Governor Brown's political career, 28-30, 68, 127, 129, 130, 306 n. 59, 312-13; controversy with Confederacy, 64 n. 72; captured by Federal forces, 119; mismanaged during reconstruction, 287, 293; leased to ex-Governor Brown's company, 293-94 and n. 8, 310, 324 n. 141, 326
State troops, Georgia, two thousand authorized by legislature, 39, 48; convention disapproves of, 61; brigade controversy, 61-63; second organization, 66, 72, 92, 163-65; organization of two regiments, 88 and n. 48; controversy over status of 1863 troops, 172-75, 181; furloughed, 179, 192, 193, 224; "loaned" to Confederate officers, 182-85, 189, 190 n. 116; ordered out to arrest deserters, 192; ordered to defend Columbus, 193; surrendered to Union officer, 193. *See* Local defense and Militia
Stephens, Alexander H., Vice President, C. S. A., in state convention and Constitutional Union party, 3, 5; joins Democratic party, 6; denies seriousness of political situation, 35; opposes immediate secession, 39, 44 n. 105; correspondence with Lincoln, 39 n. 88; member of Provisional Congress, 45; considered for president of Confederacy, 75; intimacy with brother, Robert Toombs, and Joseph E. Brown, 77 and n. 128, 130, 264; opposes administration measures, 78, 82, 83-84, 96 n. 88, 223; leads assault on habeas corpus, 194-213; premature peace efforts, 198, 199 n. 26, 224 n. 13, 229 n. 34, 235-36, 239, 263; elected governor, 1882, 213 n. 83, 292 n. 1ᵃ; receives message from Sherman, 224, 227-28; member of Hampton Roads Peace Conference, 236-37; attitude towards Radical reconstruction, 274, 322, 323; counsel for defense in Ashburn case, 285; opposes fusion with Liberal Republicans, 292 n. 1ᵃ; resigns from company leasing State Road, 294 n. 11
Stephens, Linton, proposes Joseph E. Brown for governor, 8; opposes immediate secession, 44 n. 105; intimacy with brother, 77; friendship with Robert Toombs, 77; definition of militia, 81; opposes conscription, 81 n. 11, 83-84; suggested for governor, 124; opposes levy en masse, 190; opposes martial law, 196; in conspiracy against Confederate measures, 200, 202, 205; introduces peace and habeas corpus resolutions, 209, 214, 216; suggests an explanation to the Governor, 216; refuses offer of judgeship, 218; introduces resolutions for state convention, 226, 233-35, 239; devotion to state rights, 264; opposes Radical constitution, 287
Stevens, Thad, member of U. S. Congress, opposes Democratic party's return to power, 267 n. 5
Stiles, W. H., candidate for gubernatorial nomination, 2
Substitution, in Confederate army, policy opposed by President Davis and Governor Brown, 99 n. 103, 170; in Federal army, 99 n. 103
Supreme Court, Confederate, constitutional provision, 85 n. 33
Supreme Court, U. S., not permitted to pass on habeas corpus, 231 n. 40; considers reconstruction acts, 297

Tax and funding laws, Confederate, 139 and n. 3, 140, 141, 144, 145. *See* Fiscal system
Tax-in-kind, or tithe, Confederate, law of 1863, 145; objections to, 146; value of, 146
Taylor, General Richard, commands troops opposing Sherman's march, 189; makes "unconstitutional patriots" of Governor Brown's state troops, 191 n. 116; surrenders, 193; opinion on Confederate constitution, 254

# INDEX 359

"Teacher-turnover," in South, 26 n. 38

Thweatt, Jonas, contributes to Governor Brown's propaganda fund, 217

Thweatt, Colonel P., urges Governor Brown for fourth term, 130 n. 90

Tithe. *See* Tax-in-kind

Toombs, Robert, in state convention and Constitutional Union party, 3, 5; in U. S. Senate, 4, 35; joins Democratic party, 6; comment on nomination of Joseph E. Brown, 9; leads in secession, 35, 39, 44 n. 105; member of Provisional Congress, 45; considered for Confederate president, 75; friendship with Alexander and Linton Stephens, 77; member of Confederate cabinet, 77, 78; military career, 77-78, 125, 182 n. 74, 191 n. 116; opposes Confederate war measures, 83-84, 131, 135, 144 n. 24, 146, 149 n. 52, 150, 196, 245, 255, 264; fails to receive nomination for governor, 123, 130 n. 90; declines seat in Confederate Senate, 123 n. 72; fails of election to Confederate Senate, 123 n. 72; refuses to restrict cultivation of cotton, 125 n. 77; warns Alexander Stephens against General Sherman's proposal, 227; opposes Radical reconstruction, 270, 275, 282, 283, 284, 289; sends challenge to ex-Governor Brown, 291-92, 300-2; opposes Bourbon Democracy, 292 and n. 1ª; opposes fusion in 1872, 292 n. 1ª; attempts to break lease of State Road, 294; opposes ex-Governor Brown's election to the U. S. Senate, 319; referred to by ex-Governor Brown in De Gives Opera House speech, 320

"To Our Constituents," address of Southern representatives in Congress, 35

Trammell, L. N., secures nomination of Joseph E. Brown, 7; political career in Georgia, 7 n. 28, 306, 316

Trammell, William Dugas, author of *Ça Ira—A Novel*, 302-5

Treasury notes, bonds, and change bills in Georgia, 138 n. 1

"Triumvirate," in Georgia politics, 306, 316, 319

Troup, Governor George M., of Georgia, early advocate of secession, 47

"Twelve-months men," Confederate, tendered by states, 50; their return with arms demanded by Governor Brown, 60; reënlistment, 63, 84 and n. 29

Union party, coalition in Georgia, 3 and n. 10, 4, 5

Union party, nominates President Lincoln, 222

University of Georgia, ex-Governor Brown's contributions and service to, 299, 300

Vance, Governor Zebulon B., of North Carolina, exemption policy, 89; gives opinion of Governor Brown's state troops, 189 n. 105; opposes separate state action, 198 n. 19; opposes calling state convention, 238; opinions on, 261-62

Veto, use of by Governor Brown, 21-25 and n. 33, 94

Volunteers, in Georgia, early organization of companies of, 32, 38 and n. 86, 39, 42; evidences of enthusiasm of, 49, 50 and nn. 12 and 14, 51, 53, 58 n. 44, 61-62, 66, 80, 82, 88, 96 n. 88, 105, 107 n. 1, 163, 171; Governor Brown's theory of direct tender of, 54, 55, 56-61, 72-73; number compared with conscripts, 96-97 and n. 90

Waitzfelder, Leopold and Solomon, contribute to Governor Brown's propaganda fund, 217 and n. 96

Waitzfelder & Company, financial partners of ex-Governor Brown, 301

Walker, Robert J., governor of

# INDEX

Kansas Territory, opposition in Georgia to, 1, 3 n. 1, 7
Ward, John E., speaks in opposition to Governor Brown's veto, 22 and n. 12
Warner, Hiram, candidate for gubernatorial nomination, 2; opposes secession, 44 n. 105, 45 n. 107; dissents in opinion on eligibility of Negroes to hold office, 277 n. 52; demoted from chief justice for ex-Governor Brown, 282; reappointed chief justice by Governor Smith, 288 n. 102
Watson, Thomas W., begins political career, 317 n. 104
West Point, battle of, 193
Western & Atlantic R. R. *See* State Road
Whigs, join coalition in adopting Georgia platform, 3
Whig party, wreck of, 5
Whiskey, use of in Confederate army and hospitals, 109
Whitaker, Jared, owner of *Atlanta Intelligencer,* supports Governor Brown for reëlection, 68, 128; appointed state commissary general, 68 n. 92
"White Belt." *See* North Georgia
Wilmington, fall of, 193
Wilmot Proviso, opposition to, 2
Wilson, General James H., U. S. A., receives surrender of state troops and paroles Governor Brown, 193, 246
World War, relief and military measures in, 117, 231 n. 40
Worth, Jonathan, of North Carolina, opposes Radical reconstruction, 297 n. 22
Wright, Judge A. R., of Georgia, visits President Lincoln in interest of peace, 224 n. 14

Yancey, William Lowndes, of Alabama, opposes compromise with North, 34, 47; in line for Confederate president, 75; opinion of Governor Brown's theory of state rights, 83; opinion on adopting permanent constitution, 284